GOLDMAN SACHS

THE CULTURE OF SUCCESS

LISA ENDLICH

A Touchstone Book

Published by Simon & Schuster

New York London Toronto Sydney

To Mark

TOUCHSTONE
Rockefeller Center
1230 Avenue of the Americas
New York, NY 10020

First Touchstone Edition 2000
Published by arrangement with Alfred A. Knopf, Inc.

TOUCHSTONE and colophon are registered trademarks of Simon & Schuster, Inc.

Manufactured in the United States of America

15 17 19 20 18 16 14

The Library of Congress has cataloged the Knopf edition as follows:
Endlich, Lisa, [date]
Goldman Sachs : the culture of success / Lisa Endlich.
p.   cm.
Includes bibliographical references and index.
1. Goldman, Sachs & Co. 2. Investment banking—United States.
3. Going public (Securities) I. Title.
HG4930.5.E53   1999
332.66'0973—dc21   98-31139
CIP

ISBN-13: 978-0-684-86968-1
ISBN-10:   0-684-86968-3

All acknowledgments for permission to reprint previously
published material may be found following the index.

CONTENTS

Author's Note   vi

CHAPTER I.   1986:   The Road Less Traveled   3

CHAPTER II.   1869–1976:   The Family Firm   32

CHAPTER III.   1976–1990:   The World-Class Player   70

CHAPTER IV.   1990–1991:   The Changing of the Guard   120

CHAPTER V.   1992–1993:   The Pinnacle   161

CHAPTER VI.   1994:   The Curse of Success   190

CHAPTER VII.   1995–1998:   The Road to IPO   219

1999:   The Initial Public Offering   267

Notes   275

Bibliography   291

Acknowledgments   311

Index   314

AUTHOR'S NOTE

Displayed proudly for many years on the wall of co-senior partner John Whitehead's office at Goldman Sachs was the official announcement of the Ford Motor Company's 1956 initial public offering. Goldman Sachs had masterminded the sale of stock and as the largest initial public offering to date it was one of the firm's greatest triumphs. Below the ornate script announcing that the automobile manufacturer would be selling shares was a partial listing of the underwriters, a group that totaled an astounding 722. It was a veritable who's who of Wall Street, a roster of almost every major firm and most of the minor ones.

Whitehead had framed the tombstone without any glass, and over the years each time an announcement was made that one of these established firms had ceased to exist, had merged with a former competitor, or had been devoured by a conglomerate, with his red pen he would strike off another rival. First Hornblower & Weeks went, then firms like White Weld and Blyth & Co. Slowly, the page turned red as every other major firm on Wall Street relinquished its partnership. Goldman Sachs was the last one left standing.

The end of an era came in August 1998 when the firm's 188 partners voted to sell a portion of their firm to the investing public. It was an admission that the private partnership, for centuries the model for all investment banking firms, was no longer relevant in the modern age. The change did not come about because Goldman Sachs could no longer find success as a private partnership; in fact in the first half of 1998 Goldman Sachs was having a record year and many partners vociferously argued that the partnership itself was the source of a great deal of the firm's success. Rather, the change came about because the expansion plans of top management required publicly traded shares as the means for acquiring related businesses and many partners felt they needed public shareholders to help defray the risks inherent in their business. The competitive landscape was evolving at a breakneck pace and at the height of the longest bull market in history there had never been a better moment to sell. The decision was a difficult and agonizing one, steeped in conflict and controversy, and the events that would overtake the firm were entirely unforeseen.

Goldman Sachs began the century as a little-known family business with a minor reputation and a huge dream. It ends the century as perhaps the best-known investment bank in the world, one of the greatest financial success stories of the twentieth century. Yet it was anything but obvious that Goldman Sachs would emerge as the industry leader. At any point in its first hundred years, the firm could have become a dinosaur, marginalized by competitors with more capital and better established franchises. But in the 1970s, Goldman Sachs's star began to rise. Slowly at first, gaining momentum all the time, the firm came to national and then international prominence, ultimately rising to the pinnacle of investment banking. This story is not one of a familiar rise and fall. At times the firm has stumbled—quite badly a few times—but it never relinquished its push forward. For more than a century and a quarter, Goldman Sachs thrived as a private partnership, becoming a major force on Wall Street and one of the most profitable organizations on this planet.

The firm's success has rested solidly on three legs: its leadership, its people, and its culture. Great companies have great leaders—men and women who stand out in their own age and then go on to secure a place in history. Goldman Sachs has been run by men of extraordinary vision and ability. Each senior partner has stamped his world view on the firm in a way that fit remarkably well with the times. And whether speaking to partners, competitors, former employees, or clients, the conclusion is always the same: Goldman Sachs hires the very best people in the industry, seeking out the brightest and most ambitious recruits who will fit into the confines of its culture. That culture, widely emulated across the industry, has been the blueprint for the firm's success and has remained unique.

While working at Goldman Sachs I was immersed in this culture, although I was entirely unaware of its long and colorful history. As a vice-president and trader on the foreign exchange desk I had no inkling of the controversy that repeatedly enveloped top management as they grappled for over a decade with the notion of selling the firm.

For almost one hundred thirty years Goldman Sachs has been shrouded in mystery, its finances and operations kept secret—the prerogative of a private partnership. Those working within the financial industry may have caught glimpses of the inner workings of the firm from stories in the financial press over the years, while those outside the confines of Wall Street may know little about this very private firm. This book, I can only hope, will help fill the void.

Two important caveats: I spent my career at Goldman Sachs in one of the firm's trading businesses. While I have endeavored to write about the banking side of the business, I must confess that my knowledge of this is less substantial.

Second, this book does not attempt to place a value on the role investment banking plays in our society. A debate has erupted in recent months about the part speculators and bankers have played in the world economy, particularly with regard to the many emerging economies that have recently faltered. While this is an important issue, it is outside the scope of this book.

January 1999

GOLDMAN
SACHS

CHAPTER I

1986

THE ROAD LESS TRAVELED

On Wednesday morning, October 15, 1986, John L. Weinberg, the venerable senior partner of Goldman Sachs, had a long list of phone calls to make. Before the morning was over he needed to telephone thirty-six men and one woman. His conversations would be brief; good news travels fast.

He started early, hours before the official list would be published. Thomas W. Berry would be first and Garland E. Wood last; alphabetical order was the rule. This was the phone call each vice-president on his list had waited years to receive. Each would reach for the receiver hoping Weinberg was about to extend an invitation to the most exclusive club on Wall Street—the partnership of Goldman Sachs. Weinberg's simple statement, "I would like to invite you to join the partnership," was for most the reward for a decade of grinding hard work. No one had ever refused the honor. Thirty years earlier, Weinberg's own father, the legendary Sidney Weinberg, had issued him the same invitation.

John Weinberg, with help from the eight other partners who comprised the management committee, had vetted hundreds of vice-presidents in the biannual selection process. They had deliberated for two agonizing months while speculation among the troops grew. For the hundred or so in "the zone," the inside term for those actually in contention, everything was at stake—prestige, recognition, riches. As Weinberg traveled through the alphabet, some of the dozens passed over would shut themselves in their offices, while a few would storm out of the firm's headquarters. Envy and frustration would cause one or two people to

3

resign, but the vast majority would take the disappointment in stride, hoping for another shot at a partnership two years hence.

Those telephoned that autumn morning were being offered not only vast wealth but virtual lifetime employment as well. John Weinberg himself had spent his entire career at the firm, beginning in 1950; Robert E. Rubin and Stephen Friedman, two of the more senior members of the management committee, had been with the firm for twenty years. Their tenure was not unusual. Moreover, few partners had ever been asked to leave; graceful and bittersweet departures almost always capped lengthy and prosperous careers. Barring any missteps, the young men and woman answering Weinberg's phone call could expect to retire with a nest egg worth tens of millions of dollars.

Yet those selected knew that after years of grueling sixty-, seventy-, or even eighty-hour weeks spent on trading floors, in clients' offices, or on airplanes, the real work was only now about to begin. The partners of Goldman Sachs in 1986 owned a $38 billion business, and running it was, and still is, an all-consuming job. Partnership meetings are held on weekends; vacations and sleep are routinely interrupted with conference calls whose participants span the globe. Partners felt free to call each other whenever they needed to know something about another's business. "When you made partner suddenly you had to return eighty other phone calls," says one retired partner. "Partners were much less respectful of your privacy than employees would be."

The partnership class of 1986 represented change. At thirty-seven, it was twice as large as any previous class. The all-white, all-male partnership had invited into its ranks the first African American and the first woman in its history. The pressure on Wall Street firms to become more diverse was considerable, and Goldman Sachs was one of the last to bow. Almost all partners had spent their entire careers with the firm, yet this class included two former managing directors from rival Salomon Brothers and a famous professor from MIT.

For the first time, existing partners had been unfamiliar with some of the candidates. The firm had grown and specialized. Its four divisions— equities (stock trading), investment banking, fixed income (bond trading), and J. Aron (currency and commodities trading)—had been separated into dozens of specialized departments, many members of which had very little contact with employees from outside their own department. Partners had been forced to trust the recommendations of their colleagues. Impersonality had crept into the process.

Perhaps the most atypical feature of the class of 1986 was the number of partners elevated from the ranks of salesmen and traders. Goldman Sachs's traditional strengths lay in the field of investment banking, in raising capital for large corporations or arranging mergers and acquisitions. Despite some areas of excellence, particularly in stock trading, Goldman Sachs did not have the trading prowess of a firm like Salomon Brothers. In 1986 top management determined that this would change.

Weinberg's anointed officially joined the partnership on Monday, December 1, 1986, the first day of the firm's new fiscal year. Only five days later, the management committee that so recently had bestowed this honor proposed to take it away. At the annual partnership meeting held in New York, Steve Friedman and Bob Rubin, who would be appointed co–vice chairmen the following year, announced that the firm was considering selling itself to the investing public.

In an abrupt break with one hundred seventeen years of history, the management committee was proposing that Goldman Sachs become a public corporation. No longer would the partners own their firm; no longer would they run it unencumbered by outside influences. Stockholders would own much of the firm's capital, and a board of directors, presumably with outside members, would rule on issues of policy. Partners would find themselves as employees, albeit extremely wealthy ones, of a large corporate entity. The management committee believed that in order to expand into new businesses, additional capital of a more permanent nature would be required. The pressure to sell the firm had only increased as each of Goldman Sachs's major competitors had undertaken a public sale or merger with a larger entity. Now the management committee unanimously recommended that the partnership vote for an initial public offering. Not one of the thirty-seven new partners, who had far less to gain than longtime partners from the windfall that would be created by such a sale, thought this sounded like a good idea.

The partnership had never before openly entertained the notion of a public offering, although behind closed doors the management committee had discussed and dismissed the idea many times. In the late 1960s, Sidney Weinberg had considered it briefly and sent his top lieutenant Gus Levy to canvass the partners. It would be the first time the idea was shot down. In 1971, the management committee had decided to incorporate, going as far as printing up new business cards before changing their minds and leaving the private partnership in place.

On the morning of December 6, the partners convened in the large meeting room on the second floor of 85 Broad Street, the firm's three-year-old headquarters in lower Manhattan. For days rumors had circulated but the official agenda had not been disclosed. The management committee members had been lobbying their partners, trying to line up support before the meeting. Many of the new partners were nervous; it was their first partnership meeting, and they had little idea of what to expect. Much was at stake; the future of Goldman Sachs would be decided in the next thirty-six hours.

The members of the management committee were seated around a table on a stage at the front of the room, while the ninety-five remaining partners sat facing them. Weinberg had positioned himself some distance away from his fellow members; this action sent out what many remember as a very strong signal. During the formal presentation he said almost nothing.

Most members of the management committee spoke, but when Rubin and Friedman, who were already widely regarded as heirs apparent, stood to present their vision of the future, everyone listened more closely. Goldman Sachs would be a great global firm, they told the audience, a worldwide wholesaler of investment banking services. The firm would be transformed into a trading powerhouse, one that would challenge top-ranked Salomon Brothers, which was operating with considerably more capital. Risky, capital-intensive activities like trading (some of it for the firm's own account rather than as an agent for clients), much of which was under Rubin's management, and principal investments (long-term strategic investments made by the partnership in operating companies), Friedman's latest brainchild, could not be operated easily with the firm's existing partnership capital. Earnings would be more volatile in these new businesses, and to remain competitive a fortified capital base would need to be built.

Then the issue of unlimited liability was addressed. "What would happen if we hit a bump in the road?" those on the management committee asked. In a private partnership none of the assets of partners are shielded from liability, and the individual partners are exposed down to the pennies in their children's piggy banks. Large trading losses or lawsuits could pose a threat to the firm's capital and ultimately its existence. The actions of a rogue trader could spell personal bankruptcy (one year later a lone trader would singlehandedly lose Merrill Lynch $300 million). Although 1986 had been a very successful year, the firm had suffered a few large bond trading losses, and some partners had grown concerned. Sexual harassment and racial discrimination suits, with ever larger settlements or awards for damages, were becoming increasingly common on Wall Street. Fifteen years earlier, when Penn Central railroad, a Goldman Sachs client, had filed for Chapter 11 bankruptcy protection, the firm had been plagued by lawsuits, the dollar amount of which threatened to exceed the partnership capital. It had been a frightening experience.

Goldman Sachs's capital was inherently unstable. In any given year a substantial group of senior partners with large capital stakes might retire, taking their money with them, and the drain on the firm's resources could be debilitating. If it happened in a year when the firm performed poorly, as it would in 1994, for example, the results could be extremely damaging. By inviting outside investors, in the shape of stockholders, to join the firm, its capital base could be strengthened and its risk dispersed. Friedman and Rubin strongly supported the proposal. Their boss John Weinberg did not.

For many in that room, John Weinberg *was* Goldman Sachs. He had been with the firm for almost forty years, and for eight of those had shared the top position with his friend John Whitehead. But Whitehead had left Goldman Sachs and was serving as deputy secretary of state in the Reagan administration, and, at sixty-one, Weinberg was on his own. A portly gentleman with close-cropped white hair, thick jowls, and a kind face, over the years he had inspired unswerving loyalty and total devotion. Weinberg's leadership, now in its tenth year, was unquestioned and absolute. He had kept politics out of Goldman Sachs. Under Weinberg the firm retained the feeling of a family business, and the dueling egos and unrestrained greed that had plagued and even destroyed some of his competitors was not tolerated. Only two years earlier, Lehman Brothers, a first-class name in investment banking and a onetime partner of Goldman Sachs, was crippled by a power struggle at the top and had been forced to sell itself to the conglomerate Shearson American Express.

By 1986 the relationship between Goldman Sachs and the Weinbergs—John and his father, brother, son, and nephew—extended back seventy-nine years. The emotional bond was strong. Weinberg believed passionately in the value of the partnership, in its role as the contributing factor in the firm's success. While the management committee presented a united front, many who heard the presentation doubted Weinberg's commitment to the proposal. Goldman Sachs had just closed the books on one of its most profitable years. Through the early 1980s the firm's return on equity had risen as high as an astounding 80 percent, and many partners realized that this level of profitability was unprecedented and unsustainable. The stock market was buoyant and new issues were selling well. If the firm were to go public, it would have to seize the moment. In 1986 the press was full of uncannily accurate prognostications of the gloom and doom to follow. Any knowledgeable observer could see that Wall Street was at the giddy heights of its perennial cycle and it would not be long before the inevitable downturn began. Acceding to the management committee's unanimous wishes, Weinberg agreed to set the ownership issue before the partnership.

The presentation made to the partners that Saturday morning has been described as, at best, uninspiring and weak. Others have called it haphazard and half-baked, emphasizing that its quality was far below that of presentations the firm routinely gave to its clients. Most agree that it was an amateurish effort; what was presented was little more than a concept. Partners were given written reports that outlined the proposed structure: Overnight they would be transformed into managing directors and paid a multiple of the value of their investment in the company. Veteran partners, already very wealthy, could triple their net worth overnight.

One partner who was present remembers that the numbers, in the parlance of the business, did not "foot"; those in the audience who checked back and forth between the many exhibits in the presentation package found that the numbers did not add up and they jumped all over the inconsistencies. In various scenarios, the analyses showed how the partners' capital would grow over time if the firm remained a partnership. But many of the assumptions were questioned and investment banking partners challenged the valuations underlying the proposal. Projections of the firm's earnings as a public corporation were ridiculed. In a business where almost all of the assets go down the elevators and out the front door each night, who could guess what would be left after the firm transformed itself? Calculators came out as partners estimated what their take from the initial buyout might be, but more fundamental questions remained unanswered: What would the company be worth? To whom would shares be sold? On what kind of schedule would the partners be paid? The audience was not impressed.

By afternoon, an impassioned debate had erupted. A partnership is a much more personal organizational structure than a corporation, but even Weinberg was surprised at the level of emotion unleashed. Most of these men knew each other well. The partnership was a small, intimate organization—a fraternity in the very best sense of the word—in which no one was above criticism and the more senior partners regularly challenged their leaders. What was taking place this day was open and honest conversation. Partners screamed and cried, Weinberg remembers; it was a cathartic exercise.

The newest partners could not have been expected to embrace the proposal, since for them it was a financial step backward. The dividing lines between generations of partners had always existed, but now they would be drawn in the sand. Most of the members of the class of 1986 were still in their thirties, and being a partner of Goldman Sachs was a job they had aspired to since business school. The money was not bad, of course, but for some the psychic rewards were even more important. There was a sense of affiliation, of belonging to a select group with a hallowed history and a common purpose. The newest partners had worked for, and expected, a lifelong career with the firm, and they had no interest in giving up their shot at the future.

The partners' capital at the time was a little more than a billion dollars and all members of the class of 1986 received a .32 percent stake. If the firm had been sold in 1986 each new partner would have walked away with between $3 and $3.5 million, and while that is not a bad payday it is important to consider the alternative. In its proposal the management committee had predicted that the firm's return on equity would decline to and stabilize at 40 percent, a level of return yielded by few other investments anywhere. The management committee was suggesting the transition to a public company because of the long-term growth opportunities they envisioned. But it was precisely this growth potential that would cause the very newest partners, with little invested in the company, to want to maintain the partnership. And at the end of perhaps a decade, when members of the class of 1986 had increased the size of their partnership stakes, the firm could still be sold. Of course the risks were great—a stock market crash was in fact less than a year away—but the potential for building substantial wealth was obvious to all.

A powerful contingent of banking partners, whose businesses did not require additional capital, remained unconvinced of the firm-wide need for greater resources. The merger department, which generated huge profits from the fees earned in successfully bringing companies together, was breaking profit records every year and hardly needed help. Many banking partners had not signed off on the vision of the future—expanded trading and increased principal risk—that Friedman and Rubin had presented. "I'm not sure how much they [the investment bankers] were listening either," one partner recalls. "They thought it was a terrible idea going in, and nothing was said there that would convince somebody [otherwise] who thought it was a terrible idea. If you went in with an open mind you might decide one way or the other. But if you went in totally against it, and with good reason—a firm belief in your mind that the partnership culture was in fact the essence of the firm and that this would not just be a different way of capitalizing the firm but would completely change the firm—then you would be looking for alternatives" [to going public]. Some, like former senior partner John Whitehead, believed that limits on capital were not necessarily a bad thing. Two years before he had remarked that "Everybody here knows we have restraints on capital. Capital should be a restraint. It helps you make selections. You have to make choices. We can't do leveraged buyouts and arbitrage—or we can do a little of each." Six months earlier the firm had taken an equity injection from Sumitomo Bank in Japan, and many bankers felt that additional sources of private capital could be located if necessary. This would be the best of all possible worlds, they reasoned—the partners' capital enhanced, their control undiminished.

A number of very senior partners, despite their own economic interests, took issue with their management committee colleagues. A few
stood up and spoke emotionally and at length about the value they placed
on the partnership—what it had meant to them personally. The partnership had a family feeling, which was something many were loath to part
with. A partnership at Goldman Sachs was a sacred trust, they argued.
The partners were custodians of a great lineage extending back to 1869.
Didn't this legacy belong to the next generation? What gave the current
partners the right to sell?

The arguments from the audience appeared very one-sided. Those
opposed stood up to make their points, while those in favor sat quietly,
relying on the management committee to uphold their side of the case.
Some who spoke raised the notion of privacy: Goldman Sachs did not
report its earnings, and the partners liked it that way; few wanted to pro-
claim to the outside world just how much money they made. The firm
had operated for many years under a veil of secrecy. Business decisions
were not analyzed in the press, personality conflicts were not discussed in
the trade magazines, and lifestyle features in glossy magazines complete
with pictures of second homes and second wives were not part of the
Goldman Sachs ethos.

But with the rewards of partnership come considerable risks. All partners, regardless of their stake, left the bulk of each year's earnings with
the firm, to be withdrawn only after retirement. In any given year, if the
firm were to lose money, some of those gains could be wiped out. Partners took home an 8 percent draw each year against the amount they
had in their capital accounts (the amount of the firm's profits they had
accrued but left invested with the firm) and a salary. (In 1997 it was
about $300,000.) One partner in the early 1980s asked for a $60,000
loan to do some improvements on his house at a time when Weinberg and
Whitehead were each receiving a salary of $85,000. The partner was told
to take it out of his salary. "Now how the hell could I do that? My salary
isn't that large," the partner responded. He was cash constrained perhaps, but partners are far from poor. The class of 1986 needed only to
look at the more senior partners to see what financial possibilities existed
in the partnership format. When a list of the one hundred highest-paid
professionals on Wall Street was published in 1986, Goldman Sachs partners filled twelve places.

Fundamentally, Weinberg did not believe that anyone was entitled to
cash in on the firm's legacy. With $1 billion of capital and the intangible
value of a first-class banking franchise (the firm's good name, its established businesses, and its client relationships), Goldman Sachs might have

sold for $3 billion. The firm's value at any given moment is the sum total of the contributions hundreds of people have made for more than a century. Yet the entire economic value of this legacy, worth as much as $2–3 billion, would accrue to those who owned the firm at the time of an initial public offering. In 1997 Weinberg recalled the 1986 meeting: "I always felt there was a terrific risk, and still do, that when you start going that way you are going to have one group of partners who are going to take what has been worked on for 127 years and get that two-for-one or three-for-one. Any of us who are partners at the time when you do that don't deserve it. We let people in at book value, they should go out at book value."

Although Bob Rubin strongly supported the proposal, on some level he too may have had doubts about transforming Goldman Sachs into a large public company. Two years earlier, commenting on Lehman Brothers's merger with Shearson American Express, he had said, "Wall Street has been a highly entrepreneurial arena. Lots of venture dollars are organized here. Leveraged buyouts come out of Wall Street. The merger wave, without regard to the question of whether it is a good thing for society, comes out of Wall Street. Can that entrepreneurial spirit remain alive in units as large as American Express? If not, can Wall Street remain a highly entrepreneurial world? And if it doesn't, does it make a difference? Will this source of energy diminish?" Friedman had concerns as well and did not relish the notion of running a public company, but he supported the proposal wholeheartedly, certain that the firm needed downside protection and an increased capital base with which to compete.

For every person seated in that room going public was a multimillion-dollar question, yet some had more at stake than others. The partners with more seniority, whose stakes were worth between 1 and 3 percent of the firm's capital, would find their bank accounts enriched by many tens of millions of dollars; at least ten partners had stakes that would be worth at least $50 million in a public sale. Weinberg, it was widely estimated at the time, stood to make more than $100 million if the deal went through. A contingent of older partners was very interested in selling the firm. If the firm went public the amount they would take out upon retirement would be two or three times larger than what they would receive if the firm's structure remained unchanged. With Wall Street approaching its peak, for some aging partners with high percentages this would be a once-in-a-lifetime opportunity to cash out. They were determined not to let it pass.

The night before Saturday morning's presentation the worldwide investment banking division held its annual dinner, a celebration of the year's achievements and for the division one of the biggest events of the year. Since rumors had been circulating about the nature of the following morning's meeting, the new banking partners found themselves besieged by those just under the partnership level. There was little support from the troops for going public, and the newest partners came under heavy pressure to vote against the proposal. All the vice-presidents in the room wanted their shot in the coming years, and they let their recently elevated colleagues know it.

Saturday's meeting lasted all day and was adjourned without a decision. Partners were told to disperse, meet among themselves, and carefully consider the weighty issue before them. At the partners' annual dinner dance held at Sotheby's auction house Saturday evening, there was one issue on everyone's mind. Each partner was engaged in a balancing act, an internal struggle to weigh the different factors that would affect his vote. Personally most partners wished the firm to remain a partnership; yet a judgment needed to be made as to whether the firm required a larger and more stable capital base in the near future. And then there was raw self-interest, a very personal calculation of the optimal way to enhance one's wealth. The group was to meet again on Sunday, and a decision would be made.

Without its partnership Goldman Sachs would take the first step toward becoming indistinguishable from every other firm on Wall Street. Instantly the firm would lose its ability to focus on the long term, as quarterly reporting requirements and the demands of outside stockholders would have to be reckoned with. Goldman Sachs's success in attracting and holding onto some of the most talented people in the industry might also be diminished. Without the incentive of partnership to offer young MBAs, the firm might no longer be able to pick from the absolute cream of the crop. The partnership gave Goldman Sachs a very real edge in recruiting, and the motivation it provided was unmatched at public companies. People stayed at the firm, despite being bombarded by lucrative offers from competitors, often with stock options attached, hoping one day to receive an offer of a partnership. Most partners feared that as a public corporation Goldman Sachs would find it difficult to maintain its special culture. Concern ran high that the emphasis on teamwork, low staff turnover, and an unswerving focus on clients might all come under attack if the firm was forced to meet short-term economic targets. Finally, the family feeling and collegial atmosphere might be threatened by the more formal management structure required of a public corporation.

On Sunday morning some members of the class of 1986 met to discuss the issues among themselves. Although out of strict economic self-interest they were all opposed to the management committee's proposal, they felt a weighty responsibility to do what was right for the firm. After some discussion, the presentation by the management committee was deemed to be unconvincing, and there was talk of the group voting against the proposal as a block. Their numbers and the forcefulness of their opposition could assure the motion's failure. But when the group began preparing a formal presentation outlining its disagreement with the plan, Steve Friedman joined them. Many remember that he was angry, and he made it clear that there would be no block voting; this was a matter for consideration by the entire partnership, not for·any interest group to decide. Each partner was to represent his own views and those alone. One member of the group stood up to defend the gathering, telling Friedman that he would have been proud of them, as the discussion had focused on the interests of the firm as a whole. Some of the new partners described this dressing-down as frightening—after all, members of the management committee like Friedman determined partnership stakes, promotions, responsibilities, and virtually every aspect of their partnership careers, now only six days old.

When the partners filed back into the second-floor meeting room, most still believed that there would be a vote. The management committee, and Friedman and Rubin in particular, had expressed their strong support for the idea of going public but had never forcefully pushed the idea. This contrasted sharply with the way other partnerships had gone about selling their firms to larger corporations or the investing public. When Salomon Brothers had sold itself to commodities trading giant Philip Brothers Corporation five years earlier, Salomon's executive committee had presented the idea to the partnership as a fait accompli. There were speeches by those in power and a question period for the partnership that lasted one hour. Those on the executive committee had the power to vote the merger into place on their own, and consulting the general partnership was a formality. Unlike Goldman Sachs's two days of soul searching, the Salomon Brothers meeting, which began in the evening, was so short that it left plenty of time for a celebratory dinner that same night. At no point did those Goldman Sachs partners listening to the management committee's presentation feel that the issue was being railroaded. Rubin and Friedman wisely stepped back and listened.

They got an earful. Two of Sidney Weinberg's sons were in the room that day. John, the younger of the two, was seated silently on the stage, while his brother, Sidney Weinberg Jr., known to everyone as Jimmy, was in the audience. In 1967, Jimmy had come to his father's firm in mid-career, after years with Owens Corning, to head up Investment Banking

Services (IBS), the new business development arm of the investment banking division. IBS was set up to carry on the work of Sidney Weinberg, and it was fitting that his eldest son was at the helm. Now Jimmy felt he needed to have his say. When he stood up to speak, his authority far outstripped his position. Jimmy told the group the proposal made no sense. Goldman Sachs had a heritage, and he was on the side of preserving it. He reminded the partners of their stewardship, of their responsibility to the next generation. He would feel uncomfortable reading about the partners in the newspapers, of having the details of their financial situation made available for public consumption. People stared in amazement: On the face of it the issue seemed to have pitted brother against brother. But after Jimmy spoke, it was all over. No vote was ever taken.

Geoffrey Boisi, the head of investment banking who would soon be seated on the management committee, summed up the events of the day. "We were not psychologically ready to be a public company," he says, "with all that it entailed. I found it ironical, being an adviser to corporate clients on equity offerings, our own blindness to what the impact was going to be on our own culture." Staying private cost some of the more senior partners tens of millions of dollars, and they accepted the decision with a note of regret. Others were relieved. No amount of money would compensate for the loss of the private firm to which they felt such dedication.

Many believe the proposal was doomed from the start, precisely because of John Weinberg's lack of enthusiasm for it. Despite the fact that Friedman and Rubin were managing much of the firm's day-to-day operation by the end of 1986, Weinberg's moral hold on Goldman Sachs was undiminished and his leadership absolute. Culture at Goldman Sachs was passed from one generation to the next and John along with his father Sidney had been the firm's two greatest culture carriers. Partners trusted Weinberg's motives completely; as Boisi said, "You always knew he would ultimately do the right thing." The proposal was too radical to embrace without Weinberg's unqualified commitment to it. In the assessment of one partner, Weinberg was either very brave or very smart—brave enough to take a risk that the firm would go public or smart enough to know it would fail to do so.

The partnership would remain in place, and the question of capital was left unanswered. The management committee had been both correct and incorrect in its assessment. The firm would require additional capital to pursue the expansion plans of its new leaders, but the capital did not need to come from public sources. In time a Hawaiian educational trust, Kamehameha Schools/Bishop Estate, and a group of private insurers would be willing to join Sumitomo in investing in the firm without receiving any management or policy control. Jon Corzine, a former co–chief executive, explains the miscalculation: "The two things we didn't fully consider were that we could bring in outside capital in a private format, and [that] if we performed well financially, we could retain significant capital. In any event, this firm always underestimates where it has the potential to earn. If there is a recurring theme in our thought process, it is that Goldman Sachs underpromises and overdelivers to itself."

Private capital would not come cheaply. In exchange for total managerial autonomy, over the next ten years Goldman Sachs's partners would cobble together a complex and costly capital structure. Through a combination of outside equity investors, limited partners, and employee investments, the firm would remain private but with a cost of capital in excess of what it would have had as a public institution. General partners—those actually running the firm and working for it—would find their stake of the firm's capital diminished over the period. In 1986, before the Sumitomo injection, general partners owned more than 80 percent of the firm's equity (with retired partners holding the remainder); by 1994 they owned less than one-third, although they were entitled to the vast majority of the firm's profits.

There is widespread disagreement about the effects of the December 1986 meeting. Many were elated, and more than one partner has said it was the moment he was most proud to be a partner of Goldman Sachs. A few, however, felt irreparable damage had been done, as personal greed bubbled up and open breaches between partners were aired. Yet the partners had not been asked to rubber-stamp a decision handed down from above. The senior management, as powerful as it was, had listened. For most present, a feeling of true partnership permeated the place; the partnership had reaffirmed its commitment to itself and everyone was on board.

Jon Corzine argues that much was accomplished at the two-day meeting. "I think there was something pivotal about 1986," he said in 1997. "I think the firm decided that it wanted to be a great global firm. And particularly in the post-Whitehead era, I think we reconfirmed that we believed in the global business strategy. We rejected the boutique alternative. The instincts of the organization were that, without knowing how we would be able to get the capital, there was a leap of faith that we could achieve our goals. I think it was instinctive, not a studied decision." There was an alternative route. The firm could easily have decided to cut back, particularly in its capital-intensive trading businesses, or put in place less aggressive expansion plans. These options were rejected.

In 1986 the plans for international expansion were still mostly just talk. The firm had a few foreign offices, one each in Switzerland, Tokyo,

London, and Hong Kong. They were small and relatively unimportant. In the London outpost, a few hundred bankers, traders, and support staff labored in a rundown, unair-conditioned setting on one floor of an office building. The Tokyo office consisted of a few people in search of a banking license and a seat on the Tokyo stock exchange. Zurich was still a representative office designed to service a cadre of rich individuals with interest in U.S. investments. The firm's position in international investment banking was far from established; it ranked an unimpressive twenty-fourth in managing international bond issues outside the United States. But this was only the beginning.

Thus the decision was made to expand rapidly as a private company, to travel a different road from the rest of the industry, and few partners, past or present, many of them now managing directors at publicly traded investment banks, have suggested that a public company is a superior model for managing an investment bank. The partnership is universally credited with maintaining and nurturing Goldman Sachs's unique culture, which allowed the firm to attract and keep its most talented people.

Under Weinberg's direction, Friedman and Rubin set themselves the challenge of building the premier investment banking firm that would dominate every aspect of the business. It would be an astounding feat, one that no firm had ever achieved before. In 1986 there were many investment banks in contention for the top spot, and the outcome of the race was far from assured. If Rubin and Friedman failed, the critics would argue that the firm should have concentrated its resources, capital and human, on a few choice businesses and shared the risk with stockholders. If they succeeded the rewards would be unimaginable.

On the afternoon of December 7, partners streamed out of the meeting with the sense that the discussion had just begun. Further study would be needed; other avenues for seeking capital would be explored. As one partner said, it was like reaffirming one's vows, and the effect trickled down. The following day at the regular Monday morning meeting of the investment banking department, partners spoke to those assembled, rising to say how proud they were to be associated with the firm. "Those were some of the best years I ever spent here," said a partner still with Goldman Sachs, "in part because the whole place was uplifted with the rededication."

Twelve years later the partnership would, for what it believed to be the final time, face this nettlesome issue; it would, after much deliberation, decide to go forward with a public offering. By then the firm would have doubled in size, its capital grown fivefold, and its businesses would truly span the globe. But in 1986 there was little support for such a move, and while the management committee would regularly consider proposals for a sale, the partnership would not revisit the issue for a decade.

THE FIRM FACED its moment of decision in 1986 just as it reached the top tier of investment banks. Goldman Sachs had struggled for decades to rise above its competitors on the second and third rungs of investment banking, and by the 1980s it had achieved this goal through strict adherence to the firm's core values. Sidney Weinberg had lived them, senior partner Gus Levy had followed them, and Levy's successors, John Weinberg and John Whitehead, practiced and later codified them. Goldman Sachs believed in and observed the religion of client service, and its focus remained steadfastly on the long term. Simple as it sounds, the firm's success can be traced to its iron grip on these two values, along with the incentive structure created by its partnership.

"Close client contacts gave Goldman Sachs proprietary information which in turn allowed the firm to tailor products and services which would then earn them a premium," said Peter Mathias, a former vice-president in the area of professional training and development. Even today, as many of the businesses the firm is involved in have become driven by competitive pricing rather than personal relationships, Goldman Sachs maintains exceedingly close client relations. This enables the firm to respond quickly to changing client needs and stay abreast of the deluge of innovations generated in the financial industry. As Stephen Friedman says, not everyone can be the first with a new idea, but there is no excuse for not copying a good idea quickly.

Through its strong client focus Goldman Sachs has been able to control egos and monitor arrogance. The client, not the salesman, banker, or trader, is the focus of any transaction. The banker is there to do his client's bidding. When John Weinberg was running Goldman Sachs he would quickly put new salespeople in their place with words some still remember: Clients are simply in your custody. Someone before you established the relationship and someone after you will carry it on. Weinberg, a man who walks the talk, brought in some of the firm's most important clients and retained key client responsibilities during the fourteen years he ran the firm. Weinberg, like his successors, believed that Goldman Sachs existed to serve its clients, and that not even the senior partner is exempt from this responsibility.

"Ego," Friedman once said, "was the seminal sin of the eighties on Wall Street." During his long tenure in the financial world, Friedman has watched dozens of his competitors' businesses killed by hubris born of success rather than by unsound business decisions or adverse market conditions. "If you are willing to turn down money and you keep your ego under control," says Friedman, "you can save yourself a lot of heartache in this business."

Greed, the second deadly killer on Wall Street, is best contained by focusing attention on the business five years hence rather than on the size of this year's Christmas bonus. Gus Levy's maxim—"Greedy, but long-term greedy"—became the firm's watchword. Partners reinvested almost all their earnings in the firm, so the focus was always on the future. Huge investments were made in new product lines and foreign offices years before the revenue stream to support them materialized. In the mid-1980s, long before the first American investment bank played a major role in a British acquisition, Goldman Sachs sent merger specialists to its tiny London office. Forced to justify their expensive expatriate existence, they cold-called clients and built a business from the ground up. No competitor has been able to seriously challenge the firm's early lead in the mergers and acquisitions business in the U.K.

John Weinberg never lost sight of the long-term interests of Goldman Sachs, even when it hurt. In the weeks following the stock market crash of October 1987, Goldman Sachs was staring at a $100 million loss on a single underwriting. Along with the other members of a syndicate, Goldman Sachs had agreed to underwrite the sale of 32 percent of state-owned British Petroleum for Her Majesty's government. When the U.S. stock market gapped down 22 percent in a single day, taking the world's stock markets with it, some of the other American underwriters got nervous and instructed their lawyers to review their commitments to see if there was a legal method for reducing their exposure. Weinberg never flinched. At a meeting of the syndicate members held to discuss their plight, Weinberg spoke forcefully to his fellow bankers, "Gentlemen, Goldman Sachs is going to do this. It is expensive and painful but we are going to do it. Because if we don't do it, those of you who decide not to do it, I just want to tell you, you won't be underwriting a goat house. Not even an outhouse." To Weinberg, even at $100 million (approximately 20 percent of the firm's 1986 earnings), it was an open-and-shut case. "I considered it a trading loss," he said, "but it was something that had to be done. If we were to stay in the business we had to do it." Other firms, like Morgan Stanley, withdrew for a time from the privatization business in Europe because of this unprofitable affair, allowing Goldman Sachs to garner an ever bigger market share.

By the mid-1980s, Goldman Sachs's dual strategy of focusing on clients and the long term was an unqualified success. The firm's capital, a modest $200 million in 1980, had grown to $1 billion in only six years, virtually all through retained earnings. During this period, the firm's return on equity reached as high as 80 percent, far outstripping the industry norm. In 1985 the largest U.S. investment bank, Merrill Lynch, had a return on equity of only 10 percent, while the more competitive Morgan Stanley earned 34 percent. At this point all of Goldman Sachs's capital was owned by its active and retired partners, for whom there were few better investments on earth.

As competitors folded or merged into vast corporate entities, Goldman Sachs found itself with the oldest major investment banking franchise in the United States. While useful in reminding clients of the firm's stability, the true value of this franchise lay in the length and depth of many of the firm's corporate relationships. Some of its relationships, like those with Sears, Goodrich, and General Foods, were now entering their seventh, and in some cases their eighth, decade. They had been nurtured by generations of bankers and handed down almost like family heirlooms. Devotion to the firm's clients, new and old, was considered inviolate and formed the bedrock on which the firm's investment banking division sat.

The firm's client list had not always been top tier, but three decades of intensive marketing to often uninterested prospective clients had shown results. In the biggest deals of 1986, the firm had helped General Electric purchase RCA and the British government sell British Gas to the investing public. Ford and Unilever had come to Goldman Sachs for advice that year, and the firm counted Monsanto, R. H. Macy's, and Procter & Gamble among its best clients.

The love affair with hostile takeovers that gripped corporate America in the 1980s drove many frightened targets into Goldman Sachs's experienced and unthreatening arms. The firm set itself apart from the rest of the industry by steadfastly refusing to represent any company undertaking a hostile raid. As a result, it often found the victims of such raids banging on its door for cover. Every senior partner had believed that representing hostile raiders would be bad for business—the company being raided today might have been a client in the past or could become one in the future. While some competitors considered the firm's position sanctimonious, corporate chairmen trusted Goldman Sachs not to turn on them, and the policy was a boon to business.

Ultimately, the firm's high level of performance has been due to the singular dedication of its employees, most of whom believe that one day they might become partners. Steve Friedman has summed up the value of ownership by saying, "No one ever washes a rental car." The dream of partnership has served as an unmatched source of inspiration and a great lure for attracting the best people. When graduates of top M.B.A. programs in the 1980s and 1990s compared the relative prestige and long-term financial rewards of a Goldman Sachs partnership to a managing director position at one of the other top investment banking corporations, Goldman Sachs fared well. As a public company, loyalty and performance would have to be purchased the more conventional way, with stock options and each year's bonus.

The firm's culture, the sum of its shared beliefs, is legendary on Wall Street. This more than anything else sets Goldman Sachs apart from its competitors. Widely envied and copied, the firm is sometimes vilified for being too conformist. Yet there can be little doubt that the firm's culture has worked to remarkable effect. "The firm is run like fifty to sixty small businesses, and they have the latitude to do what they want," explained one current partner. "The way you gain prestige in the organization is from the success of your business. The economic and cultural interest is to cooperate." While other firms urge departments to work closely together, at Goldman Sachs the economics of the partnership inextricably tied the partners' fortunes together, cementing that which the culture encouraged. The interests of the partners, while diverging on some matters, were entirely coincident on the issue of profitability. There was one pot from which all partners drew their income. Partners' compensation was by and large tied to the overall profitability of the firm (individual share holdings were reallocated every two years, but in any given year, the percentages already set, a partner's compensation was a direct function of the whole firm's profitability). This contrasted with other organizations where managing directors can be well paid in a single profitable department while the remainder of the firm is performing poorly.

Culture is taken very seriously at Goldman Sachs. It begins in the recruitment process, long before a formal offer is extended. Brains are not enough. The first couple of interviews determine whether a candidate meets the firm's intellectual standards; the remainder, where far more candidates stumble, are used to determine "fit." It is a grueling process that tests endurance as well as aptitude. Those candidates who do not evince a scorching ambition, total commitment, and an inclination for teamwork are quickly weeded out.

In the 1980s each successful candidate endured long interviews with at least twenty vice-presidents and partners. Interviewers were drawn from all ranks of the firm, with Weinberg conducting more than his share. For years the culture thrived in part because the firm grew its own talent. Associates were recruited directly from the very top business schools rather than from competitors. Some candidates found this process repugnant, preferring more eclectic cultures where individual performance was applauded and assimilation was less important. But fitting into the firm's culture is essential at Goldman Sachs, and rugged individualism has no place. The message is sent down by example from the top. Geoffrey Boisi says, "If you can't sublimate your ego or work with others, you have a problem."

For many years the firm eschewed Wall Street's prevailing "star" system, under which a small cadre of very profitable bankers and traders was compensated well out of proportion to the rest of the organization. As the high-profile mergers of the day become front-page news during the 1980s, the men who put those deals together became public personalities and gave Wall Street a glamour it had not had since the 1920s. For many years Goldman Sachs resisted this trend, and those interested in personal glory were urged to find employment elsewhere. "If you say 'I,' you are being abrasive," explained one thirty-three-year veteran partner of the firm. Janet Tiebout Hanson went to college with John Whitehead's daughter and several years later was fortunate enough to land a fixed income sales position immediately after graduating Columbia Business School. She was determined to make her mark at the firm. "I had the great fortune of testing out a lot of things on John Whitehead in my first year," she says. "I kept sending him copies of my trades, these ridiculous little trades. I would sell somebody $20,000 worth of three-money treasury bills, which made the firm nothing, and I would Xerox a copy of the ticket and write across it, 'I did this trade.' When John finally called me one day, he said, 'Janet, at Goldman Sachs we say "we," we never say "I" '—and he hung up. I never forgot that."

For most of the firm's history, morale was high and turnover low. Between 1930 and 1990 Goldman Sachs underwent only two transitions at the senior partner level. Staff turnover in the mid-1980s was 3 percent, substantially below the industry average. This remarkable stability was invaluable in nurturing and maintaining client relationships and raising the level of trust and comfort among the partners and their employees. As of 1986, partners had left to serve in the government, to build their own homes, or to try their hand in academia—but none had shown up in a comparable position on Wall Street.

"You cannot just be an employee of Goldman Sachs," as one former human resources vice-president explained. "The firm demands that you be a contributor. No one can survive as just an employee." There is a single-mindedness that absorbs almost every employee from the moment he or she walks through the door. Total commitment to the firm is expected. It is this atmosphere that has challenged everyone who worked there and allowed people to give the performance of their lives. The message given to young employees from the very highest reaches of the firm is explicit: The firm is special, and you are special or you would not be here. In your career you will achieve great things. Teamwork, all employees are made to understand, will be rewarded in full. For many years this was done informally, but in the mid-1980s cooperation with other departments was included in formal performance evaluations used to determine compensation. Simply doing the job you were hired to do is not enough.

"People just got it," recounts a former vice-president who left for a major competitor. "Things got done two and a half times faster than anyplace else." Business conversations start at an unusually high level; the intellectual buzz is almost audible. Ancillary functions, often staffed at other firms by second-rate employees, are considered vital parts of Goldman Sachs, and a conscious decision was made to staff them with people of the same educational background and training as the revenue-generating departments. The legal, accounting, and compliance divisions view their role as facilitating business, not forestalling action. Their focus is commercial: to find the legal, acceptable way of transacting a deal. An idea hatched on a Friday afternoon by a group of traders sitting around a bag of microwave popcorn might lead to an early morning meeting on Saturday; the lawyers and accountants would check all the angles on Sunday, and by Monday morning the salesman would be ready to put a new idea before the client. It is a fast-moving organization stripped of as much bureaucracy as possible.

Partners own and run the company, so management is up close and personal. They sit on the trading desks, work on the deals, and labor as hard as or harder than their staff. Their focus is unmatched, their commitment unfettered. When the man whose millions are at risk is sitting five feet away, it focuses the mind. What greater motivation could an employee have? A simple "How's it going?" to a trader who is losing money can feel like the grand inquisition. There can be little doubt that the owner-manager role keeps everyone on track. Goldman Sachs's competitors, who had previously relegated ownership to a larger corporation or stockholders, spent the 1980s trying to recreate the partnership atmosphere. Employee stock ownership programs, bonuses tied to the firm's return on equity, and other incentive programs were tinkered with. John Gutfreund, then head of Salomon Brothers, viewed this as one of his own firm's weaknesses and tried to increase employee ownership of its publicly traded stock, believing that this would enhance collegiality and camaraderie. "Then there will be a community of interest that will change the interpersonal relationships again," he said. "Now they are dealing with other people's money most of the time. There's no relationship between them and the capital other than the fact that they have the use of a great amount of it."

Goldman Sachs's management structure was horizontal and the style loose. Usually there have been no more than two layers to the top, and the organization plan could best be described as fluid. An organizational chart of the firm, drawn for Rubin in 1986, shows a circle with the management committee in the center and the operational divisions around the circle. Each management committee member was in the center and in a producing circle, representing their dual roles. This was a far cry from the steep pyramids that depict most large banking organizations, where those at the top operate as full-time managers.

Goldman Sachs's partners grew up together. Their paths had crossed many times over their years as associates and vice-presidents, so by the time partnership came around very few were strangers. This engendered trust, which was essential, since to run their businesses partners must dip into each other's bank accounts every day. Most crucially, management did not need to closely monitor the staff—the culture did it for them.

One of the most visible manifestations of the firm's culture is its emphasis on understatement. Bob Rubin carried a battered briefcase worthy of a law student on a tight budget; another veteran partner, Mark Winkelman, regularly rode the subway. Men of great wealth, the partners of Goldman Sachs deliberately discouraged its overt trappings even as the ostentatious 1980s descended, believing money is for bank accounts, not for flashing about. When a young trader at the firm was quoted in the *New York Times* in April 1986 as saying, "There isn't anything I see in a store that I can't buy," the entire firm cringed.

Goldman Sachs's main office, three blocks south of Wall Street, is a monument to understatement. Built by the firm in 1983, the thirty-story concrete building gives nothing away. Like private English banks or the legendary headquarters of J. P. Morgan at the corner of Broad and Wall Streets, the Goldman Sachs name does not appear on the front of its world headquarters. The sign above the door simply reads "85." Even the passes issued by security guards on the ground floor do not bear the firm's name, just the word "visitor." The cavernous, two-story lobby with brick floors and unadorned, unpolished marble walls has a cold, impersonal feeling. The firm's austere logo, a box around the words Goldman Sachs, is nowhere to be found—there are no raging bulls here, no protective red umbrellas.

The building straddles Stone Street, blocking off traffic on both sides. Archeological excavations around the perimeter of the site undertaken during construction can be seen clearly; looking through the transparent floor one can see the vestiges of Governor Lovelace's seventeenth-century tavern and the remains of an eighteenth-century cistern. Inside the building, the wooden and brass elevators open on each floor onto unprepossessing dark wood-paneled reception areas with overstuffed camelback sofas, along with a chair or two. The firm's traditional decor has a timeless quality and has remained untouched for a decade and a half; there is nothing new or flashy here. Rubin would sometimes joke about the opulent settings of the firm's competitors. When he and Friedman, as co–senior partners, visited their counterparts at the large commercial banks, Rubin would glance around the spacious waiting room outside the CEO's office, with its valuable art and oriental rugs, and ask if Friedman thought they could squeeze a whole trading floor into the space. The emphasis at Goldman Sachs is on creating wealth rather than displaying it. There is nothing to betray that this is the center of one of America's wealthiest companies and the workplace of some of its richest men and women. Discretion is everything.

Even the partners' dining room, in many firms a small elegant restaurant, is little more than an upscale cafeteria. The emphasis is on simple healthy food; alcohol, let alone vintage wines or fine liqueurs, is rarely present at lunch. The views of New York's harbor from the dining room's thirtieth-floor location are the only spectacular thing about one of the most exclusive eating spots in the world. Underneath the Limoges china, Frette linens, and Christofle silver, some of the tables are chipped or peeling, and the battered walls need a new coat of paint. Speakerphones and soundproof ceiling tiles reinforce that this is a place built for work rather than relaxation. The employees' cafeteria is underground, in a room without windows.

In stark contrast to the otherwise somber surroundings is the firm's unusual art collection. Adorning the unremarkable offices, and all the more striking for it, is an eclectic selection of American art and artifacts that includes enormous weathervanes, daguerreotypes, bright modern paintings, and a wide variety of patchwork quilts. There is also an occasional kimono. In one reception area hang the wrought-iron gates from a nineteenth-century elevator. The criteria for this collection was only that it be interesting and inexpensive.

While Salomon Brothers drew up plans for a palatial tower overlooking Central Park in 1986, and Drexel Burnham Lambert moved its most profitable traders to their own offices in Beverly Hills, Goldman Sachs squeezed more staff into a smaller space. Instead of buying more real estate and calling in the architects, when the firm's New York headquarters became crowded, management initiated a "space optimization" program. As soon as Steve Friedman discovered the cost savings of having the staff sit closer together he quickly had the extra chair removed from each cubicle, saying it had been used only as a place to set folders and hang raincoats. He estimated that reducing the size of the staff's workspace had saved the firm at least $50 million annually, and he bragged about the cost savings inside the firm and to the press.

Every Goldman Sachs office, whether in London or Tokyo, looks almost exactly alike. The same long, dark wood trading desks and the same ergonomically correct chairs are imported into any location where the firm sets up shop. Partners' offices, slightly down at the heels and showing their age, reveal remarkably few splashes of personality. A mild shabbiness seems to be almost a status symbol. If all the firm's partners were told they had to change offices in ten minutes, most could easily pick up their tastefully framed family photos and a few souvenirs of past accomplishments (mostly newspaper announcements of successful deals, sealed in Lucite), grab their papers and floppy discs, take their jackets off the back of the door, and go. Goldman Sachs partners sometimes have been characterized in the press as "the men in the gray suits," as wholly lacking the high-profile public personalities of some of their competitors.

Goldman Sachs's culture is not without its detractors. Many have argued that the collective focus has quashed innovation and original thought. As one partner summed it up, "We wouldn't be the ones to fig-ure out how you make money in Japanese equity warrants," one of the most profitable businesses of the early 1990s. Friedman, one of those whose goal was to increase the firm's receptivity to new ideas, acknowl-edges that in the 1980s innovation was a weak point for the firm. "Why should Goldman Sachs have been so much later than other firms in get-ting into derivatives? Why should we have been so much later than Salomon in getting into the mortgage business or in developing a capital markets group?" he asked in 1997. Goldman Sachs set the standard, but it did not set the pace. Even admiring competitors remarked on the firm's lack of creativity: "I love competing against Goldman because it's like going against Ohio State [in football]," says one Morgan Stanley banker. "They're predictable, they're not adaptable, and they're very, very good. You know it's going to be a hard contest, but you know how to compete against them."

Over the years, the unwillingness to create stars and to compensate extraordinary contributions financially has driven out some of the firm's entrepreneurial talent; some of these men have shown astounding cre-ativity and enjoyed successful, headline-generating careers elsewhere. While the firm made a big push to increase its creativity in the late 1980s and early 1990s, it was fighting the weight of its own culture. As one for-mer vice-president says, "I never got the sense even to the last day I was at Goldman Sachs that they really wanted you to be extremely creative. What they wanted you to do was do the ordinary things extraordinarily well." Others strongly disagree, claiming that by the mid-1990s the firm had a well-deserved reputation for creativity and innovation.

The interviewing process has been criticized for producing clones—bright, loyal foot soldiers with sharp minds and conformist natures. One partner who disagrees explains that the all-important interview process was seeking candidates with "brains, humor, motivation, a sort of restrained audacity, confidence, and maturity." One overzealous interviewer, however, asked Stanford female undergraduates whether they would advise a friend to have an abortion in order to save her career. The interviewer received a stiff reprimand, but the point had been made that one was expected to make sacrifices for a Goldman Sachs career.

Flashes of individuality have been tolerated in very brilliant or highly profitable employees but frowned upon in the masses of those who have been merely extremely bright. One trader who had made more than $50 million for the firm in his first year regularly appeared at the office in jeans and cowboy boots. When he began to lose money, he was asked to put on a suit.

Collegiality, one of the firm's greatest strengths, was taken to such an extreme within the partnership that even in 1994, when it was clear that risk management in some areas of the firm had developed problems, many partners felt unable to comment. When one young trading partner asked a member of the management committee who he knew was critical of what was happening why he did not speak out, the older partner reminded him that partners live in glass houses; if he were critical at this juncture what would happen to him when his businesses hit a rough patch?

By the late 1980s there was some recognition at the top that in fact the culture of the firm was changing. The number of employees had tripled from 2,000 in 1980 to 6,000 in 1986, creating enormous strains on the informal process of acculturation. It was increasingly difficult to create the same sense of belonging in an organization in which half the people had been there for less than two years. One member of the management committee, recognizing the problem, said at the time, "Everyone is uncomfortable with the rate of growth. We all feel that if we don't keep expanding, we'll lose our position. But if we keep growing at a certain rate, we'll lose control." A confidential study that consulted members of the management committee and other long-serving partners was commissioned by the firm in 1988 and revealed some of the partners' concerns. (The report was excerpted in the *New York Times*. The firm has declined to release its entire contents, which presumably paint a broader and much more flattering picture. Goldman Sachs spokesmen have protested that the version of the study leaked to the newspaper was only a preliminary brainstorming effort, and that the comments were taken out of context—the study itself was, they say, overwhelmingly positive—

but have never said that the quotations that appeared were inaccurate.) As one of the rare unguarded glimpses into some of the partners' true thinking, it provides insight into cultural issues at the time:

- "We've seen a lot of change within the firm—growth, international business, bringing in people from the outside, etc. It's brought a lot of things with it. Things like more backbiting, comments made about other people and other activities, and they affect what it's like to work here."
- "We get people who are excellent when they get here. They do however have an inflated sense of self and an enormous need for recognition."
- "Goldman Sachs used to be paternalistic. Now we're more businesslike. We've become tougher in a more competitive world. Some would even say we've become ruthless."
- "In the old days, when you became a partner, you would feel free to give your wallet to another partner to hold for safekeeping. I do not think it is that way today."
- "The vision of the future is as a public company."

Many believe that Goldman Sachs's future rests squarely on its culture. Bill Buckley has been with the firm for twenty-two years and is now a managing director, and co-head of Private Client Services (PCS). For years this department has been the closest thing Goldman Sachs has had to a retail business, one that served high-net-worth individuals rather than institutions. Buckley feels that culture has been and will be the key. "Our firm's culture is the most sustainable competitive advantage that we have," he says.

I also believe that we have the best people, but the magic is in the combination of outstanding people and a strong culture. This means that, through PCS, our clients are working with professionals who prefer to work in teams and are connected to many others throughout the firm. For example, a PCS representative may be up at midnight calling a colleague halfway around the world to check on an opportunity for a client. As a result, our clients have all of Goldman Sachs working for them. It's very hard to maintain a special culture, but if we can, I really think that we will be ahead of everybody else. Not only will clients get the best service, but we will achieve a superior market share. Goldman Sachs's culture was something we were always proud of, but ironically it is even more of a tangible competitive advantage today. I am convinced of that.

The firm's culture was nurtured by its partnership and sustained by the incentive structure created by its owner-managers. It would be impossible for it to remain the same if Goldman Sachs transformed itself into a public corporation.

"NINETEEN EIGHTY-SIX," *Institutional Investor* magazine proclaimed, "was the year they sold Wall Street." During the five preceding years John Weinberg had watched his major competitors incorporate, merge, or simply cease to exist. It began when Salomon Brothers sold itself to Philip Brothers in 1981. The trading muscle and formidable capital of the combined operation proved matchless. The Salomon Brothers partners became multimillionaires, and their firm, by the mid-1980s, went from strength to strength. This turn of events was not lost on the partners of Goldman Sachs just across the street. Then Lehman Brothers sold itself to Shearson American Express in 1984. In 1986, Kidder Peabody was acquired by conglomerate General Electric, and in 1981, Dean Witter was acquired by Sears. Bear Stearns went public in 1985. While all of these mergers looked as though they would create daunting competitors, most would in time encounter difficulties and would ultimately unravel.

The biggest blow to Goldman Sachs's existence as a private partnership came when archrival Morgan Stanley sold itself in 1986 to the public for 2.76 times book value. In an initial public offering worth $254 million (20 percent of the firm was sold), Morgan Stanley partners became managing directors, personally enriching themselves in the process. While First Boston and Merrill Lynch were becoming more formidable rivals, for the bankers at Goldman Sachs, Morgan Stanley was the competition, the firm most admired and feared. Morgan Stanley's partners decided to sell because they believed the firm could no longer operate as a partnership as it ventured into riskier businesses like leveraged buyouts and merchant banking. Many at Goldman Sachs grew concerned that Morgan Stanley would pull away in the race for the top, that its new access to capital would translate into access to opportunity.

Goldman Sachs, too, sold a bit of itself in 1986. The roots of the transaction took hold the year before when one morning a man who refused to identify himself telephoned Ann Ericson, John Weinberg's secretary. Would Mr. Weinberg, he asked, be in the office on a Tuesday, three weeks hence? Unable to confirm Weinberg's schedule, Ericson said she did not know, and the caller, without leaving a name or identifying trace, said he would ring back. Two weeks later the same unidentified caller contacted Ericson to confirm the date, and this time she indicated that Weinberg would be in the office. When the appointed day arrived two Japanese men, a speaker and his interpreter, appeared in Weinberg's office. The man who spoke only Japanese identified himself through his assistant: I am the president of Sumitomo Bank, Koh Komatsu told Weinberg. I came here in disguise to see you. Komatsu had tried to hide his tracks. From Tokyo he flew to Seattle, Washington. There he changed planes for a flight to Washington, D.C. From Washington, he boarded the shuttle to La Guardia. He felt certain that he had made the journey undetected. Weinberg, surprised by this clandestine behavior, then told him that every banker and lawyer in the country goes back and forth from New York to Washington on the shuttle; it was hardly the place to hide.

Weinberg was baffled by the visit. He had no way of knowing that Sumitomo Bank had long been interested in gaining a toehold in the U.S. investment banking market and had been looking at Goldman Sachs. Sumitomo, at that time the world's third largest and Japan's most profitable bank, had hired top consulting firm McKinsey and Co. to advise them on the best way to enter the market. McKinsey had recommended an investment in Goldman Sachs as the ideal mechanism.

Never in its long history had Goldman Sachs taken outside equity. For Weinberg personally it would be a difficult decision. He had fought with the Marines in Japan during World War II and had helped liberate a prisoner-of-war camp shortly after the bomb was dropped on Nagasaki. Komatsu had been a naval officer, his destroyer sunk by American forces. Weinberg was at first unsure about the alliance, but in fairness to his partners he let the negotiations proceed.

As Weinberg listened to Komatsu's proposal he was amazed. The valuation given to Goldman Sachs by Sumitomo was far above the firm's own. Komatsu was offering cash, an equity injection, in return for a share of the profits. The deal was almost too good to be true. By offering to make a $500 million investment in exchange for 12.5 percent of the firm's profits, Sumitomo was implicitly valuing Goldman Sachs at $4 billion—four times book value. Morgan Stanley had just floated itself at under three times book value, and other publicly traded investment banks were selling for less. The deal, it was stipulated, would be conducted in total secrecy, with Goldman Sachs acting as its own investment banker.

It was a big step, and Weinberg, ever cautious, proceeded slowly. Goldman Sachs had no urgent need for the capital and was in no rush. Sumitomo wanted to learn about American investment banking. Its plan was to send dozens of trainees to sit with Goldman Sachs employees and learn the business up close. The firm and the Federal Reserve balked; if the relationship was to be established it would have to be at arm's length. The Fed also decreed that Sumitomo's investment could not rise above 24.9 percent of the partners' capital. If Sumitomo invested in Goldman

Sachs, it would be as a nonvoting limited partner. Weinberg set out to explain to the new investor why it was in Sumitomo's best interest for Goldman Sachs to remain entirely independent. "I'm not being tough," he said. "You're going to end up with an eighth of Goldman Sachs's equity. We have to be the master of our own destiny. It not only has to be that we are, but it has to be perceived that we are by the financial community. Because if we're not, we will lose our reputation, our clients, and our position in the investment banking industry." The Federal Reserve Bank approved the deal on the grounds that it was a passive investment, that Sumitomo would not gain any control over Goldman Sachs, and that the two firms would not work more closely together either by exchanging employees or by increasing the amount of business they did with each other. Both agreed to the terms the Federal Reserve stipulated, and the investment was made in fiscal year 1987. The firm never regretted the move; the relationship proved both pleasant and profitable.

Weinberg's confidence in the value of his firm came in part from its competitive position in 1986. While there can be little doubt that the firm was among the very best investment banks, its stature should not be overstated. The firm was sixth in the amount of corporate debt it underwrote in the United States in 1986, behind the perennial number one Salomon Brothers and the upstart Drexel, both of whom were more opportunistic and innovative. While Goldman Sachs was struggling to establish its fixed income business, Drexel and Salomon were making headlines. Both firms had pioneered major advances in fixed income products. Salomon Brothers had broken new ground when it packaged and securitized first home and later automobile loans. Drexel had done the same with low-grade corporate debt, known unflatteringly as junk bonds. By innovating and establishing an early presence, these two firms had been able to dominate large and highly profitable areas of bond trading. The rewards had been substantial. Both firms had iconoclastic, entrepreneurial cultures that allowed new ideas to develop and flourish. Both were willing to take risks with their capital, their franchises, and ultimately, in the case of Drexel, its good name in order to make a huge leap in profitability. Referring to the firm's massive fixed income business in 1986, one member of the management committee now concedes, "Soly was eating our lunch."

Salomon's presence in Tokyo dwarfed that of Goldman Sachs, and the firm found itself in the uncomfortable role of having to play catch up. Having teamed up with Credit Suisse, First Boston dominated the very visible and highly competitive Eurobond business in London while Goldman Sachs trailed far behind all of its major American and European competitors. The commercial banks were breathing hard down the necks of their investment banking brethren. Had they not become consumed with their own loan troubles, first in Latin America and later in domestic real estate, they would have become more formidable competitors earlier. While Goldman Sachs was in an extremely strong position in 1986, there were others who, if they had played their cards right, could have overtaken it.

Yet the firm's caution was not difficult to understand. By 1986 much of Goldman Sachs's competition was protected by the shield of incorporation, but a private partnership had no such defense. Junk bonds and bridge loans were not things you would want to buy with your own money. If the firm entered these businesses in any major way, the leadership believed that it was wise to share the risk with public stockholders. While the notion of becoming a public company was not received warmly by the partnership in 1986, Friedman told those gathered at the meeting that no responsible management could fail to look at it again—it was an issue that was not going to go away.

SIX WEEKS after the momentous meeting of December 1986, outside events intervened. The insider trading scandal slowly engulfing Wall Street had had little impact on the firm over the course of 1986. Even when Ivan Boesky, the best-known arbitrageur in the business, was arrested and pleaded guilty to insider trading, the firm was not overly concerned. Still, out of prudence, it began an internal investigation. Risk arbitrage was a business invented by Goldman Sachs, and the firm was one of its savviest practitioners. Goldman Sachs was naturally involved in many of the same deals as Boesky; if there was a problem the firm was determined to locate it. Months of dissecting mountains of complex paperwork revealed nothing, however, and as the year ended the partners felt Goldman Sachs had no role to play in the growing scandal. No one could guess that only weeks later one of the firm's own partners would be arrested. For years the case would consume the attention of top management. The notion of selling the firm would be shelved until Goldman Sachs cleared its name and restored its reputation—a reputation that had first taken shape just four blocks north on Pine Street more than a century earlier.

CHAPTER II

1869–1976

THE FAMILY FIRM

For MOST OF ITS LONG and illustrious history Goldman Sachs was run by three families: the intermarried Goldmans and Sachses and the upstart Weinbergs. Members of the Goldman and Sachs families served the firm for more than a century, and after ninety years, two Weinbergs continue as partners to this day. Success for these men was defined not in terms of any one quarter's profits, or even by a couple of good years, but in leaving their heirs a stronger business than the one they themselves inherited. These unbroken chains of succession allowed Goldman Sachs to remain a family firm long after all of the other major Wall Street partnerships had transformed themselves into large public corporations.

Marcus Goldman, a former schoolteacher and the son of a peasant dealing in cattle, arrived from Germany in 1848 in the first great wave of Jewish immigration to America and thrived initially as a peddler with a horse-drawn cart and later as a shopkeeper in Philadelphia. There Goldman met and married eighteen-year-old Bertha Goldman (no relation) who had also emigrated from Germany in 1848. In 1869, with his wife and five children, Goldman relocated to New York and hung out a shingle on Pine Street in lower Manhattan, Marcus Goldman & Co., setting himself up as a broker of IOUs in a cramped basement space next to a coal chute. With an office boy and a part-time bookkeeper who spent afternoons at a funeral parlor, Goldman founded one of the greatest banking enterprises of the twentieth century.

Each morning, donning his frock coat, Goldman would call on wholesale diamond merchants in Maiden Lane and hide and leather merchants in what was called "the swamp" on Beekman Street to buy up their promissory notes. Goldman would provide the merchants with ready cash, say $4,850, and in return the merchant would sign a note promising to repay the bearer $5,000 by a specified date. The bills were discounted by between 8 and 9 percent, the standard interest rate at the time. Commission charges of one-half of 1 percent, or fifty basis points, of the face amount were also levied by note collectors, like Goldman. These IOUs were fungible, and on his travels Goldman would stuff them into the inside band of his tall silk hat for resale later in the day to the Chemical Bank on Chambers Street, the Importers and Traders Bank on Warren Street, or the National City Bank on Wall Street. It was said that a banker's success each day could be measured by the "altitude of his hat."

Promissory notes were the precursors of today's commercial paper, and the men who traded in them were known as "note shavers." From the earliest days of his business, Goldman was able to transact single-handedly as much as $5 million worth of commercial paper a year. Successful though he was, Goldman's business was insignificant compared to that of the other German-Jewish bankers of his day. Concerns like Seligman's, with working capital of $6 million in 1869, were already modern-day investment bankers immersed in underwriting and trading railroad bonds.

Goldman's youngest daughter, Louisa, married Sam Sachs, the son of close friends and fellow Bavarian immigrants. Louisa's older sister and Sam's older brother had already married. Although the second son among five children, Sam was left in charge of the family's finances after the untimely death of his parents. By fifteen he had become a bookkeeper in a small importing house, allowing his brothers Julius and Barney to finish their educations. Sam also launched his brother Harry on a business career that eventually would find him as a partner of Goldman Sachs. Emelia Sachs married soon after her parents' death and set up housekeeping for her four brothers.

In 1882, Marcus Goldman invited his son-in-law Sam to join him in the business and changed the firm's name to M. Goldman and Sachs. Business was booming—by 1880 the new firm was turning over $30 million worth of paper a year—and the firm's capital was now $100,000, all of it the senior partner's. Goldman lent Sachs the $15,000 he needed to invest in the partnership, asking for repayment in three lump sums over the following three years. Sachs worked hard and had repaid the first two installments when his third son, Walter E. Sachs, was born. In recognition of the child's birth and the junior partner's "energy and ability," the proud grandfather, in a note dated May 28, 1884, forgave the final payment. Walter E. Sachs would later write, "And thus, it appeared that on the very day of my entrance into this world, I concluded my first business deal for Goldman, Sachs." All three of Sam's sons entered the family business, but Walter's connection with the firm lasted for seventy-two years, until his death in 1980 at the age of ninety-six.

For almost fifty years after its inception all of Goldman Sachs's partners were members of the intermarried families. In 1885, Goldman took his own son Henry and his son-in-law Ludwig Dreyfuss into the business as junior partners and the firm adopted its present name, Goldman Sachs & Co. In 1894, Harry Sachs entered the firm, and in 1896 the firm joined the New York Stock Exchange.

Through the efforts of these men, Goldman Sachs would become the largest dealer of commercial paper in the United States, its dominance unrelinquished for more than a century. By 1890 the firm's annual sales of commercial paper were $31 million, and by 1894 they had risen to $67 million. By the late 1960s, Goldman Sachs would handle 50 percent of the country's commercial paper, placing more than $200 million a day with investors.

By the early days of the twentieth century the business had relocated several times and had settled into a few second-floor rooms at 43 Exchange Place, enough space for the five partners, ten clerks, and five or six messengers the firm now employed. The firm's stated capital had grown to $585,000 by 1894 and its annual profits to $200,000. Four years later the firm's capital had almost tripled, to $1.6 million. With no income tax in place, the partners' capital compounded at an astonishing rate, growing to $2.5 million by the end of 1900. In 1906 the firm had profits of $1.2 million, and the business had become so large and varied that the partners were sitting on $4.5 million of capital.

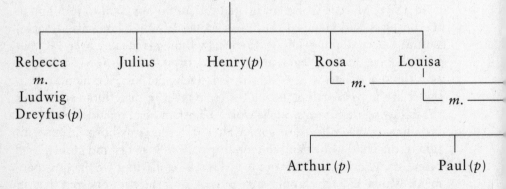

MARCUS GOLDMAN (p) m. BERTHA GOLDMAN

Rebecca   Julius   Henry(p)   Rosa   Louisa
m.
Ludwig
Dreyfus (p)

m.

m.

Arthur (p)   Paul (p)

(p)= partner of Goldman Sachs

When Marcus Goldman retired he left the firm in the hands of his son Henry and his son-in-law Sam Sachs. The brothers-in-law, Goldman and Sachs, were a study in contrast. Sam was a formal, conservative man who wore a thin alpaca office coat even on the hottest days of summer. Henry, more relaxed, worked in his shirtsleeves. Goldman was always looking for daring new opportunities to make money, while Sachs preferred to build gradually on earlier successes. Sachs concerned himself with the firm's reputation, its standing in the banking community. His sons would follow closely in this tradition. When a deal fell through with a partner about whom the Goldmans and Sachses had known very little, Sam's son Paul Sachs explained his relief: "From the very first moment, [we were] disturbed by the morale [*sic*] of these men and while I do not deny that the business might have proved satisfactory enough, we are as a matter of fact glad to have seen it fall through because as we progressed our first unfavorable impression was at every meeting strongly emphasized." Henry Goldman was more ambitious and his interests more nakedly commercial. He regularly would remind his nephew Walter Sachs, "Money is always fashionable." A risk taker, he relished trading railroad and utility bonds, successfully speculating with his partners' capital. There was a certain rivalry between the brothers-in-law, and they often rubbed each other the wrong way. On one thing, however, the two agreed. Both dreamed of developing a general financial partnership, something much greater than a simple commercial paper dealership.

Sachs envisioned an international banking firm. Like many wealthy Americans of his day, he was enamored with everything European. Traveling frequently to Europe both professionally and on family visits, his

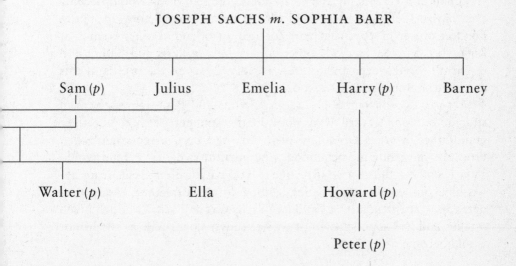

JOSEPH SACHS *m.* SOPHIA BAER

Sam (*p*)   Julius   Emelia   Harry (*p*)   Barney

Walter (*p*)   Ella   Howard (*p*)

Peter (*p*)

outlook on life was decidedly continental. American clients, he argued, would only be served fully if Goldman Sachs expanded overseas. (It would be an argument made just as forcefully by senior partner John Whitehead eighty years later.) At the time Britain had a capital surplus, and interest rates were lower there than in the United States. Money could be borrowed in England and sterling exchanged for dollars with lower interest payments, assuming the price of the sterling-dollar exchange rate remained unchanged. Of course the exchange rate was not constant, but many American borrowers were willing to take the risk. Sachs saw opportunities for his firm in transacting foreign borrowings, and in June 1897 he traveled to London and met with Herman and Alexander Kleinwort of Kleinwort Sons & Co., one of the leading merchant banks of the day.

The Kleinworts were interested but knew little of Goldman Sachs; through N. M. Rothschild's New York agent, August Belmont, they investigated the newcomers. The reply was favorable. Goldman Sachs, it was relayed by Belmont, "was a firm against whom there could not be a single word of criticism." Kleinwort was a top-tier London firm with an impeccable reputation, and the connection would prove invaluable. The joint account with the Kleinworts was established without a formal written contract in 1897 and operated successfully for many decades. Correspondence between the partners of the two firms reveals a close personal and professional relationship, with the two swapping opinions about economic and market conditions, prospective business opportunities, and warm personal regards. When in England, Goldman Sachs partners spent weekends at the country homes of their Kleinwort hosts. The Kleinworts, who also benefited greatly from the relationship, wrote to Henry Goldman in 1913, saying that they hoped the two firms would become even closer. Goldman Sachs held off for many years before opening a London office (in 1970), in part for fear of offending their friends at Kleinwort. Sam Sachs made other connections in Paris and Berlin, and the firm's foreign department grew rapidly. By 1906 the profits of this department alone were $500,000.

In 1904 two of Sam Sachs's sons, Arthur and Paul, joined the firm straight out of Harvard University. In the summer of that year their grandfather, Marcus Goldman, died. His had been a remarkable life. From the most humble beginnings, the institution he left behind would soon become a full-service investment bank. With the advent of underwriting, coupled with the existing lending, foreign exchange, and trading operations, the structure of Goldman Sachs was in place. Although much smaller and less sophisticated, it was already recognizable as the firm it would become.

WITH SAM SACHS, Henry Goldman guided the firm for many years after his father's death. He had left Harvard without a degree because of trouble with his eyesight and had arrived at Goldman Sachs at the age of twenty-eight after working as a traveling salesman. Sidney Weinberg, who was hired to assist the janitor in 1907 and would end up running the firm as senior partner for thirty-nine years, saw Henry as the creative genius who revolutionized the firm's business. It was Goldman who transformed the firm into an investment bank by taking it into a new line of business: underwriting.

During this period, from the 1890s until World War I, investment banking as it is now known came into being. The country needed capital, and a new breed of investment banker was there to help provide it. The assets of the country's financial institutions had more than doubled between 1900 and 1910, from $9 billion to $21 billion. Goldman Sachs expanded rapidly during this period, opening branch offices in Chicago, Boston, Philadelphia, and St. Louis. The early years of the century also witnessed a fantastic bull market; between 1904 and 1906, the Dow Jones Industrial Average doubled, from 36.4 to 73.5. Wall Street hit a major snag in 1907 with the banking panic that followed the failure of the Knickerbocker Trust Company. Henry Goldman would play a part in arranging the subsequent merger between the Columbia Trust Company and Knickerbocker. (The newly formed bank would later become the Irving Trust Company, a client of the firm for the next ninety years.) Goldman Sachs did not emerge from this difficult time unscathed, and Sam Sachs confided in Alexander Kleinwort that, "Owing to the fall in securities, instead of being able to say that we have four and a half million [of capital] we knock off $750,000."

The established banking firms of the day—J. P. Morgan, Kuhn Loeb & Co., and Speyer & Co.—were financing the massive expansion of the utilities and the railroads. Almost $1.2 billion of new railroad securities was floated between 1900 and 1902 alone. Henry Goldman began buying railroad shares aggressively, hoping to be noticed by the railroads' management and to muscle his firm's way into the most lucrative underwriting business of the day. Jimmy Speyer discovered Goldman's tactics and summoned him to his Pine Street office. There he informed the ambitious Goldman that the three established banking concerns would handle all of the railroad business; newcomers were unwanted. Speyer offered to purchase Goldman Sachs's railroad holdings at cost plus 6 percent interest. Goldman refused the offer, returned to his office incensed, and quickly met with his partners. As usual the brothers-in-law Goldman and Sachs disagreed. Goldman argued that the firm should take its chances and seek out railroad underwriting business, but Sachs was staunchly unwilling to upset the existing order or risk tarnishing the firm's good name. Julius Goldman, who often served as the firm's counsel, was called in to arbitrate the dispute. The younger Goldman sided with his brother-in-law, and Henry Goldman began the search for a new line of business for the firm to pursue. In retrospect, Speyer did the firm a great and lasting favor by refusing it entry into railroad underwriting. In the railroad business Goldman Sachs would have waged an uphill battle against three entrenched competitors to gain any substantial market share. By forcing the firm to look elsewhere, Goldman Sachs soon developed a new business of its own, one that would thrive long after the railroads faded in importance.

Smarting from his rebuff by the banking establishment and the lack of ambition shown by his partners, Goldman turned his sights on the growing number of large retailers. Although railroad issues continued to dominate the stock market, the number of listings for industrial and mercantile companies on the New York Stock Exchange rose steadily from twenty in 1898 to 173 by 1915. These companies, many of them family-owned businesses established after the Civil War, required outside capital to fuel their expansion. Up to this time their financing needs had been met through commercial bank loans or in some cases commercial paper (fungible IOUs), but for the first time they were turning to the stock market in large numbers. There was opportunity here, and Henry Goldman, in conjunction with his close friend Philip Lehman, took advantage of it. The friends, who lunched together almost every day on the second floor of Delmonico's downtown restaurant, considered setting up an underwriting firm of their own called Goldman and Lehman, but decided to continue to conduct business from their respective family firms as co-underwriters. Through this partnership, Goldman Sachs and Lehman Brothers would underwrite equity offerings jointly, sharing equally in the profits. The relationship rested on the fact that Goldman Sachs had the clients and Lehman Brothers had the money.

The firms' first large retailing client came to them fortuitously. Sam Sachs's sister Emelia was related by marriage to Julius Rosenwald. Years earlier, when Rosenwald had first arrived from Germany, he had lived with Emelia and her husband in New York. They had thought him a nice young man, but the family felt he would never amount to much in the business world. Eventually Rosenwald left to seek greater opportunities in the Midwest. There he met Richard Sears, a ticket agent on the Minneapolis & St. Louis Railroad, who had an idea for selling watches by mail order. The business was transplanted to Chicago from Minneapolis, and the men each took a one-third interest, with a group of individuals funding the final third of what was named Sears Roebuck & Co. The future retailing giant had expanded with funding from commercial paper sold by Goldman Sachs; in 1897 Goldman Sachs lent Sears $75,000 in commercial paper at a time when the retailer's net worth was a mere $237,000.

Nearly a decade later, when Rosenwald turned to his cousins at Goldman Sachs seeking a $5 million loan for the construction of a large mail order plant in Chicago, Henry Goldman suggested a public offering. In 1906, Goldman Sachs and Lehman Brothers joined forces to bring to the public shares in the first mail order retailer. Earlier in the year Goldman Sachs had underwritten its first public offering for United Cigar Manufacturers, and they were anxious to gain more experience and exposure. Sears's turnover at the time was $50 million, and the two firms underwrote a $10 million offering of preferred and common stock. The preferred shares would be backed by the net assets of the company and the common shares by its goodwill, a highly unusual concept at the time. Underwriters would sell the preferred stock to the public and retain the common shares for themselves. (Eighty years later Michael Milken would "pioneer" the same practice when his firm, Drexel Burnham Lambert, retained warrants—options to buy shares at a preset price later on—as compensation for underwriting risky deals.) Until this time, securities—primarily of railways and steel companies—had been valued and marketed on the basis of a company's physical assets, literally its nuts and bolts. Henry Goldman argued that the value of a retail business should be calculated based on the rate at which it turned over its inventory, or how rapidly it generated cash. This, not the value of its physical assets, would determine its ability to meet debt obligations and secure a profit. From there he went on to develop more fully the notion of valuing a company on the basis of its earning power and hence its price-earnings ratio—this is still the most widely used method for valuing common stocks. This marked a revolution in thinking that was essential to Goldman Sachs's future success. Only by valuing securities in this way could the type of companies that Goldman Sachs sought to underwrite—those with relatively few physical assets and large amounts of goodwill—be sold to an initially skeptical public.

The Sears underwriting agreement was signed in June 1906, but it took the firms several months to place all the shares. Much of the stock was placed in Europe through Sam Sachs's connections at Kleinwort. Goldman and Lehman were invited to sit on the new board of directors, lending their credibility to the fledgling company. The common stock was issued at $50 a share and a year later, in the banking panic of 1907, traded down to only $25. But in 1909, when Goldman Sachs led a syndicate that bought Richard Sears's one-third stake in the company, they had to pay him about $9 million. Only three years earlier the entire company had been valued at $10 million. When Sears Roebuck faced a large loss a dozen years later, Julius Rosenwald felt such a great obligation to his shareholders that he personally assumed a large part of the loss. Arthur Sachs commented that, "To us it seems a unique occurrence in industry for a man to present to a corporation 50,000 shares of his own stock, and in that way individually assume the burdens. I hope his action from a point of view of generosity impresses you as it does us." Rosenwald never sold his stake in the company and died a very wealthy man.

With the success of the Sears offering, Goldman Sachs and Lehman Brothers earned the mandate for an underwriting for the F. W. Woolworth Company. Despite the successful selling of both Sears and Woolworth, this underwriting business was still considered by some to be second-rate. The bankers at J. P. Morgan, the undisputed premier bank of the day, informed the Goldman Sachs partners that there was something very undignified about financing a five-and-dime shop. As underwriting was a new business for the firms, they were still finding their way, but their concern for their investors was paramount. "We have in the past made several mistakes in valuing common stock," the Kleinwort partners admitted to Paul Sachs, whose firm had priced the deals. "One mistake in the case of Woolworth common stock was on the right side, and I am delighted that the public should have benefitted thereby. The last mistake was in Goodrich common stock, which no doubt was intrinsically worth what we sold it at, and will I hope be worth very much more in time, but this is no consolation to the man who paid eighty-one for what he could have bought a few weeks later several points cheaper. No doubt our placing power will permit us to sell this new stock at a high price but I feel that we cannot be too careful not to abuse it. You will of course understand that the above is merely an opinion or if you like friendly criticism of a business in which we are just as much interested as you."

For the next three decades Goldman Sachs and Lehman Brothers acted as one on almost all underwritings. Together they co-managed one hundred fourteen offerings for fifty-six different issuers, including the United Cigar Company, May Department Stores, the Underwood Typewriters Corporation, the Continental Can Company, and Studebaker. Their early underwritings sold slowly, often taking many months to distribute, but as the team's reputation grew in the years before World War II, deals with the Goldman Sachs–Lehman Brothers imprimatur sold out even before they were priced.

The relationship between the two partnerships was profitable yet troubled, the distrust between them an open secret. During the years they were co-underwriters, the partners of the two firms lunched together almost every day. At one such lunch held at Lehman Brothers, Sam Sachs rose shortly after having arrived and turned to Philip Lehman to excuse himself, explaining that he needed to return to the firm as he had forgotten to lock the safe. Lehman looked around the room, smiled, and turned back to Sachs saying, "Don't worry, Sam, we're all here." For years, Goldman Sachs argued strenuously that it brought in the bulk of the business and therefore should receive credit and fees greater than the 50 percent that originally had been agreed to by Henry Goldman. Without Goldman Sachs's customers, the firm reasoned, Lehman Brothers would have little business to underwrite. Lehman Brothers, not surprisingly, did not see it this way, instead viewing its partner as greedy, selfish, and interested in having its name alone on the top line. The relationship deteriorated in the late 1920s, became openly hostile, and was formally dissolved with a memorandum of understanding in 1936. The large client list was split, with forty-one firms going to Goldman Sachs and the remaining nineteen to Lehman Brothers. For many years afterward great bitterness existed between the two companies—retired partners to this day still recall how as young men they were taught to disdain Lehman Brothers—although each firm honored the other's turf, as agreed.

Sam Sachs's and Henry Goldman's vision of a general investment company was taking shape. The commercial paper business and the relationships it had generated provided a steady stream of underwriting business. New issues were being sold overseas through the firm's partnership with Kleinwort and others and domestically to an ever more enthusiastic buying public. Goldman Sachs was now a full-service investment bank, but the cohesive structure the partners had worked so hard to establish was about to be shattered.

World War I divided Europe and Goldman Sachs. Henry Goldman, highly conscious and fiercely proud of his German-Jewish heritage, was a staunch and vocal supporter of Germany and its war efforts. An intense, high-strung, and didactic man, his outspoken support and deep admiration for everything German did untold damage to the firm's reputation. When Sam Sachs returned from Europe shortly after the outbreak of the war, after assuring the Kleinwort partners of the firm's pro-British stance, he was horrified by his brother-in-law's open support for the enemy. The Sachs's German origins were just as recent and just as strong, but their allegiance was to England and France.

In 1915, Goldman, despite pressure from his partners and sisters, rejected Goldman Sachs's participation in the $500 million J. P.

Morgan–sponsored Anglo-French loan to fund the war effort, to which virtually all the leading Wall Street firms of the day were subscribing. The firm had a longstanding policy requiring unanimous agreement of the partnership for participation in any piece of business. Out of their own strong beliefs and to save face for their firm, Sam and Harry Sachs marched down to the offices of J. P. Morgan and personally subscribed $125,000 toward the loan.

As the war continued, the ill will between Goldman and the Sachses grew. One can only imagine the uncomfortable atmosphere that must have prevailed in the firm's small offices. Even after the United States entered the war, Goldman continued to speak out publicly in support of Germany, despite the fact that two of his partners and one of his partner's sons were on duty in Europe. The episode was a painful one for the Goldman and Sachs families both personally and professionally. Finally, Kleinwort cabled Goldman Sachs that it was in danger of being blacklisted in London. The British merchant bank had been embarrassed when called before the Ministry of Blockade and shown a large number of cables between Goldman Sachs, its partner of two decades, and German banks. It was clear to the Kleinwort partners that the firm was doing an active exchange business with the Germans. They wrote to Goldman Sachs in 1916: "We were frankly astonished at the evident importance of these operations, and we are therefore not surprised to find the authorities skeptical as to the possibility of entirely avoiding any indirect connection between such business and your sterling account with us." The Bank of England eventually prevented Kleinwort from doing exchange business with Goldman Sachs, cutting off much of Goldman Sachs's London business until after the war.

The firm's business had come to an almost complete standstill, despite its growing stature in the financial community. This was due in part to Goldman Sachs's belief that the economic expansion the country was undergoing was driven by the war and was almost certainly near its peak. The firm was unwilling to leap at new opportunities, since it believed that less prosperous times would soon follow. "Some of our neighbors do not seem to share this opinion of ours," Arthur Sachs wrote in early 1917. "Almost without exception, there has been no new business done which has not at one time or another been in this office and it is a great trial of patience to run, as Mr. Goldman expresses it, 'a turning down office.' "

Shortly after this, Henry Goldman announced his departure on Goldman Sachs letterhead with the words "Save & Serve. Buy Liberty Bonds!" emblazoned in red at the top of the page. He wrote, "I am not in sympathy with many trends which are now stirring the world and which are now shaping public opinion. I retire with the best of feeling towards the firm (and all of its members) with which I have been associated for thirty-five years and to which I have given all there is in me." Goldman offered his partners his apology and his resignation. They accepted both.

The loss of Goldman's services was a damaging blow. Some felt that the firm was harmed more by the withdrawal of his talents and sizable capital than it had been by his pro-German sentiments. Paul Sachs, who had worked closely with Goldman, had resigned his partnership in 1914 to become a professor of fine arts at Harvard, so there was no one to fill the gap. The rift between Goldman and Sam Sachs (and Henry's sister, Louise Goldman Sachs) was not mended, and the two never spoke again. According to Stephen Birmingham, a chronicler of the saga, "The hostilities continued in the next generation and to this day [1967] there are hardly any Goldmans who are on speaking terms with any Sachses."

Henry would be the last Goldman to work at the firm bearing his family's name. He left the firm an extremely wealthy man and subsequently made several large and successful investments in the Commercial Investment Trust Company, May Department Stores, and Sears Roebuck & Co. Like many other members of the Goldman and Sachs families, he had a deep love of art and assembled a spectacular collection of Renaissance and baroque paintings, including works by Rubens, Van Dyke, and Rembrandt, some of which now hang in the National Gallery in Washington. He helped to found a chair of German art and culture at Harvard University and quietly made many generous contributions to charity. When Goldman and his wife heard the child prodigy Yehudi Menuhin perform at Carnegie Hall, they invited the twelve-year-old to lunch. The banker asked Menuhin what he would like most in the world. The response was, "a Stradivarius," and his wish was granted. On one trip to Germany, Goldman was the guest of President Paul von Hindenburg, and he visited Albert Einstein, presenting him with the gift of a yacht (which was confiscated by the Nazi regime in 1933). In 1922, Goldman was commended by the German Republic and was made an honorary citizen. In the early 1930s he returned to his beloved Germany with the intention of settling there, but as Hitler rose to power, Goldman, his family believes, was subjected to many humiliations. He returned to New York where he died in 1936 a disillusioned man.

IN SEARCH OF A NEW PARTNER to run the underwriting business, Goldman Sachs found Waddill Catchings, a friend and Harvard classmate of Arthur Sachs. Catchings was tall and slim, with a thick head of white hair, and he possessed enormous charm and personality. A native of

Sewanee, Tennessee, and a Harvard Law School graduate, Catchings worked for Sullivan and Cromwell as a lawyer and at J. P. Morgan buying munitions and other supplies for the war effort. Catchings was openly disappointed in his Harvard education, arguing that it failed the test of real life. Professors, he complained, had "casually explained that their theories would hold true in the long run. But what people are interested in is the short not the long run. So I made up my mind that as soon as I had enough money I would set about reconciling these two phases of business—theory and practice." His words, widely published and read, might have served as a clear warning of his views and an almost precise blueprint of his future actions. He was one of the most popular economic writers of his day, authoring books with titles such as *Profits*, *Money*, and his best-seller, *The Road to Plenty*. Business, Catchings argued, must be agile, able to move quickly out of unprofitable sectors into moneymaking areas: "If business is to be kept zooming production must be kept at high speed whatever the circumstances." The business cycle was dead, Catchings declared. America's economic prospects were limitless, he believed; nothing could stand in the way. Yet it would be the business cycle, the boom and bust of the 1920s, that would destroy Catchings's future with Goldman Sachs.

Catchings's optimism and confidence were infectious, and in 1918 the partners of Goldman Sachs asked him to join them to reignite the firm's dormant underwriting effort. In the 1920s, American industry underwent a merger boom, and with Catchings's wide circle of contacts Goldman Sachs was able to participate in this new business. Many of the companies formed through Catchings's efforts during this period, such as General Foods and National Dairy Products (which went on to become the Kraft Company), would remain clients of the firm for decades.

Catchings was particularly interested in the trading side of the business. He organized a number of trading accounts and installed a ticker tape in the office of the senior partner. During his tenure the firm became increasingly active in foreign business and traded and arbitraged foreign currency prices, hampered by the fact that there were no direct telephone lines to Europe. Their greatest success came in Germany, where, the partners believed, they were doing as much business as their competitors. The partners felt further disadvantaged in their trading by the fact that their competitors in this business, Guaranty Trust (now part of J. P. Morgan) and National City Bank (now Citibank), had considerably more capital to employ.

Catchings's success went to his head, and his relationship with his partners soured. Arguments ensued about his position within the firm and ownership percentages among the partners. Walter Sachs explained that as "he [Catchings] became successful, he became more and more difficult and imperious, he became ruthless and made all kinds of demands as to his position in the firm." Walter Sachs, over the vocal protests of his brother Arthur, acceded to many of Catchings's demands for a larger stake in the partnership. By 1928, Catchings owned the largest stake in Goldman Sachs, and his actions would therefore become increasingly difficult to overrule.

In December 1928, when the bull market was very long in the tooth, Catchings, with the agreement of his partners, formed an investment trust that he proudly named the Goldman Sachs Trading Corporation (GSTC). Investment trusts that pooled investors' capital for the purchase of shares, much like today's mutual funds, increased in popularity throughout the 1920s; as the market rose, investor interest rose commensurately. By 1928 investment trusts were being formed at the rate of one a day and were engaged in a feeding frenzy of stock buying. These trusts were barely regulated by today's standards, but the GSTC was sponsored, operated, and controlled by a reputable investment bank with a published list of its holdings, and many considered it safe.

The original plan called for a $40 million to $50 million trust, with the Goldman Sachs partnership retaining ownership of between 20 and 25 percent. However, demand for the shares was so strong that the partnership stake of $10 million—roughly half the partnership capital—remained constant while issuance grew to $100 million. (The speculative trust sold out in a single day.)

Each of the one million newly issued shares had a face value of $100 and were all sold by the GSTC to Goldman Sachs & Co. (in time the corporation would issue almost six million shares). The firm then resold 90 percent of these shares at the price of $104, for a quick profit in excess of $3 million. The profit alone totaled 15 percent of the firm's capital. Put into today's terms, this would be like Goldman Sachs earning a fee of $1 billion on a single transaction.

The stock took flight. By February 2, 1929, it was trading at $136.50; five days later it had rocketed to $222.50. Investors suspended disbelief. At that price it was worth twice the value of the underlying cash and securities held. As investment trusts increased in popularity, the corporation sold more stock to the public. The GSTC also began buying its own shares and by March had spent in excess of $57 million in this pursuit. "It is difficult not to marvel at the imagination which was implicit in this gargantuan insanity," John Kenneth Galbraith wrote in his classic work, *The Great Crash of 1929*. "If there must be madness something may be said for having it on a heroic scale."

Catchings was on his own, having by now abandoned the long-held principle of unanimous agreement by all partners before entering into a major transaction. In July the trading corporation gave birth to another investment trust, the Shenandoah Corporation, which was seven times oversubscribed. The shares were issued at $17.50 and closed the first day at $36. The GSTC owned 40 percent of the corporation, and Goldman Sachs & Co., in turn, owned 10 percent of the GSTC. Thus began the process of leveraging the trusts. In August the newly minted Shenandoah Corporation sponsored the even larger Blue Ridge Corporation (worth $142 million). Eighty-six percent of the common shares of Blue Ridge were owned by the Shenandoah. John Foster Dulles, who later became secretary of state, was the GSTC's lawyer and sat on the boards of the Shenandoah and Blue Ridge Corporations. So popular were these shares that Goldman Sachs made a special offer whereby an investor could swap any unwanted stocks, such as shares of AT&T, General Electric, or Eastman Kodak, directly into Blue Ridge Preference and Common. Many accepted the offer. Through the GSTC and its investments, Goldman Sachs & Co., with roughly $20 million in partnership capital, obtained sole or joint control of funds in investment companies worth $500 million.

In the space of a month, the GSTC had issued more than a quarter of a billion dollars of securities, "an operation that would not then have been unimpressive for the United States Treasury," Galbraith wrote. This level of leverage left the firm brutally exposed to the events that unfolded only a few weeks later.

Goldman Sachs, spurred on by Catchings, had expected to profit from this tower of trusts in three ways. First, there would be the original underwriter's commission, a phenomenal fee by the standards of any day. Second, Goldman Sachs would hold shares in the trust and was confident that these would continue to increase in value. Finally, the GSTC's holdings in various industrial and utility concerns would throw off investment banking work to Goldman Sachs & Co., and the corporation would use the firm as a broker, paying it fees for the execution of securities trades.

Both Sachs brothers were away in Europe during the summer of 1929 when the Blue Ridge and Shenandoah trusts were born. Walter received a cable in Italy informing him of the deals. He was worried sick by it, and when he returned to New York he went straight to see Catchings at his apartment in the Plaza Hotel. Now, only weeks before the crash, with the shares already sold in the marketplace, Sachs told Catchings that the pyramid scheme was crazy. Catchings, by this time in full flight, dismissed him out of hand, saying, "The trouble with you, Walter, is that you've no imagination."

When the crash came in October 1929, the Goldman Sachs Trading Corporation took the full force of the market decline. The shares in the trading corporation, which had reached a high of $326, fell to as low as $1.75. Some of the shares had options embedded in them, which meant that as the price fell the GSTC was forced to buy more shares, dramatically extending its losses. These obligations were met by selling some of the GSTC's holdings, further depressing prices. The firm's actions stand as a testament to the lethal combination of poor timing and high leverage. As one of the greatest investing debacles of the twentieth century, the outcome of the GSTC brought the Goldman Sachs name into disrepute.

When asked many years later what sparked Goldman Sachs's desire to embark on this frenzy of activity, Walter Sachs sadly replied, "To conquer the world. Not only for greed for money, but power sparked it and that was the great mistake because I confess to the fact that we were all influenced by greed. We were carried away by the bull market, we thought these values were going to be justified . . . and the bottom fell out of everything as we were caught with our pants down."

Catchings was unrepentant. Early in 1930 he had a brainstorm that he felt certain would solve the firm's financial difficulties. Full of enthusiasm he called young Sidney Weinberg, who had been made a partner three years earlier, to sound him out. "Look, we owe $20 million to the banks and we have certain other obligations amounting to about $10 million," said Catchings. "We ought to fund this debt in a two-year convertible note. We ought to sell $50 million of two-year convertible notes and with the balance of the money, twenty or thirty million dollars, Frank Taylor (an investment trust manager in California) out here can make a world of money." In the midst of the worst bear market in history, Catchings was suggesting the firm issue debt to make further investments in the stock market. Weinberg and Sachs were baffled by his audacity and for the first time recognized the major weaknesses in his judgment. With the benefit of hindsight, Catchings's earlier words seemed prophetic. He was determined to keep Goldman Sachs "zooming at high speed, whatever the circumstances."

The GSTC and the Goldman Sachs company had become one in the public's mind. Weinberg and Sachs knew it would take a decade of hard work to disentangle the two—gradually liquidating the GSTC and rebuilding the partnership capital—but both were certain that was what needed to be done. Catchings, clearly, had another view.

Walter Sachs became president of the disgraced Goldman Sachs Trading Corporation in June 1930, and he and Weinberg began the slow and painful process of liquidating the corporation's assets. In less than twelve months, the corporation had acquired majority ownership stakes in a number of banks, insurance companies, and real estate holdings scattered throughout the country. The stock market rebounded slightly, and they used this breathing space to sell every possible stock owned by the corporation. This was not a matter of good market judgment, but a move driven by the necessity of raising cash. The GSTC had $20–30 million in bank loans which needed to be paid off. It was a long and arduous process; there were few buyers, and Goldman Sachs was a forced seller.

By 1933 the Goldman Sachs Trading Corporation's 42,000 investors had lost close to $300 million off the market's peak. Eddie Cantor, one of the biggest theatrical stars of the day, sued the firm for $100 million and used the name Goldman Sachs as the butt of jokes on stage and in a popular book. Hundreds of millions of dollars' worth of other lawsuits were filed against the firm, and the ensuing legal tangle took a decade to straighten out. None of the legal actions were successful, but the partners settled some of the suits. The firm's eight partners had not sold any of their 10 percent holding in the original trust, and by the end their extensive legal costs coupled with the trading losses amounted to about $13 million. In the aftermath, the firm's capital was reduced to $5 million by 1936, a devastating blow considering that the partnership capital had been $4.5 million thirty years earlier. With the Depression and World War II, it would take decades to rebuild the firm's business, and it was not until the mid-1950s that the firm's capital would again rise above $10 million.

Weinberg found a buyer for the disgraced GSTC, but the sale required the approval of its aggrieved stockholders, and this proved difficult to obtain. The investors who had put their faith in Goldman Sachs had lost 92 percent of their original investment and were not in an accommodating mood. At a meeting of shareholders, Walter Sachs addressed his hostile audience for hours trying to persuade them to accept the offer from Floyd Odlum's Atlas Corporation. Odlum, who specialized in buying battered businesses, was the only serious bidder; there were few who had the cash or the temerity to take on such an investment. Finally, in frustration, Sachs put the point to the rebellious crowd. Goldman Sachs had made some frightening errors in judgment, he conceded, but having lost more than any other single investor, it had stood by the wreckage. Forcefully, he told the group that Goldman Sachs wanted to sell, and that the shareholders should acquiesce. Ultimately, the corporation was sold to Odlum, and the shareholders realized a paltry $8 on their original $100 investment.

In the crash of 1929 the name Goldman Sachs came to symbolize much of what was wrong with Wall Street. The GSTC debacle was an enormous blow to the reputation of the firm, one from which many competitors believed it could not recover. So damaged was the firm's name that it did not lead an underwriting for five years, and the partners waited until 1935, when the firm had ceased losing money, to involve themselves in the distribution of securities brought to market by other firms. The damage would reverberate through the firm for decades. When Goldman Sachs reentered the money management business in the 1980s, the management committee debated long and hard about attaching the firm's name to the new business. The lessons of 1929 died hard.

In May 1930, under Sidney Weinberg's guidance, the partners demanded Catchings's resignation, which he reluctantly submitted. In the space of a year, Catchings had almost singlehandedly destroyed Goldman Sachs. With the benefit of hindsight, Walter Sachs later wrote, "Most men can stand adversity; very few men can stand success. He was not one of them. Success went to his head. He was a man who had had no money. He suddenly thought himself to be a rich man. He was a rich man on paper. In that very year—it all happened in twelve months—he just went haywire. We weren't smart enough, perhaps—or perhaps we were too greedy, too—but anyway we didn't stop it in time." Catchings was paid an astronomical $250,000, despite the fact that his capital account was negative, and he was asked to leave the firm six months before his partnership contract ended. He moved to California, where for a time he was a radio producer and later wrote a book entitled *Do Economists Understand Business?*

Weinberg never shied away from his responsibility for the fiasco. When asked for an explanation of his role as treasurer he said, "I just wasn't very bright." The experience had a profound effect on Weinberg's outlook toward risk, the role of the partnership's capital, and the value he would place on the firm's reputation. The fact that Goldman Sachs rebounded and thrived can be credited to one man. Still in his thirties, a high school dropout, a kid from the streets, in 1930 Sidney Weinberg assumed the leadership of the firm he would head for the next four decades.

SIDNEY WEINBERG WAS, without question, the father of the modern Goldman Sachs. Reigning as its chairman from 1930 until his death in 1969 he would take the firm through the aftermath of the Depression, raise its name to national prominence, and leave it with a solid-gold reputation. He was a larger-than-life figure whose influence within the firm can still be felt today.

A tiny man—five feet four inches tall, with legs only twenty-six inches long—Weinberg had immense stature both within and outside the firm. "As the senior partner of the venerable and powerful investment-banking firm of Goldman Sachs," reported *The New Yorker* at the peak of his influence in 1956, "as a director over the years of more big corporations than any other American, and as an adviser to whom not only the country's industrialists but its Presidents listen attentively, Weinberg, though largely unknown to the man in any street but Wall, is among the nation's most influential citizens."

A fierce patriot and a loyal banker, Weinberg was an intimate of almost every major business leader of his day. Dressed in a three-piece suit, gold chain peeking out of his vest pocket, he was immensely proud of being a self-made man. At high-level business meetings or on other occasions when he felt the plain speaking for which he was so famous was needed, he could be heard to quip, with the touch of a Brooklyn accent, "I'm just a Brooklyn boy from Public School No. 13."

Sidney James Weinberg was the third of eleven children born to Pincus Weinberg, an immigrant and wholesale liquor dealer of moderate means. Born in 1891, Sidney grew up in Brooklyn and was indeed educated at P. S. 13, to which he remained steadfastly loyal throughout his life. One part Horatio Alger, one part Sammy Glick, he entered the workforce at the age of ten selling newspapers at the Manhattan-Brooklyn ferry terminal, shucking oysters, and carrying feathers for a milliner. By the age of thirteen Weinberg was employed as a summer runner for a brokerage house, but finding the one job insufficient, he obtained similar jobs with two other brokers in violation of the long-established custom that a runner worked for a single house. When a bank teller discovered his ruse, Weinberg was out of three jobs. He completed the eighth grade and his formal education in the spring of 1906.

His first real job on Wall Street was waiting in line at the shaky Trust Company of America during the banking crisis of 1907. As desperate depositors fought their way through the melee on Wall Street, Sidney held their places at the paying teller's window for $5 a spot. Seeking more stable employment, later that year he took the elevator to the top of what was the tallest building in New York, the twenty-five-story tower at 43 Exchange Place, and worked his way down asking at each floor if work was available. After twenty-three refusals Weinberg arrived at Goldman Sachs's offices on the second floor, and there the chief clerk hired him to assist Jarvis, the porter, at $3 a week. His first responsibilities at Goldman Sachs were to clean the cuspidors, brush the partners' silk hats, and wipe the mud from the partners' rubbers. Weinberg's first promotion was to office boy in the partners' room. There he filled the inkwells each morning and polished their enormous silver tops. For many years Henry Goldman and Sam Sachs did not know his name and simply addressed him as "boy." While delivering a flagpole to the Harlem home of Paul Sachs, Weinberg made the acquaintance of the son of the firm's founder, who urged the young man to continue his education and handed him $25 to pay for a course at New York University. "Paul Sachs was the first partner who ever really gave me a second glance," Weinberg later recalled. "Until he took me in hand, I was an awful kid—tough and raw." Even after Sachs left the firm to teach at Harvard he never lost touch with the Weinberg family. During Weinberg's two sons' college years at Harvard, Sachs frequently invited them to dine at his family home in Cambridge.

Sachs was so impressed when Weinberg suggested ways to modernize and improve the mailroom that he placed the young man in charge. For many this would have been a welcome advancement, but Weinberg was bored, found his duties unchallenging, and wiled away the time playing practical jokes. He put tacks on the chairs of the company's clerks and once placed a want ad in a local newspaper announcing that Sam Sachs was assembling a chorus for a new Broadway show. Interested applicants were to report to the august partner's office for personal interviews. A stream of young women arrived at Goldman Sachs headquarters, disappointed to learn of the joke. In an industry known for personal conservatism, where men take themselves with the utmost seriousness, Weinberg's willingness to poke fun at himself and others was unusual. His irreverence never dissipated, and to many on Wall Street he was a breath of fresh air. Weinberg spoke his mind truthfully and humorously, never worrying about public relations fallout. "Somebody's got to call you an s.o.b. in life or you haven't made good," he would say.

Although he had enormous respect for higher education he never failed to note that education did not confer intelligence. Weinberg would sometimes buy Phi Beta Kappa keys in pawnshops and hand them out to executives with whom he was not impressed. "Here, bright boy," he would say good-naturedly, "maybe one of these will help."

During World War I, Weinberg left Goldman Sachs to serve as a cook in the Navy aboard Henry Goldman, Jr.'s boat and was later transferred to inspect cargo for naval intelligence. After the war Sidney approached Henry Goldman, who by then had left Goldman Sachs, about a job. He had long considered Goldman the genius behind Goldman Sachs and wanted to assist him in whatever new venture he was about to undertake. Goldman demurred, telling the young man that he was not reentering the investment business and urging him to return to Goldman Sachs where his future would be brighter. Weinberg followed Goldman's advice and rejoined the firm in a $28-a-week position as a salesman for commercial paper accounts. Gradually his responsibilities grew, and by 1920, when he married Helen Livingston, he was making $5,000 a year. Helen and Sidney Weinberg had two sons, both of whom would serve as partners of

Goldman Sachs. After Sidney started work in the firm's corporate finance department his financial acumen became increasingly clear. Soon he was forming syndicates to sell underwritings, determining the pricing of new issues, and supervising trading. In 1927, at the age of thirty-five—twenty years after he set foot across the threshold—Weinberg was made a partner of Goldman Sachs.

After Catchings's departure the firm's capital was largely owned by the Sachs family. Arthur had withdrawn from the business when he and his cousin and brother could not agree on the direction it should take. Arthur had favored a contraction while Walter, Howard, and Weinberg preferred a policy of expansion, despite the difficult economic climate of the 1930s. It was only through the fortitude of Walter and Howard Sachs, who despite the unprofitable times left their capital in the firm, that Goldman Sachs exists today. In 1931 the more senior partners bailed out the junior partners who now had deficits in their capital accounts. The cost to each partner was between $200,000 and $300,000—a considerable sum at the time. Goldman Sachs, family or not, was a partnership, and no one was going to begin his career in debt.

That the Sachs family chose Weinberg to succeed Catchings is a testament to their sound business judgement. Others with larger egos and lesser intelligence might have taken the job themselves, ignoring the fact that one of the greatest bankers of the twentieth century was in their midst. Walter Sachs was the first to admit, "There's been three geniuses in this firm. There was Henry Goldman, there's been Waddill Catchings and Sidney Weinberg—and Sidney Weinberg alone went through fire." It would be more than a decade before the firm operated profitably again— the firm lost money every year for the first half of the 1930s—but the Sachses believed in the firm, its clients, and Weinberg's talents.

In April 1934, the firm's co-founder, Sam Sachs, died. In the years just prior to his death he had repeatedly asked his son Walter how the Goldman Sachs name was regarded. To Sachs this was an issue of paramount importance. In the last year of his life, as the cloud over the firm began to lift, his son was finally able to give him the reassurance he so wanted to hear.

Although Weinberg was the man in charge, Walter Sachs acted as the firm's managing partner. Sachs had joined the firm in 1908 and, in addition to his other roles, was the unofficial chronicler of the firm's fortunes. In his unpublished autobiography he recounted the life of the firm through the story of the Goldmans and the Sachses. Sachs managed the day-to-day operations of the firm, leaving Weinberg free to concentrate on developing clients, doing deals, and serving Presidents. Sachs betrayed a rare note of jealousy when he described how his caretaker role at the firm freed Weinberg up for serving on dozens of corporate boards.

Weinberg was aggressive, ambitious, and did little to promote Sachs outside the firm. He tended not to share his glory, yet he recognized whose firm it was and whose capital he was using. For many years Weinberg and Sachs sat in richly decorated adjoining offices of equal size and importance, each with walnut paneling and wood-burning fireplaces. A dignified gentleman and a one-time treasurer of the NAACP (the Sachs family had long been concerned with civil rights), Walter Sachs had a box at the opera and a lifelong love of music. Everything about him, even his name, was bound up with Goldman Sachs. Reminiscing about his life he recalled, "We rebuilt it, so that today I can say, without fear of contradiction, that the name and the reputation of the firm is greater than it's ever been in its history. Well, that's been my satisfaction in life. That's worth more than dollars. Other people may be a great deal richer than I am but that's, to my way of thinking, unimportant." There is no doubt that he was Sam's son.

The 1930s and much of the 1940s at Goldman Sachs were a time of very little business and virtually no profits. The firm's reputation had been pulverized and the country was mired in a deep depression. John Whitehead, who joined Goldman Sachs at the end of this period and would later become co–senior partner, estimates that the firm's combined profits from 1930 to 1945 were zero. During the 1930s, Weinberg's contribution to the firm was so great that he was accorded one-third of the firm's profits. But as his son John pointed out more then sixty years later, one-third of nothing is still nothing.

In a brave move that suggested great optimism about the future, Goldman Sachs bought its main commercial paper competitors in 1932, enhancing and solidifying its reach into the Midwest. Later a Boston competitor was absorbed as well, and with it a customer base among the southern textile companies. These moves, which at the time might have been seen as foolhardy, allowed Goldman Sachs eventually to dominate the commercial paper business in the United States. Marcus Goldman had admonished his son and son-in-law never to neglect the firm's commercial paper businesses, and the firm he founded never did.

The pace of life on Wall Street was different in the 1940s. There were long stretches of time when there was very little to do. Summers were particularly quiet, and the firm's associates sometimes spent the afternoons playing bridge or poker. With few pressing demands on their time, the partners of Goldman Sachs did undertake a few bold measures that would lay the foundation for their future profitability once the economic haze lifted. Gus Levy was hired to wrench Goldman Sachs into the world of trading, and he soon created a profitable arbitrage department that subsidized some very bleak banking years.

The business began where Henry Goldman had left off forty years earlier. By positioning and trading railroad and utility bonds, one of Goldman Sachs's most profitable departments, risk arbitrage, was born. During the Depression many of the country's railroads filed for bankruptcy protection. Yet during World War II they operated at full capacity and, although technically bankrupt, were flush with cash. Railroad bonds, on which payments were not being made, were therefore trading at enormous discounts. Levy became a master at accurately valuing these securities so underrated by the market, a skill he would later apply to utility holding companies and corporate mergers. Levy would make his name as one of Wall Street's greatest arbitrageurs. Later, with the help of his assistant Bob Rubin, Levy would establish Goldman Sachs's unchallenged preeminence in the world of arbitrage.

During these lean years the firm established its municipal finance department and a retail sale operation (selling stocks and bonds to an extremely wealthy clientele), although the buying public was very small and very nervous. Having such an operation was viewed as essential; if the firm eventually reentered the underwriting business, distribution would be a key factor in any future offerings. Investment banking in those days was a simple operation. There was the buying department and the selling department. The first bought securities from companies and the latter sold securities to institutional and, to a lesser extent, individual investors. The trick to successful investment banking was to line up a buyer for any issue before you bought it, or, as Levy would quip, "Something well bought is half sold." It was the way business was conducted, and it saved firms from horrific underwriting losses. During the 1940s the cautious Weinberg ensured that the firm steered clear of any major losses, but it also realized few gains.

Throughout his tenure as leader of the firm, Weinberg assiduously pursued the firm's interests with his far-flung contacts throughout the business world. Among his personal friends were the chairmen of General Electric, Owens-Corning Fiberglas, National Dairy Products, Ford Motor Company, Procter & Gamble, and dozens of other huge companies. For many years these contacts yielded little or no business, but Weinberg persevered. He knew that the future of the firm rested on its ability to cultivate a client list made up of the top U.S. corporations. He bequeathed the firm a list of clients—rivaled only by that of Morgan Stanley—that would serve as the cornerstone of the firm's phenomenal profitability in the years to come.

Weinberg sat as a director on the boards of more than thirty corporations. Originally this activity had been seen as a way to redeem Goldman Sachs's reputation after the GSTC fiasco, but he continued it long after this was necessary. Weinberg became the guardian of Goldman Sachs's good name, the keeper of its reputation, although for many years his own name was the better known. Acting as the firm's ambassador to the world of industry, for more than twenty years Weinberg attended an average of two hundred fifty board or corporation committee meetings a year. *Fortune* magazine dubbed him "the directors' director," but to many he was known as "Mr. Wall Street."

To Weinberg, service on corporate boards was almost a religion. While others took their fees and made an appearance at the required meetings, Weinberg, with the help of young bankers at the firm, prepared carefully for each of his many board meetings. He enshrined his strong opinions on the responsibility of directors in a 1933 memorandum on the subject. In views that were radical at the time, Weinberg stated that directors are supposed to direct. Their obligation is to the company and its shareholders, and therefore they must be privy to all corporate information. From the vantage point of youth, Weinberg also asserted that by the age of seventy all directors should retire, vacating their positions to make room for younger men. He would live long enough to regret this statement; as he approached the end of his seventh decade he would tell Whitehead, "I'm not like these guys, some of them are in wheelchairs, they fall asleep at meetings, I'm not like that." Weinberg remained a member of the Ford Motor Co. board of directors until his death at the age of seventy-seven.

One of the most notorious recipients of Weinberg's memoranda was Donald Coster, president of McKesson and Robbins, a pharmaceutical company. So impressed was Coster by Weinberg's views that he invited him to sit on the company's board. Weinberg graciously accepted the invitation. Coster, it was later revealed, was a con man by the name of Philip Musica. In his incarnation as Coster he had fabricated $21 million in company assets through the creation of dummy corporations. When Walter Sachs heard of this ruse it seemed familiar, and he went back through some of the firm's old files. There he found an old credit memo on a company called A. Musica & Sons. This company had been accused of irregularities by the U.S. Customs Department, and Sam Sachs had red-penciled the file and indicated that the firm should no longer do business with this company. Musica had been undeterred, and posing as Coster—with Sam Sachs retired from the business—had approached Goldman Sachs about a financing that the firm turned down.

Musica had fooled all of the companies' directors, their outside auditors—and Sidney Weinberg. Once Musica's crimes had been revealed, the board, including Weinberg, met to dismiss him officially from his duties. During the meeting a message was brought to the directors saying that Musica had just committed suicide. There was a moment of grim silence before Weinberg called out, "Well, come on, gentlemen, let's fire him for his sins anyway."

Weinberg and his fellow McKesson and Robbins directors avoided litigation by voluntarily donating $600,000 of their personal resources in a payment to the company. Weinberg's share amounted to $75,000. Later, with the help of John Whitehead, Weinberg wrote an article for the *Harvard Business Review* in which he unabashedly recounted the scandal: "In the investigation that followed the McKesson and Robbins ruckus . . . the attorney brought [my] memorandum forward and asked me why I had not operated as a director of that company in accordance with the standards I had set up in the memorandum. I pointed out to him that Moses had brought down the Ten Commandments from Mount Sinai, that we all believed in them, but unfortunately few of us live in accordance with all of them."

Despite his humor, Weinberg was deeply affected by the McKesson scandal and in response decreased the number of boards on which he sat and redoubled his efforts to serve them better. His devotion to the companies he served, most of which were or would become Goldman Sachs's clients, was legendary. Weinberg was fanatical about using only the products manufactured by the companies he represented. Cheese was only fit for consumption if it was Kraft, his light bulbs had to be made by General Electric, and he bought his kitchen appliances at Sears. He even insisted that Goldman Sachs purchase all its paper from Champion Paper and Fiber once he was seated on its board. And once he joined the Ford Motor Company board, he sold his Cadillac and Oldsmobile, replacing them with a Lincoln and a Mercury. Once, on a sailing trip with fellow National Dairy Board member Paul C. Cabot, Weinberg was devastated to learn that the ship's galley had stocked rival Borden's instant coffee. Weinberg refused to be unfaithful, even on vacation, so his host Cabot bought some Maxwell House at the next port. When the contents of the Maxwell jar were depleted Cabot refilled it periodically from his stock of Borden. Those on the voyage remember that "Weinberg ecstatically made himself several cups a day, and kept asking his crewmates if they had ever tasted anything so delicious."

Weinberg was one of the few Roosevelt supporters on Wall Street in 1932 and 1936, and the president often sought his services as an informal advisor. Many in the financial community believed that it was Weinberg's sound advice that tempered the New Deal's assault on the country's capitalist system. A parody of a Kipling poem was written to reflect this concern:

> *Oh it's "Sidney this" and "Sidney that"*
> *And "Boy, what do you say?"*
> *And "Sid, please ask Ole Franklin*
> *Not to take our shirts away."*

Acting as a one-man headhunter for Presidents Roosevelt, Truman, and Eisenhower, Weinberg served in Washington during both World War II and the Korean War as vice-chairman of the war production board. He soon became known as the "Body Snatcher," recruiting leaders from industry to serve the government as "$1-a-year men" as the country mobilized for war. Often those in positions of power demurred, arguing that they were serving their country through their company. Weinberg refused to accept this argument, which to him smacked of self-interest. Once he had decided that a particular executive was well suited to the government's needs he brought considerable pressure to bear, and when all else failed, he was not shy about asking the president to intervene. Most of Weinberg's victims were afraid to offend him, and those who were not could hardly say no to the president. By all accounts Weinberg's recruitment efforts were very successful. When Roosevelt approached Weinberg for the job of ambassador to the Soviet Union, Sidney at first accepted the posting and began to commute to Washington learning about Russia in preparation for the assignment. Yet later, he turned the president down and is said to have replied, "I don't speak Russian. Who the hell could I talk to over there?" In truth, however, Weinberg did not feel he could leave his wife and sons, and with his passionate interest in education, he did not wish his sons to be tutored abroad.

THE BIGGEST THREAT to the securities industry during the Truman administration was the antitrust case brought by the Justice Department against the seventeen largest banking houses of the day. The case absorbed Wall Street from its announcement in 1947 until its conclusion in 1953. In its intent to prove collaboration and restraint of trade the government provided the first look at what would later be called league tables—rankings of investment bankers by the dollar value of their underwritings. Weinberg and the partners of Goldman Sachs were concerned at being implicated in the case; their livelihoods were at stake, and the case would consume time and resources for many years. For up-and-comers like John Whitehead, being included in the suit was a relief; to have been neglected would have been a disgrace, an announcement that the firm was nowhere. In a ranking of underwriters by market share for the years 1938 through 1947 Goldman Sachs was in twelfth place and accorded a market share of 1.4 percent of all underwritings. By contrast, Morgan Stanley had 16 percent of the market, and First Boston had 13 percent. These were two of what were known as the bulge bracket firms. With Dillon Read and Kuhn Loeb they constituted the top group, the managers of almost every major syndicate and the leaders on all high-profile takeovers. The ranking prepared for the hearings on the case held before Judge Harold Medina may have overstated Goldman Sachs's importance in the marketplace. In a 1950 list of leading syndicate heads of underwritings, Goldman Sachs did not even make it into the top seventeen. At this point Goldman Sachs can only be described as an also-ran, a firm with a few good clients and many dreams.

Judge Medina, in his landmark decision against the government, described the investment banking industry as one with many leading players and plenty of competition. Goldman Sachs, in its combative relationship with Lehman Brothers, was singled out as a particularly good example of the vicious competition that existed among Wall Street bankers. The trial had been costly in terms of partners' time and legal expenses—between $600,000 and $700,000—an enormous amount at that time, as the partners' capital in 1948 was only $7.5 million. Walter Sachs wrote of the verdict that, "After the Medina trial, the skies really cleared for the first time in years."

Surveying the investment banking world of the 1940s, there were few signs of the great changes to come. By the 1990s six of the firms ranked above Goldman Sachs would no longer exist. Two others were marginalized and can no longer be considered serious competition. Only Morgan Stanley, First Boston, and in some cases a reincarnated Lehman Brothers contend with the market leader, Goldman Sachs. (Merrill Lynch, a major competitor in the 1990s, did not even figure into this listing.) But for the genius of Weinberg, the fortitude of Walter and Howard Sachs, and the staggering talents of some of those who would come after them, Goldman Sachs might easily have been relegated to little more than a footnote in books describing the trading catastrophes of 1929.

IN JANUARY 1947, Sidney Weinberg met Henry Ford II, and the two undertook a deal that, after years of hard work, finally put Goldman Sachs on the map. Upon the recent deaths of his father Edsel and his grandfather Henry, the young Ford heir found himself at the helm of the largest privately owned company in the United States. The fifty-five-year-old Weinberg was already a nationally respected business leader, and Ford began to look to him for business advice. (The relationship became so close that Ford later described Weinberg as his best friend.) Weinberg began to make regular trips to the family headquarters in Dearborn, Michigan, and was an invited guest at private family gatherings held at the home of Mrs. Ernest Kansler, Edsel Ford's widow and the mother of the four Ford heirs. The matriarch, who presided over all of the meetings, was the doyenne and acknowledged leader of the family. Weinberg was in a very privileged position—Henry had taken him into his confidence. The Ford Motor Company was the largest company in the United States, but as it was privately held, almost nothing was known about its financial situation.

In an effort to avoid the mammoth estate tax that would be due upon his death, Henry Ford, Sr., had placed almost 90 percent of the company's shares into a foundation. These were nonvoting shares, so the foundation did not receive dividends and, as a result, served almost no function. All of the voting rights, and thus the control, remained with the family's shares. The young chairman was troubled by this and consulted with Weinberg. On the face of it, the problem was simple. The foundation wanted to sell some of its stock in order to have funds to disburse, the family wanted greater percentage ownership in the company, the stock exchange wanted voting rights vested in whatever stock it listed, and the Internal Revenue Service wanted its fair share.

For two years Weinberg, with the help of Whitehead, slaved away in secrecy, ultimately devising fifty alternative plans for restructuring the Ford Motor Company. Technically, Weinberg was the family's advisor. The foundation had asked him to serve in a similar position, but Henry Ford II let its leadership know that Weinberg was taken. Throughout the years that Weinberg worked with the Fords there was never a formal agreement, a contract, or any discussion of the fees Goldman Sachs would charge for the services he offered. Few within Goldman Sachs were even aware of the project. Weinberg and Ford developed a code to use in cabling each other with developments. Ford was "Alice," Weinberg "Edith," the foundation "Grace," and the company "Agnes." Weinberg dictated no letters or notes on the subject, committing everything to paper in his own hand. The veil of secrecy was lifted when a society columnist spotted Weinberg and Ford together at a charity function, chatting with the Duke and Duchess of Windsor.

It was decided that $650 million of stock would be made available—the largest public offering ever—and, except for Morgan Stanley, which was General Motors's primary banker, every major investment bank was included. The underwriting list included an astounding 722 names. On the morning of the offering, in January 1956, Sidney's round, smiling face

stared out from the front page of the *New York Times* as he was revealed
to be the man behind the throne. Alongside his friend Paul Cabot, the legendary Boston banker, Sidney became one of the first two outside directors of the company. For many years Ford did not use any other
investment banker and, in turn, was Goldman Sachs's most important
corporate client. The Ford offering catapulted Goldman Sachs into the
limelight and was the pinnacle of Sidney Weinberg's long and distin-
guished career.

"During the first years that I was at Goldman Sachs the only person
who ever produced any investment banking business was Sidney Weinberg," recalls John Whitehead. "I don't believe that anybody else brought
in a public offering or a private placement or any kind of investment
banking business except for Sidney Weinberg. He knew everybody; he
was the best-known businessman in America, and when someone wanted
to deal with an investment banker they tried to get an appointment to
come see Sidney Weinberg. He didn't do much traveling, because everybody came to him."

Whitehead grew increasingly concerned as Sidney passed his seventi-
eth birthday. Despite the fact that the firm had sixteen partners and four
hundred employees, Goldman Sachs was a one-man show, and it was
clear to Whitehead that others would need to begin selling the firm's services if it was to survive the inevitable loss of its leader. Carefully, in an
official blue-covered memo (the color indicated that it held confidential
information), Whitehead outlined his suggestion for a sales department
located within the investment banking area but did not circulate the
document. Later that year, after he had joined the partnership, he distributed the memo to all of his partners, including Weinberg. "I knew the
memo had to be approved by Sidney," says Whitehead, "so I wrote it in a
delicate way. I said nobody will ever duplicate Sidney Weinberg; we don't
have anybody here and couldn't get anybody, but if we could have ten
people who each produced 20 percent of the business that Sidney Weinberg produces every year, our business would be twice as big as it is
today." One of the main recommendations was that Whitehead detach
himself from Weinberg and head a new business development effort that
would be charged with going out and finding clients, not simply waiting
for the phone to ring, which was the standard practice in the industry at
the time.

The memo suffered from inattention, since no one dared say a word;
only Weinberg could pass judgment on such a radical plan. A few months
later, despairing of hearing anything, Whitehead asked Weinberg if he
had received the memo. Weinberg opened his top desk drawer, pulled out

the controversial document, looked at it, and said, "What a crazy idea, we don't need anything like this. Do you really want to do it?"

Whitehead persisted and brought the proposal up at a partnership meeting, where it was finally approved. Modeling itself on a manufacturing, rather than a service, industry, Goldman Sachs would build a sales department that would do nothing but sell. Taking a radically different approach from that of its competitors, the members of Investment Banking Services (IBS) would fan out and cultivate business, then turn over its execution to specialists. The new salesmen were initially rather limited in their expertise; they were familiar with only one product, commercial paper, but that would soon change.

It was hard going at first. The new salesmen called on companies all over the country trying to persuade them to issue commercial paper through Goldman Sachs. After much persistence a salesman would finally get a foot in the door of the assistant treasurer, a man tucked away in a small office who had primary responsibility for dealing with the banks and managing the cash needs of the company. Goldman Sachs would offer the prospective client money at a lower rate than that available from loans from the commercial banks. Many corporations were deeply conservative and it would take years for Goldman Sachs and the other investment banks to make them see the advantages of raising funds through the capital markets. The assistant treasurer would inevitably shake his head slowly and respond, "Oh, I don't know about that. We've never used this commercial paper before, and who is Goldman Sachs? How can we be sure that you will really give us this money?"

Whitehead is a man of extraordinary creativity and vision, and this slow start did not dissuade him from the certainty that this was the way forward. Now well established, IBS is a cornerstone of the firm and is widely credited for Goldman Sachs's ability to gather and retain clients all over the world. Each IBS representative soon had a list of 200 to 300 companies in his region, and his job was to get to know the business and the leadership well and to bring in specialists to meet any of the companies' financial needs. In creating IBS, Whitehead began the process of specialization, first in selling, later in mergers and acquisitions, and finally in every conceivable industry. By creating specialists early on, Goldman Sachs had a head start on the competition that in many areas of investment banking it never relinquished. IBS made Goldman Sachs a brand name—something other than Weinberg's back-up section. In its selling ability Goldman Sachs is second to none, and it all derives from Whitehead's plan for life after Sidney Weinberg.

Weinberg shaped Goldman Sachs in his image, and for decades after his death many of his personal beliefs were held sacrosanct. By way of example, for many years the firm did not manage other people's money; in Weinberg's words, "Goldman Sachs does not manage any investment trusts—open end, closed end, or no-end." The firm's one experience in the fund management business had almost been its ruin.

Weinberg also bequeathed to Goldman Sachs his personal style. Weinberg made much of the fact that his wealth came largely from his personal compensation, not trading profits. "I never traded," he claimed. "I'm an investment banker. I don't shoot craps. If I had been a speculator and taken advantage of what I knew I could have five times as much as I have today." Although blessed with a Midas touch, Weinberg's highest priority was establishing a top investment bank with a first-rate client list—not making money for himself or Goldman Sachs. The firm's decidedly understated style was set by Weinberg himself. The Weinbergs lived simply, residing in the modest Scarsdale home they bought shortly after their marriage. On one occasion his friend Floyd Odlum convinced Weinberg to invest in the Broadway production of *The Pajama Game*. When the show became a hit and the dividends rolled in, Weinberg held up the latest check and said, "Money! Keeps coming in all the time and hardly means anything at all."

Above all, Weinberg showed unswerving devotion to his clients. The customer reigned supreme, and Weinberg passed this mindset on to the firm. He had restored the firm's good name and laid the groundwork for its later profitability. For decades to come Goldman Sachs would benefit from the goodwill generated by this one man. Sidney Weinberg was the embodiment of Goldman Sachs; no one would ever play a comparable role and his imprint on the firm can still be felt. The day after Sidney died on July 23, 1969, his obituary ran on the front page of the *New York Times*, alongside news that U.S. astronauts Armstrong, Aldrin, and Collins were returning from the moon.

GUSTAVE LEHMANN LEVY was the obvious and only choice to succeed Weinberg as senior partner of Goldman Sachs in 1969. Gus Levy's stature as the number two profit maker after Weinberg dictated the decision. "Whoever produced the clients and produced the dollars, that is what counted at Goldman Sachs in that era," says Whitehead. "It was the only thing that counted. But that didn't mean that Sidney had to like it." Weinberg's style of doing business had no place in Levy's rough-and-tumble trading world. While Weinberg strove to associate Goldman Sachs's name with the finest corporations in America, those closest to Levy say his aspirations were more mercantile—he simply wanted to do all of the business. Weinberg never believed that Levy had the stature or the business standing to lead the firm and was worried about leaving a trader to do what he considered to be a banker's job. "Sidney looked down his nose at Gus," Whitehead adds. "But Sidney, I'm sure, acknowledged to himself that there was no other choice, and therefore selected Gus."

Weinberg's office with its walnut paneling, thick carpets, and oil portraits of the firm's founders was a place where gentlemen spoke in muted terms, transacting the business of the day. Levy operated from a glass-fronted office situated on the firm's main trading floor. In a chaotic world of slamming phones, chattering telex machines, and screaming traders, Levy was the loudest of them all. Weinberg could not imagine clients sitting in Levy's office, with its small sliding window banging open and slamming closed a dozen times a day, like a drive-through hamburger joint. Weinberg may have worried about how this would look to clients; those who sat at the nearby desks simply worried that the glass might shatter.

At the same time he appointed Levy senior partner Weinberg established a six-member management committee and stacked it with older partners, many of them bankers of his own generation. Their job was to watch over Levy and keep him under control. Levy always worked for Weinberg, and when Weinberg would visit the trading floor, Levy would dash to put his jacket on and run around the floor like the boss was in for inspection. Levy's respect for Weinberg was so great that he never addressed him as anything other than "Mr. Weinberg."

The choice of Levy to head an investment bank was an unusual and ultimately pivotal one. The senior partners of all of the firm's major competitors at the time were bankers. Goldman Sachs's business and culture were heavily weighted toward banking as well, but with a trader at the helm Goldman Sachs would become prepared for the trading-oriented world that would emerge in the early 1980s. One of Levy's greatest contributions was to prepare the firm psychologically for the risky world of proprietary, mortgage-backed securities, and derivative trading that he himself could never have foreseen. Decades later, John Gutfreund, the legendary head of Salomon Brothers, would argue that on Wall Street only Goldman Sachs had gotten right the balance between trading and banking.

Levy was born in New Orleans in 1910, one of three children of Sigmund Levy, a manufacturer of wooden crates, and his wife Bella. After his father's death, the sixteen-year-old Levy and his two sisters were taken by their mother to Paris, where he was educated at the American School. He was unsupervised and undisciplined and could often be found at the race track rather than in the classroom. Returning to the United States he entered Tulane University, where he played football and again pursued his interest in betting on horses. After only three months, Levy was forced to drop out because the insurance money from his father's policy had been spent. At eighteen he moved to New York and began his career as a runner, ferrying bundles of securities between brokerage firms during the day and studying business and finance at New York University at night. His firm failed during the Depression, and Levy found himself broke and without a job. A friend referred him to Goldman Sachs in 1933, where he was hired to work on the foreign bond desk, as a one-man trading department, at a salary of $27.50 a week. The following year he married Janet Wolf, a commercial artist from a wealthy family; their son Peter would become a partner of Goldman Sachs. Levy served in the Army air corps right after Pearl Harbor as a nonflying officer and was discharged as a lieutenant colonel. He returned to the firm in 1945 and was named a partner the following year.

Levy brought trading risk to Goldman Sachs and thereby set the firm on an entirely different path from the one Weinberg had steered. Lacking the painful firsthand experience of the Goldman Sachs Trading Corporation, he was able to see the value to the partnership of risking its capital, sensibly and in a controlled manner. Weinberg had averred risk, arguing that it had once almost fatally damaged the firm's name. Levy, too, was concerned about the firm's reputation, but he was aggressive and ambitious and wanted Goldman Sachs to make money. Like Henry Goldman, he was always searching for creative and profitable ways to do business. "More growth occurred during his period of leadership than during Sidney's period of leadership," says Whitehead. "Sidney saw to it that the firm survived and that its reputation reached a high level, but it was Gus who saw to it that the firm had the thrust and drive to grow during this period."

Levy was an impatient, almost hyperactive man, and stories of his management style abound. One standing joke within the firm is that he was always called "Gus" because in the time it took to say "Mr. Levy" he was on to something else. Famed for his impatience with longwindedness and endless meetings, employees would think up "Gus-a-grams" before entering his office. This was the shortest number of words that could be used to convey a thought or problem to the man in charge, who might listen for only a few seconds. Steve Friedman remembers Levy as a "one-man electromagnetic force field" whose energy never seemed to wane. Levy had two secretaries on the theory that he would never need to wait for one to be free. He had no interest in strategic planning: "To Gus short range was what's happening this morning and long range what's going to happen this afternoon," says Whitehead.

During his earliest days in the arbitrage department, Rubin got a taste of Levy's famed impatience. Rubin, analytically minded, had discovered a complex trading opportunity involving warrants that would allow the firm to buy stock at an attractive price in the future. Levy, who himself thrived on elaborate deals, hated long explanations. Rubin took the idea to his boss, who listened for about a minute.

"Stop! D'ya wanna buy or d'ya wanna sell?" Levy shouted at Rubin in his New Orleans drawl.

Rubin tried again. "Gus, it's not that simple . . ."

"I don't care!" Levy hollered. "D'ya wanna buy, or d'ya wanna sell? Don't waste my time."

Management committee meetings, the mechanism Weinberg had bequeathed to keep tabs on Levy, were scheduled every Monday morning from 8 to 9 o'clock, but some who sat in on the meetings remember them ending after only fifteen minutes. Levy insisted on brevity; if it could not be said in that time it was not important. Even the fifteen minutes may have been too long for him; he often held a telephone and gave trading orders while the meeting carried on around him.

People who worked for Levy, including some of those who went on to run the firm themselves, describe his ability to inspire terror, admiration, and intense loyalty. His acts of personal kindness to employees are remembered, as well as his ability to court clients. Yet he could be a demanding taskmaster, flying into rages when he was disappointed with an employee's performance. Yet Levy expected no more of those who worked for him than he did from himself.

Each morning he rose at 5:30, jogged for fifteen minutes, said prayers, read the papers, ate breakfast (he claimed it was sometimes orange juice and leftovers), and headed down to Wall Street. He arrived at 7:50 in order to have the office to himself. For the better part of an hour he made phone calls to clients, usually reaching them at home. As one former CEO remembers, Levy would call, give his appraisal of the world in three minutes or less, ask the client if he had any business to do, and then ring off, often with the client having said little more than a yes or a no.

Some mornings Levy began his day even earlier. Although the firm had a long-established practice of hiring M.B.A.s, Levy, a man without a degree, had his own system for staff recruitment. Early in the morning, before the markets opened, he would invite high school seniors into the office to play bridge or poker with him. He would play whichever game each visitor knew best, watching how his opponent's mind worked. Did he remember which cards had been played? Could he judge risk? Under pressure, could he keep his wits about him? These were the skills he sought. Successful trading, Levy believed, rested on ability as well as steely nerves, integrity, and luck. For years many of the firm's best traders had no higher education, but had passed Levy's entrance exam.

During the first hour in the office Levy wrote his plan for the day on a yellow legal pad and would not rest until every item of the plan was crossed off. Levy sat on about twenty corporate boards and was a trustee of a dozen charitable and cultural organizations, all of whose meetings he attended regularly. The stock exchange closed at 3:30, and Gus departed shortly thereafter. By 4 most afternoons he was on the subway heading uptown to Mount Sinai Hospital to convene a meeting of its staff for the next two hours in his role as chairman of the hospital, the medical center, and the school of medicine. He ran Goldman Sachs and Mount Sinai, both huge, complex business enterprises, for many years, seemingly unaware each was a full-time job.

Afterward he would head home, have a couple of martinis, and almost every night don his tuxedo and go out with clients to the 21 Club or with his wife to one of those "damn testimonial dinners," as he called them. At midnight he would arrive home, in time to sleep and rise again at 5:30— or 4:30 if he wanted to get in a little extra work before heading downtown. He had so much energy that he was known to finish a business meeting in Los Angeles, board the overnight flight to New York, disembark, and drive straight to his club for a round of golf. On those mornings, after he returned to the office, his employees avoided him, as his temper was apt to be short. When asked about the pressure to work hard at Goldman Sachs, Levy simply said, "Well, we do demand a full day."

BLOCK TRADING, which revolutionized the exchanges and is now the predominant method for buying and selling large stock holdings, was Levy's brainchild. After World War II the country's assets had become institutionalized. Many companies set up self-administered pension funds that pooled savings but invested only in bonds. Slowly, as the wisdom of diversifying into equities spread and the painful memories of the crash receded, these funds began to purchase stocks. As the first sizable investors they found the market too small and illiquid to accommodate their transactions. The New York Stock Exchange had been established to facilitate the business of the individual investor and had operated that way since its inception. Specialists who had provided a bid and an offer for stocks from the exchange floors were unable to handle the increasing volume. Levy proposed a novel solution. He would split trades with the specialists, taking part of the price risk and opportunity for profit onto Goldman Sachs's books. For a time this system worked, but the transaction size continued to increase, and even half became too large for the specialist system. Levy stepped into the fray again, committing Goldman Sachs to buying large blocks of stock, often in advance of finding a ready buyer. By situating itself in the flow of information and trading, the firm put itself in the best position to locate the other side of any transaction.

Levy had a sixth sense for everything done on the trading floor. He wanted Goldman Sachs to be involved in every major trade and didn't spare his wrath when he felt the firm had missed a major piece of business. A sign reading "A 250,000 Share Block a Day Keeps Gus Levy Away" hung on the trading room wall, and traders knew that you missed a big block trade at your peril. Even when charged with responsibility for the entire firm, he watched this part of the business extremely carefully: "It so happens that I sit next to the trading room," he reminded his traders. "Don't forget we have a lot of our money on the line and our position is pretty huge. I think the partnership wants to know that it is watched very carefully."

For Wall Street the early 1970s were wretched times. In January 1973 the Dow had stood at 1,051 and by December 1974 it had almost halved to 578 and would not rise above 1,000 again until 1980. For Goldman Sachs, which would struggle with low earnings and a spate of lawsuits, this would be a particularly difficult time. The low point in Levy's management of the firm came in February 1970, after the Penn Central Railroad reported dismal earnings. An official of the National Credit Office (the agency that rated commercial paper) telephoned Goldman Sachs, Penn Central's commercial paper issuer, to discuss the railroad's creditworthiness. The firm reassured the official of its generally positive view of the situation, and the paper's "prime" rating was left in place.

Goldman Sachs continued to sell Penn Central paper, but took steps that minimized its own exposure to the securities. While still recommending the commercial paper to customers, the firm feared that there would be little customer demand and insisted that henceforth it would provide customers with Penn Central paper from a "tap"—that is, the railroad would issue a specified amount whenever Goldman Sachs brought them an interested buyer. In this way Goldman Sachs would have no more than $8 million in inventory.

When Penn Central plunged into bankruptcy, panic engulfed the commercial paper market. Investors concerned about the solvency of other issues by Goldman Sachs—the firm had about 300 issuers at the time—rushed to redeem their securities. Corporations all over America had to borrow from banks to repay these short-term debts, and the Federal Reserve was forced to act to ensure continued liquidity.

Goldman Sachs had assumed, incorrectly, that the Federal Reserve would rescue the railroad by providing it with the needed liquidity. The $3 billion in assets held by Penn Central, they believed, were sufficient to cover its debt—the company simply lacked available credit. Levy testified later that at no time was he concerned about the solvency of the railroad. Regardless, Goldman Sachs was censured by the Securities and Exchange Commission for its actions and required to give customers more detailed information about issuers in the future. Despite the fact that Goldman Sachs had access to a great deal of adverse financial information about Penn Central, the SEC said that it "did not communicate this information to its commercial paper customers, nor did it undertake a thorough investigation of the company. If Goldman had heeded these warnings and undertaken a reevaluation of the company, it would have learned that its condition was substantially worse than had been publicly reported."

For Goldman Sachs the episode was nothing short of a disaster. The firm's good name, nurtured for so many decades by Sidney Weinberg, was once again tarnished, its credibility damaged, its finances precarious. These were scary times, and, ironically, it fell to Sidney's son to make amends. Levy sent his lieutenant, John Weinberg, who had joined the firm in 1950, to meet with many of the firm's clients in the South and offer them a deal, fifty cents on the dollar. Word of his deal arrived at each town before he did, and everywhere he met with hostile creditors who were angry and unwilling to negotiate. Weinberg's mission was a failure, as Levy knew it would be, but the firm had to extend some offer, no matter how unpalatable. Goldman Sachs could not be seen walking away from its clients. If that happened there would be no going back.

Clients lined up to sue the firm, with Goldman Sachs named in at least forty-five lawsuits. The railroad had defaulted on $87 million worth of commercial paper at the time of the bankruptcy, and the firm faced potential lawsuits for an amount greater than the partners' capital, which stood at only $53 million at the time. It was a frightening time for the forty-five partners, because their personal liability was unlimited. Although the firm did not admit liability, it eventually settled with many clients, buying their paper back for between twenty and twenty-five cents on the dollar and granting them some participation in any recovery of funds that might be made from Penn Central. In October 1974, Welch's Foods and two other plaintiffs sued the firm, and the case went to trial. A federal jury found Goldman Sachs guilty of defrauding its customers by selling them Penn Central commercial paper in 1969 and 1970, when the railroad was going broke. The firm was forced to buy back the commercial paper from the plaintiffs at its face value plus interest. The immediate results were damaging both to Goldman Sachs's reputation and its finances, but the firm had bought back much of the paper at a heavy discount to the face value, which later rose sharply, and this helped mitigate the level of losses eventually sustained.

In 1973, because of poor market conditions, the firm had suffered losses for the first nine months of the year, and the newest partners faced the prospect of their capital accounts moving into deficit. When Levy suggested that the existing partners indemnify the new partners against loss, there was unanimous agreement in favor. Once again, as had happened after the stock market crash, the senior partners decided to wipe out the deficits in the junior partners' capital accounts. It was a partnership, recalled one thirty-year veteran, and everyone knew what that meant. Troubles or not, no Goldman Sachs partner should begin his career in debt. (The recollections of those who were partners at the time were that by the end of the year the firm had not sustained a loss, and this act of generosity turned out to be only symbolic.)

In October 1976, Levy suffered a stroke and collapsed while chairing a board meeting of the New York & New Jersey Port Authority. Slipping into a coma from which he never recovered, Levy lay unconscious but alive at Mount Sinai Hospital. This was the second time in eight years that a strong and beloved leader had been lost, and although Levy had publicly indicated that there were heirs apparent, he had never named names. Leaderless, the firm was left in turmoil.

CHAPTER III

1976–1990

THE WORLD-CLASS PLAYER

W HY EXACTLY LEVY failed to name a successor will remain a mystery, but perhaps there simply was no single obvious choice to
inherit his mantle. The "two Johns," as Whitehead and Weinberg were
always known, were the only contenders. John L. Weinberg and his
friend and colleague John Whitehead had worked together since the day
Weinberg stepped out of Harvard Business School and into the firm his
father had been running since he was five years old.

Whitehead had arrived at Goldman Sachs, also from Harvard Business
School, three years before Weinberg. He had sought a job in investment
banking, viewing it as further training for an eventual career in industry,
and Goldman Sachs just happened to be the only firm to interview on
campus during the spring of 1947. The son of a telephone linesman,
Whitehead was raised in then working-class Montclair, New Jersey, and
served in the Navy in World War II fighting in the battles of Normandy,
Iwo Jima, and Okinawa. He is of moderate height and build, well-
tailored, with gracious manners, and from the earliest days his patrician
appearance belied his upbringing. A calm, exceedingly well-spoken man,
the respect and admiration in which he was held would only increase
throughout his lifetime. After thirty-eight years with Goldman Sachs,
Whitehead would begin a second career, serving in the Reagan administration and later as the chairman of the board of the Federal Reserve
Bank of New York, the International Rescue Committee, and the United
Nations Association of the U.S.A. In time, with his full head of white hair
and gentlemanly ways, he gained the status and appearance of the elder
statesman he had become.

Whitehead arrived at the firm's headquarters at 30 Pine Street—by coincidence the exact site on which Marcus Goldman had opened his first office—to find his desk located in the partners' squash court. Goldman Sachs was cramped for space, and the firm's six associates and their secretaries worked in the court. Each time Sidney Weinberg brought in a piece of business he would call down to the squash court in search of some young Turk to handle it. As time went on the elder Weinberg got into the habit of calling on Whitehead; the young man's keen mind, polished presentation, and ambitious nature impressed the senior partner, and Whitehead eventually became his assistant. During Whitehead's first nine years with the firm there were few profits, and when Whitehead was made a partner in 1956 he invested his life savings, all $5,000 of it, in Goldman Sachs.

John Weinberg, three years younger than Whitehead, came from the same school but a different world. He had worked at the firm during summer vacations, but had lived with it all his life. Raised in Scarsdale, he had attended Deerfield Academy, and been toughened by his two tours of duty with the Marines, first as a teenager during World War II and then as a captain during the Korean War. Weinberg was so influenced by his famous father that as a Princeton undergraduate he wrote his senior thesis on "The Status and Functions of Corporation Directors." Despite a childhood steeped in privilege and prosperity, John Weinberg is a plain-spoken, disarmingly honest, and unpretentious man. Like his father, he never minces words when describing friend or foe. Once described as "a block of a man with the battered square-jawed appearance of an ex-boxer," he is the leader of one of America's great banking families and a man who has inspired unswerving loyalty and personal devotion from those who have worked for him. Long on substance and short on style, sentences tumble out, phrases sometimes awkwardly worded, but the meaning entirely clear. Weinberg exudes such warmth and sincerity that he is impossible not to like.

Many employees love Goldman Sachs because of the status it has conferred upon them or the wealth it has bestowed; others feel a genuine sense of loyalty to a company in which they fervently believe. Weinberg loves Goldman Sachs as the family heirloom that it is for him, something to be prized, cared for, and bequeathed to the next generation. He believes that people and relationships are paramount—all else is a distant second. Even during some of the firm's darkest moments he was able to imbue partners and employees with a sense of pride and optimism.

As his graduation from business school approached, John was casting around for direction, so his father sent him to see the heads of the reigning banks—J. P. Morgan, Morgan Stanley, and First Boston—all men

Sidney knew personally. Finally Sidney sent John to see Floyd Odlum, the man to whom he had sold the Goldman Sachs Trading Corporation. Odlum was an aggressive entrepreneur who bought and sold businesses that had failed in the 1930s, a shrewd and successful businessman, who became a millionaire in the decade when millions of people lost their shirts. He had bought so many failing businesses during the Depression—like the GSTC—at a fraction of their break-up value, that Sidney Weinberg nicknamed him "Fifty Percent." While the other meetings John attended may have produced some sound advice, Odlum's words still ring in John's ears some fifty years later. While praising Sidney, Odlum offered the younger Weinberg these prophetic words of advice: "I am going to do something for you. I will give you this book, but you have to promise me that for the whole rest of your career, you will keep a copy of this book and refer to it. Read it once and then from time to time refresh your memory with the table of contents." The book was *Popular Delusions and the Madness of Crowds* by Charles McKay, originally published in 1841. "Watch for the excesses," Odlum warned. "No one is going to tell you what they are or when they will arise; each time they will look different." Excesses will be taken care of by the marketplace, he told the younger man, but as each generation forgets the lessons of the last, the same mistakes are made again. He cautioned that success would come only to those who could recognize and correctly value risk. Weinberg took the book and the elder man's advice to heart. To this day he keeps a copy of the book in each of his offices, referring to it from time to time. As his father's son he was well versed in the history of the Goldman Sachs Trading Corporation, and he made sure its lessons would not be lost on a new generation.

Decades later, as Goldman Sachs sailed into the 1980s financially secure, its reputation second to none, John Weinberg kept his eye out for the excesses. Odlum's words of advice ultimately saved Goldman Sachs from hundreds of millions of dollars of losses in business the firm walked away from. Goldman Sachs's success in the 1980s can be attributed not only to what it did but perhaps, more important, to what it did not do. Goldman Sachs steered clear of making hazardous bridge loans (short-term loans made by investment banks until public funding becomes available) and involved itself in few failed leveraged buyouts.

Sidney Weinberg wanted his son to join the business, but he would never give him an easy ride. "I worked for my father all my business life, but he never made it easy for me. No strawberries for lunch, he used to say to me," says John. At the same time, the affection and admiration he felt for his father is plain.

From his first day at the firm John Weinberg was seated at a desk facing Whitehead, only inches apart in the old squash court. For lunch the pair walked over to Scottie's Sandwich Shop, which served the thickest corned beef sandwiches. There, Whitehead recounts, they would "talk about how poorly Goldman Sachs was run, how inefficient and unaggressive and old-fashioned. And, by god, if we ever had a chance to have any influence we certainly would do it a lot differently." The partnership operated informally in the 1940s and 1950s, with no scheduled meetings other than the understanding that all partners would lunch together every Monday. Information about clients, complimentary or critical, was circulated among the partners in a notebook called "the red book," a system abandoned when the partnership grew too large. Over and over Weinberg and Whitehead would reorganize the firm in their heads, making plans for how it would be different if they ever got their shot.

At the time of Levy's death in 1976 the two Johns had been working together for two and a half decades. Weinberg and Whitehead had become partners on the same day in 1956, and their long careers had moved in lockstep. They had the same salary, the same partnership percentage, the same titles. After Levy, Whitehead and Weinberg held the largest percentage of the firm. Although they were the obvious heirs, the question remained: Which one? Whitehead was the older and more experienced of the pair, with a higher profile outside the firm. He had chaired the Securities Industry Association and was chief banker to Ford Motor Company, the firm's most important client. He was the strategist, the visionary many looked up to and admired. But John Weinberg was the soul of the firm and its major developer of new business. As Sidney's son, there were some who believed his succession was a foregone conclusion; he would be the link. His father had worked for the Goldmans and the Sachses. Sidney Weinberg had assimilated many of their values and passed them on to his sons. With John Weinberg at the helm the link to the firm's foundation would remain unbroken for almost a century and a quarter.

While Levy lay unconscious, Whitehead and Weinberg met alone without consulting their partners and summarily decided to anoint themselves the firm's leaders. The pair presented the plan to the management committee, which rubber-stamped the decision and paved the way for another smooth transition of power. Shortly after his death Levy's will was read, and it was discovered that he had named Weinberg and Whitehead as joint executors of his estate. They took it as a nod.

Upon hearing the news of their ascendancy, Marvin Bower, then head of the highly respected consulting firm McKinsey & Co., called immediately to offer the pair his congratulations and issue a warning. While both were men of great talent and either could lead the firm capably, the structure they had put in place, he informed them, simply would not work. Bower told them that when their plan failed, as it certainly would within a few months, he and the considerable resources of McKinsey would be at their disposal to straighten out the mess they had created. The three agreed to have lunch in one year to discuss the progress. But when the time came, two of them would eat lunch, the other would eat his words. Bower congratulated the pair, and the three have remained in touch to this day.

The two new leaders had long felt that Goldman Sachs was sloppily run. Responsibility was not clearly defined, and discipline was lacking. Expenses were high and inadequately restrained. Neither Sidney Weinberg nor Gus Levy had concerned himself much with management systems, budgets, or organizational structure. Weinberg and Whitehead were determined to change all this. For years a limousine had stood at the front door of Goldman Sachs at 4:30 every afternoon to ferry partners from their downtown offices to Grand Central Station. It had long been one of the perks of partnership and was enjoyed by many. The first warning shot of the new regime was fired with a succinct memo: "Effective today the limousine to Grand Central Station that has historically left at 4:30 is discontinued." There would be no hierarchy of partners, expenses would be watched, and 4:30 was now the middle of the afternoon, not the end of the day.

Management committee meetings changed dramatically once the two Johns were in charge. Instead of a fifteen-minute session during which the senior partner was both chairing the meeting and trading stocks, the meetings took on substance and length. Every Monday morning at 9, the eight men met at a round table. The meeting was now a forum for a real flow of information and decision making, though there was no doubt what would happen in the absence of a consensus. "John and I would decide," said Whitehead bluntly. "There'd be no question of a vote."

Being a partner in Levy's day did not mean you were in charge of a particular department or division of activity. That would change. "When you became a partner," Whitehead remembers, "you were sort of above everything and the organizational structure was down there somewhere. And once you were a partner, you were free to do almost anything you wanted—and most partners did. So we tried to bring about a division of responsibilities, and make people responsible for doing the kind of things they did best and not have them cross over into things they weren't very good at." Whitehead and Weinberg distributed authority more widely, giving greater responsibility to the pool of talented partners below the management committee level.

Weinberg and Whitehead led by example. By meeting with clients, working on deals, and putting in long days of traveling, they sent out the message that everyone at the firm gets their hands dirty; managing is only part of the job. Weinberg feared the day when any partner or vice-president would feel they were too important to transact the real business of the firm. "All these people who came out of these [business] schools were very talented, at the top of their class upon graduation. We spent many hours recruiting them. We wanted people who were not only out-standing performers, but also who were able to work well as members of a team. When they came aboard we worked them very hard. Arrogance and politics are everyplace, always. I'm not part of management at all [anymore], but I still keep telling these people—arrogance and politics will kill you, someday it will kill you."

Weinberg and Whitehead decided to run the firm together. Rather than carving it up into spheres of influence they undertook joint responsibility for the whole. Instead of adjacent desks in the squash courts they now had adjoining offices. From the start they let it be known that a decision of one was a decision of both.

Their strengths meshed perfectly. Whitehead was the planner, the man who focused on the firm's long-term direction, shaping its business, some of its major clients and its budget. Weinberg focused on the clients and on drumming up new business. The pairing was a complete success. Out of a small family business, they created a professional organization complete with operations in many of the world's major business centers, one that thrived in the increasingly fast and complex environment of the 1980s.

Sam Sachs's dream of an international firm had died in the aftermath of the 1929 stock market crash, but Whitehead revived that dream and made it his own. Goldman Sachs's first push on the road to international expansion, however, came not from the inspired foresight of the firm's new management but from a disgruntled client. When General Foods approached Goldman Sachs with an offer to acquire a French food company, the firm was forced to turn the business away. At that time, Goldman Sachs had no offices and few business contacts in France— or anywhere else in the world. "We had correspondents," Whitehead recalls, "and they might pay us a finder's fee. But it wasn't our business, it was their business." Thus Morgan Stanley did its first piece of business with General Foods, which had been a Goldman Sachs client since the company was founded.

At that moment Whitehead realized that without an overseas opera-tion the firm's domestic business would suffer, although this wisdom was not universally accepted by the partnership. Many felt the opportunities at home were more than adequate to sustain the firm's growth. Others worried about maintaining the cultural integrity of the firm as it became geographically diverse. Most balked at the costs. Moreover, opening offices abroad was not easy; neither London nor Tokyo welcomed the arrival of American banks. It would prove difficult and hugely expensive to wean clients away from their traditional compatriot bankers. Some of these relationships were centuries old, many of them resting securely on ties of family, friendship, shared school days, and everything but good business sense. The two Johns were forced to assert their seniority.

"All of our international activities lost money and partners regularly complained," Whitehead remembers, "so I changed the accounting system. Instead of having an international division which had a separate P&L [profit and loss statement], we accounted by product line and we didn't have an international division at all anymore. Each department had to absorb its share of international losses, and now that these were no longer visible, things went a little better."

The international expansion plans for some American investment banks were derailed at just this point. The rewards of establishing a presence abroad, if any, seemed too remote and the price too high. Nonetheless, Goldman Sachs—and some of its competitors—persisted. Whitehead and Weinberg were both prescient and stubborn, and the benefits they reaped were phenomenal. The decision was a pivotal one, laying down the firm's strategy for the remainder of the century. Goldman Sachs was not going to be a good or even a great American bank; it was going to be world class. "Now we are a truly international firm, the leading firm in London—not the leading U.S. firm, but the leading firm," Whitehead says proudly.

At the end of 1984, after thirty-seven years with Goldman Sachs, John Whitehead retired. John Weinberg tried to convince his co-senior partner to reconsider his decision and stay but Whitehead felt that at sixty-two it was time for him to move into the nonprofit sector. Shortly after leaving the firm he joined the Reagan administration. In the years following Whitehead's departure, Steve Friedman and Bob Rubin played increasingly important roles in the management of the firm. In 1985 they were asked to head fixed income and when they were appointed co–vice chairmen and co–chief operating officers in 1987, few suspected they would bring radical change to Goldman Sachs. Both men, lawyers by training, had spent most of their working lives with the firm. Their appointment was seen as a way to ease the sixty-one-year-old Weinberg's considerable workload and signal the eventual transition of power. But new management brought new intensity, and the two leaders, both in their late forties, injected a strong sense of dynamism into a naturally cautious organization. While still valuing the firm's culture they exhibited a greater interest in the firm's profitability and little tolerance for what they viewed as clinging to the past. Nothing was beyond scrutiny, and change was inevitable.

Rubin and Friedman ran the two most profitable areas of the firm. Rubin had spent his entire career in risk arbitrage, taking on responsibility for J. Aron after the merger with the commodities firm in 1981. Friedman had been one of the first members of the mergers and acquisitions department. Both businesses were fast, transaction-oriented areas where speed and good judgment were essential.

Rubin's lightning career path at Goldman Sachs began on Halloween Day in 1966 after Yale Law School, the London School of Economics, and two years practicing law. Rubin was elevated to the partnership after a mere five years with the firm and was seated on the management committee fourteen years after walking through the door. Extremely thin, with dark eyes and thick dark hair that over the years has become peppered with gray, Rubin's youthful looks became familiar to many Americans when he joined the Clinton administration in 1992.

Inevitably Rubin will be remembered in history as a committed Democrat with strong views on the value of public service. A highly successful fund-raiser for every Democratic presidential campaign since the 1970s, Rubin was instrumental in bringing the 1992 Democratic National Convention to New York. Rubin is a native New Yorker who was raised in Miami, and his love of politics is rooted in his own family. His wife, Judy, was an advisor to former New York City Mayor David Dinkins. His father was a socially concerned and financially successful lawyer; his grandfather was a Democratic Party leader in Brooklyn. Rubin's extraordinary career took him to the highest circles of power, where he became the secretary of the treasury in 1995.

Despite his public profile, Rubin is a very private man who handles even the greatest crisis with total equanimity. Although those at the firm were long familiar with his grace under pressure, this attribute came into public view in the budget crisis in the fall of 1995, when many feared the U.S. government would default on its debt for the first time in history, a crisis Rubin deftly averted. A deeply humble and unpretentious man, Rubin exhibits few of the trappings of his vast wealth. When people talk about him, they usually mention his lack of ego. Searingly smart, he is renowned on Wall Street and in Washington for his self-effacing nature.

"To me Rubin's and Friedman's legacy is absolute intellectual honesty," says Goldman Sachs CEO Hank Paulson. "Some leaders say I want every side, I want a real debate. I hate to say it but the vast majority don't. Rubin and Friedman always did. We used to kid Friedman because he would say, 'I'm 51–49 on this.' " Even when Rubin agreed with someone he was often known to take the other side in order to provoke debate. Rubin kept his fellow management committee members on their toes. "I've never seen a combination of a guy that intellectual and commercial," says Paulson. "Usually people who are like Bob are academic, but they are not commercial. And I just think that is a rare combination."

A skilled listener in a world where everyone is trying to grab the floor, Rubin is universally admired for his ability to get to the heart of any matter with probing and thoughtful questions. A practical flexibility seems to be at the heart of his success. "He has enormous patience for people who disagree with him if they have good argumentation," says Steve Friedman. "He was amazingly ready to switch his thinking."

One of Rubin's greatest contributions to the firm was his deep understanding of risk and his ability to manage it. He knew the necessary components of a first-class trading operation and passed this understanding on to the partners who worked for him. Rubin seemed to have an intuitive feel for setting the right psychological conditions in which traders and salespeople could function best; this accounts, in part, for the phenomenal success of both risk arbitrage and J. Aron.

The walls of Rubin's office at Goldman Sachs were lined with signed photographs of presidents, while the floor was piled high with papers and his desk strewn with half-filled plastic cups of coffee. A workaholic, he raised the standards for everyone with whom he came into contact. A number of European traders recall trips to New York when, up before dawn because of jet lag, they wandered onto the New York trading floor at an insanely early hour and found Rubin already there. His intensity was masked by an air of unruffled calm that belied the pressure cooker in which he lived. In taking his leave of a group, Rubin would turn around and with a quiet smile raise his index and middle finger in a V and say "Peace."

Steve Friedman, who was Rubin's partner at the top, is an intense, intellectually voracious man with the youthful appearance of the wrestler he once was. When Friedman says that Goldman Sachs is different because of its intensity, he is certainly speaking of himself, too. Friedman exudes relentless energy; his forceful handshake seems almost a challenge to arm wrestle. Jacket off, sleeves rolled up, he never stops moving. Friedman thrived on the grueling schedule that was the life of a merger specialist. He can barely sit still. When quietly discussing the firm's history, pen and yellow legal pad always on hand, Friedman is frenetically diagramming his thoughts as if preparing a blueprint for the firm's future. Even in retirement from the firm his desk is piled so precariously high one dares not slam his office door.

Friedman was an agitator for change. His challenge was, as he put it, "to get them to think of change as a constant." Like Rubin, he arrived at Goldman Sachs in 1966 after Columbia Law School—where he was on the Law Review and was a national AAU wrestling champion—and a few years with a law firm. At the time, mergers and acquisitions was not a mainstream business, and he was an outsider within the organization. It was a mindset he held onto for the next thirty years. Probing every situation, Friedman was never satisfied with pat answers. As his successor, Jon Corzine, remembers, "When I think of Steve, it's 'stand by for twenty questions.' "

Friedman's goal was for every employee to be able to answer correctly his "3 a.m. wake-up call." If he telephoned members of the firm in the middle of the night and asked what Goldman Sachs stood for, most would have answered, bleary-eyed and half-asleep, "client service, integrity, and teamwork." Once he was in charge, he did not want anyone going back to sleep until he or she had also answered, "strategic dynamism and a commitment to change." There can be little doubt that, with Friedman's intensity, he considered 3 a.m. part of the working day for anyone committed to a career at Goldman Sachs.

Resolved to unleash the firm's creative potential and enter new businesses more aggressively, Friedman accelerated the pace of change. The firm had been slow to innovate, slow to adapt to many of the changes in the financial markets in the 1980s, and even slow to copy. The firm had never suffered a major failure upon entering a new business—evidence, Friedman felt, that it was getting in much too late. During his years in mergers and acquisitions he had seen the value of establishing an early and unchallenged lead in a new business. Goldman Sachs had practically invented the raid defense business. During the 1970s and into the 1980s the firm had more than a 50 percent market share in this hugely profitable business; and maintains its leadership position to this day. Its early leads in businesses like commercial paper, risk arbitrage, and block trading had also hammered home the benefits of being out in front. Friedman was determined that Goldman Sachs should follow this model in its other businesses, but such a path would require a massive overhaul in the firm's thinking. Many partners believed that the firm should enter new businesses cautiously, only after the profit potential had been proved by others. More adventurous institutions would have both failures and spectacular successes. Friedman was a demanding boss, constantly pushing Goldman Sachs to do better.

DESPITE A SLOW START, one of the major drivers of the firm's success in the 1970s and early 1980s was the burgeoning mergers and acquisitions

(M&A) department. For many years, merger activity at Goldman Sachs was a largely informal business, a matter of quietly selling family-owned businesses to public companies. "John Weinberg would say that he *was* the original merger department, in the sense that the bottom left-hand drawer held the buyers and the bottom right-hand drawer the sellers," Geoffrey Boisi explains. In these early days the business was simple; doing deals was a matter of matching up the two. Had this gentlemanly approach to business continued, Goldman Sachs might have chipped away at its formidable rivals and over time built up a small, respectable mergers and acquisitions business. Instead, in 1974, Morgan Stanley handed Goldman Sachs the business opportunity of a lifetime and by doing so lifted the firm out of the second tier of investment banking and placed it on the road to the top.

Prior to the 1970s, a company or its bankers might propose a merger with another firm, it might even cajole or attempt to persuade its target, but it would never actively and openly pursue a merger uninvited. But beginning in the early 1970s, the civilized world of investment banking came to an abrupt end as major U.S. companies and their investment bankers cast aside more than a century of tradition that dictated all takeovers must be friendly. Boisi recalls, "The notion that you would raid a company was so ungentlemanly that in the early stages it was almost considered an immoral act. In the late 1960s and early 1970s it was considered improper by the generalist banker to even suggest to a CEO that he consider selling his business. It was like asking him to sell one of his children. It was the worst thing that you could suggest."

It is generally agreed that in July 1974, Morgan Stanley, the investment bank with the finest reputation, fired the first salvo when, on behalf of its Canadian client International Nickel—INCO, as the company was known—it raided Electric Storage Battery (ESB), the world's largest maker of batteries. INCO had decided on the attack and went to Morgan Stanley for assistance and advice. Morgan Stanley justified the extraordinary move by arguing that it was merely assisting a longstanding client. Morgan Stanley had a lock on many of the largest U.S. corporations in relationships extending back to the days before the investment bank was split off from its commercial banking parent J. P. Morgan in 1935. Hostile takeovers would now create a new world order, forever shattering the traditional lineup.

When Fred Port, the head of ESB, learned of Morgan Stanley's headlong assault, he called Steve Friedman, then in charge of Goldman Sachs's mergers and acquisitions department, and asked for help. On the day of the attack, Friedman had arrived home at midnight to find an urgent message from Port saying, "Call no matter the hour." At 9 the following morning Friedman was seated in Port's Philadelphia office. ESB began by condemning Morgan Stanley in a letter they issued publicly. When Friedman learned of the $28-a-share bid, a $9 premium over the last trade, he advised his client to fight INCO with a white knight (a friendly bidder brought in by the target company) or an antitrust suit. Goldman Sachs, with white knight United Aircraft, drove the price up so that INCO eventually paid $41 a share, earning the shareholders a 100 percent premium. But from this day forward the battle lines were drawn. In conflict after conflict Morgan Stanley, and soon afterward First Boston, would represent the acquirer and Goldman Sachs the target.

This new business, defending companies from unwelcome predators, would require all the specialist skills the firm had and a much heightened emphasis on interdepartmental teamwork. To Friedman, a raid defense is like stalking a mastodon, and Goldman Sachs's culture was perfectly suited to taking on such large prey. "For years the investment banks had operated as small hunter-gatherers," Friedman says. "Guys were out there in their fur loincloths, hunting small animals. Each could pretty much exist by himself, maybe he had a spouse that could cook for him or something like that. But you start hunting bigger game, you can't do it alone as a hunter-gatherer, it cuts across too many specialized areas. You can't do a raid defense as a hunter-gatherer. You've got to have a lot of little guys running around beating the brush, starting a fire to get the mastodon running, and a bunch of other guys in their furry loincloths digging a big pit so he'll fall in and break his leg."

Friedman, along with partner Corbin Day, created the first merger and acquisitions department on Wall Street in the mid-1960s, operating it as a small subsection of the firm's investment banking division. Long considered a backwater, the department had trouble getting the best talent at the firm to work on its deals. When Geoff Boisi joined Goldman Sachs in 1971 there were just enough men in the M&A department to make a bridge game. But the department was a small revolution; no other firm had a department dedicated to this single service. Goldman Sachs reasoned that the merger business had become too specialized to be someone's sideline. In establishing Investment Banking Services, a department focused only on marketing new business, and thereby separating the relationship and execution sides of the business, Whitehead had laid the groundwork for Goldman Sachs's bankers to specialize. While other firms still operated on the generalist model, with one banker covering the range of a client's needs, Goldman Sachs surged ahead by designating specialists who could remain abreast of every development in a particular market. By the late 1970s the merger business was evolving so rapidly that each new deal seemed to hinge on an innovative offensive or defensive tactic. Anyone who had not worked on the last big deal, among them generalists who had other responsibilities, quickly found that their tactics were already out of date.

The INCO-ESB fight earned Goldman Sachs its battle stripes, with first-hand experience on the first hostile takeover. For Goldman Sachs this was a portentous stroke of good luck, a chance to jump ahead in the pecking order. "People thought of Goldman Sachs as a strong, emerging firm working with the smaller to middle-size companies and a few Fortune 100 accounts," Boisi remembers. "We were not in the elite category. I think we were viewed as a high-quality, sort of up-and-coming firm, nowhere near the dimension that we evolved into. We certainly weren't recognized as a national championship team, no less a world-class player."

In time companies under attack would call Goldman Sachs for help, but in the early days the firm needed to bang on a few doors. When Aztec Oil, the Dallas oil and gas company, was raided in January 1976, Aztec was not interested in Goldman Sachs's services; they had their lawyers, and the situation was under control. Friedman asked them to rethink their decision and told them that his team was on its way to the airport; they could discuss it in a few hours in person. Friedman remembers, "We ran to the airport and flew to Dallas and they still didn't want to see us. We camped out on their doorstep and then we got in and told them a few things that they hadn't thought through. But they said, 'We still don't want to hire you,' so we said, 'We'll be back tomorrow.' Every day we'd go to the Brooks Brothers near the office and buy another shirt, a pair of underwear, and a set of socks." Finally, as the company realized the depth of its troubles and the staying power of its new bankers, Goldman Sachs was hired. The packed schedule that these early days brought would only accelerate. For Friedman and Boisi the pace would not let up until the day they left the partnership.

It is hard to overstate the value of raid defense work for the Goldman Sachs investment banking franchise. In 1966, the year Friedman came to Goldman Sachs, M&A revenues were $600,000. When he ceded day-to-day control of the department to Boisi in 1980, M&A revenues had risen to about $90 million. By 1989, M&A was bringing in $350 million, and eight years later it would be a billion-dollar business. But the business brought more than just profits to the firm.

Suddenly, CEOs across America were scared stiff. Everyone apart from the very largest corporations felt vulnerable to the hostile takeover. Goldman Sachs presented defense strategies to the CEO and board of directors of its clients (many of them CEOs in their own right). The message was simple, Friedman and Boisi would tell prospective clients. They should figure out what the raider would do and do it themselves. "It was life's happy confluence of events that the best advice for clients—not being passive and generating shareholder value—happened to be very good for us," says Friedman. "It was a wonderful, wonderful way to get close to a lot of clients."

Like Boisi, Friedman is enthusiastic when he talks of those days, and he describes running investment banking as one of the happiest times of his life. The exposure was invaluable. Brainstorming sessions with top management about a company's defense would result in a variety of assignments for different parts of the firm. M&A was hugely profitable in its own right, but now it had become a new business development arm of the firm. In time it would spawn other businesses, including leveraged buyouts, high-yield debt, and stock repurchasing. "Fear was driving the corporate decision makers a little bit because they wanted to protect their perceived long-term growth strategies," Boisi remembers. "We then took advantage of this concern and started to look at how to enhance the value of their businesses in order to protect them from raiders. It gave us an opening to learn their innermost strategic thinking. Together we'd sit down with the CEO, who would say, I have got this problem, this opportunity; you know, we used to get into these great and important conversations and we would come out of these meetings with four or five different actual assignments."

As the 1980s unfolded, Friedman was squarely in charge of all investment banking, and his number one lieutenant was Boisi. Aggressive, direct, the consummate player, Boisi had a perfect pedigree. This was not some scrappy kid from the streets but a high-class banker. One of six children and the son of a retired vice-chairman of Morgan Guaranty, deals were in his blood. "When I was a kid the conversations at the dinner table were very wide-ranging. But I remember hearing about big real estate deals, the intense negotiating process. It intrigued me." After a summer internship with the firm the twenty-two-year-old Boisi returned to the Wharton School to complete his M.B.A. before heading right back to Goldman Sachs as the first M.B.A. hired into M&A. Friedman and Boisi set the pace for the department. "It's a difficult life," Boisi has said. "There have been more times than I care to remember when the phone rings, I just pick up my briefcase and go out to the airport. No clothes. No toothbrush. A couple of days later the clothes arrive. The deal dictates your schedule."

No star shone brighter than Boisi's. He was dyed-in-the-wool Goldman Sachs, a culture carrier of the first order and a formidable money generator. Like most of those who rose to the top of the Goldman Sachs banking hierarchy, Boisi was intensely ambitious, with an understanding wife and family. The claims of the job seemed to have no limit. The father of four worked up to eighteen hours a day and was named partner at the age of thirty-one. In 1980 when Friedman was promoted Boisi took over as merger chief, and again in 1986 he succeeded Friedman as head of all investment banking. The tall, dark-haired banker was respected and feared in the profession as a tough boss and a ruthless, but honest, competitor.

By pursuing unwilling targets, Morgan Stanley and First Boston were earning record-breaking fees, but early in the merger boom Goldman Sachs separated itself from the rest of the investment banking world with a strict policy of refusing to aid in a hostile tender offer. The firm would defend the victim, but it would not attack. Some said the policy was a legacy of Sidney Weinberg's values (although in his day there were no hostile takeovers), but it was viewed by many competitors as a sanctimonious act designed to grab headlines and lure clients.

Debates raged within the firm over the wisdom of this policy, but for John Weinberg and Whitehead, both of whom had worked in investment banking, it was an easy decision. Whitehead felt strongly that the firm was acting in the long-term interest of itself and its clients. There were those who felt Goldman Sachs was leaving enormous buy-side merger fees on the table for other firms to swoop down and grab. The debate grew heated, but Weinberg and Whitehead were adamant. Short-term profits would not be earned at the expense of long-term relationships.

Boisi and Friedman both argue that the firm's policy made good business sense. "Look at the statistics and you'll see that most often the raider loses out to a white knight. Since fees are structured to reward success rather than failure, the investment bank loses out when its raider client loses out," says Friedman. Goldman Sachs's strategy was to get a foot in the door of the senior decision maker, says Boisi: "This was not a moral decision, simply a pragmatic one. No client was going to give you confidential information if they felt you would later return with a predator." John Thornton, who in the mid-1980s was in charge of M&A in London, suggests that the firm's policy was unexpectedly fortuitous: "The bank [Goldman Sachs] didn't realize then the power of the defense niche. While [other] banks had about a one in six chance of getting the work [hired by the bidder] we were the only one who fought for the other side."

With success, ironically, came change, and the firm gradually altered its stance. Clients' needs, says Boisi, not greed, motivated the change. "As we got more successful, as the years went by, we started to win over the lead adviser relationships with these very large companies. They would say 'Well, hey, perhaps we shouldn't use [Goldman Sachs] because you won't do a raid when we want to.' That's when the compromises started to come in. 'Well we won't be a dealer manager of a [hostile] tender offer, but that doesn't mean that we won't keep advising on the buy side.' "

WHILE THE FIRM'S merger business in New York boomed, its investment banking activity in London languished. For many years London was the Siberia of investment banking, a place to banish those the firm hoped to forget. Management may have acceded to Whitehead's plans for overseas expansion, but this did not mean they would send their best people. One partner who was there characterized London at that time as out of sight, out of mind. Despite a small presence in London since 1969 the firm had broken little ground by the early 1980s, and the whole office was staffed with only 268 people. John Thornton, a young merger specialist who viewed London differently in the mid-1980s, recognized, years ahead of his American banking competitors, that the British market was not a frozen tundra but a promised land.

Thornton, who at thirty-five was running the firm's European M&A business, is widely tipped—with John Thain—to succeed Hank Paulson as one of the next generation of leaders. (Thornton and Thain were named co–chief operating officers in early 1999.) Peter Sachs, a great-nephew of Sam Sachs and son of former partner Howard Sachs, was a partner in his family's firm, a race car driver, and, in the mid-1980s, a merger specialist working in London. Thornton and Sachs could easily see that the situation in London was similar to what it had been in the United States a decade earlier. Stock prices were low relative to intrinsic values, and therefore the desire among companies to acquire rather than build was high. The gloves came off when a group of conglomerateurs, led by BTR and Hanson Trust, pounced on their unsuspecting targets. The British merchant banks did not have separate M&A specialists, and the early deals had all the hallmarks of amateurs. For Thornton and Sachs it was like watching a movie they had seen before, and wondering why everyone else did not remember the ending. It was INCO and ESB all over again.

Thornton knew that at first the firm would have to play second fiddle to the less-experienced U.K. merchant banks. This was not Ohio, business was done differently, and while he recognized that his English counterparts would at first take the lead, he knew he would have an opportunity to step in. Initially Goldman Sachs was brought in as a second or third banker on a number of major deals, the firm selling itself on its U.S. experience. But a vast number of the tactics used in the mergers business were transplanted to London and adapted easily to the local market. There was no way the British competition could hope to compete on either experience or expertise.

"Big Bang," the deregulation of the London financial markets in 1986, was just the opening Goldman Sachs needed. British merchant banks facing the upheaval of foreign competition on their own turf were fish in a barrel for American bankers flush with profits from a booming U.S. stock market. The British brokers were capital constrained, and their industry was suffering a major consolidation. It was a wonderful time to attack, knowing the opponent could not retaliate on your home base.

There can be little doubt that the Americans were unwelcome in London in the mid-1980s. "Honestly, it perplexes and bewilders me that Goldman Sachs has been retained by U.K. companies here," said a director and corporate finance specialist at Morgan Grenfell. Another British banker added, "We fail to see what the American firms add in U.K. situations, but we're not complacent. We're twitching twenty-four hours a day." But complacent was precisely what they were. After centuries of having the market to themselves they vastly underestimated the threat from New York. When BTR launched a hostile bid for Thomas Tilling in 1983, the target's traditional British investment bankers did not even call their client for three days. Thornton had been virtually camped out in Tilling's office for seventy-two hours before his British counterpart arrived. Another banker, choosing to speak anonymously, said that Goldman Sachs was "nothing more than high-priced interlopers who produce a massive stream of impractical ideas that have no relevance to the U.K. market. I give them credit for making a lot of noise."

"The British disease is that there's always an excuse not to do something," shot back Thornton, unimpressed by the local talent. "When we get on the scene the patient is half dead already. At that stage we need emergency action." In the mid-1980s a British takeover took four to five months to complete. It was an excruciating process that left everyone enervated. In 1986 Goldman Sachs was hired, along with other British bankers, to defend Imperial Group in a hostile attack by Hanson Trust. The defense was ultimately unsuccessful, and on the day when it was entirely clear that the cause was lost, Goldman Sachs was invited to attend a lunch with the British bankers at the company's headquarters, Imperial House. This was the funeral lunch; in hours it would all be over and the company and its headquarters would be Hanson's. The former management would be forced to vacate the premises at the close of business. A feeling of nostalgia spread across the room; none of these bankers would ever sit here again. As the meal wound down the conversation turned to life after the deal, now only an hour and a half away. One British merchant banker told of his plans to walk Hadrian's Wall for two months; another was jetting off to Mauritius. The conversation worked its way down the table to the Goldman Sachs bankers who were seated in the least-prestigious spots. Their British counterparts asked what they would be doing next. One Goldman Sachs banker looked at his watch and then up at his colleagues. "Guys, it's 2:30. Woolworth Holdings was raided by Dixon's yesterday and we've been hired. We're doing a meeting at 4:00. We'll see you later." As he recalls, "While they went to Hadrian's Wall, we took the food off their plates."

By 1987, Goldman Sachs was ranked among the top ten financial institutions in its market share of mergers and acquisitions business in the U.K. By then, the firm had securely established its credentials with the British Airways–British Caledonia merger. This would be the first time an American investment bank acted as the sole advisor to a U.K. corporation involved in a takeover. British Airways had agreed to buy its ailing competitor, but when the stock market crashed and it looked like rival bidder SAS Airlines would not be allowed to proceed for regulatory reasons they tried to lower their bid. In what the *Financial Times* called "a well-played hand of financial poker," Goldman Sachs thought of a clever strategy to revive the rival bidder and British Airways paid the original £250 million price tag. Yet the success of reaching the top ten was not enough, and the firm's goal began to shift. No longer would it be satisfied with being the number one U.S. institution in a foreign country; it wanted to be the number one investment bank, regardless of nationality.

This goal would only be achieved when Goldman Sachs became a full-service investment bank in London. Until then, the firm would find itself paired with a British institution that could provide these services. Initial efforts to recruit top talent to perform these functions were unsuccessful. In the United States, Goldman Sachs was considered deeply conservative and part of the establishment, but in Europe the firm was seen as a daring new arrival.

With its high-profile successes in mergers between two British companies, like advising the shareholders of Virgin Music Group in the sale to Thorn EMI and defending Standard Chartered Bank from a takeover by Lloyd's Bank, the firm's ability to recruit improved. During the 1980s the firm had heavily staffed its foreign offices with expensive expatriates (costing up to half a million dollars a year, before compensation), yet over the course of the 1990s it would intensify its efforts to recruit locals. The U.S. investment banks took advantage of centuries of British snobbery by hiring bright Oxford and Cambridge graduates from middle-class and working-class backgrounds. One salesperson who came to the firm at this time remembers, "The American way of doing business was a breath of fresh air." By 1990, Goldman Sachs could have the pick of the crop; a move to the U.S. firm was now widely seen as a move up. The London gamble had paid off, and in 1990 the firm was the number one advisor on cross-border European deals, edging out a dozen European investment banks with relationships that spanned centuries. The Goldman Sachs London strategy soon became its European strategy, and the firm sought top billing and a dominant market share in every country it entered. Goldman Sachs's merger department remains one of its largest profit centers and greatest successes. In attaining this success the firm followed the steps that characterize its other triumphs: jumping into the business early with a highly aggressive approach, focusing squarely on the client, reaping the benefits of teamwork, and maintaining the very highest reputation.

"CAN WE MAINTAIN our esprit de corps as we continue to grow? That's the question which worries me most," Weinberg admitted in the early 1980s. Early on Whitehead and Weinberg spotted the impact that expansion would have on the firm's culture. The firm built a new headquarters in 1983 to unite a staff that was spread across four downtown locations, but physical consolidation would, of course, not be enough. For most of Goldman Sachs's history, its principles and values had been passed along by osmosis, through unofficial mentoring relationships, but as the firm expanded Whitehead grew concerned that this informal mechanism would no longer suffice. People had worked together because they knew or liked each other and because the firm was their team. As the organization expanded globally, this level of informality became impossible to maintain with so many new people. "So just for fun one Sunday afternoon," Whitehead says, "I sat down with a yellow pad and wrote down the things that I thought Goldman Sachs stood for. I tried to keep it from being a sort of motherhood thing, where we stood for all the good things and against all the bad things; I tried to make it realistic." His list focused on what was unique about Goldman Sachs. It was not meant to be a marketing tool but an internal reminder. The principles as they were then written have remained largely intact, although, as Whitehead notes, "As I read them today I can see the hand of lawyers, and some of its succinctness has been destroyed. I wrote twelve and now there are fourteen."

"Goldman Sachs's business principles are a sure-shot way of making money," says management specialist Peter Mathias, who in the mid-1980s was hired as an internal consultant to the firm. He carries the list of principles with him everywhere, which includes,

- Our clients' interests always come first. Our experience shows that if we serve our clients well, our own success will follow.

- Our assets are people, capital, and reputation. If any of these are ever lost, the last is the most difficult to regain.
- We stress teamwork in everything we do. We have no room for those who put their personal interests ahead of the interests of the firm and its clients.
- Our profits are the key to our success. They replenish our capital and attract and keep our best people.
- It is our practice to share our profits generously with all who helped create them. Profitability is crucial to our future.

An unwritten yet closely adhered to fifteenth principle is that of secrecy; it is understood by almost every employee that the firm's business is confidential.

Mathias would be responsible for developing an introductory training session for new employees, entitled "Goldman Sachs in Perspective," but dubbed the "Culture Club," to teach the firm's history and business principles to the uninitiated. New employees, M.B.A.s as well as lateral hires, would spend a week simply learning about the firm. Time would be devoted to explaining the firm's organization, its method of conducting business, and the role of each key player. The firm's history would also be taught. In mock games resembling Trivial Pursuit, new employees would need to learn the answers to questions such as, "Are the retired general partners of Goldman Sachs called: 'unemployed,' 'special partners,' or 'limited partners,' or 'reserve partners'?"; "Carrying on a longstanding tradition started by his father, which of the following cars does John Weinberg drive?: a Cadillac Seville, a BMW 325i, a Chrysler New Yorker, or a Jaguar XJS?"; and "Steve Friedman describes the members of which committee as 'intelligent men from Mars'?: Innovation Committee, Ad Hoc Profit Maximization Committee, Diversity Committee, Ad Hoc Problem Solving Committee." (Hints: After retirement liability is limited; Jaguar is owned by Ford Motor Company; Friedman felt the firm needed to focus some of its best minds on new profit opportunities.)

Twice a year the firm would formally review its commitment to its principles. Weinberg and Whitehead required department heads to hold discussion groups with all the professionals under them. Conversations would center on any possible violations of the principles that may have occurred and how the principles applied to their day-to-day work. Department heads would then send the minutes of these meetings to the management committee. This gave management direct input from employees about the operation of the firm, and according to Whitehead, a great many changes and improvements grew out of this process.

In 1980 the Goldman Sachs annual review summarized the travails of the previous decade. Nineteen-seventy had been one of the firm's best years ever, and looking ahead, management had been optimistic. Alas, "The ten years to come were a decade for which, had we known in December of 1970 what lay ahead, we would likely have feared the worst," the 1980 annual review reads. In the space of a decade oil prices increased tenfold, causing inflation and interest rates to soar; the country's largest railroad went bust; and the Dow did not recover its 1970 level until 1980. Fixed commissions on the sale of equities were scrapped, causing earnings for the industry in this area to drop precipitously and leading to many bankruptcies among brokerage companies. Goldman Sachs had lost the leadership of Sidney Weinberg and Gus Levy, and the firm had to battle the Penn Central lawsuits. Still, for Goldman Sachs the 1970s were a remarkably successful decade. The partnership grew from thirty-seven to sixty-three, and its capital expanded from $49 million to $200 million. In 1979 the firm's pre-tax profits exceeded $115 million, and three years later it had tripled; meanwhile, the firm's standing over the decade had been greatly enhanced. But the world had changed dramatically, and Goldman Sachs would need to do so as well. It would begin the 1980s with a surprising acquisition unlike anything else in the firm's history.

ON NOVEMBER 16, 1981, in an unprecedented move, Goldman Sachs bought one of its clients, J. Aron & Co., a small, family-owned commodities trading company. The two firms knew each other well, sharing what one J. Aron partner termed a "sympathetic cultural attachment." Goldman Sachs was J. Aron's investment banker and acted as one of its futures brokers. J. Aron considered Goldman Sachs one of its customers and vice versa. Gus Levy had known Jack Aron, J. Aron's chairman of the board, for many years, as both were leaders in the Jewish community and deeply involved with Mount Sinai Medical Center. Aron had sought Levy's advice from time to time about the possible sale of his family business. John Whitehead, as one of the firm's investment bankers, had been brought into these discussions. In 1979, Goldman Sachs came close to buying J. Aron, but the handling of a tax liability on a large unrealized gain that J. Aron held caused the talks to fall apart. The J. Aron partners felt their business had expanded as far as it could as a small independent company, and some of the older partners hoped to retire, so they asked Goldman Sachs in 1981 to find a buyer. Yet the more closely Whitehead looked the more he became convinced that Goldman Sachs should not help sell J. Aron but should acquire it. Commodities, precious metals, and foreign exchange trading would all fit well with Goldman Sachs's existing businesses and those that he and John Weinberg envisioned for the future. Most investment banks had little or no exposure to traditional commodities businesses. Gold trading was conducted by specialist firms like Johnson Mathey or Mocatta Metals and the major Swiss banks. The world of foreign exchange was dominated by the money center commercial banks. That did not intimidate Goldman Sachs.

In 1898, Jacob Aron had founded J. Aron as a New Orleans coffee trading company with $10,000 in capital. Twelve years later he relocated his company and family to New York, opening offices at 91 Wall Street. Like the Goldman and Sachs families, the Arons and their cousins, the Israels, ran their coffee businesses largely with family members and family money. Only later, when the J. Aron business expanded to include cocoa, copper, rubber, and even hides would outsiders be included. J. Aron's early business was arbitrage in the textbook sense of the word, buying, for example, rubber or sugar in New York and selling it immediately in London for a marginally higher price.

J. Aron was an extremely conservative operation. It was a family-owned business, so capital had to be husbanded, and there was an unwillingness to do anything that even resembled gambling. The firm specialized in riskless trading, in locating market discrepancies that others had overlooked: There was no speculation or market risk, and credit risk was kept to an absolute minimum. As Jack Aron said, "Our plan of operation calls for being long or short up to a maximum of twenty seconds." The irony is that J. Aron eventually would become Goldman Sachs's greatest vehicle for speculation. Many of the firm's riskiest and most daring trades would be made in the J. Aron department of Goldman Sachs. It is here, in the late 1980s and 1990s, that the firm would earn some of its most fabulous returns and suffer a few spectacular losses.

J. Aron's big breakthrough came in the late 1960s when the firm ventured into precious metals trading. The company grew rapidly, and the partners' capital compounded from $4 million in 1925 (or roughly a fifth of Goldman Sachs's size) to $12.5 million in 1965 (or about half of Goldman Sachs's $25 million). J. Aron & Co. was recapitalized in 1970 with a mere $400,000, and in one exceptionally profitable decade the partnership capital had grown to $100 million by 1981.

In September of 1981, Goldman Sachs brought to J. Aron a tender offer from Engelhard Minerals Corporation. Engelhard, which had once been part of the mighty Philip Brothers and was looking to compete with its former owner, saw the acquisition of J. Aron as one way to increase its size, trading expertise, and profitability. J. Aron's partners were not impressed. The offer, as one partner recalls, "was a relatively full offer, which meant that we would become part of a public company, there would be employment contracts for three years for key employees, and we would get a lot of money in shares. We just couldn't do it. We couldn't become part of a public company because we didn't think our business was right for it. But the big issue was one of being part of a public company. Aron's philosophy was, 'Never tell anybody how much money you make, just smile on the way to the bank.' In a public company we would never have been able to do that." One of the major sticking points in the deal were the employment contracts Engelhard demanded from all J. Aron's principals. Shortly after J. Aron rejected the Engelhard offer, Goldman Sachs's senior management made up its mind to try to buy the company itself, now that the tax liability problem had been solved. From the perspective of J. Aron, acquisition by a privately held firm like Goldman Sachs would not pose the same kind of concerns about privacy as those raised by the proposed Engelhard purchase.

Goldman Sachs's sudden interest in the commodities business was a sign of the times. By the late 1970s inflation in the industrialized world was raging out of control, and there was money to be made in those products that would retain their value. Inflation was very much on the minds of the partners of Goldman Sachs, who had expressed an almost religious desire to rid the country of its menace. In the 1979 and 1980 annual reviews, management wrote, "Our most fervent hope for [the coming year] . . . is that the nation will not just continue to attempt to control inflation, but will succeed in attacking its causes." Some believed that J. Aron would be a small but real hedge against inflation. Traditional investment banking businesses—equity underwriting, bond underwriting, stock and bond sales—all dry up when inflation and interest rates soar. At least if the firm had a commodities division focused on a market whose prices might rise with inflation, one department might be making good money while the others waited for more auspicious times.

Despite the arguments in favor of the proposed merger, opposition among Goldman Sachs partners was tremendous. Some believed that the firm could and should build its own currency and commodities division. With little knowledge about J. Aron's business few felt able to judge its intrinsic value. And many were alarmed about the proposed price, in reality only a tiny premium to the book value. Some of the opposition was simply snobbery—partners looking down their noses at those who had not gone to Harvard Business School and yet were running a highly successful business. If there had been a vote of the partnership the acquisition would probably not have been approved, but top management believed strongly that J. Aron would enhance the firm's business, and the deal went through.

Whitehead was determined to internationalize Goldman Sachs, and buying J. Aron was one of the first major steps in that ultimately successful process. But in addition to seeking a countercyclical hedge, Goldman Sachs was motivated by archrival Salomon Brothers's position in the commodities business. In 1981, Salomon Brothers had been acquired by Philip Brothers, and many at Goldman Sachs feared that with the merger Salomon Brothers would pull further ahead in the trading businesses. J. Aron provided a shortcut, a fast track to the world of commodities. Unfortunately, Goldman Sachs was never a firm to take a shortcut, and its haste would prove costly.

Crucial to the transaction was J. Aron's phenomenal profitability. J. Aron's precious metals trading, its largest business, had made approximately $60 million in 1981 on firm-wide capital of only $100 million. By comparison Goldman Sachs had earned $150 million on partnership capital of $272 million. J. Aron's costs were a fraction of Goldman Sachs's, as it had only a fifth the number of employees. But J. Aron's profitability was even more incredible than it looked on the face of it. The return on equity of roughly 70 percent was achieved with no market risk and little country or credit risk.

"The way we made money was so simple that we couldn't speak about it. Anybody could do it. We were sworn to silence," one former J. Aron partner confesses. J. Aron made most of its fortune from classic arbitrage, small but steadily profitable deals overlooked by others in the marketplace. London was the center of the gold market, and for a time J. Aron was the only New York dealer with a direct telex to London. This made J. Aron the only dealer in New York who always knew the price of gold, and the firm moved in and out of trading situations as the opportunities arose. When the price of silver rose, the firm booked smelting time at all the available refineries and made profits simply by reselling the reservations, which, because silver could only be sold in bars, had become almost as valuable as the metal itself. When silver prices fell, J. Aron established a platinum leasing operation with oil refiners. And the firm made steady returns arbitraging the price of silver against the silver futures contracts traded in New York and Chicago.

J. Aron merchandised gold coins in the United States for foreign governments, beginning with Mexican pesos, moving on to a gold Russian chervonetz (the recast of a coin that had been minted in 1925), and then Canadian maple leafs. The firm eventually handled about half of the South African government's chamber of mines distribution into the United States. J. Aron would buy Krugerrands from South Africa but not pay for them for three months; maple leafs were held without payment for up to a year. The central banks let J. Aron have the gold and extended interest-free credit for these periods, which made this business extremely lucrative. The banks were, quite simply, naive. "Leasing gold was a license to print money," explains one former J. Aron gold trader. But all of these opportunities were temporary, depending as they did on unsophisticated customers and competitors or on highly unusual market conditions.

For a short time, J. Aron had one of the most profitable businesses on Wall Street. It is no wonder that the company kept it to themselves. As one former senior trader puts it, "We were convinced that we were the smartest people in the universe because we were making all that money. There was a hubris which just infected the place."

"After we sold our one millionth Krugerrand, the Chamber of Mines of South Africa came to New York and took us out to celebrate at 21," recounts another senior J. Aron trader. "J. Aron was the largest whole-saler of bullion coins in the U.S. and they had come to say thank you. Anyway, during the dinner they gave us each a set of Krugerrand cuff-links, a token of their appreciation. You've got to remember that at this time gold was worth $500 or maybe $600 an ounce, and each of the coins weighed one quarter of an ounce but as jewelry would have retailed for $500 or so. After dinner we walked out onto the street, and a guy came up to us begging for some change. I was married at the time to a Jamaican woman, and basically couldn't stand the South Africans, so I gave them to him. I just gave them to a guy on the street begging for a quarter. That's when I knew we were making too much money."

In November 1981, Jack Aron stepped down as chairman of his family's firm, and J. Aron became part of Goldman Sachs. Although it was widely reported that J. Aron was sold for $200–$250 million, Gold-man Sachs in fact paid a mere $120 million—a small multiple of book value—and gave up six partnership spots and one seat on the manage-ment committee to J. Aron partners.

With one or two notable exceptions the only route to the management committee had been through the firm's ranks. Now men who had not worked a day of their lives at Goldman Sachs and who were completely unfamiliar with the firm's businesses had been granted direct decision-making responsibilities. The fact that one of the most coveted spots in the financial world was bestowed upon a J. Aron partner suggests the seri-ousness with which Goldman Sachs approached this acquisition and the role it hoped the division would play.

J. Aron's partners were paid most of the purchase price up front and were to receive the balance over a few years. There was no contingency for performance, no review, and no need to earn the remaining sum. In an effort to retain the top J. Aron people under the partnership level, golden handcuffs were put in place for five years. Some immediately below the partnership level were incensed. Their chance at riches had been yanked out from under them. J. Aron had been openly studying plans that contained some profit-sharing element for its top employees, allowing the benefits of the firm's fantastic profitability to accrue before actual partnerships were conferred. Nothing like this would exist at Goldman Sachs.

Soon after the purchase of J. Aron the deal took on a sallow complexion. J. Aron's profitability rested heavily on the soaring and volatile price of precious metals. Arbitrage trading requires volatility. Prices fall out of line only when they are moving. In a static environment few such opportunities exist. When the price of gold plummeted from $800 to $500 an ounce, customer interest evaporated and with it J. Aron's spectacular arbitrage opportunities. Gold eventually settled into a very narrow price range, where it would remain for the next decade and a half. "People thought we had made the sale of the century," one J. Aron partner recalls. "The price of silver peaked, I think, in January of 1982, and we sold the company at the end of October of 1981. With the benefit of hindsight, the way the business went sour, with all the people that we had, I don't know what would have happened. It would have been a very difficult time if we had not sold the company." In 1982 the J. Aron division's profits would be half of what they had been when J. Aron was an independent company, but by 1983 profits had shrunk to nothing. It was not until the division built a more stable business in the form of foreign exchange trading that it would recover its previous levels of profitability.

By the time Goldman Sachs had relocated J. Aron to its new headquarters at 85 Broad Street, real competition had arrived. J. Aron's initial competitors had been small, specialized metals firms, but now the big boys were getting into the market. Citibank, Chemical, and J. P. Morgan all had begun trading in precious metals. Drexel Burnham Lambert, which was just beginning its streak through the 1980s, had hired disgruntled former J. Aron traders and set them up in their own organization, Drexel Trading. Now, not only were J. Aron's secrets out, but they were being practiced by some of the traders who had perfected them. It was not hard to see that enormous margins on riskless trades would soon be a thing of the past.

On the face of it, J. Aron and Goldman Sachs seemed the perfect match. Both were highly successful, paternalistic organizations that greatly valued their private status. The firms' histories were strikingly similar. They were established in the nineteenth century by German Jews looking for opportunity in America's infant capital markets. Their founders lent their names and their offspring to the operations. J. Aron was a family firm, much like Goldman Sachs had been in the 1940s, but Goldman Sachs had changed greatly since then, and initially the fit between the two firms was a disappointment.

If Goldman Sachs were the men in the gray suits, J. Aron was a pea-cock. Unlike Goldman Sachs's collegial atmosphere, Aron functioned according to a strict hierarchy. If you were the new kid on the block, part of your job was getting lunch for the guy who had been there a little bit longer. Aron was a secretive, autocratic, and colorful organization in which a small number controlled the rest by keeping the flow of informa-tion to a minimum. Information was shared on a "need to know" basis. Clients had code names, either numbers or nicknames; using their real names in anything but the most private conversation was forbidden.

The J. Aron trading floor was a world of uncontrolled chaos and excitement, a far cry from the quiet, cultured halls of investment banking. In the high-pressured environment of fast-moving markets, gold traders often began a sentence to a subordinate with "You idiot!" as they pounded their fists on the desks and threw their phones. Foreign exchange traders shrieked prices to salesmen who were either frantically pacing the floor with phone receivers seemingly glued to their ears or huddled under their desks with their telephones, trying to hear their clients. Dozens of speaker boxes blared the sounds of trading pits in Chicago and New York, and there was almost no time of day when obscenities were not being piped full blast into the air. There was an unstated link between decibel level and profitability. The floor was too close to the ceiling, and the room was often overheated; unlike the purpose-built fixed income and equities trading floors, J. Aron was using a space that was designed to be offices. By 10 o'clock in the morning, everyone, no matter how he had started the day, looked a physical wreck. Ties were pulled loose and shirtsleeves shoved up; haggard, sweaty looks adorned most faces. This was not Goldman Sachs.

J. Aron would be the greatest cultural challenge that Goldman Sachs had faced. Not only was it the single largest expansion to date, incorpo-rating four hundred people into a firm of twenty-nine hundred and adding six new partners to a partnership of sixty, but J. Aron had its own culture. For a firm that was meticulous—sometimes excruciatingly so—in its hiring practices, forcing every candidate to endure fifteen, twenty, or even twenty-five interviews, it was something of a shock to find a division full of people who would not have made the first cut. Most J. Aron employees did not have the minimum educational background required to be considered for a professional position at Goldman Sachs. Hiring practices at J. Aron had been eclectic, and an assortment of characters were given opportunities in the firm's own Wild West. The management of J. Aron looked for entrepreneurs, those more interested in building a successful business than in being associated with one that already existed.

One senior J. Aron trader recalls how he obtained his first position as a currency trader after a single interview. Both firms had long prided themselves on training their own, on bringing people up through the ranks. For J. Aron this meant creating traders and salespeople from secretaries, position clerks, and back-office staff who were short on formal education and long on brains, guts, and ambition. For Goldman Sachs it meant paying for a one-way ticket and moving expenses from Cambridge, Massachusetts, and starting their newly minted Harvard M.B.A.s at the bottom.

"J. Aron was a graft on the body which never took," explains a former partner of Goldman Sachs who spent many years in the currency and commodities division. The division has been described—by those within it—as earthy, street-smart, and rough around the edges. So uncomfortable was the J. Aron group in its new surroundings that for their picture in the 1983 Goldman Sachs annual review the men all donned red suspenders in mockery of their more serious banking brethren.

"You had the combination of people not really blending well together," one former J. Aron and Goldman Sachs partner remembers. "There was defensiveness on the part of the Aron people. If you were making $50 million it would not have mattered but we weren't making any money, we were just sort of surviving. I remember speaking to one elder Goldman Sachs partner once about some of the tensions and the pressure . . . and he said, 'Anybody can be your partner when things are going well. Now you'll find out who your good partners are and who are not.' I have never forgotten that and I still think about it today. He was right."

Soon after the merger, a battle broke out between top J. Aron management and the partners of Goldman Sachs over the location of a bond arbitrage operation. J. Aron's partners believed that this trading operation fit well with their other arbitrage activities, while Goldman Sachs saw it as part of its fixed-income trading department. J. Aron lost the battle, and shortly after the acquisition a few J. Aron partners tendered their resignations, leaving Bob Rubin to represent the newest division on the management committee. Management realized immediately the enormity of the problem and sent a young partner named Mark Winkelman to clean up the place, like a deputy sheriff dispatched to an unruly Western town.

In 1980, Winkelman became one of the first non-American partners of Goldman Sachs. A blond, blue-eyed Dutchman, he had a runner's build and could be seen leaping over chairs and sprinting across the cluttered trading floor whenever his secretary hollered, "Mark, it's Bob Rubin on the phone." Winkelman had come to Goldman Sachs from the University of Pennsylvania's Wharton Business School via the World Bank and had a well-deserved reputation for analytical brilliance. Unabashedly willing to speak his mind, he was a towering intellect in an organization with exceedingly high standards. He was elevated to the rank of partner because of his pioneering work in government bond arbitrage, one of the first types of trading undertaken on the basis of computer analysis.

The computer would change Wall Street forever, and Winkelman was one of the first to realize it. While others were still trading on gut feel, he was programming the first Apple personal computers to calculate the precise differential between the value of a U.S. government treasury bond and the price at which the newly created treasury bond futures contract was trading in Chicago. As the prices of these two fungible instruments fell out of line with each other, which they did often in those early days, there were almost guaranteed profits to be captured. The computer added two things to the equation: speed and precision. These were all Winkelman needed to turn his tiny bond arbitrage unit into a major profit center. He took an early and abiding interest in the firm's operational capabilities. Most considered this boring stuff, but Winkelman knew that failures of technology could be fatal—when traders cannot accurately value instruments, systems do not pick up pricing irregularities, or customer interfaces are unreliable, the cost can be tens of millions of dollars or more. The best systems can help detect fraud, the deadly "ticket in the drawer" (where traders hide their losses by either not submitting, or falsifying, their trade tickets) that every trading manager dreads. In 1995, Nick Leeson, a futures trader in Singapore, through his trading activities bankrupted 232-year-old Baring Brothers with hidden losses of more than $1 billion on what was described as risk-free arbitrage trading. (Many have noted that Goldman Sachs's culture also helped the firm avoid this scourge. As one long-serving trading manager argues, "Part of the reason why people never tried to hide things was that Goldman was one of those places where, certainly in the areas that I ran, we accepted losses as well as profits, and management didn't kick your butt if you lost money.") Winkelman never let up in his efforts to perfect Goldman Sachs's technological capabilities. By the mid-1990s the firm was miles ahead of the competition and had gained a valuable advantage in monitoring risk and executing business; this edge was an important part of Winkelman's legacy to the firm.

Winkelman is a wise man and was a skilled manager of traders. He knew from personal experience when to encourage, express doubt, or pull the plug. He was an uncannily accurate judge of both individual talent and character, and had no difficulty separating the two. A tough but fair boss, Winkelman (like most successful Goldman Sachs partners) demanded no more of his employees than he did of himself. He seemed entirely unfettered by distractions, second thoughts, or a desire to be anywhere else but on Wall Street; his ambition was white hot. Even after he failed to be named senior partner of Goldman Sachs his loyalty to the firm never wavered. Winkelman poured his enormous energies into two causes, the firm and his family. A devoted family man with a down-to-earth, charming, and personable American wife, he rode the subway, drove a beat-up Saab, and jogged with staff members in the morning. Entirely without pretense, he valued substance and had little time or regard for the superficialities of style.

Winkelman began every annual J. Aron departmental meeting with a reading of the firm's business principles, in which he believed with an almost religious fervor. He repeated them to his employees with all the solemnity of the pledge of allegiance or grace before a meal. Staff were adjured to look at them, think about them, and practice them in their daily business. In his eighteen years with the firm Winkelman lived by these principles, recognizing that example rather than recitation was what mattered. Later, after Winkelman left Goldman Sachs, he returned to Wharton to teach business ethics. Goldman Sachs's business principles formed the cornerstone of his curriculum.

By 1983, J. Aron was a problem Goldman Sachs had to contain, and before the second anniversary of its purchase Winkelman and the other partners of J. Aron undertook the first mass firing Goldman Sachs had ever known. In a single week in August, Goldman Sachs fired almost 20 percent of the J. Aron division's employees, forever destroying the firm's reputation for benevolence. (Although some of those fired found other jobs within Goldman Sachs, those closely associated with the firings describe this period as the worst in their professional lives.) The firings were done at the behest of the original J. Aron partners, who were extremely concerned about the high level of overhead in this unprofitable time. Yet the Goldman Sachs management committee had a great deal more patience with their new acquisition and was not as anxious to trim costs.

Winkelman had opposed the J. Aron purchase from the start. He was among those who felt that Goldman Sachs had the expertise to establish the new business successfully on its own and that the necessary talent could be hired, one person at a time. Yet he revised his opinion when he took a closer look at the business. Commodities trading is a physical business. Cargoes of oil, truckloads of gold, and bags of coffee actually change location once the trader has shouted "Done!" Goldman Sachs traders were "paper traders." The nuances of matters like insurance or shipping are often lost on people who wire money or call a runner to carry share certificates from one location in lower Manhattan to another. Paper traders simply have the wrong mentality for the world of physical products. In this light, some believe that the expertise and contacts acquired through the purchase of J. Aron were important assets and were used to the firm's best advantage. This, however, overlooks Winkelman's contribution, along with that of Bob Rubin, in remaking J. Aron. During the early difficult days, and for five years after that, no one foresaw the earnings powerhouse that these two men would create.

While Goldman Sachs's bankers scoured America, J. Aron's visited clients in Brazil or Ghana. Each firm was looking to the other to help it conquer the globe. J. Aron had close contacts with a grab bag of central bankers—in the Soviet Union, South Africa, and Austria—with whom it traded precious metals, while Goldman Sachs had opened new offices in Zurich, London, and Tokyo. Fifteen years after the merger, Goldman Sachs partners credit the J. Aron operation with helping it to internationalize, and vice versa.

To become the international organization that Whitehead envisioned, Goldman Sachs needed a foreign exchange business. Whitehead knew that without expertise in the volatile world of foreign currencies, the firm would be unable to give clients the best advice. Looking forward, he could see the folly in completing an international transaction, be it a merger, a bond trade, or an equity offering, and then allowing, in fact advising, the client to go to another institution to complete the incumbent currency trade. Whitehead foresaw foreign exchange as the enormous client business it would become. Precious metals and even coffee would be extras in the J. Aron acquisition, and if these operations profited, all the better; if not, the growth in foreign exchange, he felt, would more than compensate.

At the time of the merger, J. Aron's foreign exchange business was small and relatively insignificant. Currency futures recently had been introduced on the International Monetary Market exchange, and J. Aron had established a trading operation to exploit the tiny price differential that existed between the currency futures contracts and the much larger and more liquid cash market. The futures contracts were too small for the large commercial banks to bother with, so J. Aron had the market largely to itself. The department made between $10 million and $15 million in 1981 and $20 million the following year. Operations like this almost never lose money because, like most of J. Aron's businesses, positions were rarely held for more than a few seconds. Many feared the business would not last—that, like all good arbitrage opportunities, margins would collapse and the business would disappear. Margins did shrink, but volume exploded, compensating somewhat for the smaller profit earned on each trade.

The simple J. Aron arbitrage business, with its shrinking profits, had a limited future, so the foreign exchange department was retooled in the quest for greater profits. Rubin and Winkelman put in place a first-class client business staffed by a group of bright young lawyers who developed new foreign exchange products and a large client base to sell them to; later, speculative trading profits would be the fuel for growth. Winkelman also revamped J. Aron's recruiting process. The road to a professional position was now through the M.B.A. programs at Harvard, Stanford, Wharton, MIT, and Columbia, not through a clerk's job on the gold traffic desk.

Winkelman continuously expressed confidence in his salesmen and traders, urging them to build on their successes. "Leveraging the franchise" would become the bywords; watch the flows of customer business, analyze the economic trends, then jump in with both feet. By prodding a few traders to increase their risk tolerance from Jack Aron's twenty seconds to a few days and then a few weeks, Winkelman and Rubin returned J. Aron to the black. As the firm expanded internationally, foreign exchange became an integrated part of Goldman Sachs's business. By the end of the decade foreign exchange would earn fifteen times what it had when J. Aron was a separate firm and would account for 80 percent of the division's profits.

When opportunity presented itself in March 1988, the foreign exchange desk at J. Aron was ready. During that month the British government capitulated to overwhelming market forces and allowed sterling to soar beyond the level of three German marks to the pound. For months, Chancellor of the Exchequer Nigel Lawson had been trying to depress the value of the pound in order to alleviate the growing trade deficit; for weeks the Bank of England, on the instructions of the government, had been intervening, selling sterling in the open market and buying marks. The rising pound had been hurting British exporters, as it increased the cost of their goods, and the government had begun a deliberate policy of shadowing the mark. Yet Lawson had recently raised British interest rates, which had only increased the high level of capital inflows into Britain from investors attracted to the economic boom created by Thatcher's revolution. The pound had been rising for weeks against the West German currency, with only the Bank of England standing in its way. But the bank's efforts proved futile, and early one morning it stepped back and let sterling fly. Traders all over New York heard the news from their London counterparts and rose from bed at 5 a.m.

J. Aron's trading floor was filled before the sun was up. For weeks the department had been buying British pounds and selling the mark, waiting for this day.

John Weinberg went downstairs to the fifth floor and congratulated each trader on a job well done. But one of the men most responsible was not on this or any trading floor. Winkelman and Rubin had two years earlier hired one of the world's best currency economists, and his presence could already be felt. David Morrison had for weeks been reassuring the traders of sterling's inevitable rise, and he had given many just the confidence they needed. He had told his loyal following not to panic even when facing the seemingly unlimited resources of the Bank of England; economics, not market manipulation, would prevail. (Central bank intervention, because of the overwhelming size of international capital flows, is rarely successful in fighting an economic trend. The Bank of England proved this once again, five years later, when it tried unsuccessfully to support the pound from a speculative pummeling. Again Goldman Sachs benefited from central bank action that went against economic fundamentals.) Later Morrison would put his bullish views in the *Sunday Times* and be widely credited with pushing sterling even higher. There were many lessons of the celebrated day. Management confidence in top-flight economists, traders, and salespeople was strengthened. There was an even deeper recognition that only with real risk would spectacular profits accrue.

Morrison and his partner Gavyn Davies had been hired from British broker Simon & Coates in the winter of 1986. They were the firm's first full-time economists to be assigned a non-U.S. portfolio, and they would be made partners in a record-breaking two years, testament to their talents and the rising importance of the firm's international activities. Both men had been named top-ranked analysts year after year by *Institutional Investor* and other financial magazines and their names were well known in the industry. Clients loved them and so did the firm's staff. Among U.K. clients, Davies and Morrison lent the fledgling London operation immediate credibility that might otherwise have taken years to build. Their economic analysis would serve as the sales force's calling card.

Davies grew up in Rhodesia, the son of a headmaster of an African high school, and worked as an economics advisor for Labour Prime Minister James Callaghan. Davies would renew his government service when Tony Blair appointed him an advisor to the Bank of England in 1997. An academic sort, educated at both Oxford and Cambridge, Davies is known for being mad about sports. His passion led him to bid—as part of a consortium—for ownership of an English football club.

Morrison, a charismatic Scot, has an accent so thick most Americans have trouble understanding him at first. The son of a bus driver, he hails from the fading industrial town of Greenock in western Scotland, and while he would travel far from his roots as a partner of Goldman Sachs, the world of his childhood deeply colored his economic views.

Until Morrison's arrival, Goldman Sachs's economists were concerned, not surprisingly, only with economics. Now Morrison, along with his economic forecasts, made predictions about short-term price movements. Using technical analysis, the study of past trends and price patterns, he published both long- and short-term currency forecasts. He soon had a large following and had become a central fixture in the firm's trading operation. Traders carefully studied his forecasts, and salespeople sounded him out before talking to clients. As Morrison's influence grew, a simple comment of his reported by Reuters, Telerate, or Bloomberg could move the market.

Morrison remained approachable long after he became one of the world's hottest financial gurus. Even after he was sought out by the financial cognoscenti and the very rich, he seemed to have time for a drink and a chat with the cadre of salespeople and traders he had cultivated. His conversation was irreverent and humorous in a partnership long known for its circumspection. It was Morrison's eccentric side that made him even more attractive to the men in the gray suits. A racing car enthusiast, Morrison built a collection of Ferraris, and not content to watch them gather dust, he began racing them himself. Morrison showed up at his first partners' dinner dance wearing a skirt—never mind that it was a kilt; no male partner had ever failed to don trousers for the occasion.

The addition of Morrison and Davies were not the only big changes in London. Mark Winkelman hired Michael O'Brien to run London's foreign exchange department. Recruited from Wells Fargo in 1982 to lead a small bank the firm had acquired the year before, O'Brien had never heard of Goldman Sachs. O'Brien is a small, quiet man, known affectionately as Obi, short for Obi-Wan Kenobi, the *Star Wars* character. His gentle manner belied his bold approach to trading. O'Brien was comfortable with risk and urged his young traders to adopt a more aggressive stance. "Bet the ranch," O'Brien would advise, and when they were successful he would urge them on: "Bet two ranches." On the most profitable days London traders could be heard mooing like cows. O'Brien would go even further, encouraging his traders to expand their horizons and speculate in any financial market in which they felt they had an edge. The proof was in the profits, and as each year's expectations were exceeded, O'Brien and his traders were given more and more latitude. J. Aron had become the embodiment of proprietary trading, where the firm risked its own capital not in the service of clients but simply to achieve handsome returns. The results were nothing short of spectacular. Risk made money, and more risk made more money.

J. Aron's way of making money was a departure from the firm's traditional approach to its other trading businesses. "Until Mike O'Brien took over in London," one U.S. government bond trader from New York said, "equities traded equities, fixed income traded fixed income, and the two shall never meet. Aron broke that mold." Bonds, stocks, options, even precious metals—nothing was off-limits to O'Brien's proprietary traders. The small band of traders he put in place all sat within ten feet of him on the trading desk. Risk was monitored, as it was in other parts of the firm, with relatively crude analytics, but also with an in-depth knowledge by management of the trading going on around their desks. In the 1980s managers were so close to those taking the risk, and the areas in which the firm speculated were so limited, that the challenges of monitoring traders had not yet arisen.

Rubin's and Winkelman's transformation of J. Aron was complete. The division had gone from a losing operation to a roaring success in a few short years. By the end of the 1980s, J. Aron had trading operations in London, New York, and Tokyo and was operating with just over two hundred people (a little more than half the size it had been at the time of the merger) at a time when the firmwide headcount was more than sixty-three hundred. In 1989, J. Aron contributed more than 30 percent of Goldman Sachs's $750 million in profits. Not surprisingly, other parts of the firm took notice of the division's activities. Winkelman was invited to join the management committee and asked to co-head the giant fixed income division.

WHEN GUS LEVY sent John Weinberg down to run the firm's then tiny fixed income department in the early 1970s he had issued a single warning: "No surprises. I want no surprises." What Weinberg discovered was a department short on fixed income trading talent; he knew he would need to hire from the outside. In the early days the firm rarely looked to its competitors for new staff and resistance to lateral hiring among the existing staff was strong, but Weinberg persisted. "This is what I want to do, this is what Mr. Levy would like me to do, and if you don't like it, in fifteen minutes I think you ought to be out of here," Weinberg told the handful of people who made up the corporate bond department. The following morning when he arrived at the office he found a row of empty desks and a list of the department's positions. Eric Sheinberg, already a veteran equity trader, was recruited on the spot to run the department.

At its core, Goldman Sachs had always been a banking and equity firm, its bond business historically second- or even third-rate. There was little product innovation in fixed income and the firm was often in a position of playing catch-up with less prestigious but more innovative competitors. Although long a leader in commercial paper and municipal finance, the firm worked hard to build up its businesses in government and corporate bond trading and sales. Within the firm, fixed income did not have the same standing as, say, block trading or mergers and acquisitions. Top management was unfamiliar with the business and at one point questioned the wisdom of devoting serious resources to a business where there were no commissions or fees, where profits were made by earning the spread between the bid and offer in the market.

Just as Levy had done with him fifteen years earlier, Weinberg sent Rubin and Friedman down to straighten out fixed income in 1985, although neither man had any experience in the area. Rubin, a lifelong trader, had spent his career in equities—and bonds were an entirely different world. Friedman, the consummate banker, had no trading experience.

Goldman Sachs's fixed income department was living in the huge shadow cast by Salomon Brothers, and Rubin and Friedman were tired of it. In 1984, Goldman Sachs ranked fifth in total underwritings behind Salomon, Drexel, First Boston, and Merrill Lynch. Salomon had a 26 percent share of the undewriting market while Goldman Sachs had just under 10 percent. But the fixed income business was becoming integral to every other part of investment banking; unless the department could be brought up to the standards of the rest of the businesses, the entire firm would suffer.

When Rubin and Friedman arrived in fixed income they were shocked at the state of the business. At first they recruited heavily from other departments within the firm, but their efforts met with enormous resistance because fixed income was widely deemed to be a step down. As they approached experienced vice-presidents one by one, few considered the job offer a compliment and all resisted the move. But the two leaders could be persuasive; they did "some pretty violent arm-twisting," according to Friedman. Holding out a carrot, they made it perfectly clear that those staying put would not be penalized, but that switching to fixed income was a partnership-track move. Rubin and Friedman were the obvious heirs to Weinberg's mantle, and no partnership candidate wanted to risk their disapproval. Friedman contends that the career of every person who made the move to fixed income benefited. Still, even after some internal repositioning, it became clear that the firm lacked sufficient expertise to run a top-flight bond business. Rubin and Friedman, like Weinberg before them, would need to go outside.

Friedman is an intellectually voracious man who constantly seeks the lessons of other disciplines to provide insight into managing his own business. In talking with Nobel Prize–winning scientist Murray Gell-Mann, he found a valuable metaphor for his experiences with fixed income. "The standards of fitness for individuals within an organization should be conducive to achieving fitness for the organization. He [Gell-Mann] is using fitness in the evolutionary biological sense, in the sense that 'You survive' and 'You don't,' " Friedman says. Friedman knew that until the financial interests of the firm's fixed income salesmen and traders coincided with the financial interests of the firm, the department would never be a success. For many years, fixed income had operated under almost a commission system. What made the individual wealthy—selling certain bonds—was not necessarily what enriched the organization. The test of fitness was not being correctly applied, and despite strenuous objections by those who had profited by the old system, Friedman and Rubin instituted a subjective compensation system that would bring the two into line. Salesmen would earn the most when the firm earned the most, but the decisions would be made on a subjective basis, taking into account a wide range of factors above and beyond simple profitability.

Just months after Rubin and Friedman took over, the fixed income department suffered an extraordinary $50 million loss on a single corporate bond position. (Considering that the year before the entire firm had made $360 million, a loss of this magnitude was exceptional.) The firm had handled some bonds without correctly valuing the option imbedded in their structure. What most disturbed Friedman was not the money but the inexperience and lack of knowledge regarding many of the newest products. Losing money from time to time was to be expected, but losing it without knowing why was a very serious concern. The following year bond traders took another large hit when they hedged a corporate bond position with some treasury bonds, and the relationship between the two changed dramatically. It became clear that the firm would need to raise the level of its bond math sophistication and trading acumen, and that outside expertise was needed.

In 1986, Salomon Brothers was the king of fixed income trading. The undisputed market leader, Salomon Brothers had always been a trading firm. John Whitehead called it "an interest rate shop, period. Most of Salomon's emphasis is placed on offering the best terms to a client once that company has already decided what to do." Salomon Brothers had become a trading powerhouse not by coincidence or good luck, but because all the pieces were in place. Steeped in a trading culture, risk was in its very nature. With less emphasis on teamwork and more on short-term profitability, the more entrepreneurial elements of the firm had sniffed out, and capitalized on, every trading opportunity. A macho, winner-take-all attitude prevailed, manifesting itself in an aggressive trading style still foreign to Goldman Sachs. John Gutfreund, the firm's chairman, sat on the main trading floor and could not help but listen to the heartbeat of the firm. But it was in the development of the mortgage-backed securities market, the bundling and reselling of millions of individual home loans, that Salomon Brothers would hit pay dirt. By securitizing mortgages early Salomon Brothers owned this business, just as Drexel owned the junk bond market (the market for sub-investment-grade corporate debt). In both of these markets Goldman Sachs was far behind. At first wary of the default risk involved with bonds rated below investment grade, the partners had demurred. Then when the business became too large and profitable to ignore they struggled to catch up. Goldman Sachs had slowly started to make money in the bond business, but rivals Salomon Brothers and Drexel were far ahead. Still, Goldman Sachs looked down on upstart Drexel; even at this early juncture, it was widely rumored in the markets that something was amiss with its business. Instead, Goldman Sachs's new fixed income management turned its sights on mighty Salomon Brothers.

Expertise could and would be bought. Rubin and Friedman hired Tom Pura, David DeLucia, and later Michael Mortara from Salomon Brothers, luring them with the possibility of partnership. Each was already a managing director (the corporate equivalent of a partner) at Salomon Brothers, with an excellent reputation in the market. For at least one of the recruits from Salomon Brothers, Goldman Sachs's bond business was a huge disappointment. He remembers that when he first arrived it was immediately clear that Goldman Sachs was a better managed and better balanced firm than Salomon Brothers, but that its fixed income department simply did not compare. The traders from across the street would quickly make their mark on Goldman Sachs's bond business. Pura was a hard-driving trader who would be widely emulated. A contender in the annual "Iron Man" triathlon, he would bring to the department a new intensity and a risky style of trading that was bolder and more aggressive than anything Goldman Sachs fixed income had ever seen. In time De-Lucia would build up a $200-million-a-year business trading emerging market debt (that of countries with newly formed capital markets throughout Eastern Europe, South America, and Asia), a business no one could have even envisioned when he was hired. Mortara would outlast his colleagues, ultimately running the division with Lloyd Blankfein, a longtime Goldman Sachs partner.

By the end of 1986, it seemed that many of the department's troubles had been straightened out. The largest M.B.A. class ever—with 160 members—was hired into fixed income as the division returned to profitability. But by 1988 it was clear that fixed income was in trouble again. Part of the problem was London. Nineteen-eighty-six had been the year of the deregulation of the British financial markets, which seemed to be great news for foreign banks who now had a chance to play on a level field with the British institutions that had for so long dominated their own market. The number of gilt (U.K. government bond) dealers in London went from seven to twenty-seven in the fall of 1986. But in an almost precise repeat of Mayday in 1975, when fixed commissions were abolished on the New York Stock Exchange, the financial markets discovered that deregulation meant lower fees almost immediately. Goldman Sachs had invested heavily in its London trading and sales operation and now it was watching the margins on this business collapse. Few doubted that, if the costs could be endured, a top position in the London markets would be a treasure; the problem was getting there.

At the global managers' meeting for fixed income in 1989, the head of each department spoke. It had not been a good year, and many felt the need to offer inspiring remarks about the bright prospects for fixed income in 1990. Winkelman stood up and walked to the podium. Many remember his words: "Ladies and gentlemen, you should all know that fixed income, with a thousand people in the division, made $1.5 million for the firm this year. This is a completely unacceptable result, and it will not happen again." With that he sat down. Few could fail to guess that Corzine and Winkelman were determined to turn the division around. The firm had made three-quarters of a billion dollars, and fixed income had contributed virtually nothing.

Layoffs in fixed income, until this point an extremely rare event in the firm's history, followed in London and New York. It would be three years before the division was expanded. "You see, Winkelman had this notion that you keep on cutting people until you cover your costs. And he was right," explains one departmental manager from fixed income. "Mark is the most impressive businessman I have ever met. No one comes close. Really, I attribute about 70–80 percent of the success of Goldman Sachs in London fixed income to Mark. He inspired people, and not really through fear, [but] just by being smart and by asking smart questions, making people think, and not accepting mediocre results." Many of those who worked for Winkelman feel he was the best manager they had ever encountered. Steve Kim, a former fixed income salesman and now a portfolio manager at Rosenberg Capital, says, "He had his hands on the pulse. He was one of the few people who were visionary and the instrument of change."

Hiring managing directors from Salomon Brothers had been a bold move. Now, under Friedman and Rubin, the firm would dedicate itself to innovation in the bond business, what Friedman calls the "first mover" advantage or at least the benefits of being a "very quick follower." The difficulties in the 1980s came from a lack of innovation and the sluggish adoption of new approaches. With a new outlook in 1990 profitability would improve, and in 1991 the division would be responsible for almost 40 percent of the firm's profits. A large part of these profits would come from businesses like junk bonds, mortgage-backed securities, and proprietary trading, all businesses the firm had barely been in two years earlier. By 1993, under Corzine and Winkelman, these three departments of the fixed income division alone would earn Goldman Sachs more than $500 million, and the firm would stand in second place in its underwriting of Eurobonds and investment-grade debt.

IN STARK CONTRAST to fixed income, risk arbitrage was one of the firm's major engines of profits throughout the 1980s. Invented by Gus Levy in the 1940s and popularized by Ivan Boesky forty years later, risk arbitrage was Goldman Sachs's second most profitable department after mergers and acquisitions, and it was a jewel in the firm's crown. The risk arbitrage business, in its most simplified form, involves the purchase or sale of securities deemed to be mispriced, often because of their complexity or some change occurring in the company of which the shares represent ownership. Many of these opportunities arise as a result of a takeover by one company of another. After the public announcement of a bid, there can be considerable price movement in a stock because of a spirited defense waged by the target, doubts about the bid's successful outcome, the chance that a new bidder will emerge, regulatory and tax implications, and many other unknown factors. Risk arbitrageurs jump on such opportunities, pitting their analytical and trading skills against the market. But risk arbitrage is all about risk. Deals often fall apart in the negotiations, terms are changed, and the economics of the situation are always in flux. "You had to stick to your discipline and try to reduce everything in your mind to pluses and minuses and to probabilities," Rubin remembers. "If a deal goes through, what do you win? If it doesn't go through, what do you lose? It was a high-risk business, but I'll tell you, it did teach you to think of life in terms of probabilities instead of absolutes. You couldn't be in that business and not internalize that probabilistic approach to life. It was what you were doing all the time."

In most investment banks risk arbitrage is practiced by a small cadre of highly trained individuals who maintain a low profile. By all accounts arbitrage was Levy's and his successor Rubin's first love. In its essence the business has changed little since Levy first put it into practice a half century ago, although the deals have become dramatically more complex. His brief description, in his characteristic plain speaking, described the situation then: "The work itself, of course, is mostly financed by bank loans. The profit is very quick but small, and if you can convince a bank to put up 80 percent of the money, your profits increase fivefold. Since it's quick the interest you pay is no hindrance."

By the 1970s, Levy's legacy had passed to consummate trader Rubin, who was so fond of his mentor that even as secretary of the treasury he still has Levy's picture hanging on the wall. "There is probably no extended period of time when he does not come to mind," Rubin said about Levy in 1996. For Rubin the marketplace would change with new competition emerging every day, often in the form of small, stand-alone boutiques. Yet Goldman Sachs had an early lead in this area that it never relinquished. A highly analytical business suited to quiet geniuses, risk arbitrage thrived at Goldman Sachs. Throughout the industry Rubin was known as one of the best in the field. His careful research and unemotional trading style were legendary in a world where voices are often raised and expletives heard constantly. "We weren't plungers," he says. "We tried to be cool and hardheaded—not scared, though, because if you were scared, you couldn't function effectively." After every unsuccessful deal Rubin would pull out his everpresent yellow legal pad and write out everything that had gone wrong and why. Rubin likes to joke about the lack of sophistication in the early days of the business: "There was something called Roan Selection Trust. It was a stock that was listed on the New York Stock Exchange, and it was liquidating. You got about five or six different securities. You got cash. You got an American Metals warrant. You got a Zambian 6 percent bond and something called Botswana common stock. We didn't even know where Zambia was, so one of the fellows called the consulate and said, 'Where are you?' And they said, 'Fifty-seventh and Madison.' And he said, 'No I mean where is the country?' "

The 1980s would mirror the 1920s with an eerie déjà vu. The market rally, the ensuing crash, the financial scandals, the merciless government investigations—all had been witnessed sixty years earlier. Goldman Sachs had been dealt a body blow in the final days of the 1920s, and it would not escape the 1980s unscathed. The takeover wave would bring new and unimagined opportunities, as hostile tenders and "greenmail" provided price aberrations of the kind that arbitrageurs thrive upon. Working with a $1 billion portfolio of securities, Rubin and his half dozen assistants immersed themselves in the takeover mania of the 1980s. Robert Freeman was Rubin's number one assistant, soon becoming a partner in the division. Bright and well liked, he was a master of the techniques used to value takeover situations. Even at a firm that professed to have no stars, he was one.

For years the "Chinese wall"—the veil of secrecy intended to keep confidential information from traveling from one department to another— between banking and arbitrage was paper thin. Bankers all over Wall Street hopped the divide with frightening regularity, consulting with traders about the market's perception of a deal, and if no confidential information was discussed the exchange was legal. The risk arbitrage department at Goldman Sachs acted as in-house consultant to the firm's merger specialists in a way that was entirely legal. Arbitrageurs provided expert advice in evaluating the complexities of a deal and calculating the potential market reaction. This was an invaluable service to bankers attempting to structure a client's defense. Consultations between the two departments would continue until 1986, when the trading environment on Wall Street and what was considered acceptable practice changed radically.

On May 12, 1986, Dennis Levine, an investment banker at Drexel Burnham Lambert, was arrested and charged with making $12 million on insider trading. The SEC, the government body charged with prosecuting such crimes, made arrests like this from time to time. The stories briefly filled the front page of the *Wall Street Journal*, while those who worked on the street wondered why anyone would be so foolish as to risk everything for a suitcase full of cash. Almost always, the episode was soon forgotten. This time, however, the stories remained on the front pages of newspapers across the nation until the end of the decade. By then, dozens of individuals had been arrested, their firms humiliated, as billionaires traded in their mansions for jail cells, and the public lowered its estimation of the financial world yet another notch. The SEC investigations that began in 1986 changed the entire climate on Wall Street. Previously accepted and legal practices came under scrutiny as firms tightened their internal controls in response to a more thorough and aggressive SEC. Many of the accepted practices at Goldman Sachs and other firms that allowed arbitrageurs unimpeded access to information— talking with the bankers working on a particular deal, for example— would be closely scrutinized and after 1986 changed dramatically. Although heads shook and tongues wagged in May, no one dreamed of the damage a minor figure at a second-rate firm could do to Goldman Sachs.

Information provided by Levine resulted in the arrest of a group of relatively junior bankers from Shearson Lehman, Lazard Freres, and Goldman Sachs. These young men had made relatively little or nothing from their illegal activities but would pay a huge price. The Goldman

Sachs banker, who pleaded guilty, was very junior and left the firm immediately. And while the situation was disturbing to those in the industry,
during that summer, when the weather was perfect and the stock market
kept rising, concern did not run too high.

Then, in a desperate plea bargain agreement, Levine offered up Ivan
Boesky, the best-known arbitrageur of the day. Boesky had preached
greed, financial success, and self-interest as acceptable, even morally
laudable goals. Emblematic of the age, he was admired by many. "Boesky
had a substantial impact because he raised the profile of the business and
then trained a lot of people who then ventured out and set up their own
boutiques," says Rubin. "He contributed to the enormous influx of
money into the business." For years there had been whispers of Boesky's
insider trading, his implausible profitability, but most had labeled the
man a genius. Boesky, quite literally, had written the book—*Merger
Mania*, in which he describes in painstaking detail the methodology he
claimed to have used to become a successful risk arbitrageur.

On November 14, 1986, Boesky was arrested, pled guilty to charges of
insider trading, and paid the then unheard-of fine of $100 million. He, in
turn, implicated Martin Siegel, a well-respected and successful banker
and merger expert who recently had moved from solid Kidder Peabody to
more daring Drexel. Siegel had accepted suitcases of cash in exchange for
tipping Boesky about upcoming takeovers. Siegel then pointed his finger
directly at Robert Freeman, chief of risk arbitrage, head of international
equities, and trusted partner of Goldman Sachs.

After Siegel's arrest Goldman Sachs undertook, with the help of outside counsel, an exhaustive internal investigation. The firm wanted to
check its own books before the government did. "No surprises," as Gus
Levy had often warned. All trading records were reviewed and Freeman
was interviewed for two months about his extensive trading activities,
but nothing surfaced. According to Lawrence Pedowitz, Goldman Sachs's
lawyer and a former chief of the criminal division of the U.S. attorney's
office, "These were transactions that any firm that was in the arbitrage
flow would have been trading in substantial volume. Virtually all of the
trades were explainable in light of public record information. The transactions did not look irregular." Other members of the arbitrage desk
were interviewed. Endless hours were spent by lawyers trying to recon-
struct the past and explain every action taken by Freeman and others
over a two-year period. It was a difficult and complex task. Conversations, many of which had occurred years earlier, had to be reconstructed
without the aid of tapes. Special attention was paid to trades or phone
calls involving either Siegel or Boesky. (Many of Goldman Sachs's businesses routinely tape-record conversations between traders as a final

check in any dispute with a counterparty. An irate equities partner once cornered Winkelman, complaining that a counterpart had begun to use tape recorders, and the partner was thinking of discontinuing the relationship. Investment banking was a gentleman's business, he felt; trust was the cornerstone, and he was not certain his division wanted to deal with people who did not hold the same values. Reluctantly, Winkelman had to inform his partner that J. Aron routinely taped the telephone conversations on its trading desks, as was the norm in currency trading, and had done so for years.) The investigation was fruitless, and the management committee and Freeman proceeded secure in the knowledge that the growing scandal was unlikely to envelop the firm.

On the snowy morning of February 12, 1987, special deputy U.S. Marshall Thomas Doonan and two postal inspectors, all armed, walked onto the twenty-ninth-floor trading room of Goldman Sachs. They quickly located Freeman and asked him to step into his glass-fronted office. There they lowered the blinds and told the shocked Freeman that he was under arrest. He was made to empty his pockets, and he was informed of his rights. While he waited they searched his desk and files, and confiscated his Rolodex. "I was having a hard time fathoming what was going on. I felt almost like Dorothy [in the *Wizard of Oz*]," Freeman recalls.

Freeman called Goldman Sachs's lawyer. "Someone's here to arrest me," he told Pedowitz.

Pedowitz was preparing for a Utah skiing trip to celebrate his fortieth birthday, and this was not what he wanted to hear. "Bob, I'm about to go away; this is a joke, right?"

"No. I'm serious," was Freeman's response. "There is someone from the U.S. attorney's office named Tom Doonan, and he is here to arrest me."

Pedowitz and Doonan knew each other from their days in the U.S. attorney's office. "Let me speak with Tom," Pedowitz asked. Freeman handed over the phone, and Doonan informed Pedowitz of his intention to arrest Freeman. Pedowitz told his former colleague, "Tom, Bob is a really fine person; you don't need to put handcuffs on him." The publicity of the arrest would be humiliating enough, and Pedowitz wanted to save his client the further embarrassment of appearing on the evening news in handcuffs, like a teenage thug in need of restraint. Freeman was led through the trading floor, into the reception area, down the elevator, where they handcuffed him and led him to a waiting car. Doonan stayed behind to search Freeman's office. Freeman was driven to federal court and arraigned. His passport was confiscated, he was fingerprinted and photographed, and his bail was set at a quarter of a million dollars. "I thought I was being remarkably cool," Freeman remembered, "but when they asked me my Social Security number, I couldn't remember."

Goldman Sachs and much of the financial world was in shock. This was a partner of the firm with the cleanest reputation on Wall Street. The forty-four-year-old Freeman was a model partner. A Dartmouth College and Columbia Business School graduate, he had arrived at Goldman Sachs in 1970 as a junior analyst and was offered a partnership eight years later. An intense and talented trader, Freeman was also a suburban dad who coached Little League. His seventeen years at the firm had been a remarkably successful tenure.

When Freeman returned to 85 Broad Street, he went straight to the management committee meeting room where Steve Friedman, Bob Rubin, and Larry Pedowitz were waiting. Freeman had had an opportunity to review the charges in the arrest complaint and felt that he was innocent. Walking into the room Freeman was furious and said (referring to Martin Siegel), "That liar, that liar, I didn't do anything wrong." He told his partners, including Rubin, who had been his mentor for most of his career, "It's not true, it's just not true."

Freeman's personal nightmare lasted for the next six and a half years. The question of his guilt, never examined in a trial, was the subject of countless newspaper articles and chapters of books. "This was a real tragedy," Pedowitz says. "Bob was sitting on top of the world, with a prominent position at Goldman Sachs. You can imagine what it was like having reporters all over your front yard. He was an involved and caring father with three young children, two of whom were old enough to be quite impressionable."

From the first, the firm protested Freeman's innocence and proclaimed its intention to fight. John Weinberg, traveling on business, was unaware of his partner's arrest until his plane landed in Tokyo hours later. He has described the years that followed as "one of the most excruciating and difficult periods I have experienced in my career. All of us will have scars from it." Weinberg's unswerving devotion to his partner and to the firm's reputation would, by the end of the ordeal, cost $25 million of Goldman Sachs capital.

Freeman was a high-ranking partner who had worked personally for years with both Rubin and Friedman, and Goldman Sachs would not distance itself from him. To this day many of Freeman's partners believe that he was entirely innocent. Many within the firm have suggested that it was this and the culture of the firm, its commitment to sticking by those in trouble, that caused the firm to pursue Freeman's defense so doggedly. A more cynical explanation is that in a private partnership, where liability is unlimited, there is a strong incentive to diminish the guilt of any member of the team. An equally important point is that the partners of Goldman Sachs *are* Goldman Sachs. And while Marty Siegel may have been an employee of Kidder Peabody, which in turn was a division of the mammoth General Electric, Freeman was part of the fabric that made up Goldman Sachs.

For two years the firm's top management was consumed with Freeman's defense. One member of the management committee readily admits that the case distracted management, but the stakes were too high for the firm to act differently. The damage to the firm's reputation, had the government proved that a Goldman Sachs partner was involved in a systematic pattern of insider trading, would have been insurmountable. Recent history has shown that investment banking firms cannot withstand a criminal conviction; the list of firms that have fallen victim to criminal proceedings and later failed or were forced to merge includes Drexel and E. F. Hutton. The damage to reputation, morale, and ability to recruit, not to mention the possibility of having operating licenses revoked, is simply too great. Most within the firm think that Freeman was defended so vigorously because his partners believed in his innocence. This may be true, but Goldman Sachs would have had to fight—and win—the battle in any case.

On April 9, 1987, Freeman was indicted on federal charges of conspiracy to violate securities laws. The firm kept employees posted through a series of memos like this one: "Bob has been at Goldman Sachs since 1970. He maintains his innocence. Based on all that we now know, we continue to believe in him and to believe that he did not act illegally." The length of Freeman's tenure and the firm's confidence in his innocence might seem like a non sequitur, but in fact the two points are integrally related. He had been one of the family for a long time. Freeman remained a partner, and the firm paid for his considerable legal expenses, including the services of two of the country's top attorneys. The firm never flinched. "No one within Goldman Sachs broke ranks, a reflection in part of an institutional culture that had placed the firm ahead of its institutional partners for generations," observed James Stewart in *Den of Thieves*, his best-selling book on the insider trader scandals. The memo to the firm's staff continued, "We have been advised by counsel that the result at trial is likely to turn on the jury's assessment of witness credibility and its interpretation of circumstantial evidence." This last sentence would be crucial.

Almost immediately after the arrest the proceedings ran into difficulty. The indictment itself had taken two months, and Paul J. Curran, one of the former U.S. attorneys defending Freeman, said, "It would appear the government is now doing an investigation after his arrest." On May 12, the government asked to delay the trial, pleading for additional time to prepare its case. The judge refused. The following day the government sought to dismiss the indictment, declaring that it would seek a new, expanded indictment that would show an eighteen-month conspiracy between Freeman and Siegel, and that the dismissal should be seen as only a delay. The indictment was dismissed without prejudice, and the government was free to seek a wider indictment. The firm viewed this as a victory; its adversary was clearly unprepared, and the claims for an expanded indictment might just be a bluff.

The government fell silent while it proceeded to work on its case. Freemen returned to Goldman Sachs, this time to the merchant banking department. He retained his title as head of risk arbitrage, but in truth his time was consumed planning his defense. Freeman's and Goldman Sachs's lawyers met repeatedly with the government, focusing on the firm's generally high level of integrity and the fact that Siegel's allegations against Freeman, whether true or false, could all have alternative explanations. When presented with another plausible story, sufficient doubt would be raised in a jury's mind, the lawyers argued. Yet inside the firm the story was different. Freeman's lawyers had polled prototype jurors, and the results were troubling. Those polled were asked their views of Wall Street, investment bankers, and traders; names like Ivan Boesky's were mentioned to solicit reaction. "Arbitrageurs were thought of somewhere below lawyers," Pedowitz remembers. Whatever Freeman's lawyers were telling the government, and no matter how strong they believed their case to be, going to trial was not an appealing option.

On February 12, 1988, the first anniversary of Freeman's arrest, James Stewart and Daniel Hertzberg, both Pulitzer Prize–winning editors and writers for the *Wall Street Journal*, wrote an article that would change the course of events. The two journalists had been out in front of the story all along, uncovering vital pieces of information even before the government. Their dogged and comprehensive reporting would become a nightmare for the firm. Based on their own investigation, the story alleged a detailed catalogue of misdeeds by Freeman in his relationship with Siegel, all but one of which Freeman would staunchly deny. (The allegations all remained unproven, and the firm blocked access to information filed by the court that could have shed further light on Freeman's actions. Freeman testified under oath before the SEC about these additional transactions, after which the commission decided not to proceed.) It was the final allegation—the one concerning the now famous "bunny" comment—that would be Freeman's undoing.

In October 1985, the leveraged buyout firm of Kohlberg, Kravis, Roberts and Co. (KKR) had offered almost $5 billion, at $45 a share, for

Beatrice Corporation, in what was the largest leveraged buyout to date. (KKR borrowed money and used it to buy back all of the shares in the publicly traded Beatrice, converting it to a private company.) Martin Siegel was one of KKR's investment bankers. The bid was raised to $47 on October 29, and Freeman purchased shares of Beatrice for both the firm's arbitrage account ($66 million) and his personal accounts ($1.5 million) after details of the increased offer were made public. On November 14, Beatrice and KKR announced an agreement on a price of $50 per share, $43 in cash and $7 in securities. Freeman was so confident that this bid would go through that he invested almost 40 percent of his family's "at risk" trading accounts in Beatrice.

On January 6, KKR began to fear that the deal could not be financed at that lofty price. The next morning, Freeman bought an additional 22,500 shares in Beatrice for his own account. During the day, trading volume was heavy (Beatrice was the second most active stock on the NYSE that day) and the price edged downward, which concerned Freeman. At the end of the day, Goldman Sachs's position was worth approximately $66 million, or $16 million over the usual limit for friendly takeover situations. The position consisted of 1,360,100 shares of stock and 4,074 calls expiring in March. On January 7, Goldman Sachs executed a large sale for a well-known arbitrageur named Dick Nye. When Freeman learned of this trade he grew even more concerned. During the course of that afternoon Freeman spoke to Marty Siegel three times and once to Henry Kravis of KKR, who Freeman remembered as "very abrupt and anxious to end the conversation." Freeman then proceeded to sell all the shares he had purchased that morning. The following morning, January 8, Freeman put orders in the market to sell his entire personal holding and to reduce Goldman Sachs's position to below the $50 million level. Later that morning, a floor trader known as Bernard "Bunny" Lasker called Freeman to say he had heard that there was a problem with the Beatrice deal. Freeman telephoned Siegel, KKR's banker. According to Freeman, "I told Mr. Siegel that I had heard there was a problem with the Beatrice LBO. He asked from whom I had heard that. When I answered Bunny Lasker, Martin Siegel said, 'Your bunny has a good nose.'" Freeman relayed this amusing anecdote to an assistant on the desk and then sold Beatrice calls that he had bought for the firm's account. Early that afternoon, an announcement was made that the deal would be restructured to include only $40 in cash and $10 in securities. The share price of Beatrice immediately dropped $4, closing the day at $43.25.

In the firm's internal investigation a trader reminded Freeman of the "bunny" remark, but neither the firm nor its lawyers believed that this constituted insider trading. Siegel, when questioned by the government, had not remembered the conversation. In the course of its prosecution the government immunized Frank Brosens, one of Freeman's top aides. When Brosens appeared before the grand jury his testimony yielded little for the government. In frustration the prosecutor finally asked Brosens if there was anything else he could remember. Brosens requested a chance to consult with his counsel. After their discussion, Brosens repeated the story Freeman had told him, corroborating the "bunny" remark. The options sales that had followed Freeman's conversation with Siegel had saved the firm $548,000.

By the summer of 1989, worn down by the lengthy legal process, Freeman was ready to plead guilty to the "bunny" charge. He told Weinberg in a letter, "I recognize that I should not have initiated any trading after Siegel confirmed the rumor that there was a problem with the Beatrice deal, and I am prepared to take full responsibility for what I did," while continuing to insist that he was guilty of no other wrongdoing. Pedowitz says, "Bob was capable of analyzing this as well as any of us. He would switch from being emotionally involved to being the perfect arbitrageur. No emotion, just analyze A, B, C. Make a chart, right-hand side, left-hand side, weigh them out, figuring out the probabilities. When you took the probability of a conviction at trial in light of juror attitudes toward Wall Street and multiplied that by the effect from Bob's point of view on his family, there was only one right answer." Freeman summarized his calculation, "When I balanced the risks and costs, both legal and personal, it was to put it in financial terms a very high negative expected value."

Freeman's willingness to plead guilty to a single criminal count of using nonpublic information for trading was prompted by many factors, one of which was the fear that a fair trial would not be possible. No jury would be sympathetic, and there was some doubt as to whether one would be fair. "The atmosphere," Freeman recalls, "was extremely poisoned. For anyone who had anything to do with the eighties, there was no sympathy." On April 17, 1990, Freeman was sentenced to one year, with eight months suspended, of which he served one hundred nine days (including time off for good behavior) at Saufley Federal Prison Camp in Florida. He was also fined $1.1 million by the SEC—the $548,000 he had saved by selling the options and seven years' interest.

The admission of guilt shocked the firm, which had staunchly defended Freeman's innocence, and spent tens of millions of dollars on his defense. Goldman Sachs now had to face the unprecedented fact that one of its own was serving time in a federal prison. In a memo to "the people of Goldman Sachs," the firm put a brave face on it. The memo said in part that, "Bob has made an exceedingly difficult decision in the face of highly complicated issues of law and fact." Freeman insisted that the guilty plea was simply a way to put the matter behind him, to save his family and the firm further grief. In Freeman's resignation letter to Weinberg, while thanking the firm for its support, he did not convey any sorrow for having damaged the firm's reputation.

After Freeman's admission of guilt, the government dropped any further investigation and Goldman Sachs sought to put the entire episode behind it. After the publication in 1991 of James Stewart's *Den of Thieves*, which detailed further allegations concerning Freeman's trading, the SEC briefly increased the scope of its investigation, later deciding to focus only on the "bunny" charge. Freeman's lawyers wrote to the book's editor and detailed their belief in his innocence, calling Siegel a con man, a liar, and a felon whose only interest was in reducing a lengthy jail sentence by falsely accusing others.

Any thoughts of a public offering or other ways to enhance the firm's capital, which were actively being considered at the time, were pushed aside, although Goldman Sachs was neither fined nor censured. The legacy of the Freeman experience would be Rubin's and Friedman's commitment to "zero defects." They had lawyers and accountants go through the operations procedures used by every business at the firm looking for any holes in the system. Although it is virtually impossible, they attempted to put in place infallible systems that would eliminate the possibility of impropriety, whether deliberate or accidental. As an outgrowth of this episode the firm has state-of-the-art compliance procedures.

In its letter to the staff the management committee showed its abiding support for Freeman. "We do not condone even a single act of wrongdoing. However, it remains true that over the past thirty months, Bob had been subjected to an arrest that the prosecutor has since characterized as a mistake, a withdrawn indictment, and a series of highly publicized formal allegations and innuendoes that far exceed anything he actually did. . . . He and his family have our heartfelt sympathy." The culture of partnership ran deep. Even as Freeman served time, his partners would not abandon him.

CHAPTER IV

1990–1991

THE CHANGING
OF THE GUARD

Tʜᴇ ᴄʜᴀɴɢɪɴɢ ᴏꜰ ᴛʜᴇ ɢᴜᴀʀᴅ, heralded for so long, finally came to pass on December 1, 1990, when Steve Friedman and Bob Rubin were named senior partners and co-chairmen of the management committee. John Weinberg had given them a five-year transition period, gradually handing over more and more responsibility for the firm. "I believe in succession planning," Weinberg said at the time, "and I decided that when I did it I was going to do it correctly and as best I could. The big question was to decide whether [Friedman and Rubin] would be able to do what John Whitehead and I did." It was textbook good management, and Goldman Sachs once again was saved the kind of wrenching political upheaval that had engulfed other investment banks, like Lehman Brothers, in the transition of power.

Friedman viewed the change as business as usual. He and Rubin in effect had had their hands on the controls since Weinberg had made them vice-chairmen three years earlier. Since Whitehead's departure in 1984, they had functioned informally as chief operating officers. The pair would not need to put their stamp on the firm; they had been running large parts of it for years.

Weinberg, like his father, was one of the firm's great developers of new business. He is credited with adding some of the world's largest companies to Goldman Sachs's client list and focusing on the long-term interests of the firm. But mainly he is remembered for reinforcing the firm's culture and preserving its legacy. When Weinberg announced his retirement after forty years he was a vigorous sixty-five years old. He joked that he wanted to go out "a master of my own destiny, and not drooling." He explained his timing in words reminiscent of his father: "These guys are ready, and I'm ready. This is the logical time. When the goose is cooked, you better go ahead and eat it."

During Weinberg's tenure the firm's earnings had increased tenfold, and the partners' capital had swollen from $60 million to $2.3 billion. Within the partnership Weinberg was universally admired; he was a true leader who embodied everything the firm stood for. As one partner summed it up: "John Weinberg was the heart of the place." It was, by any standards, a remarkable career.

Rubin's and Friedman's ascendancy was not viewed by everyone as an entirely positive change. Some argued that when Weinberg retired some of the firm's values went with him, that under the new leaders the firm maximized rather than optimized profits. One former member of the management committee explained that the pair brought with them a more focused profit orientation that was new to Goldman Sachs. With a note of nostalgia, some former partners explain that when Weinberg left, Goldman Sachs ceased to be a family business, although it maintained some of the same collegial feel. The new leaders embodied a more aggressive and dynamic approach and were determined to create a growth company on the cutting edge of investment banking. When a partner from outside New York missed his first annual partners' meeting and dinner dance because of his daughter's birthday, Weinberg sent his wife roses and called to congratulate him on his sense of values. A few years later when the issue arose again Friedman let the same partner know that skipping partners' meetings was not looked upon kindly.

Against the odds, the co-CEO structure worked a second time, and the Friedman-Rubin pairing was a complete success. Rubin described the arrangement as a source of strength: "If a co-chairmanship works, one plus one equals far more than two." It was an unusually close association developed over many years of working together. A deep mutual respect pervaded their relationship, and they were so intellectually compatible that many partners have described them as interchangeable. One partner remembers asking Rubin a question at 9 one night about a complicated issue that would need consideration and consultation. At 7 the next morning Friedman gave her the answer.

The two men had been negotiating over complex issues for decades. In every major takeover situation the firm could either act as a banker, or take a trading position (in Rubin's risk arbitrage department), but not both. The issue would arise many times, and to Rubin's credit he more often than not opted for the banking business, knowing that it would enhance a client relationship and might lead to additional work in the future. It is difficult to imagine many companies with $60 billion in assets that would be able to operate successfully with two leaders, but it worked. Like Whitehead and Weinberg before them, the new senior partners did not carve up the firm into spheres of influence—although each took certain geographic responsibilities—but rather ran the entire organization together. A decision of one was binding; it was not necessary to consult them both.

Rubin attributes their success in this highly unusual arrangement to the fact that "Neither of us has an ego structure that is invested in the notion of being chief executive officer." Friedman puts it more simply: They just agreed on most things. Neither man seemed to need top billing, and each, along with his wife and family, was happy to have someone to share the burdens of the office. Partners who worked closely with them say that differences of opinion rarely arose, but that when they did each yielded to the one who felt most strongly about the particular issue. Their styles were similar in that both probed a new issue tirelessly by asking an exhaustive string of questions. "Facts are extremely wiggly; they're like greased pigs," Friedman has said, "so you have to ask a lot of questions." Their approach was legalistic, and no detail was left unexamined. "They have different questioning styles," explained their partner Rick Adam. "Steve tends to ask a lot of lateral associative kinds of questions. Bob is more vertical, more probing. So Bob will go deeper down on the issue, and Steve will try to correlate it to something he already knows." Partners reporting to the pair would be asked to submit memoranda in advance of any presentation. The unwitting executive, arriving at the meeting expecting to reiterate much of what had been written earlier, would be greeted by the senior partners who, with their ever-present yellow legal pads and sharpened pencils, would seat themselves across the table from the nervous presenter. "Assume we have read the memorandum," Rubin would say, and the rapid-fire succession of questions would begin.

After Weinberg's retirement, Rubin and Friedman moved from their noisy offices on the fixed income trading floor to the sedate executive suite on the twenty-second floor. After twenty-four years immersed in the chaos of the trading floor, Rubin was not entirely at home when surrounded by the wood-paneled walls and oil portraits of the firm's founders. Like his mentor, Gus Levy, Rubin had a small glass window installed in his office that he would slide open when he needed to speak to his secretary, and slam shut when a client entered his office.

Weinberg's successors made decisions and took action faster than he had. Strategic dynamism—upping the pace of change in a firm accustomed to carefully measured movements—is what the pair had in mind. "If you are not constantly working for constructive strategic change, then you are the steward of something which must erode," Friedman would say. "Competitors will leapfrog over you, and clients will find you less relevant. If that was your approach, why would you even want the job?"

Rubin and Friedman knew all too well they would be working against the firm's natural complacency. Goldman Sachs, with its sixty-five hundred employees, was highly successful, and the partnership was by its nature conservative. After a decade of astounding prosperity, the impetus for change was low. "We were moving too slowly, or not at all, to face some serious competitive threats, with too little internal coordination between divisions and too much self-satisfaction," Friedman remembers. "Too many crucial things were on autopilot and were not being reexamined. If we waited to fix them it might get to be too late. The challenge for my generation was to institutionalize a continuous process of reinvigoration."

When Friedman and Rubin came to power, the quality of the firm's businesses was uneven, which the new leaders considered unacceptable. The two shared a vision of creating the premier investment bank with beachheads all over the world, a firm larger and more sophisticated than anything their predecessors imagined. Goldman Sachs would not be a boutique firm, like Lazard Freres—a small, first-rate investment bank that focuses on a limited cadre of top corporate clients, acting as their agent and servicing the needs of the largest corporations. Instead, often acting as a principal, Goldman Sachs would take on the largest banks all over the world, including the so-called universal banks in Europe and the Far East, and build a critical mass that would allow it to compete for any major piece of investment banking business anywhere on the globe. The firm now had ten foreign offices, most of them relatively small, and the new leadership would focus on their expansion. As part of this broad reach, Goldman Sachs would pursue the financing business of national governments with unmatched vigor, especially the spate of privatizations sweeping the globe. Goldman Sachs facilitated the highly complex process of selling government-owned assets to the public in twenty-five different countries including Argentina, Germany, Mexico, Finland, India, and Thailand. Only a handful of other investment banks had the international research, trading, and sales expertise to complete these major asset sales. This high-profile business, which the firm dominated by the mid-1990s, would serve as its calling card in every new country it entered. In 1990, Friedman and Rubin presented their vision of the future to the partnership. They would create a world-class business in every major sector in which the firm competed, even if they had to drag along the organization kicking and screaming.

During the 1980s the business of investment banking ramped up sharply, and everyone was forced to climb faster up ever steeper hills. Whatever was good enough before was no longer sufficient. Friedman puts those who resisted into three camps: "You have the Barons, who perceive change as a risk to their fiefdoms and personal importance. You have the Creationists, who feel comfortable with things as they are and distrust evolution. And you have the Romantics, who hark back to some imagined Camelot, when every subject in the kingdom was happy and prosperous." Anyone continuing to resist change under the new leaders would be cajoled, convinced, and finally pushed aside.

Rubin and Friedman were in a hurry, in part because neither man might be staying with the firm for long. Rubin's political interests were widely known, and many of his partners expected to lose his leadership the next time the country sent a Democrat to the White House. And Friedman had confided to Rubin his plans for a limited tenure as senior partner. He wanted to usher in some monumental and lasting changes and then hand the reins over to the next generation. No one else in the organization had a clue that, at age fifty-two, Friedman did not have a lengthy career with Goldman Sachs ahead of him.

The pressure for speed also came from the outside world. With the gradual weakening of the Glass-Steagall Act, the 1933 legislation separating investment and commercial banking businesses, commercial banks became "margin-reducing, risk-heightening" competition. (Glass-Steagall had been a boon to investment banks, separating underwriting and lending powers and thereby keeping the well-capitalized commercial banks away from their lucrative business. One partner remembers that at his first partners' meeting in 1981 two large portraits of old men with long beards were held up. The audience was told that these were the two most important men to the firm's business and was challenged to guess who they were. After the names Goldman, Sachs, and Weinberg had been discarded, the answer was revealed: The portraits were of Senator Carter Glass and Representative Henry Steagall.) With Glass-Steagall eroding, the giant commercial banks could have bought their way into many of Goldman Sachs's businesses by offering to lend corporate clients huge chunks of money at highly competitive rates in exchange for a greater share of the client's investment banking business. Bankers Trust was already considered the premier name in derivatives; J. P. Morgan had begun to capitalize on its first-rate client list; and mammoth Citibank was flexing its substantial trading muscle. Many commercial banks had global networks in place, with locals and expatriates on the ground in hundreds of offices throughout Europe, Latin America, and Asia. But commercial banks, just emerging from the burdens of their Third World loans, now found themselves choking on domestic real estate loans.

Despite Friedman's concern, the firm had a bit of breathing room before these competitors invaded its turf.

GOLDMAN SACHS entered the 1990s in an extremely strong position relative to its American investment banking competition. The 1980s had ended, like all great parties, with scattered debris and a blinding hangover. After years of indulging in speculative financing vehicles, there was now a price to pay for the excesses of the decade. For Drexel there would be Chapter 11, scandal rocked E. F. Hutton, and Kidder Peabody would be sold. First Boston, one of the firm's major competitors in mergers and acquisitions, would be stretched to the limit by ill-advised bridge loans (short-term unsecured loans, many of which looked good in the 1980s and failed in the early 1990s) and later aided by its wealthy parent, Credit Suisse. Lehman Brothers, once one of Goldman Sachs's most formidable investment banking competitors, would be torn apart by political infighting and forced to sell itself to the American Express conglomerate. The SEC investigation of Salomon Brothers's activities in the government bond market followed by the departure of its chairman John Gutfreund would weaken this once-insurmountable competitor, allowing Goldman Sachs's fixed income department to escape from its enormous shadow. By avoiding many of its competitors' mistakes, Goldman Sachs was well positioned as the new decade began. Weinberg had recognized the excesses of the era early on, and his caution had paid off. One could almost see Floyd Odlum smiling.

Some within the partnership argued there was no reason to rush into new businesses. Early profits, they maintained, are often illusory, eaten up by teething problems and the expensive infrastructure necessary to support a product that may still have little volume. Clients, too, can become alienated by the difficulties that often plague the introduction of new products. Friedman did not believe this for a moment. Experience had shown him that when Goldman Sachs had entered a new business at its inception it had been an indomitable force, grabbing and maintaining a sizable market share. On the other hand, he could list businesses where the firm was still playing catch-up, and he was determined there would be fewer of these on his watch. By management's own admission, the firm had been slow to enter some of the most profitable businesses of the late 1980s. Goldman Sachs set the standard for the industry but not the pace, and other more innovative institutions were streaking past. The firm had a widespread reputation for letting its competitors dip the first toe into the water. If the temperature was right, Goldman Sachs jumped in after others had proved the existence of a viable business. But under Rubin and Friedman, the firm would dedicate itself to innovation. "If you consider

the advantages of being the first mover, if you look at people in our industry who have innovated a product, you will find the advantages are significant. Creativity has a substantial payoff," says Friedman.

One of the biggest changes in investment banking over the course of
the 1980s was the role of the client. For more than a century, from the
days Marcus Goldman roamed the streets of New York collecting his
primitive commercial paper, securities firms had made their profits by servicing their clients. At Goldman Sachs the job of salesperson traditionally
carried greater prestige and often a higher salary than that of trader.
Salespeople determined what would happen on the trading floor; their
work drove the firm's activity.

As the 1990s began this was no longer the case. While clients were still
vitally important, they were now only part of the profit picture. For
Goldman Sachs, this was a cataclysmic transformation. In the 1970s, Gus
Levy had sold the firm's asset management business because he did not
want to compete with the firm's clients. "We're striving to be a client-
driven service business with worldwide trading capabilities," Weinberg
would explain during his tenure as senior partner, "so we can't start competing with our clients." Long after every major Wall Street firm was
busy collecting a steady stream of fees from managing large pools of
investors' cash, Weinberg was still unwilling to risk alienating his clients.
He stuck by the firm's first business principle, "The client's interests
always come first," even at the expense of a profitable business. The
notion of not competing with clients, however, would soon become ludicrous as clients began to compete with their investment bankers and the
margins on many client businesses collapsed. Companies like General
Electric would initiate their own asset management business, and American International Group (AIG), the insurance giant, would become a
major force in derivatives products.

A public clash with a client, an extremely rare event, came about when
Goldman Sachs opened the Water Street Corporate Recovery Fund,
named for a street two blocks south of the firm's New York headquarters,
in the fall of 1990. Bankruptcy investment funds, known unflatteringly as
"vulture funds," invest in the bonds of failing companies. They were in
great demand in 1990, and Goldman Sachs jumped onto an already
crowded bandwagon. With a $100 million investment of its own capital,
Goldman Sachs had no trouble raising $683 million from institutional
investors, such as the pension funds of DuPont and Ameritech. For the
firm this was a substantial commitment of capital and an evolutionary
milestone in the firm's progress toward becoming a major principal
investor. The fund, it was planned, would operate for four years and aim

for lofty returns of between 25 and 35 percent. Goldman Sachs's track record of successful investing suggested that such returns were possible.

Water Street was a problem from the start. The fund sought to acquire controlling positions in the debt of financially distressed companies and then influence a restructuring, leading to a reallocation of the company's assets. Often, profits were accrued by squeezing other debtor classes or diluting existing equity holders. The problem was that many of the investors subjected to these tactics were the large money management firms that bought stocks and bonds from Goldman Sachs every day. The firm had said it would take action to avoid such situations, but the conflict arose almost immediately.

The press sneered that Goldman Sachs was once again entering a new business too late, and when the market for distressed debt fell and the fund showed early losses it was quickly dubbed "the underwater fund." But the most devastating criticism came from the firm's own clients. Surprised clients wondered if Goldman Sachs had changed its stripes. Was it a different organization than they had thought? Among those angered were Tonka Toys, USG Corp., and even the mighty Fidelity Investments. In one deal, Water Street acquired approximately half the bonds of Tonka Toys. The fund tried to negotiate a higher price for the bonds when Hasbro, Inc. acquired Tonka and blocked the deal while it sought better terms. The negotiations were gut-wrenching, and the firm created some ill will. This was an uncomfortable position for a firm still refusing to aid or advise on hostile takeovers, and it seemingly flew in the face of Goldman Sachs's longest held and most sacred principle.

"The perceptions surrounding this activity were much more intense, far outside the range that we had thought they would be," explained a spokesman for the firm. Angry clients and bad publicity were not what Goldman Sachs needed, and the firm acted swiftly to remedy the situation. When the market for distressed securities rallied in early 1991 and the fund was solidly profitable, Goldman Sachs took the opportunity to shut it down and sell off the investments, returning a profit to their investors. The entire episode lasted less than a year. While in the end the Water Street fund was little more than a public relations difficulty, it highlighted an important way in which the firm appeared to have changed. Rubin and Friedman's predecessors would not have risked the ire of those who for so long had paid the bills. But a closer look at Goldman Sachs's finances revealed that principal transactions in which the firm risked its own capital to make a profit, as opposed to purely client-driven business where the firm acted as agent, had become increasingly important to the firm's profitability.

At this point Friedman could easily have walked away from the principal investment business and returned to the less controversial form of investment banking, acting simply as an agent for clients. But there was no doubt that Goldman Sachs was ideally suited for principal investments and that they could be successfully balanced with the firm's client businesses, and no one contemplated abandoning this new business.

From his first days at Goldman Sachs, Friedman had been a constant force for change. He never let up, relentlessly questioning and probing those around him, pushing management to improve itself. Long after he knew he was leaving the firm, at a time when others might have put their feet up on the desk and reviewed their accomplishments, he continued to challenge his partners to question every assumption they had made about their businesses in a perpetual effort to improve the firm. Friedman had a vision of a principal investments area that would be an integral part of Goldman Sachs and would serve as a source of customer businesses while capitalizing on the firm's financing expertise. Early in his investment banking career, Friedman came to believe that Goldman Sachs, in arranging financing deals for others, was passing up first-rate investment opportunities. Not everyone agreed with him. John Whitehead, as co-head of Goldman Sachs, felt that the firm needed to remain cautious in entering this business. "The minute you exchange the role of agent for one as principal," he explained, "you change the traditions of your business. If you're out looking for deals for yourself, you can't do the best for your client."

Principal investments would require bankers to broaden their notion of what a business opportunity was for the firm. In one of his characteristic anecdotes Friedman explains that the firm sent down its coal miners, otherwise known as investment bankers, into the mines to look for the black stuff. They were so focused on their goal that when they stumbled upon veins of gold embedded in the coal they simply left them alone; coal was what they were after. Many did not recognize new business opportunities outside their narrow purview, and they were not given the proper incentives to do so. Bringing in business for other departments was not yet a route to promotion. Friedman had seen the problem before. When he ran private investments, it had been difficult to get generalist bankers to recognize new specialized financing opportunities for the firm. Friedman, with a flash of humor, explains, "We would go to the marketing people and we would say, 'Look, we don't want to make it hard for your guys. You don't have to understand the product; all you have to do is ask the question.' It still wasn't working, so we said, 'Let's make it simpler. If you go to visit the client and there is a huge hole outside next door to his office—a big hole, not a little hole; a giant hole—could you get them to say, Sir, we see an enormous hole there. Does that mean you are building a new headquarters building? If so, I have someone I want you to talk to.' "

Friedman was not surprised when he found a lack of internal support from management for his plans for a principal investments department. "It is harder to get a good idea accepted than to get a good idea," he says. The partnership was divided on how enthusiastically to pursue this business. But Friedman persevered, having learned many lessons from the early years of building the mergers and acquisitions business: "Here I am getting more and more frustrated because—wait a minute, let me get this straight—we've got the client, we had their confidence, we had priced and negotiated the transaction, knew how to finance it, and we were going to get a fee, not starvation wages, but let's figure out where the real profits are in this business—in the capital gains. I tried to get some of the most imaginative and creative guys to go into that area. I couldn't understand why the hell they weren't excited about it. The answer was, culturally, it was not perceived as the right career move. We did not have enough strategic dynamism to say, 'Hey this is a fantastic opportunity; let's go for it.' "

Many partners were reluctant to embrace such a risk-taking mentality, and few employees were enthusiastic about joining a start-up business with no track record and no assurance of success. The opportunities that interested Friedman would require large commitments of capital in illiquid investments that the partnership might not be able to sell easily or quickly. Earlier Whitehead had stated that he felt the firm needed to proceed cautiously because of the tremendous demands on capital and the longer-term nature of principal investments: "I think it's important to keep our capital liquid for use in serving our customers and clients," he said at the time. But Friedman was convinced that by using its expertise to value companies accurately, Goldman Sachs would be able to locate undervalued companies or special situations in the market and achieve enormous excess returns on its own capital and that of its investors. The business started slowly. On the first deal Friedman persuaded the management committee to invest the fee the client would have paid the firm back into the client's business. With the success of such deals, Friedman was slowly able to recruit another kind of talent, true goldminers, to the business.

Principal investments signaled a return to the firm's roots. On many of Goldman Sachs's early underwritings, partners had functioned as outside directors while the firm held large chunks of stock and retained a close attachment to the company. When the firm underwrote the Sears Roebucks IPO, eight decades earlier, it owned a chunk of the preferred shares. When it brought Ford Motor Company public, Sidney Weinberg took a seat on the new board of directors. When Goldman Sachs bought a stake in the Ralph Lauren Company in 1994, Goldman Sachs's Richard Friedman (no relation to Steve) became a director.

In 1991, Rubin and Friedman had asked Richard Friedman, a personable young banker, to run the firm's budding principal investments area. Like Steve Friedman, Richard Friedman's enthusiasm for the firm's investment activities can barely be contained. Goldman Sachs had a number of distinct competitive advantages: close industry relationships, sophisticated financial knowledge and resources, and an unmatched window on the flow of deals. Capitalizing on these advantages, the firm would invest in minority stakes in established operating companies through negotiated transactions that were friendly on both sides. Many viewed Goldman Sachs as an ideal financial partner. The firm's studied discretion and financial acumen are desirable characteristics for privately owned companies seeking outside investors. Principal investments would also help the firm in its client business. When a client was looking for capital the firm's bankers could now offer it an equity underwriting, a bond underwriting, or an investment from one of the firm's own funds. In the fall of 1991 the firm raised an investment fund, called GS Capital Partners I, and this time committed $300 million of the $1 billion fund. In 1995 the firm raised $1.75 billion for GS Capital Partners II, contributing a second $300 million. Principal investment revenues rose almost tenfold between 1990 and 1993, while the investment banking division as a whole saw its revenues double.

The goal of the principal investments area is to seek investment opportunities—generally between $25 million and $250 million, located anywhere in the world—that will yield an excess return. Desirable investments have a five- to seven-year time horizon after which the firm, through a public offering, sale, or merger, can exit with its cash. These are not venture capital opportunities, but rather partnerships with existing operating companies looking to expand. The area has become central to Goldman Sachs, spinning off new business opportunities to many other departments—something Steve Friedman, in his early attempts to establish the department, had argued would happen. Goldman Sachs also offers banking services to the companies in which the firm is invested. When Ralph Lauren looked to sell a portion of his privately owned business, his largest outside investor, Goldman Sachs, was there to help him execute the sale with a team of experts in initial public offerings. Principal investments and the business it generates is now the largest single client of the firm's investment banking division.

The firm's investments are eclectic and opportunistic. They have included everything from an Indonesian telephone company to an Israeli oil company. In 1996, Goldman Sachs, in its largest transaction to date, bought the privately owned bowling chain AMF with a group of investors for $1.35 billion. Richard Friedman is now the chairman of AMF, and his office at Goldman Sachs is decorated with bowling pins and balls. It was not an obvious match, the top-drawer investment bank teaming up with a sport always considered to be a little rough around the edges. But the firm operates as a hands-on investor, helping set policy and strategy. Its vision for the company is to have AMF become a brand name in entertainment, with thousands of AMF entertainment centers around the country. Goldman Sachs hopes to develop bowling as a family pastime, and plans to see its centers become venues for birthday parties and weekend visits with grandparents—a far cry from the dimly lit, smoke-filled lanes reeking of overcooked hot dogs many remember from childhood.

The Ralph Lauren investment was accompanied by a great deal of publicity. The firm made a substantial initial investment of $135 million in 1994 in exchange for a 28 percent stake in the clothing designer and three years later led an initial public offering. Goldman Sachs received $48.7 million at the time of the sale, and its remaining 22 percent stake in the company was valued at more than $530 million. Steve Friedman was right. The returns from this business would far outstrip what could be achieved simply by serving clients. The principal investments area has grown to between $4 billion and $4.5 billion in assets, and its annual compounded return exceeds 30 percent.

In 1992, Goldman Sachs lifted the veil on its shrouded finances and gave the world a glimpse of its astounding profitability. For the first time the firm revealed publicly some of the ways in which it made money. Although the firm was still viewed as a traditional investment banking firm in the client service mold of Morgan Stanley, it was now clear that Goldman Sachs's trading businesses had become substantially more important. In 1989 investment banking accounted for 35 percent of the firm's overall profits; by 1993 that number had slipped to 16 percent. Within investment banking, the areas with the greatest increase in revenues were businesses in which the firm takes some or all of the risk of each transaction onto its own books. Mergers and acquisition fees, which in the late 1980s represented fully 40 percent of investment banking revenues, had declined to 17 percent of the department's revenues by 1993. In each of the firm's other divisions, arbitrage and proprietary trading for the firm's own account had become the engines of profit growth. Unlike income generated by client fees, these transactions involve risking the firm's own capital. The importance of the change was lost on no one, and top management readily acknowledged that the firm would not prosper simply by doing agency and advisory business for clients.

In the five years between 1985 and 1989, Goldman Sachs consistently earned between $500 million and $750 million a year. Steve Friedman and Bob Rubin never believed that this was a profit plateau, although some of their partners did. Wall Street lost money in four out of the five quarters between December 1989 and March 1991, and in 1990 the securities industry had its first losing year since 1973. The combined loss of the seven largest firms (including Goldman Sachs) was $678 million, but for Goldman Sachs it was a year of record profits. Under its new senior partners, Goldman Sachs was firing on all cylinders. In 1990 the firm earned $886 million, breaking all previous records by a substantial margin. The following year its profits exceeded a billion dollars. Friedman and Rubin, however, had even greater ambitions.

For their efforts, Rubin and Friedman earned more than $25 million each in 1992 on stakes estimated to be worth 2.25 percent of the firm's equity, although they probably deposited into their bank accounts only a few million dollars, reinvesting the remainder in the firm. Partners' compensation is determined solely on the basis of ownership, and these numbers represent their share of Goldman Sachs's pretax profits rather than a discretionary bonus such as that received by the firm's professional employees. In *Financial World*'s annual listing of the one hundred highest-paid executives on Wall Street in 1991, Friedman, Rubin, and long-serving partner Eric Sheinberg held the top three spots among traditional Wall Street firms (only thirteen men who ran highly leveraged hedge funds were better compensated). Forty of the firm's partners would have fallen within the top one hundred spots, so rather than dominate the list and leave only sixty places for the rest of Wall Street, the magazine gave Goldman Sachs a separate list. In 1992 and again in 1993 the firm had its own listing, with twenty-six and twenty-seven names respectively. Morgan Stanley, in second place, had only six executives on the 1991 list, the first of whom was in fifty-fourth place. The compensation of other CEOs on Wall Street trailed far behind Goldman Sachs as well. The head of Merrill Lynch, Daniel Tully, earned $12.8 million in 1991, while Richard Fisher of Morgan Stanley was paid $7.7 million, and Deryck Maughan of Salomon Brothers took home $5.3 million.

From the lofty base of $1.15 billion in 1991, Goldman Sachs's profits leaped to $1.46 billion by Thanksgiving of 1992. The firm's return on equity—more than 35 percent—dwarfed that of its nearest competitor. One of the main engines of profitability was tiny J. Aron, the firm's currency and commodities division. By 1990 the performance of J. Aron was nothing short of spectacular. From an insignificant operation in the early 1980s, Rubin and Mark Winkelman had, by the end of the decade, created a trading powerhouse. With fewer than four hundred people, J. Aron accounted for more than 40 percent of Goldman's pretax earnings in 1990 and for approximately one-third of the firm's earnings, in excess of $300 million, in 1991. Part of the division's success rested on its ultra-lean operation. Winkelman had preached the religion of cost containment from his earliest days at J. Aron, and nothing had dimmed his belief.

Although by mid-decade J. Aron would be melded into the much larger fixed income division, in the early 1990s it still operated in its own world. Early on, Rubin and Winkelman had risked entering new businesses, like petroleum and grain trading, outside Goldman Sachs's traditional bailiwick. They encouraged those who worked for them to experiment and take risks, which was easier to do in a small division with a less rigid culture and more malleable structure. By 1990 the newly created oil trading department was up and running, and a proprietary trading unit speculating with the partners' capital had been established alongside the foreign exchange business. J. Aron traders speculated in coffee and grains, while the foreign exchange sales force produced a steady stream of innovative financial products to place before a client base with a growing appetite for sophisticated hedging techniques. Winkelman kept tight control of his operations, insisting on state-of-the-art technology to monitor traders' positions and measure risk.

When the London foreign exchange traders suffered their first major trading loss, manager Mike O'Brien was devastated. Rubin, unconcerned, told O'Brien not to worry. He offered the younger trader a story about losses he had incurred on a large trade designed to benefit from rising oil prices and inflation in 1979. On an unrealized basis, the risk arbitrage department trade had lost more money in a single month than the entire firm had made in any year prior to that. "It was sort of like an earthquake," Rubin remembers. But Rubin never lost his nerve, and although year-end bonuses for the entire firm rested on this single trade, he rode out the storm. "You go through enough of those kinds of situations, you learn to live with difficult decisions," Rubin said. Rubin gave O'Brien reassurance of his support. Despite occasional setbacks, risk arbitrage went on to become the second most profitable department of the firm, after mergers and acquisitions.

The message was clear: Losses are a part of trading; learn something from them and move on. Rubin grew up with trading risk. He believed in well-researched bets and carefully analyzed risk-reward calculations. Entirely comfortable with the downside, he argued that "as long as there are risks there will be losses. If the day ever comes when there are no risks, there will also be no profits." In difficult times Rubin and Winkelman showed understanding, and in good times they pushed even harder. But the setbacks were few, and the division profited from frighteningly successful currency speculation and the turbulence created in the oil markets by the Gulf War. In 1991, with international economist David Morrison issuing a string of accurate predictions, J. Aron had a small stable of experienced traders and a well-connected sales force, with the market's prevailing winds at their back.

With higher profits and greater financial disclosure came increased pressure. When the Goldman Sachs partnership was a small, closely held organization far from the media's gaze, a difficult year was its own business and spectacular years could be kept under wraps. For decades all that was known about the firm's profits was the ambiguous statement published in each annual review—"the average [earnings] of the last five years was above $20 million." The firm was still making modest claims in 1979 when profits had already reached $117.5 million. Now in the glare of *Wall Street Week*, CNBC, and even the British tabloid newspapers, much would be made of a bad quarter, and a bad year would generate a mountain of unfavorable publicity. A good year yielded a crop of stories speculating on partners' personal wealth. Still determined to stay out of the limelight, Goldman Sachs initially refused to comment on its financial results. The firm took pains to maintain a low profile, until recently preferring to keep its name, its profitability, and its growing financial power out of the newspapers. Many within the firm declined to be interviewed, and those partners who did converse with the press spoke in vague terms that revealed little about the firm. Partners still hoped that as part of a private company they might lead quiet lives, with their businesses and their personal fortunes shielded from public view. But the press had become increasingly interested in the most profitable investment bank in the world, and stories that attempted to shatter the image of a completely harmonious organization with almost infallible management appeared with increasing regularity.

The Goldman Sachs mystique was born of secrecy and success. Nothing like it exists on Wall Street. Long after all the other major Wall Street firms had gone public and been forced to disgorge once-confidential information to their shareholders, Goldman Sachs kept its counsel. Even after partners retired from the firm, a few under acrimonious circumstances, no one spoke publicly; it was instilled in the culture—and in most cases the firm still had their money. (Until 1996, partners who retired and became limited partners took half their capital out at retirement and the remainder over five years. Many chose to leave their capital with the firm for much longer periods of time.) Nothing was explained unless it became a public relations problem, because revealing anything might create such a problem. The firm called this its passive-defensive approach and expended almost no effort on image building. While its competitors spent millions on shaping their public images—including television campaigns in which Smith Barney boasted about making money the old-fashioned way, and the Merrill Lynch bull wandered loose in a china shop—Goldman Sachs just went about the business of investment banking, paying little more attention to the media than it had for the past half of a century. (It was not until after Jon Corzine took over as senior partner in 1994 that the firm established an internal office of corporate communications designated to deal with the press in 1996.) By 1991 the Freeman episode was ancient history, and Goldman Sachs had an almost pristine name. The Water Street venture was a blip on the radar screen and had left the long-term reputation of the firm undiminished. Little was known about the last major Wall Street partnership, and many found it intriguing.

The mystique only grew with financial success. Everyone on Wall Street wanted to be a Goldman Sachs partner. As Michael Lewis, author of *Liar's Poker*, pointed out, for anyone who could not make it as a professional sportsman or a rock-and-roll star, there was no better-paying job in the world than working on Wall Street. And there was no better-paying job on Wall Street than being a partner of Goldman Sachs. Long a mark of prestige and accomplishment, a Goldman Sachs partnership took on even greater luster as the firm's returns soared. But it was not an easy honor to obtain. In 1990 the firm's four thousand vice-presidents were all competing for the same thirty-two coveted partnership spots.

GOLDMAN SACHS anoints new partners every other year. The carefully constructed and painstaking process by which individuals are selected to join the club begins two months before the announcements are made. In August of even-numbered years every partner is asked for a list of nominations from the ranks of the firm's vice-presidents. Written nominations are submitted to the management committee, and a preliminary list, including up to one hundred names, is assembled. Endorsement letters are filed from all over the firm, and the partnership selection subcommittee takes weeks to sort through the paperwork. For each candidate in serious contention a background check is conducted. Quietly, with the candidate presumably unaware, the firm looks for any sign of trouble—unpaid taxes or student loans, minor infractions—that might have slipped by in the initial hiring process or occurred since. Then what the firm calls "cross ruffing" begins: For three weeks division heads and management committee members seek information on candidates from outside their area, looking to construct a full picture of each candidate.

The process is watched closely inside and outside the firm. Up for grabs in 1992 was a salary of more than $150,000 and 0.25 percent of the firm's future profits. For a first-year partner in 1993, this amounted to total compensation of more than $4 million.

The list is winnowed down, and in the early fall a more select list, with sixty or so names, is compiled. On a Sunday in October, the management committee meets at a midtown hotel. There, in total seclusion, the penultimate list is formed. The Sunday meeting often lasts well into the night. The future of the firm is shaped in these meetings. The individuals chosen, their values and personalities, determine the course of the firm's history. Equally important are the messages conveyed by this selection process—messages that can alter the behavior of the remaining managing directors and vice-presidents waiting in the wings.

More than once, Steve Friedman used the partnership process to make a point to the firm's top professionals. He thought it would be nice if all the firm's employees liked their jobs, admired their bosses, and felt loyal to Goldman Sachs. But he knew the organization would thrive only if the actions that made each individual successful also made the firm successful. He also knew that his sermons about the firm's priorities often caused his audience's eyes to glaze over. So he sent his message in such a way that it could not be ignored—through his partnership selections. "You will be rewarded for doing what is best for the organization," was Rubin's and Friedman's message. A banker who went willingly to Japan, after others had offered excuses ranging from fear of flying to worries about their pet surviving the trip, was promoted ahead of his class. Overseas assignments, once looked upon as a ticket to nowhere, were now tracks to partnership. Teamwork was emphasized in this highly subjective process. As Friedman remembers, "This is not some schmaltzy, feel-good talk. I have looked people in the eye and said, 'You did not become a partner this time despite your basic abilities, your candle power, your energy. You had all the goods to have achieved it, but you didn't become a partner because you were perceived as having too damned much of your own agenda, and you were not focusing on what we were telling you was in the broader interest of the firm.' " The message came across.

On the following Monday, the management committee presents its list to the entire partnership. Although there is no specific number of partnership slots to be filled, it is understood that the management committee's list will be trimmed. Efforts have been made in recent years to increase

the number of non-U.S. nationals and minority candidates. To jog partners' memories, a fact sheet is distributed on each candidate, along with a
photograph and a few lines of description. Partners are encouraged to
speak for or against the candidates as their brief vitae are presented
alphabetically. Having an articulate defender never hurt, but anyone can
be blackballed. While most have praised the process, suggesting that by
and large the best candidates are selected, it is in this final stage where
politics come into play. The growth in the size of the firm means that
partners no longer can be personally familiar with all the candidates, and
a certain amount of horse trading has crept into the game.

The management committee meets Monday night to prepare the final
list, and on Tuesday it is presented to the entire partnership for approval.
Although even at this late date a name can be deleted from or added
to the list, in practice few alterations are made. Later in the day the list
is made public. Those selected are telephoned by the senior partner
and given the good news. Many of those passed over are taken aside by
a partner and told to sit tight. Others are left to infer what they will,
and there is usually a small contingent that beats a hasty retreat, after
bonuses are paid, to managing directorships at one of the firm's major
competitors.

At the end of 1991, Rubin and Friedman had every reason to be proud
of their firm's achievements. The reputation of Goldman Sachs was of the
highest caliber, the firm had made more than a billion dollars, and it was
on its way to becoming one of the first truly global investment banks.
During the course of the year the management committee revived the idea
of taking the firm public, but before a proposal could be placed before the
partnership, events overtook the firm, and the idea had to be dropped
once again.

ON OCTOBER 22, 1991, Eric Sheinberg met with Robert Maxwell for
the last time. Goldman Sachs was fed up. Maxwell's loan payments to the
firm were months overdue, and the firm began to make threats. If Goldman Sachs was not paid immediately it would begin to sell Maxwell's collateral in the market to realize the value of the loans. After months of
begging for more time, making excuses, and proffering lies, Maxwell's
response was succinct: "If you do that, you'll kill me."

When the British media tycoon fell off his boat on November 5, 1991,
his empire went over the side of a cliff, dragging with it the reputation of
the companies, among them Goldman Sachs, that had worked with
Maxwell during his rise to fame and fortune. The firm had had close ties
with the Maxwell organizations, and some partners of Goldman Sachs's
London office had feared this day for years.

When Goldman Sachs took on Maxwell it failed to follow the first rule of Wall Street: Know your client. Maxwell's professional reputation was far from unblemished and much about his empire was hidden from view. First in 1954 and again in 1971, Maxwell was censured by British financial authorities. In 1971 inspectors from the Department of Trade and Industry (DTI) were adamant about his conduct and in a report whose findings were made public concluded, "In reporting to shareholders and investors, he had a reckless and unjustified optimism which enabled him on some occasions to disregard unpalatable facts and on others to state what he must have known to be untrue. We regret having to conclude that, notwithstanding Mr. Maxwell's acknowledged abilities and energy, he is not in our opinion a person who can be relied upon to exercise proper stewardship of a publicly quoted company." Maxwell challenged the inspectors' findings but was defeated in the Court of Appeals.

Maxwell's business practices had never changed. As his son Kevin admitted at his own trial (at which he was acquitted), "My father would stretch the law as far as it would go to achieve his business ends. There was the letter of the law and the spirit of the law." While Goldman Sachs was aware of Maxwell's sullied name, they believed from the outset that they could safely do business with him in an arm's-length manner, always keeping at a safe distance.

Robert Maxwell was a financial legend. A Czech immigrant, born Jan Ludwig Hoch, he came to Britain in 1940 and in the immediate postwar period built a vast publishing empire. He served in Parliament for the Labour Party, pledging allegiance to socialism while assiduously reaping the benefits of his new capitalist homeland. He was the father of nine; his two youngest sons, Ian and Kevin, eventually took leading roles in his businesses. Robert Maxwell had a reputation for brains, daring, imagination, and egoism that seemed to know no bounds. He inspired admiration, jealousy, contempt, and fear. He created and recreated his own image: the devoted father, the philanthropist, the brilliant publisher, the survivor. He was a raider before it was fashionable and suffered paper losses of £300 million on the day of the 1987 stock market crash. Throughout the 1980s, Maxwell bought and sold companies, tearing the pieces apart and capturing the windfall. Like so many other empire builders, he acquired ever more expensive properties at the height of an economic boom, all with somebody else's money. The highly predictable results were financially disastrous and personally devastating. Although he spent a lifetime carefully constructing his public persona, his final and lasting image—that of a thief and a swindler—would be out of his hands.

Goldman Sachs's relationship with Maxwell began when the firm rented space in an office building owned by the publisher in the Holborn area of London, just up the road from Fleet Street. Although the London office had moved to larger premises in 1985, down the block from the Old Bailey, the small office was overcrowded with 268 employees, and the firm rented extra space in Maxwell House, the headquarters of Maxwell Communications Corporation (MCC). Goldman Sachs undertook its first piece of business with Maxwell in 1986 when Eric Sheinberg bid on a £200 million portfolio of shares Maxwell was offering. Sheinberg had never heard of Maxwell and the deal was a minor success, but the business was welcomed as the firm was trying to establish itself as a major player in the London market.

When Maxwell had large blocks of shares to sell, it was no surprise that he sought out Sheinberg to do his business. Sheinberg and Goldman Sachs had already made a name for themselves in block trading in London, which was dubbed by *Euromoney*, a trade magazine for the international banking industry, "the most macho game in town."

Sheinberg, a trim man with gray hair and a Brooklyn accent, loved Goldman Sachs. He had come to the firm as a college student in 1956 with Peter Sachs, and the two began their careers, like so many others of their era, as outdoor runners, delivering securities between banking houses. After one week in the hot sun, Sheinberg and Peter Sachs convinced his father Howard Sachs that they were meant for better things, and they became indoor runners. The job was not any easier, but at least there was air-conditioning. For the next two summers Sheinberg worked for Goldman Sachs, and shortly before he returned to Wharton for his senior year, Gus Levy insisted that he come back permanently once he had a degree. Levy taught Sheinberg many things, but the most important was about risk. Never worry about how much money you are going to make on a trade, Levy would warn his disciple; focus instead on how much you are going to lose if you make a mistake.

By 1991, Sheinberg had been with Goldman Sachs for thirty years, twenty of them as a partner. Working in the firm's London office, he brought Levy's legacy to Europe. Although the business had been thriving in the United States for four decades, block trading in Europe was still in the dark ages. When a European company or investor had a sizable block of shares to sell, it quietly approached its banker and asked for a price. The banker, after much deliberation, agreed to purchase the shares for perhaps 10 percent below the market price. In most cases the deals were pre-placed, buyers lined up even before the banker took delivery of the stock. To Sheinberg this antiquated market spelled opportunity. He said: "If a client called you up and he wanted to sell $50 million of stock, Fidelity calls Goldman, and you bid it down 10 percent, and you would probably never hear from Fidelity again. Stocks in the United States trade on an organized exchange. It's around the last sale, give or take some-thing, a half a percent, 1 percent, probably maximum. In the U.K. and in Europe, it was the most fantastic thing in the world. Anytime somebody wanted to buy a block of stock, he paid up 10 percent, and any time he wanted to sell it he sells down 10 percent for the market. It was the crazi-est thing I ever saw." This kind of trading had died years ago in the United States, where investment banks vied to buy large blocks of stock in an extremely competitive price environment. Few of the European bro-ker dealers or the foreign subsidiaries of U.S. banks had the capital or appetite for risk to take on very substantial blocks of stock for a competi-tive price. Goldman Sachs had done a number of notable European block trades before 1991; this was a market made for Goldman Sachs.

One of the trades that caught the market's attention and solidified Goldman Sachs's reputation came in 1991 when the Vuitton family of France wanted to sell 400,000 shares (worth 3.2 percent of the company) of Moët Hennessy Louis Vuitton (LVMH). The French bank Paribas had for years served as banker to both LVMH and the Vuitton family. It had been rumored that a large sale was in the works, and Paribas probably thought it had the business sewn up. Sheinberg, through Goldman Sachs Paris, met with representatives of the Vuitton family and presented the firm's trading credentials. A few weeks later Goldman Sachs was asked to bid against the rival French bank for the shares. Sheinberg learned that the other bankers involved in the competition had bid below the prevail-ing price—in other words, business as usual. When Goldman Sachs bid the market price, the last sale, they walked away with the deal.

The transaction had been widely anticipated in the market. Traders had been selling LVMH shares short in the expectation that a huge supply of shares would swamp the market, driving prices sharply lower. Later they hoped to repurchase shares at the deflated price, thus locking in a profit. (In order to sell shares short, traders must borrow them from a market participant who is already holding them. Once the shares are repurchased in the market, the borrowed shares are returned.) Shein-berg's long experience came into play; he had seen this many times before. Aided by France's computer-driven stock trading system, Sheinberg—now the owner of $320 million worth of LVMH—made a very public bid for additional shares, a bid that could be seen on the screens of all the major market participants. The audacity of this move was monumental. At first, the short sellers did not believe it and continued to sell. Shein-berg, meanwhile, continued to buy, ultimately purchasing in the market an additional 2 percent of the company. Initially the firm was simply recycling stock that it had sold to investors, who were now selling as well, but as the market realized that Sheinberg was there to stay the selling dried up and the price began to rise. Dealers who had shorted the stocks and reached their pain threshold began to panic and cover their shorts. Goldman Sachs, in turn, sold all of its shares, not through the thin and transparent broker's market, which would have been unable to absorb such volume, but through an institutional placement to large investors all over the world. The shares were actually sold at a premium to the prevailing market price, with Goldman Sachs arguing convincingly that they had "antique value" and it might be many years before a block of similar size in this closely held company would be available again. Goldman Sachs's profits on this single deal were estimated at $10 million. The firm had brought real competitive pricing to Europe, changing the market for block trading forever.

In the late 1980s, Sheinberg had undertaken a number of block trades for Robert Maxwell, and the firm had acted as underwriter on a few small flotations by Maxwell-owned companies, including the Berlitz language schools and the Overseas Airline Guide (OAG). In 1989 the partners of the Goldman Sachs London office met in Maxwell House to discuss the burgeoning relationship. They argued strenuously that Maxwell was not someone with whom the firm should develop a close relationship. They acquainted the firm with the DTI investigation and its censure. They felt the official reprimand had substance, and that the management committee should take this warning very seriously.

Some investment bankers in London had found the Maxwells— Robert and his son Kevin—to be difficult clients. "Both Maxwells behaved appallingly," recalled one banker. "Kevin worst of all. We soon hated them." The London partners sent their warning to the management committee in New York. After considering the warning, the answer came back: Goldman Sachs could do business with Robert Maxwell, but only in a limited and circumscribed way. As one London partner remembers, this was the last time the partners in London held any formal discussion of their relationship with Maxwell. The next time the issue was raised would be after the publisher's death two years later. In 1989, Maxwell's business and the possibilities it held were thought too profitable for the firm to ignore. The London office was still trying hard to establish itself. Maxwell was one of the biggest trading forces in the City (as the London financial district is called), and his empire threw off a huge number of investment banking deals, including buying and selling companies, currencies, and real estate. The management committee decided the firm would conduct what they call "plain vanilla" securities transactions—the buying and selling of shares—with Maxwell, as the risk involved in this kind of business was deemed negligible. Between 1989 and 1991, Goldman Sachs traded hundreds of millions of pounds worth of MCC shares back and forth with Maxwell.

In choosing to do business with Maxwell, Goldman Sachs was in good company. While Maxwell singled out Goldman Sachs as one of his favorite brokers, he spread his profitable business to others. Almost every major bank in the City, many of them American, lent Maxwell money, so that when he disappeared over the railing of his yacht he collectively owed his bankers £2.8 billion. One American banker and longtime Maxwell counterpart in London explained his allure: "Maxwell paid over the odds. His business was hugely profitable, and so many were willing to ignore what they knew." Maxwell presented his bankers with financial information that was incomplete or often misleading; the precise relationship of his myriad of companies was often difficult to discern. Yet many top institutions failed to heed the flood of well-founded rumors when faced with a client so willing to pay their hefty fees. Goldman Sachs makes much of the value it places on its reputation, working hard to maintain it and stating its importance in every annual review. Yet the firm took a risk with this intangible asset when it developed a close yet combative relationship with the shady Maxwell. As the *Economist* noted shortly after the publisher's drowning, "Of all the reputations smudged by the scandal, that of Goldman Sachs, an American investment bank, was the brightest."

Maxwell's closest relationship at Goldman Sachs was with Sheinberg, who at the time believed that there was no reason to be overly concerned about Maxwell's reputation. "I took it on faith that Robert Maxwell was an honest person," Sheinberg said later. "Now he turned out to be a crook, I can't help it—I didn't know. Here's somebody who's supposedly one of the richest people in the world, a good client of Goldman Sachs, a good client of many other firms, a good client of many banks, running around with kings, queens, and presidents, you know."

In 1990, Goldman Sachs began active trading in the shares of MCC. MCC was at the center of a web of four hundred private companies, spun by Maxwell with the help of his lawyers. For Goldman Sachs, which was trying at the time to establish itself as a major player in the U.K. equity market, the large trades provided both credibility and commissions. For Maxwell this was a chance to do business with the big boys. Goldman Sachs was on its way to the top of the world league; no British institution came close. Other market participants would see Goldman Sachs purchasing shares and take note. Part of what Maxwell was buying with his commissions was the reflected glory of Goldman Sachs's reputation.

Maxwell wanted the world to know he was a billionaire. He lived in a world of private jets, helicopters, an exclusive London penthouse, tight security, a huge personal staff, and his famous yacht, the *Lady Ghislaine*, on which he traveled the world. His personal fortune was estimated at £1.2 billion. While his wealth was acknowledged by all, most of his companies were private, and few hard numbers existed.

Yet, Maxwell's empire rested heavily on a mountain of bank debt which was in turn secured by the share price of MCC. Maxwell had offered these shares as collateral to banks in order to secure large loans. The price of MCC was the key to his empire's solvency. If the price fell too far, additional collateral in the form of liquid securities or cash would be required by Maxwell's legion of bankers. This in turn would cause the share price to drop further and fuel a vicious circle that could not easily be broken. The price of MCC shares had to be maintained at all costs.

The share price was also psychologically important to Maxwell. MCC was in the prestigious FTSE-100 index (the British equivalent of the Dow Jones Industrial Average), an important badge of success, and if the share price declined too much, the market capitalization of the company would fall and Maxwell would suffer the humiliation of having MCC booted out of the index. To Maxwell, the price of MCC was also a barometer of the investing public's esteem, a referendum on his personal performance.

Sheinberg and Maxwell were both acutely aware of this situation and both used it to their best advantage. In Maxwell, Sheinberg had a client who traded in huge volume and often acted in an uneconomic manner. Maxwell, on the other hand, assumed that he could borrow money from and trade with Goldman Sachs even if he failed on payments and delivered shares late, because the firm would not want to be seen harassing clients or dumping their collateral in the market, especially in London where it was a newcomer. So it began, two titans playing a game of chicken that each assumed the other could afford to lose.

In 1991, Sheinberg was the third most senior partner at Goldman Sachs. At fifty, he was older and more experienced than most other traders. Yet he brought to his trading a young man's intensity—with screens at home he would trade securities day and night, taking advantage of opportunities wherever he could find them. "It used to be when the phone rang at two o'clock in the morning, someone died," says Sheinberg. "Now someone wants to do a trade." Sheinberg was an old-fashioned trader, relying heavily on gut feel and instinct to guide him. He hailed from a trading era with less technology and more trust, from a time when most of the major players in the market would have known each other. "Listen, I've never been involved in a situation like this," he explained, lapsing into his familiar tough trader talk. "To me, your word is your bond. If you lie in this business, you're dead meat, all right."

In 1985, Sheinberg had become co-head of international equity trading with Robert Freeman. After Freeman's indictment, Sheinberg assumed sole responsibility for the division. During these years Sheinberg spent about a third of his time in London, living in a hotel. He was well known to all the members of the management committee and had wide discretionary powers. By his own admission he was on a long rein, and his seniority meant that few in London could question him.

The publisher and the trader had many interests in common. Both were involved in Jewish philanthropy and both loved the financial markets. Sheinberg was closer in age to Maxwell than to the legions of twenty-five-year-olds seated on trading desks all over London, or to their thirty-year-old bosses. As a trader Sheinberg chose to speak to few clients, and Maxwell was probably flattered to be dealing with such a long-standing partner of the firm. Over time, Sheinberg became Maxwell's main point of contact at Goldman Sachs, and it was to Sheinberg he turned again and again when he was in trouble.

Throughout 1990 and 1991, Sheinberg repeatedly bought large amounts of MCC shares in the market—five, ten, twenty million shares at a time—which he in turn sold profitably to Maxwell's private companies. The buying escalated. By August 1990, Maxwell already owned more than 50 percent of the outstanding shares of MCC. For Sheinberg the relationship appeared to have limited downside. If he bought MCC shares and the price rose he could simply sell them in the market. If the price declined, Maxwell might buy them, as he had in the past shown his readiness to take them off Sheinberg's hands, although there was no prior agreement or guarantee that this would be the case. But markets are about risks and rewards and one does not exist without the other.

In 1991, Goldman Sachs dominated the market in trading shares of MCC; in the first seven months of the year the firm on average traded more than 50 percent of all MCC shares. In July the firm figured in 72 percent of the transactions. As an article in the *Economist* explained shortly after Maxwell's death, "Goldman was the biggest market-maker in MCC shares and its keenness on the otherwise unpopular stock kept its price up late in 1990 and in the first half of this year [1991]." Market participants certainly would have noticed if Goldman Sachs made large public sales of MCC stock, but Maxwell could ill afford that and he continued to buy the shares from Sheinberg. Some Goldman Sachs partners have since questioned the wisdom of such trading, asking if this was really the way Goldman Sachs should be making money, but it was entirely legal.

Maxwell believed there was a bear raid on the shares of MCC, and he claimed Sheinberg had told him so. A bear raid occurs when traders act in concert to sell shares short, forcing the price lower. Although illegal, bear raids have been known to happen. A group of savvy traders working together could have an excruciating effect on a thinly traded share like MCC. Maxwell was predisposed to believe in the bear raid because it would explain the dramatic fall in the value of MCC. Rather than focus on the company's economic fundamentals—MCC's large borrowings had severely strained its finances, and its credit rating had been downgraded in 1990—Maxwell found it easier to believe that a conspiracy lay behind the decline in his share price. Frightened by what this would do to his empire, Maxwell, according to the testimony of his son Kevin, "agreed to follow the advice of Eric Sheinberg and to engage in a concerted and sustained pattern of purchasing shares in MCC, i.e., in an attempt to drive the price up by forcing the bears out of the market."

Sheinberg, Kevin said, had told him and his father that if the raid failed and the bears could be stopped they would be forced to buy back their shares to cover their exposure at skyrocketing prices. According to Kevin, Sheinberg estimated that the price of MCC could double or triple under such conditions. This would have been music to Maxwell's ears. If the price of MCC rose in any meaningful way, some of the financial pressure his empire was under would be eased. Over the course of 1990 and 1991, Maxwell spent an incredible £400 million purchasing shares of MCC, much of it through Goldman Sachs.

Sheinberg strenuously disagrees with Kevin's testimony. "The only recommendation I ever gave Robert Maxwell, and this is what gets me PO'd when the London papers say I was his advisor, the only advice I ever gave him was to tell him not to buy his own shares, and he wouldn't listen, but that's life. . . . [What Maxwell] could never understand is why nobody wanted to own the shares. Probably one of the reasons I got along with him was because I told him the truth—nobody liked him."

Sheinberg had three reasons for buying the shares. First, he was generating profits for his department, and this would look good to management in New York. Second, by such substantial trading Sheinberg would establish himself and his firm as a "player" in a London market long dominated by British institutions. Finally, Sheinberg believed that the large number of short positions in the market were vulnerable. Sheinberg testified to the SEC that he did not intend to "squeeze the shorts" but recognized that his buying did have a positive effect on the price of MCC. Sheinberg regularly held positions of up to 20 million shares, worth at times $50 million, and if Maxwell's continued buying forced the price to rise, Goldman Sachs stood to make a killing.

In March 1990, Maxwell approached Sheinberg about buying a call option on 10 million shares of MCC. Goldman Sachs had never done an options trade with Maxwell, and Sheinberg was surprised by the request. An option, Maxwell was incorrect in assuming, would not need to be reported publicly, and thus the extent of his buying could be hidden. An option would also allow cash-strapped Maxwell to delay payment for the shares. The call option Maxwell purchased from Goldman Sachs gave him the right but not the obligation to buy 10 million shares of MCC from the firm three months hence, at a price agreed upon at the time the option was written. A premium, a sort of fee for the privilege, would be due up front, but the shares would not be paid for in full until the end of June if the option was in fact exercised. Maxwell hoped Goldman Sachs would enter the market and buy MCC shares to cover the exposure created by this option (the shares the firm might need to sell Maxwell three months hence), thereby putting upward pressure on the price. He was to be disappointed. Sheinberg was already holding most of the shares.

In thirty years of trading Sheinberg had never priced an option, so he went to one of the firm's options traders asking for a fair price. When Sheinberg presented the price to Robert Maxwell, Kevin objected. By his calculations Goldman Sachs was charging too much; the agreed price would be 10 percent lower. Hedging an option requires precise knowledge of an array of complex market factors. Yet despite knowing little about options, Sheinberg did not transfer the deal to the options experts but instead managed the risk himself.

In August 1990, Sheinberg wanted to dispose of another 15 million shares of MCC and did another option with Maxwell, but this time he priced the deal himself. "I'd done one, so to me it was just numbers picking out of the air," he said later. Goldman Sachs's knowledge in the field of options is second to none. Fisher Black, a partner of the firm at the time, had co-invented the model for pricing options. His discovery of the mathematical method for valuing this instrument brought about a revolution on Wall Street. The Nobel Prize for economics was awarded in 1997 to Robert Merton and Myron Scholes, two of Black's MIT colleagues, for just this discovery (Black had died in 1995). Fair options prices cannot be made up.

Sheinberg used his HP12C calculator, rather than the proprietary software the firm had spent a great deal of time and money over the years developing and perfecting, to calculate that paying 5 pence per share for the right to sell MCC shares three and a half months later at 19 pence above the current market price was a good deal. (Goldman Sachs was buying rather than selling this time.) For a first effort Sheinberg did quite well. The option he had valued at 5 pence was, according to the SEC, worth 31.83 pence; the firm bought the option for £4 million less than it was intrinsically worth. This time Kevin did not interfere but allowed his father to sell Goldman Sachs an option priced at a sixth of the option's true value. Sheinberg justified the incredible prices Maxwell was willing to pay by saying, "First of all, you didn't know the animal, meaning Mr. Maxwell. If he was in the type of a mood where he wanted to buy, you could name your price. He didn't quibble. He just said, 'Done.' " In the fiercely competitive world of investment banking, where counterparts fight over a mere basis point, Maxwell was willingly selling at a remarkable price. A more experienced options trader might have grown concerned; only a savvy investor in trouble or someone well out of his depth would commit to a transaction at such a ludicrous price.

U.K. law forbids the purchase of shares by insiders in the two months prior to the formal announcement of a company's results, the so-called closed period. As Maxwell entered the closed period in September 1990 his empire was in serious trouble. Throughout the summer the price of MCC had continued to fall, not because the company did not have valuable businesses—including Macmillan Publishing Company, Pergamon Press, and OAG—but because of Maxwell himself. Investors did not trust him, and the "Max factor," as it was known, depressed the price below what it might have been under different leadership.

As the closed period grew nearer Maxwell urgently needed to take some action. "Now you have to know with his ego, he loved a fight," Sheinberg recalls. "And since he thought there was a conspiracy going on he was going to fight. Now he was going into the closed period, and he said, Do you have any suggestions. . . . In any event we sold him 20 million [MCC shares before the closed period began]." During the closed period, with Maxwell's purchases at a standstill, MCC shares dropped in value from 152 to 132 pence.

Goldman Sachs's management committee was reconfigured on December 1, 1990, and at its very first meeting the newly assembled body took a hard look at many of the firm's businesses and exposures. Sheinberg received a phone call. The firm was still holding OAG shares from the flotation a year earlier, the foreign exchange department had open contracts with Maxwell for future settlement, and Sheinberg was holding MCC shares. All told, the firm's exposure to Maxwell was estimated by Sheinberg at between $120 million and $160 million. The OAG shares could not be sold; if they could have been, the firm would not still be holding them. On his open foreign exchange positions Maxwell was looking at potential losses of $10 million, and nobody wanted to force him to realize these. Sheinberg's exposure would be the easiest to shrink, and the message from above was clear: Cut it back.

In the early months of 1991, Sheinberg was mystified by the price action in MCC shares. He knew the size of his and Maxwell's holdings, and he knew what buyers friendly to Maxwell held. This combined number was fast approaching 100 percent of the shares. Yet despite all of the buying, the supply continued, and the price declined. "I'm strictly a numbers guy, and this is plain arithmetic to me," Sheinberg explained later to the SEC. "If Maxwell owns 68 percent then I assume that in his ESOP [employee stock option plan] and the pension fund there's probably another 10 or some odd percent and the public must own some." The notion of a free float, or a real market in MCC shares, was disappearing. "At some point in my mind there weren't going to be any more shares," says Sheinberg. Then the shares could go to any price that Maxwell was willing to pay for them. If such a scenario had transpired—the price of MCC rising sharply, perhaps doubling or tripling—the potential profits to anyone holding large blocks could be very substantial.

Reflecting in 1993, Sheinberg said, "I believe that in the beginning of April 1991 it became evident that the short positions in these shares were substantially in excess of anything I could have dreamed." Yet the short sellers had continued to find a source for borrowings despite the fact that Maxwell had many times offered Sheinberg assurances that his own MCC share certificates were in a vault, away from the speculating hordes. Both men had expected the supply of shares to dry up much earlier. Who could still be lending shares to those selling in the market? Sheinberg wondered.

Sheinberg decided it was time to give the market a push, because, he explained, "If the shorts were out there, I was going to participate in getting the shorts." For two months, Sheinberg went through the list of counterparts who had sold MCC shares to Goldman Sachs without arranging the borrowing and delivering the shares. He then issued buy-ins, which allowed him to go into the market and buy the required shares, regardless of the loss to the original counterpart. Although this enforcement procedure was not widely used at the time, Sheinberg remembers, "I decided to enforce it just to squeeze the shorts more, which is in my interests, or Goldman Sachs's interests, because we had the shares."

The tactic seemed to work. Sheinberg's buy-ins, a large divestiture that brought the company £400 million of much-needed cash, along with the news that a well-respected businessman and former Conservative Party cabinet minister, Peter Walker, had agreed to take over as CEO of the company, caused the price of MCC to rise 60 percent from the end of March through the third week in April. Yet Sheinberg admitted that he was a crucial factor in pushing up the price of MCC. As the price rose he continued to buy, accelerating the upward pressure. Now that he had the shorts on the run, he was going to make it hurt. "I think I probably did transactions with the attempt to get shorts to buy shares from me,"

Sheinberg admitted to the SEC. "And the only way you do that is to scare the shorts. . . . At a given point in time, [you ask] do they feel enough pain, because I know I've felt enough pain in my life where I've been short shares and I just say, the hell with it, and I cover my shorts and I go on and do something else."

In the battle with the bears, Sheinberg had made one major miscalculation. Both Maxwell and Sheinberg assumed that the culprits were poorly capitalized minor British stock traders or, as Sheinberg calls them, "spivvy brokers." (Sheinberg's lawyers were asked to explain his vernacular to the SEC. Spivs are street-smart traders. The term originated in the immediate postwar period to describe those who sold rationed items on the black market. Now it is used for "someone who sails very close to the wind and from time to time on the wrong side of it.") Maxwell and Sheinberg were wrong. The second week in April, on a day when the price of MCC rose steeply, Goldman Sachs received four surprising phone calls. U.S. fund managers, some of them major hedge fund operators with billions of dollars under management, turned out to be some of the shorts. Maxwell was at war with powerful forces—those with pockets as deep as his and traders with much greater savvy. Better financed and more sophisticated, these were the kind of players who could and would outlast Maxwell.

The British authorities later investigated Goldman Sachs for an alleged illegal share support scheme. They cleared Goldman Sachs of the charge of helping Maxwell buoy the price of MCC by disguising his purchases. Their conclusion was that Sheinberg did in fact buy independently rather than at Maxwell's behest, only later offering the shares to Maxwell, and that there was "not evidence to support an argument that Goldman Sachs was illegally supporting the MCC share price." Goldman Sachs was exonerated of any illicit activity with Maxwell and his companies.

By early 1991, Maxwell held 68 percent of the shares in MCC, up from 52 percent only nine months earlier. Legally, he was barred from holding more than 70 percent of the company. Once Maxwell hit his limit he directed Sheinberg to other buyers who, he assured Goldman Sachs, were unrelated to Maxwell. Sheinberg assumed they were simply investors "friendly to management."

The procedure Maxwell and Sheinberg followed was usually the same. Once Sheinberg let Maxwell know he had shares to sell, Maxwell would often send him to a Dr. Werner Rechsteiner of Zurich acting on behalf of trusts in Liechtenstein, where it also happens that the Maxwell family fortune was said to reside. Rechsteiner never explained the purpose of his purchases of MCC shares, and Sheinberg did not feel that he needed to ask. "I'd never had a problem with Robert Maxwell," said Sheinberg.

"Maybe other people did, I never did. To the best of my knowledge, every transaction we ever did with him, there was never a question of owner- ship, there was never a question of settlements, everything went like clockwork. That he could be introducing me to somebody who wasn't good for the money or who wasn't, you know, legitimate—what it all turned out to be in 1992 after he went overboard—it was a rude shock for me. To some extent, it still is."

On March 27, 1991, Goldman Sachs made a loan to Maxwell of £25 million secured by 33 million shares of MCC worth about $80 million. The one-week loan was at terms favorable to Goldman Sachs so was never called but instead rolled over every week. The MCC collateral, as the firm would have known, was difficult to value. As the largest market maker in MCC shares, Goldman Sachs itself was the major price discov- ery mechanism. If there were ever a problem it would be hard to say exactly what the collateral was worth. In making the loan the firm was confident either in Maxwell's ability to repay his obligation easily or in its own ability to dispose of the collateral without attracting widespread attention. Either way, Goldman Sachs was mistaken.

In this high-stakes game of brinkmanship, Maxwell had counted on Goldman Sachs miscalculating its own risk. He was in possession of information, particularly about his own unsteady finances, that the investment bank did not have. Maxwell carefully calculated what Gold- man Sachs stood to lose each step of the way. He knew the difficulty the firm would have in selling any collateral and had counted on an unending series of delays if and when Goldman Sachs sought repayment. From his son Kevin's court testimony, it is clear that Maxwell had in mind a series of hurdles he would throw up each time the firm grew impatient with the game.

By April, Maxwell was desperate for cash, and he was going to have to steal to get it. The publisher telephoned Sheinberg with an unusual request: He wanted Goldman Sachs to stand between two buyers and two sellers on some shares of MCC. It would be a simple agency transac- tion. Maxwell would bring Goldman Sachs both sides, and the firm would earn a small commission of £110,000. Sheinberg did not ask Maxwell why he needed Goldman Sachs for the trade. "I didn't see any reason to ask him," he told the SEC. "We are brokers. Our business is shares between buyers and sellers." This is a somewhat unfair characteri- zation. Goldman Sachs's business is to *find* buyers and sellers; they are rarely matched up in advance. It was the first time Maxwell used Gold- man Sachs to steal money, but it was months before the firm uncovered the theft.

Goldman Sachs bought 25 million shares of MCC from two Maxwell pension funds on April 26, 1991, at a total cost of £54.9 million. When the trade settled a month later, the proceeds of these sales were repaid not to the pension funds but, as Kevin Maxwell had directed, to BIT, Maxwell's privately owned company, with which Goldman Sachs had done the earlier options trades. At the time Kevin was no longer a pension fund trustee.

Maxwell had provided the names of two Liechtenstein trusts, Servex and Yakosa, that would purchase the 25 million shares from Goldman Sachs on the same day they bought them from the pension funds. The trusts were in fact indirectly controlled by Maxwell. The payment for the trusts' shares came from BIT—the same entity Goldman Sachs had paid for the shares only hours earlier. In a memo to his father Kevin Maxwell described this arrangement as "self-financing." The money simply moved back and forth from Goldman Sachs to BIT, and then back to Goldman Sachs again, all in the same day without any economic function. Meanwhile, Maxwell had shifted 25 million shares of MCC from his employees' pension funds to his personal companies. These shares could now be used as additional collateral for borrowings for his increasingly illiquid empire.

Correspondence between Goldman Sachs's back office and Kevin Maxwell indicates that payment for the shares on behalf of the trusts would be made by the Maxwell-owned BIT. If someone outside the back office had looked at this document they might have raised questions about why Maxwell's private company was funding share purchases for two trusts with which he allegedly had no connection. But Sheinberg saw this document only after Maxwell was dead and the theft had been uncovered. If he had seen it earlier, he told the SEC, things might have been different. He might have realized that Goldman Sachs was being used to cover Maxwell's tracks, that the deal was cleverly designed to steal shares from the pension fund. If nothing else, it would have been difficult to continue to believe that Rechsteiner and the Liechtenstein trusts were financially independent of Maxwell.

According to Maxwell biographer Tom Bower, someone at Goldman Sachs did indeed recognize the peculiar nature of the trade. It was reported that two back-office employees can be heard to say on tape on the settlement day, "We can't get the purchase money from BIT until we pay the money for the sale to BIT." Yet the trade sailed through unimpeded.

In the summer of 1991, Goldman Sachs had a client to whom it was highly exposed. The client was the source of a great deal of bad publicity, some of which had already reflected poorly on the firm. Yet Goldman Sachs would in the end achieve a dominant role in all areas of investment banking in the British capital ultimately in spite of, rather than with the help of, Maxwell.

Sheinberg returned to New York from a vacation in Europe on July 15, 1991, and was startled when his phone rang at 2:30 a.m. It was Maxwell's secretary calling; she had Mr. Maxwell on the line. "I said 'What the hell does this screwball want at this hour?' " says Sheinberg. "And I didn't want to disturb my wife so I said, 'Tell him I'll call him back.' I got out of bed and I went to my lounge and called him back after counting to about twenty because I'd start to scream and yell, 'What's so goddamn important?' "

Maxwell was distraught. Once again he turned to his broker in a panic. "They're attacking, they're attacking," Maxwell cried. He explained to Sheinberg that there was an article in that morning's *Independent* saying that the newly appointed chairman, Peter Walker, who had provided MCC with so much credibility, would not be taking up his position.

To Sheinberg, this was worrying news. Walker was a key asset, and without him Sheinberg was not as interested in holding MCC shares. Sheinberg determined to keep his positions down, not letting them rise above 10 million shares.

Once again Rechsteiner purchased more shares of MCC. The trades had been booked for accounts with names like Jungo Stifftung, Kiara Stifftung, and Baccano Stifftung. Goldman Sachs has both corporate and individual accounts. Sheinberg's secretary had looked at the names and operated on the assumption that the accounts were for individuals. When Rechsteiner telephoned one day she asked, "How many individuals are there in the Stifftung family?" Rechsteiner answered, "It's not a family, it's a foundation." Then he asked her to keep it a secret. She immediately put him on hold and walked into Sheinberg's office to tell him what she had learned. She was upset; thinking the accounts were for a group of individuals, she had sent out the wrong new account form; everything would now need to be amended. Initially, Sheinberg assumed the problem to be an administrative error until a few days later on the golf course. "I started to think that weekend," he said, "you know, why the heck would a foundation be buying the shares? And then it dawned on me, Jesus, could this—that was the first inkling I had that maybe somehow Maxwell was connected with these." Sheinberg had asked both Maxwell and Rechsteiner if there was a connection; the answers had always been no.

On July 24, Kevin and Robert Maxwell asked Sheinberg if he would do a program trade for them. Goldman Sachs would buy and later resell a basket of hundreds of shares, from a dozen different countries, all for one price of £37 million. Normally on such trades the firm receives the shares

Marcus Goldman gave his name and progeny to the small family firm that would become one of the greatest financial success stories of the twentieth century.

Samuel Sachs joined his father-in-law in 1882, thus creating Goldman Sachs & Co. He was the voice of conservatism at the firm, nurturing the commercial paper business, developing European contacts, and sometimes reining in his more daring brother-in-law, Henry Goldman.

Goldman's first office, opened in 1869, was in the basement of 30 Pine Street in lower Manhattan. In the 1930s, by coincidence, the firm relocated to the same spot.

The youngest son of Samuel Sachs, Walter (left), was connected with the firm for seventy-two years. Here, h is testifying in Washington, D.C., before the Senate Banking and Currency Committee in 1932.

This photograph was taken to commemorate the golden wedding anniversary of Marcus and Bertha Goldma in 1900. The family photo includes seven partners of the firm. Henry Goldman can be seen in the top row o the far right.

The Goldman Sachs Trading Corporation, an investment trust established on the eve of the stock market crash of 1929, was developed under Waddill Catchings. The firm and its 42,000 investors would lose 92 percent of the value of their investment.

Sidney Weinberg, the father of the modern Goldman Sachs, worked for the firm for sixty-two years, reigning as its senior partner for thirty-nine years.

Goldman Sachs's first management committee in the late 1960s. Sidney Weinberg (center, talking) would be succeeded by Gustave Levy (standing to his left) in 1969, and later by John Whitehead and his son John Weinberg. Levy was known for his trading genius, stamina, benevolence, and temper.

One of the firm's early trading floors where Goldman Sachs pioneered some of the most daring trading practices, such as risk arbitrage and block trading. (Robert Rubin, future co-senior partner of Goldman Sachs and Secretary of the Treasury, can be seen on the phone at the very rear.)

The "two Johns," as senior partners Whitehead (seated) and Weinberg were known, brought modern management and organization to a small family firm, internationalizing its business and elevating it to the top tier of investment banking. Weinberg was to many the "heart of the firm."

John Weinberg's management committee presented a united front when it proposed that the partnership sell the firm, yet many doubted the senior partners' resolve. Events then overtook the firm and the partnership did not reconsider a sale for another decade.

Robert Freeman, the firm's head of risk arbitrage, was arrested in 1987 on charges of insider trading. Here, he is seen in 1989 after pleading guilty to a single charge. He served 108 days in jail.

Stephen Friedman (left) and Robert Rubin, who began their tenure as co-senior partners in 1990, took the firm into new businesses, dramatically increased its profitability, and brought it to the very pinnacle of investment banking. Rubin joined the Clinton administration and Friedman departed in 1994.

Friedman, here with Ralph Lauren, accurately foresaw the opportunities for the firm in investing directly in ongoing businesses. Over the vocal opposition of many partners, he established the firm's principal investments area. Goldman Sachs made a major investment in Lauren's fashion business and later led the successful initial public offering.

Goldman Sachs's worldwide headquarters, located three blocks south of Wall Street, is built over the remains of a seventeenth-century tavern. The firm's name does not appear on the front of the building, only the number "85."

Peterborough Court, on London's Fleet Street, serves as the firm's European headquarters. Behind the old facade of the *Daily Telegraph* rises a towering steel-and-glass structure.

Robert Maxwell, the disgraced media tycoon, traded heavily through the firm's London office in the early 1990s. Goldman Sachs received a great deal of adverse publicity because of its dealings with him.

The heartbeat of capitalism can be heard on the firm's massive modern trading floors, like this one in New York. Although the technology has advanced rapidly, some things—the piles of financial reports, trade tickets, personal photos, newspapers, bottles of aspirin, half-finished cups of coffee and half-eaten meals that are stacked on every horizontal surface—have remained unchanged.

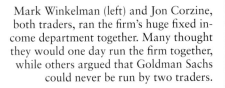

Mark Winkelman (left) and Jon Corzine, both traders, ran the firm's huge fixed income department together. Many thought they would one day run the firm together, while others argued that Goldman Sachs could never be run by two traders.

Hank Paulson and Corzine reengineered the firm in 1994 and brought it out of its darkest days since the Depression. While the pair have been credited with aggressively pursuing new markets and new business opportunities, they will undoubtedly be remembered for generating a consensus in 1998 for taking the firm public. Corzine stepped down as co–chief executive in early 1999.

before it pays out the funds, but Robert Maxwell was anxious to do this trade for settlement the following day. He wanted the funds immediately. The Maxwells lived in a world of crisis management, leaving everything to the last minute, and Sheinberg assumed once again that this was the case. The Maxwell empire was indeed in crisis, as the need for cash loomed larger. Despite Sheinberg's developing concerns about Robert Maxwell's honesty, he decided to pay out the money in advance of the delivery, telling Larry Woods, the head of the London back office, that "a deal is a deal." On July 30, when Sheinberg came to London, Woods was worried; payment had been made but the shares had never arrived. Woods had more bad news. Maxwell had failed to deliver on a foreign exchange transaction for £29 million. Sheinberg was furious: "I had a major problem at that point in time. I had paid out, I think, $40 million [*sic*]. And all I had was air. I was holding air."

Sheinberg reached Maxwell by telephone on his yacht and said, "Listen, how the hell can you do business like this? You can't sell shares and not deliver them. I've already paid you the money. This is not the way this business works, and you won't be able to do business with anybody if you do this." Maxwell had been operating in the financial markets for many decades, and he should have needed no reminder of how things worked, but his were the actions of a desperate man. Maxwell told Sheinberg, "Go over and see Kevin, and he'll come clean with you." The two offices were in walking distance of each other, but before Sheinberg set out Woods gave him another piece of troubling information. The Goldman Sachs back office had determined through the market grapevine that the shares in question had been loaned out by the pension funds. This was not an administrative foul-up; Maxwell could not deliver the shares because he did not have them. A few minutes later Kevin expressed bewilderment at the missing shares, Sheinberg remembers, and blamed the management at the bank vault where they were stored.

Sheinberg mentioned to Kevin that his father said he would come clean with him. Kevin confided that their credit lines were being cut by some banks because of the bad publicity surrounding Walker's resignation. Then Kevin told Sheinberg the truth: Maxwell's MCC shares, the ones Robert had told him again and again were tucked away in the safe, were actually pledged as collateral to two other banks. Kevin said they had been forced to pledge the shares when their bank lines had been cut. Suddenly, Sheinberg understood what had baffled him for months. The steady source of shares available for borrowing by the short sellers was Maxwell himself. He was fueling the bear raid he so feared.

"You pledged shares! How could you be so stupid?" Sheinberg asked Kevin. "I thought the only shares you had pledged were the ones with us." Maxwell, when he had offered the MCC shares to Goldman Sachs in February in exchange for a loan, had assured Sheinberg that he had not pledged MCC shares anywhere else. And Sheinberg had believed him. Goldman Sachs had even agreed not to lend out the shares in its possession.

It was a vicious circle of heinous proportions. As MCC's share price declined, Maxwell bought shares in the market. Then, strapped for cash, he used those shares as collateral to raise more cash to buy additional shares. The banks took the shares they held against the loans and lent them to speculators who used them to go short MCC. As the speculators sold the shares short the price moved down further, and Maxwell went into the market to purchase more shares. For Sheinberg it all began to make sense.

Even as Goldman Sachs was waiting for the remaining shares from the already completed portfolio trade, the Maxwells telephoned Sheinberg on Sunday, August 4, to request another one-week loan.

"For how much?" Sheinberg asked.

"Thirty million dollars," answered Kevin.

"No, make it $35 million," Robert said.

Sheinberg did not want any more MCC shares—the firm already held too many—so they agreed that the guarantee would come from the shares of Mirror Group News (MGN), the recently floated British newspaper chain owned by Maxwell, to the value of 200 percent of the loan.

"How long do you want the loan for?" Sheinberg asked.

"Three days," answered Kevin.

"No, make it seven," Robert said.

"Well listen. Don't tell me it's three. Don't tell me it's seven. If it's three weeks—if it's three weeks, tell me it's three weeks because this is how we're going to do it this time," Sheinberg replied.

"Seven days, my word," Robert solemnly answered.

Sheinberg was loaning money to a man who was a liar and in serious financial trouble, and one who quite possibly was also in violation of securities laws. It was hard to see how it would work out well. In sworn testimony Kevin Maxwell said, "There was no way that he [Robert Maxwell] could honor that obligation to repay the margin loan in the period of time he had originally negotiated it. Although initially he did not see that as a problem, and Eric Sheinberg did not see it as a problem, the partners of Eric Sheinberg were unhappy that the margin loan had not been of the short duration that clearly internally they thought it was."

Despite the alarming revelations and his growing concerns, Sheinberg put the wheels in motion for the final loan that Sunday afternoon, and on

Monday the firm agreed to the conditions for collateral and repayment. On Friday, August 9, at the behest of his partners, Sheinberg sat down to a quick breakfast with Robert Maxwell, and the two discussed ways that Maxwell could raise the money he owed Goldman Sachs. Sheinberg was also sounding him out; if there was going to be trouble with repayment on Monday he wanted to let his partners know as soon as possible. There had been an unflattering article about Maxwell in the *New York Times* the day before, and concern within the firm was growing. Sheinberg naively suggested properties that Maxwell could sell, unaware that all had been mortgaged to the hilt. Goldman Sachs recently had moved out of some Maxwell-owned premises and the firm owed Maxwell £1.8 million for dilapidation. Goldman Sachs issued a check that day for the payment, but rather than give it to Maxwell, Sheinberg put it in his desk drawer, he says, "Because if he wasn't going to pay us on Monday, we weren't going to give him that money." The check stayed in Sheinberg's drawer for the next two months.

DURING THE FIRST WEEK in August, Robert Katz was vacationing with his family in South Carolina. The dark-haired, dark-eyed Katz is a marathon runner and a former partner of the prestigious law firm Sullivan and Cromwell, Goldman Sachs's lawyers for most of the twentieth century. Although not yet a member of the management committee, as the firm's general counsel and a partner since June 1988 he regularly sat in on the committee's meetings, providing guidance on many complex legal matters. He planned to leave his family Sunday night and fly to New York for what he thought would be the management committee's routine Monday morning meeting. But before making his way to the airport, he received a phone call from one of his assistants informing him that Robert Maxwell had failed to repay a margin loan that had come due. Katz was genuinely surprised. He had long been aware of Goldman Sachs's heavy involvement with Maxwell, but until this moment there had never been a problem.

When the management committee sat down for its meeting on Monday morning, they asked investment banking partner Ken Brody to assume day-to-day responsibility for the developing Maxwell situation. He was assisted by the co-head of equities, Roy Zuckerberg, Katz, and Sheinberg. But Sheinberg was being edged out of the situation. His partners felt he had not taken a tough enough line. They hoped that Sheinberg would cease communications with Maxwell. Now that real problems had developed, Brody and Katz took over. Katz was to become a debt collector—a man who would bang repeatedly at Maxwell's door first asking to be repaid, then demanding, and finally making threats.

Goldman Sachs still hoped to work out a repayment schedule that Maxwell could meet. In August the firm was holding £106 million worth of MCC and MGN shares as collateral, and no one was interested in selling it and starting a downward spiral in prices.

At the very highest levels, Goldman Sachs now knew that Maxwell was mired in serious financial trouble and had lied to the firm. On August 27, Katz wrote to Rechsteiner and received written confirmation of the verbal assurances he had given Sheinberg that the trusts Rechsteiner was buying for were unrelated to Maxwell. The firm's investment banking division continued dealing with Maxwell in an effort to sell some of his remaining assets. But Goldman Sachs undertook no further trades with Maxwell or his associates. In refusing to trade with Maxwell, Goldman Sachs unknowingly cut his lifeline. No longer could he steal from his pension funds to feed his need for cash.

"Starting sometime in September," Sheinberg said later, "it became quite obvious that we were dealing with people who were either—who were a combination of liars, sick in their heads, desperate, or all three. And they would just tell you anything you wanted to [hear], they were stalling for time. Brody was convinced the guy was broke. Now, Brody had experience dealing with people who were broke." As Brody and Katz closed in on him, Maxwell demanded to appeal directly to the firm's senior partners. His request to take his case to Rubin and Friedman was summarily denied.

By early October the loans had still not been repaid, and on October 10, Brody, Katz, and Bob Hurst (a co-head of investment banking) went to see Maxwell at the Helmsley Palace Hotel in New York. Maxwell used his triplex suite at the hotel year-round as a personal headquarters and residence. The three partners and the extremely overweight Maxwell rode upstairs in a tiny elevator designed for two normal-sized adults. After a few moments of pleasantries, Brody reviewed the history of the unpaid loans. Maxwell offered a range of pie-in-the-sky solutions, all of which would take time to materialize, but the men from Goldman Sachs were tired of giving Maxwell time. Maxwell tried to impress on the Goldman Sachs partners that there was nothing fundamentally wrong with his companies; these were mere liquidity problems, temporary cash constraints that would be sorted out by December, or at the end of the year at the latest. The deadline for repayment was the following day, and that, they reminded him, remained unchanged.

When there was no repayment on the eleventh, they extended the firm's deadline once again until Monday, October 21, and Katz and Brody were back on collection duty. On the twenty-second Maxwell called and asked to meet with Brody and Katz. The pair refused to see him. Goldman Sachs was no longer interested in meetings, only in payment. There was nothing to discuss.

Later the same morning, Katz received word from the ground-floor security guard that Maxwell was seeking to gain entry to 85 Broad Street. With his powerful mixture of ego and audacity, Maxwell did not take no for an answer. Maxwell had showed up on the doorstep assuming that the well-mannered partners would not risk an incident by refusing him entry. Maxwell, the consummate gambler, was betting that face to face the lawyers and bankers of Goldman Sachs would stop short of pulling the trigger, and he would be able to bargain for a bit more time.

Maxwell rode up to the twelfth floor where the firm had its legal department. There in a conference room he and his attorney met with Katz, Brody, and Sheinberg. Maxwell, far from showing signs of anguish or remorse, asked the bankers to remind him once again how much money he still owed. He let them know that while this may have been important to them, to him it was trivial, and the details were a bit fuzzy. Maxwell made a call to Chase Manhattan on his cellular phone and wire-transferred an amount to pay off a small debt he owed the firm. Five minutes later the funds were confirmed to be in a Goldman Sachs account, and Maxwell's ploy had proved successful.

Now Maxwell again offered the story that he would be more liquid by year-end and would be able to repay the loans in full. In response, Brody offered the publisher a story of his own. "There is a famous story about the Sultan and the condemned man," he began. Everyone perked up, surprised at the conversation's turn and curious to hear what Brody would say. "The man is condemned to be executed but he says to the Sultan: 'If you do not execute me for a year I will teach your dog to talk.'" Katz recalled, "The point of the story that Mr. Maxwell and Mr. Brody seemed to click on together quite readily was . . . after all, in the course of the year the man might die anyway, the dog might die anyway, the Sultan might die anyway, or God knows, the dog might learn to talk. In any event, the year would have been bought. I think this was Mr. Brody's way of suggesting that we had had a lot of talk about things that would happen if we granted more time, and it was time to talk about payment." Maxwell pleaded with his bankers not to liquidate the collateral: "If you do that, you'll kill me."

The tension lifted, and Maxwell made an offer. He would repay the $35 million loan within a week, and "In addition I will pay you £3 million, or if you push me, £5 million, on the £25 million loan." The bankers met privately and came back with the announcement that the one-week time frame was acceptable, but they would release only a portion of the collateral from the repaid loan. Maxwell was delighted with the deal and shouted, "Done!" He had gambled and won.

Rumors were now swarming through the banking communities on both sides of the Atlantic that MCC was insolvent. Legions of bankers from major American, British, and European banks had been begging for repayments on loans to Maxwell, all overdue. He had barely been able to hold them off. Without consulting Maxwell, Goldman Sachs tried to sell the MGN collateral to a large London broker, but the message came back, not interested.

Once again Maxwell's promised payment never came. On Wednesday, October 30, Katz and Sheinberg telephoned Maxwell and informed him that the firm would begin liquidating the collateral, responsibly and in the firm's own self-interest. Maxwell seemed unfazed by this announcement. It was the moment he had tried so hard to postpone, yet he was businesslike in his response and did not protest, offer new excuses, or plead for more time. Maxwell simply said to Katz, "I must of course reserve all of my legal rights." That night Maxwell left London for Gibraltar to board his yacht.

Sheinberg was surprised. "I thought I would definitely get a phone call from him that night, 'Isn't there something you can do to stop it?' But I never heard from him again in my life."

The situation was dire for the Maxwell empire, and Kevin Maxwell, in a last attempt to halt its collapse, sent Katz a letter detailing the desperate state of affairs. When MGN was floated, there was an agreement that Maxwell would continue to hold more than 50 percent of its shares. Goldman Sachs's sale of collateral would put Maxwell under that threshold. This would create an "event of default," and the directors of MGN would then ask the stock exchange to suspend trading in the shares. Maxwell was telling Katz that if Goldman Sachs kept selling, the shares would cease trading, and the firm would no longer be able to sell. Robert Maxwell, in a final gamble against any action by Goldman Sachs, had told Kevin what to say. "He [Robert] told me to threaten them with a large problem," says Kevin, "namely a default or a suspension of shares. He basically calculated it would not be in Goldman Sachs's interest, they would do nothing to precipitate the suspension of shares because then they would have no value as collateral at all. . . . My father believed that by committing that concept to paper it would basically frighten off Goldman Sachs from taking any precipitous action in terms of selling the shares." Goldman Sachs consulted with outside counsel, whose advice was, you can do whatever you want with the shares.

True to Katz's word, Sheinberg began to sell collateral on Thursday. Katz and Sheinberg were surprised and delighted when they sold 2.2 million shares of MCC the first day. They informed Kevin Maxwell and at the same time implied that Goldman Sachs would refrain from selling more shares if repayment were forthcoming immediately. In truth, further sales would hurt them, as they were still in possession of 24.2 million shares that would almost certainly decline in value once the initial sales became known. For better or worse the firm was now intertwined with Maxwell in the eyes of the market; if it was seen to be deserting him, all would assume the worst.

Goldman Sachs contends, as proof that it was still in the dark, that by selling the collateral they risked damaging Maxwell's fragile empire and bringing down the scrutiny of regulators. This, they point out, is hardly the action a company would take if it felt that it played any role in Maxwell's illegal activities.

On Tuesday, November 5, at 1:05 p.m. London time, the announcement appeared on trader's screens all over the globe: Goldman Sachs had reduced its holdings of MCC. Less than two hours later, trading in MCC shares was suspended. Maxwell had fallen into the sea.

Maxwell died on the day that Goldman Sachs abandoned him. Many have speculated that his death was a suicide, a fact never confirmed because it coincided with so many of his bankers demanding the repayment of loans that he could not make. Maxwell headed for his boat shortly after speaking to Sheinberg and Katz for the final time. His death occurred just hours before the public announcement that Goldman Sachs had abandoned him. His failing empire could not withstand Goldman Sachs dumping loan collateral on the open market. Bankruptcy was imminent.

The first time Katz spoke to Kevin Maxwell was thirty-six hours after Katz learned of Robert's death. Robert Maxwell might have been gone, but the firm was still hoping for some repayment. Sheinberg, standing in Kevin Maxwell's office, dialed Katz at home. Katz offered the younger man his condolences, and the two eased into a discussion of their unfinished business. Kevin told Katz that there were two transactions afoot that Katz would find as "credible" sources of repayment. Goldman Sachs would be repaid in full out of the proceeds. The two spoke many times that day, learning how each other operated and ironing out the details of how to proceed. Goldman Sachs was long past dealing; the firm would commit to nothing that tied its hands in dumping the remaining Maxwell assets. Katz was suspicious and told Kevin that he wanted confirmation, that he wanted to speak to the bankers working on these credible deals.

Kevin laughed and said, "Well, I think you better ask the other side of your own house." In spite of everything that had happened, the firm was in the process of selling QUE, a Maxwell-owned company.

"Are you referring to the QUE transaction?" Katz asked.

"Yes."

"Is not QUE a company or an asset that is owned by the public companies?"

"Yes, but that is no problem, because there are intercompany accounts between the public and private sides," Kevin explained.

Kevin provided assurances that MCC was in compliance with all of its loan covenants and was therefore free to do with its assets what it wished. Before they hung up Katz reminded Kevin that payments had to be made by the following day. Kevin told the lawyer he heard him loud and clear.

Unbeknownst to Goldman Sachs at the time, Maxwell's death was just the beginning of the firm's troubles. In the weeks and months that followed, the full magnitude of Maxwell's illegal behavior would be revealed, and over the next three years Goldman Sachs would be hounded by bad press and a spate of lawsuits on both sides of the Atlantic. From the first, the firm put a brave face on it, insisting it had done nothing wrong. They hoped the furor would quickly die down. But as the extent of Maxwell's dealings became public, partners close to the situation soon realized that this was only wishful thinking.

CHAPTER V

1992–1993

THE PINNACLE

THE EUROPEAN HEADQUARTERS of Goldman Sachs on Fleet Street is one of the strangest buildings in London. For years the firm housed its London staff in a scattering of rented offices around the City, most recently near the Old Bailey, a few feet away from the Crown Court. Late in 1991, Goldman Sachs opened its own office on a street better known for newspaper publishing than investment banking. The building was once the home of the *Daily Telegraph*. Its Corinthian columns and enormous clock, jutting out at a ninety-degree angle from the building, have been restored to their early-twentieth-century grandeur. But they are little more than a facade. Situated a dozen feet behind this front is a stainless steel and glass tower that houses the firm's twenty-two hundred London-based employees. Outside all is perfectly restored tradition, inside is modern technology.

By the early 1990s, London had become increasingly important to Goldman Sachs. The profitability of the firm's largest foreign office was established and, at its height, would reach more than 25 percent of total profits. The firm's trading businesses in Europe were a major force, no longer playing second fiddle to domestic competitors. The firm was now taking a major role in some of the largest U.K. mergers and advised on more European cross-border transactions than any other bank in the world. London was Goldman Sachs's launch pad into the rest of Europe, and it was here that the firm would find some of its greatest success and failure between 1992 and 1994. In 1992 the firm's association with Maxwell, and the negative publicity it generated, remained the single dark cloud on an otherwise bright horizon. It would not be until 1995, when all of the lawsuits were finally settled, that the firm could put this difficult episode behind them.

Throughout the 1970s and into the early 1980s the London office had been an unprofitable backwater, little more than a drain on resources. The competition in Europe's financial capital was greater, the margins thinner, and the firm's market share smaller. Any bank with international aspirations begins with an office in London; it is the playing field on which all the world's banks compete. As each new foreign bank arrives, trying to eke out a profit, spreads on traditional trading businesses and banking fees are squeezed further. Goldman Sachs would bring American know-how, be it in mergers or block trading, to an arthritic and outdated marketplace. In both of these businesses the firm would revolutionize existing practice, gaining a sizable market share along the way.

To the merger business Goldman Sachs brought not only expertise but a worldwide network of clients which would prove invaluable in cultivating business. When the British maverick entrepreneur Richard Branson decided to sell Virgin Music, his privately owned record label, it was no surprise that he turned to an American investment bank, as the popular music business had long been dominated by American interests. Branson's eight-year-old upstart airline, Virgin Atlantic, was in serious financial straits, so Virgin Music was now expendable. Nineteen-ninety-one had been a terrible year for airlines. As a result of the Gulf War and a recession fewer people were flying and aviation fuel costs had doubled. Small independent airlines have a history of failure and Branson, fully versed in this history, was determined that Virgin's fate would be different. While many naysayers doubted the viability of the airline, Virgin Music, with its stable of successful artists, including the Rolling Stones, Janet Jackson, Bryan Ferry, and Phil Collins, was a commodity that John Thornton, head of Goldman Sachs's European mergers and acquisitons business, could certainly sell.

Branson and Thornton were a good match. Thornton, whose high profile positions include seats on the boards of Rupert Murdoch's British Sky Broadcasting and the firm's once traditional seat at the Ford Motor Company, brought an underdog's aggressiveness to the marketplace with a healthy disrespect for the status quo. Selling Virgin Music would not be business as usual and Branson, who has sought out the new and different in all of his businesses, was not a typical Goldman Sachs client. A hot-air balloon enthusiast with a very un–Goldman Sachs-like high profile, his bearded face can be seen in his companies' advertisements for products as diverse as cola, savings plans, and bridal wear (although he shaved to pose as a bride).

This was a delicate assignment. Thornton would need to maintain the mystique that Virgin Music had developed over decades, and which would in turn keep up the price, while allowing potential suitors to sift through the company's finances. In many ways it was a return to the firm's mergers and acquisitions roots, selling family-owned businesses to larger publicly-owned entities. Branson had hoped to sell to a British buyer and Thorn EMI, a British record label and a client of Goldman Sachs, was Thornton's first stop. Thorn EMI was interested in buying Virgin but was far less interested in the £500 million valuation (the intangible value of its name, record contracts, and back catalog of recordings) that Goldman Sachs had given the company. Thornton had initially hoped that Thorn EMI would pay Branson's figure and that the deal would sail through, but he now knew that to get a top price for his client he would need to bring in a rival bidder. MCA, the American record giant, was extremely interested but also balked at the price tag. Their first bid came in so low Thornton refused even to pass it along to his client.

Now, Thornton had a problem. Branson needed to sell but the two most interested parties had no interest in the lofty price he and Goldman Sachs had affixed to the business. While under pressure from his bankers, Branson was not eager to sell the business he had spent most of his adult life building. He never stopped Thornton's search, but showed very little enthusiasm for it. To keep the deal alive and moving forward Thornton used a highly unusual technique with the rival bidders. He made the negotiations totally transparent and kept each side fully informed of the other's interest. Perhaps most important, he never let either Thorn EMI or MCA say "no" and walk away from the table. By year's end Thorn EMI was offering £425 million with an earn-out beginning from the second year. But the client was not happy. Other comparable record labels had sold for much more and Branson, despite the pressure from his lenders, was not impressed. By playing one party against the other Thornton was able to drive up the price and on a Concorde flight bound for New York he and the chairman of Thorn EMI agreed to more favorable terms for Branson—£560 million, equal to $1 billion, at the time. It would be a triumph for the firm. Thornton's aggressive approach and unswerving focus on his client would result in the type of headline-grabbing success that would earn Goldman Sachs a place as the top merger specialist in London.

When Mark Winkelman sent Mike O'Brien back to London in 1985 to set up a foreign exchange trading business, O'Brien was certain of one thing—he was not going to join the fray. Goldman Sachs would not be just one more bank trying to make a living by quoting currency prices in a market with collapsing spreads. If the firm was to establish a business in London, it would go about it differently. O'Brien, a small, quiet man with an unlined face and a thatch of light brown hair, had been schooled by Winkelman and knew the dangers of creating an infrastructure that his new business would be unable to support. From the start his traders made money, speculating on the relationship between European currencies and interest rates. Slowly a sales force was added, focusing on specialized and innovative currency products. The firm would aim for high-margin business, and overhead would not race ahead of profits. The existing trading businesses—fixed income, equities, and foreign exchange—had all been established as "flow" businesses in which traders stood ready with a bid and offer for the firm's clients (or other market players) and then offset the price risk with other dealers in the market. The trader sought to make a small profit on each transaction while risking little, and to repeat the process hundreds of times. Traders, along with specialist salespeople, focused on an individual market, and their expertise and the quality of the firm's client business paid off. Goldman Sachs's service to its clients over the years had yielded an enormous flow of business. Slowly it became clear that this flow was in itself a source of valuable market information, an early indication of developing trends. It would provide a real edge if the firm was willing to risk some of its own capital. This proprietary activity was seen as "leveraging the franchise" and an opportunity to take advantage of and supplement the firm's established client businesses.

While in theory proprietary trading marked an abrupt break with the firm's largely risk-averse past, it was approached in a very Goldman Sachs–like fashion. The firm carefully combined talented, trusted traders with top economic analysts and attentive management. Risk levels were increased incrementally, and caution was shown at every turn. There was no reliance on gut feelings, no macho stunts. The guys jumping up and down and gesticulating wildly on the exchange floor were clerks executing customer orders. They were amusing and made good footage for the evening news, but the real money was made by highly educated professionals with access to the most up-to-date technology and research, quietly taking risks with the firm's own capital. Goldman Sachs hired some of the world's best economists and "rocket scientists" (mathematicians, physicists, and computer experts) and most skilled traders, and it all went right.

Goldman Sachs's proprietary trading operation was an unqualified success in both New York and London, with an unbroken string of profitable years. No other investment bank, with the exception of Salomon Brothers, traded more aggressively in this period, and no other investment bank found as high and consistent a level of profitability in this dangerous sphere. Friedman liked the business. He understood that Goldman Sachs, with its world-class economists and top-notch traders, had natural advantages in this area. Because of the breadth and depth of its client relationships, the firm also had a unique window on global capital movements.

Management was enthusiastic about the business and encouraged O'Brien to locate and hire the best proprietary traders he could find. Prior to this the firm had brought along its own M.B.A.s, moving them into trading spots once they felt the recruits were ready. O'Brien hired an experienced trader named Larry Becerra in the fall of 1991. He would come to personify some of what happened in the firm's proprietary businesses in fixed income and J. Aron, as his trading advanced from cautious, measured bets to enormous, daring gambles that would make and lose the firm tens of millions. Like the firm's proprietary business, Becerra ultimately would be successful and his career at Goldman Sachs profitable, but the roller-coaster ride that he and the firm would take would prove to be more than some partners could bear.

Most people liked Becerra. He had a relaxed manner, as if he hailed from some small California town instead of Chicago. While most Goldman Sachs employees commuted to work on overcrowded trains or through impassable city streets, Becerra, dressed in his signature cowboy boots and faded Levis, rode to work on his Harley-Davidson. With his deep voice, flat American accent, and mane of thick graying hair, Becerra was hard to miss. There was no way his picture would be found in the annual review. Outspoken, ebullient, confident, even arrogant, he attracted everyone with the edge of danger that seemed to cling to him. His booming laugh could be heard three desks away. Smoking an endless string of cigarettes and gazing at the legs of female colleagues as they passed, Becerra was anything but politically correct.

Becerra was not brought up at Goldman Sachs. If he had been, he never would have been able to display the brash disregard for authority that made him an irresistible personality on the trading floor. With no M.B.A. and a patchwork career that included time selling bonds and trading Eurodollars at Continental Bank, speculating with his own capital, and a stint with a sugar broker, he was not a typical Goldman Sachs recruit. Hired as a senior proprietary trader, he felt his mandate was clear; as Becerra remembers it, he was hired to take risk, to trade anything and everything, and to bring others on the trading floor along with him. Becerra started slowly, easing his way into the new job. "Mike O'Brien," says Becerra, "who was probably the most optimistic person I have met in my life, said, 'We brought you in here to help beef this thing up.' So I said, 'That's not a problem.' " The firm's trading management does not remember it this way; Becerra, they argue, was hired to make money. The leadership role he took on himself, as he soon developed a following.

Becerra made $58 million for Goldman Sachs in his first nine months on the desk. "That year I made a pretty significant amount of money for them," he says, "an amount of money that an individual trader hadn't really made on the proprietary side before, in, like, nine months. And with that came some notoriety." Becerra was forthcoming about his positions, and soon everyone knew what he was doing. His trading became a spectator sport, and in no time he was a visible force on the firm's trading floor and in the London marketplace. His colleagues, the market, and even some of the firm's clients watched in amazement. Soon a host of "would-be" Becerras emerged, all trying to imitate his style, trading approach and success. As Becerra threw himself into his work at Goldman Sachs, the size and riskiness of his positions grew steadily. Those who worked with him closely claim that by the end of his Goldman Sachs career his positions were as large as those of the rest of his department combined.

When British Prime Minister John Major called an election in March 1992, the Labour Party was thought likely to unseat a Tory government of which the public had grown weary. The gilt market, Britain's equivalent of the U.S. Treasury bond market, declined steadily as the election drew near. The last Labour government had left office in 1979 amid high inflation, unemployment, and interest rates, and now the markets were wary. Gavyn Davies, Goldman Sachs's senior U.K. economist, a partner then and now, thought that, if victorious, the Labour Party would pursue conservative economic policies, and that the risk premium being built into U.K. bond markets was unwarranted; it was a short-term panic that would soon correct itself.

Henry Bedford, a thin, soft-spoken, serious man who in 1992 had been a Goldman Sachs trader for twelve years, agreed. An American, Bedford had been sent to London to trade U.S. government bonds and was later put in charge of the firm's gilt trading operation. Bedford had grown up under Corzine and Winkelman and was a highly respected trader. In the weeks leading up to the general election, Bedford and the other traders in London bought gilt futures contracts betting on lower interest rates. Going into the election many of the traders had sold out their positions, but Bedford still held 5,000 contracts. It was an exceptional position because of its size, but the firm's appetite for risk had increased, and Bedford was keeping up with the times. As the election approached the markets became increasingly concerned about a Labour victory, and Bedford's position, in a word, tanked. Corzine called Bedford daily to discuss strategy and indicate his support. But even as the position lost more and more of its value, no one told Bedford to liquidate it. Management, while supervising closely, rarely told a trader what to do, allowing those on the front line free rein.

Bedford's position became one of the first "house" positions—it was so large and widely known that everyone on the floor was rooting for the market to go his way. "The gilt price was the first thing everyone checked each morning," another proprietary trader at the time remembers. When some traders on the desk suggested establishing a short gilt position—after all, the price was falling quickly—conversations were ended abruptly. A short position was unpatriotic; the firm was long. On the evening of the election, Bedford's position hung in the balance, dependent on the voters' will. At the close of business on election day the position had an unrealized loss of $8 million, which at the time was considered very substantial. Anything could happen—the final polls had been close.

In a throwback to an earlier age, British ballots are counted by hand. In gymnasia and public halls around the country, large paper ballots are read aloud and tallied. Through this painstaking process an industrialized country of almost sixty million people elects its leaders in the last decade of the twentieth century. It is quaint if you are a lover of tradition, agonizing if you have a position. By 1 a.m. the town of Basildon, a bellwether for the country at large, came in solidly for the Tories; when all the votes nationwide were counted, the Tories also came out on top. The unrealized loss had been transformed into a profit within hours and in two days had recouped $20 million. Bedford was a hero.

Bedford's trading was deemed a huge success, and Goldman Sachs's comfort with risk was raised a notch. The London partners, meeting shortly after this, praised Bedford for keeping his nerve, and word of his success traveled instantly across the trading floors of Goldman Sachs's offices around the world. Building a business was still important, but short-term trading profits were ascending. Traders' views on risk evolved rapidly during this period, as each new success emboldened those who watched from the sidelines.

A few traders voiced concern, arguing that this sort of trading was not the firm's style, that traders should make measured bets but never risk a year's profits on a single trade. Chipping away, building up profits gradually was more in keeping with the firm's trading past. Others argued that Goldman Sachs had a new style, that there were few market players with better information and analysis or with more skilled and experienced traders, so wouldn't it be foolish not to try to capitalize on these advantages when the opportunities arose?

Just as the firm established itself as a major trading force in the fixed income and currency markets, a number of experienced traders and economists, many of them partners at the peak of their careers, departed Goldman Sachs for the riskier world of the hedge fund. Even the firm's long-serving head of research and money management left after twenty-five years to establish his own hedge fund in 1992. One reason they did so was that despite the astronomical sums the firm paid its proprietary traders, Goldman Sachs was not competitive in the marketplace. Hedge funds compensate their traders based on a formula of their profits—something Goldman Sachs has never done. For many the financial allure was impossible to ignore.

Throughout the 1980s hedge funds were on the cutting edge of risk. Set up originally as stock trading funds that would take long and short positions, by attempting to remain hedged they mutated into some of the riskiest trading vehicles in the marketplace. As offshore funds for rich investors, hedge funds seek to earn high rates of return (above 30 percent) by taking huge trading bets in any financial or physical asset anywhere on the globe. Their generous pay structure attracted many risk-seeking traders by the end of the 1980s, forcing pay packages upward throughout the industry.

Goldman Sachs had no set structure for compensation, and the firm prided itself on the use of subjective measures. Some of the firm's competitors had paid their star traders enormous sums upwards of $10 million. Banks with such compensation practices had met with mixed success, as some of these traders later incurred large losses and others left their firms. Compensation tied directly to personal profitability seemed to encourage "plunging," taking on excessive trading risk for a marginal increase in return, while discouraging teamwork and loyalty. "With the exception of one area [private client services, selling to rich individuals], today all professional employees' bonuses are subjective," Friedman says, describing Goldman Sachs. "No one at a trading desk gets a share of the profits. No one in the merger area gets a share of a fee. We wanted everyone to think more about the firm's interests, as opposed to their own personal interests."

As proprietary traders made ever-increasing profits for their employers, their own compensation as a percentage of those profits generally declined. This meant that they stood to earn significantly more at a hedge fund that had a strict link between profits and compensation (most hedge funds got around the issue of excessive risk taking by requiring that traders earn back their losses before being compensated further). A successful Goldman Sachs trader making $50 million in profits for the firm might receive between $2 million and $3 million at year's end. The same trader who generated $50 million for a hedge fund might receive a Christmas bonus between $10 million and $15 million. Thus, the defections began; by 1994 two international economists from the London office, three senior London traders, the chief government bond trader in New York, a group of fixed income partners, and several others had left the firm to join hedge funds. Their numbers may not have been large, but their trading experience was vast. With the firm's increased focus on proprietary trading, Friedman, for one, grew concerned at the loss of key people in this important area.

Management believed that the firm needed a hedge fund of its own. Speculating in a leveraged risk-taking vehicle was a business that potentially could earn the firm hundreds of millions of dollars. While seemingly at odds with the firm's unwillingness to pay traders according to a formula, the possibility of setting up such a fund was explored. The problem was one of trading talent. In order to start the hedge fund the firm would need to pull traders off its existing proprietary trading desk and reassign them to the new area. While many would have undoubtedly clamored for such a transfer, at the time the firm did not have a deep enough pool of trading talent to move anyone out. The firm explored the option of making a $100 million investment in Long-term Capital Management. The firm hoped for a close relationship in which it could learn more about the hedge fund business, yet the negotiations foundered when the two parties could not agree on the form the investment would take.

The defecting traders, most of whom had spent their entire careers with the firm, would be replaced by experienced recruits from other institutions. But those hired into the firm at a senior level had not come of age at Goldman Sachs—a distinction that would become apparent in a short time. Lateral hires were not the firm's strong point. Goldman Sachs is a place of intense personal relationships; midlevel hires, coming late to the game, sometimes found it hard to fit in. As one former member of the management committee explained, lateral hires are like foreign bodies. They do not speak the language, do not understand who to go to, and most importantly do not know how things are done. While many would find enormous success, some would not be steeped in the firm's culture. And at Goldman Sachs it was culture that monitored people's behavior.

THE BRITISH GOVERNMENT was more than kind to Goldman Sachs's bottom line in 1992. Britain had joined the European Exchange Rate Mechanism (ERM) two years earlier, and the pound was now tied to the other major European currencies. Periodically, because of diverging economic policies or political events, the ERM comes under pressure. Exchange rates that are supposed to be held in predefined bands drift toward or outside their limits, and the result is that governments have their hands forced into a devaluation by turbulence in the market. Between 1979 and 1992 the system had to be realigned nine times. By the summer of 1992 pressures were building again, and predictions of an explosion began to surface.

The British pound has had a long and unhappy relationship with the ERM, and market participants do not quite trust the pound's resolve—the British government's commitment to stave off devaluation even in times of turmoil. David Morrison never liked the ERM. In his view, artificially holding currencies together results in unnecessarily high unemployment and interest rates as governments tailor their economic policies to the needs of their currencies rather than their economies. A government with high unemployment may be unable to lower interest rates to stimulate the economy for fear of the potentially damaging effect on its currency. The son of a bus driver, Morrison had watched four uncles lose their jobs in the Scottish shipyards. That, he says, "had a big influence on me. In my head unemployment is the greatest disease."

In the spring of 1992, Morrison had published a piece of economic research in the *Goldman Sachs Currency Analyst*, a publication distributed to the firm's clients, stating that the Italian lira would need to be devalued by year-end. Italy's minister of finance saw the piece, took issue with Morrison's conclusions, and publicly labeled the firm's research rubbish. The lira, he announced, would not be devalued. An Italian journalist received a copy of Morrison's next piece and an Italian newspaper ran the headline, "Goldman Sachs Predicts Lira at 1000"—a rate considerably lower than its value at the time. Morrison was undaunted, and when John Major stated publicly that he would make sterling the stongest currency in Europe, Morrison could no longer contain himself. He published another research piece in the *Analyst* concluding that Major's chance of strengthening sterling was less than that of Eddie "the Eagle"—Britain's only entrant in the ski jump at the Winter Olympics that year—winning a gold medal.

By early September 1992 both the pound and the lira were falling steadily against the German mark. Major's new government signaled its resolve to keep sterling in the ERM whatever the cost, saying that to abandon the system would be "a betrayal of our future." The European Community made a formal statement ruling out a realignment. Yet the European governments were hamstrung—to raise interest rates to support their currencies in the midst of a severe recession was to risk throwing their economies into a depression. The British government had narrowly staved off a crisis when the Italian government raised interest rates only to unilaterally devalue its currency a few days later. The pound came under renewed selling pressure in the currency markets. John Smith, the Labour opposition leader, publicly railed against the Tory government's intransigence in Parliament, waving Morrison's piece in the Goldman Sachs publication as ammunition.

By the second week in September the British government foolishly decided to do battle with the market, and the Bank of England was forced to buy billions of pounds on the foreign exchange market (selling German marks against them in the vain hope of counteracting the actions of speculators), thereby burning up its foreign currency reserves. In what amounted to a quick transfer of resources from taxpayers to speculators, the Bank of England made a wholehearted attempt to defend the pound through purchases at an implausibly high level. Speculators from around the world, among them the traders of Goldman Sachs, sold the pounds that the Bank of England continued to buy, knowing that if there was a devaluation they would be able to repurchase them cheaply. For the firm, it was an almost perfect trade. If the Bank of England was successful, the pound would probably rise slightly and then stabilize at a relatively low rate. The prevailing economics would not permit the pound to rise by much; the Bank of England's motivation for holding the pound in place was purely political (based as it was on the U.K.'s commitment to the other European countries in the ERM), not a recognition of the demands of the British economy. If the Bank of England failed—and the odds seemed overwhelming that it would—the bottom would drop out, and those who had sold the currency stood to make a fortune. This type of risk-reward situation does not occur often, and the firm took full advantage of the opportunity.

On Wednesday morning, September 16, the Bank of England set aside £7 billion of reserves to defend the pound until the weekend; it was gone by lunchtime. If things continued at this pace, the Bank of England would expend all of its reserves in two or three days. That afternoon, in a dramatic move, the chancellor of the exchequer raised interest rates by 5 percent in an effort to save the flagging pound. The market viewed this as further evidence of the government's weakness, a desperate measure certain to fail, and continued its assault on the beleaguered currency. Finally, later that evening, Britain walked out of the ERM. The pound went into free fall, and the speculating community made a fortune.

For most Goldman Sachs currency traders, the ERM explosion was the most exciting trading opportunity of their careers, and management concurred. There was widespread agreement that the European central banks had presented speculators with one of the most positive risk-reward scenarios, on a grand scale, that anyone had seen in years. Despite the rhetoric and the patriotism governments ascribed to their currencies, it was hard to see how they would continue to defy gravity. Goldman Sachs's foreign exchange traders, who up until this point were having a solid but unremarkable year, saw their fortunes change overnight. The firm was in the right place at the right time, and in a matter of weeks the foreign exchange department made about $200 million, those who were there recall, more than they had in any previous year. Management and traders had become comfortable with much greater risk just as the market presented an unusual opportunity. Most of the major hedge fund players would be involved as well (one of them, George Soros, would later be dubbed "the man who broke the Bank of England" for his aggressive selling of the pound), and some of them were clients of the firm. Goldman Sachs had front-row seats on the action and joined in with vigor.

This was Becerra's trading debut, the first time he had an opportunity to show Goldman Sachs the stuff he was made of, and in a matter of weeks he had made approximately $50 million. As risk taking had increased, foreign exchange profits had more than doubled between 1991 and 1992, topping $350 million by year-end. While firm-wide profits rose 27 percent, fixed income proprietary trading profits in London quadrupled. The amounts of money were unprecedented, and the adulation was untempered. Those responsible for the windfall were transformed overnight into stars.

"Be big and be real" is the phrase many have used to describe the change in style that occurred around this time. Suddenly the possibilities seemed limitless, and going into 1993 the firm brimmed with confidence. When the market presented trading opportunities, Goldman Sachs grabbed onto them with both hands. A year's profits could be made in a matter of days or weeks if you were willing to take some real risk. The old approach to trading—churning out gradual, steady profits while accepting some small losses—would give way to a more aggressive style where sizable losses would be endured for the sake of even bigger gains. When Becerra entered a buy order onto the futures exchange without stating the amount, the floor trader naturally demurred; he could not responsibly execute an order without a price and an amount. The answer that came back was, "Buy them 'til your hands bleed."

From the firm's point of view the timing of the sterling and lira crises could not have been better. The profits from the ERM tumult could be used to fund the firm's energetic expansion into Asia over the next two years. The firm's financial success in 1992 meant that it had the resources available to invest in new businesses—and thus pulled further ahead of the competition.

"I hate to say this," says one former partner, "because I was a partner for years, but there is one thing you have to understand about the partnership. Greed changed the firm, and the view was to take as much risk as we can, and make it as fast as we can." All over Goldman Sachs, departments were earning hitherto unheard-of profits and management believed the firm had a real "edge" in trading. The firm had always focused on long-term profitability and on building a successful business for the future. Many have suggested that as trading opportunities presented themselves the focus shifted somewhat and short-term profits increased in importance.

Rubin and Friedman were *not*, in fact, driven by mindless greed. In their worldview, if Goldman Sachs was not surging ahead, it was falling behind. The firm's geographic expansion, its aspiration to be a global brand name, and the mathematics of the partnership all required more income as the engine of growth. As the partnership grew the pie would need to grow even faster. To maintain a constant level of income for the partners and their employees, profits would need to rise commensurately to compensate for the rapid dilution in equity, the escalating costs, and the deteriorating fee structures in many investment banking businesses. During the 1980s the returns on client business were compressed. The fees earned on underwriting corporate bonds in the late 1980s were one-third less than they had been at the beginning of the decade. But in the standard trading businesses the declines were even more dramatic, with revenues for selling uncomplicated instruments like U.S. government bonds falling by as much as 75 percent. Lower-cost competitors, namely commercial banks, had entered the market in the 1980s, driving fees down further. At this point Goldman Sachs's steady fee-generating business—like the money management operations or private clients' services departments that would be vastly expanded during the 1990s— were still relatively small, so additional income would be earned through the development of more innovative (or value-added) products, expansion into new markets, and proprietary investments and trading.

Before they left the firm, Friedman and Rubin would make John Whitehead's dream of a worldwide operation a reality. By the end of 1992 more than 30 percent of the employees and almost 10 percent of the partners were citizens of countries other than the United States, and the firm was staffed by people from ninety-one countries. Friedman believed that there was a window of opportunity, a short period in which an American investment bank could establish itself in emerging markets all over the globe. Once the window closed, competition would be insurmountable and newcomers would struggle for a foothold. So Goldman Sachs surged ahead, almost doubling the number of foreign offices, founding new offices throughout Asia, Latin America, and Europe. After the firm was named to the hotly contested position of financial advisor to the Russian Federation on foreign investment, it set up a small office in Moscow. The rapid expansion required an enormous investment and increased the firm's need for profits.

GOLDMAN SACHS had been expanding the size of its partnership steadily for decades. There had been fifty partners in 1973; there were seventy-five in 1983 and one hundred fifty by 1993. If the firm was to cover the globe, geography and increased specialization would demand that the expansion continue. When the partnership classes had been small, twenty or fewer, shares in the firm from retiring partners, many with stakes of 2 to 3 percent, could be redistributed to new partners without diluting the holdings of existing partners. But as the size of the partnership increased, the profits of the firm had to grow at breakneck speed if existing partners' income levels were to be maintained.

With his ascendancy in 1990, Rubin openly discussed with the partnership the need for an expanding pie, stating that the management committee would not have created so many new partners if it had not been confident that comparable growth in earnings could be achieved. Friedman, too, made it clear he had little interest in pursuing rankings in league tables or market share as an end in itself, unless these efforts resulted in increased profitability. He asked his partners to focus on the primary reason for endeavoring to be in business—namely, to maximize shareholder capital.

Before 1986 the active partners of Goldman Sachs were entitled to almost all of its profits each year. This is no longer the case. In addition to the firm's limited partners (retired partners who choose to leave capital in the firm), Goldman Sachs has taken on three groups of financial partners. Sumitomo's investments in 1986 entitled the Japanese bank to 12.5 percent of the firm's annual profits. Kamehameha Schools/Bishop Estate, the giant Hawaiian education trust, which also made two major cash infusions into the firm, first in 1992 and again in 1994, receives about 11 percent of what the firm makes every year. Finally a group of insurers has injected $225 million into the capital structure. Limited partners do not receive a percentage of the profits, but rather receive interest rate payments as compensation for the use of their capital. Payments made to outside investors, before the partners see a dime, have run between $300 million and $400 million a year. Before the Sumitomo capital injection, general partners owned more than 80 percent of the firm's equity, with limited partners holding the remainder; by 1994 general partners owned a mere 28 percent although they were entitled to 74 percent of the firm's profits, down from 88 percent in 1990 when the firm had almost fifty fewer partners.

Goldman Sachs will go down in history as the last major partnership on Wall Street, but even at this stage, few argued that it could or would stay that way indefinitely. Many viewed the strenuous push for increased profits as driven by the firm's inevitable future as a public corporation. If you are going to sell a house you spruce it up; if you are going to sell a business it does not hurt to string together a couple of exceptional years. A public listing will require even greater financial disclosure, and thus it becomes especially important that the results are impressive.

The arcane financial structure of Goldman Sachs has been a mystery even to some of those closely associated with the business. Detailed questions about it led inevitably to deep breaths and long, complicated explanations. Every two years the partnership was dissolved and a new partnership reconfigured accounting for the new class and any retirements. Each partner was accorded a certain percentage of the firm's equity, and that number was published in the partnership agreement for all the current partners to see. The management committee set these percentages, and there was no appeal.

Friedman and Rubin believed in individual accountability. Some people performed at a higher level than others, and, they felt, their compensation and responsibilities should reflect this difference. For years Goldman Sachs had smoothed over disparities in performance, compensating partners in lockstep and placing enormous emphasis on seniority. The process of naming partners at Goldman Sachs was a meritocracy, but once inside the partnership seniority rather than performance was the defining feature in determining compensation. Beginning in 1990, however, differentiation within classes was introduced based on performance. Each class was divided into thirds based on a subjective assessment of the partners' contributions. So the top performers in one partnership class might hold larger stakes than the bottom of the class ahead. A good performance in any given year could result in an increased percentage, while a rough year could cause a demotion. With a solid performance almost any career could be revived.

Friedman's and Rubin's goal of creating a world-class organization could only be accomplished by those capable of world-class performances. The differentiation would serve other functions as well. When the average size of the partnership class leaped from ten to almost forty, there was an acknowledgment that "mistakes" might be made more easily. Grading partners as they progressed would be one method for rectifying any errors that had occurred and edging out those who were not, for a variety of reasons, making the grade. New partners would be given four to six years to prove themselves. Those deemed to be a little "slow in their step"—leaving for the Hamptons a touch early on a Friday afternoon or suffering what management called "a career slowdown"— would have their ownership percentages reduced and be nudged toward the door. A few others deemed to have exhibited unacceptable behavior would be pushed in the same direction. Differentiation would be a chance to, as one former partner says, "clear out the mezzanine layer"—the partners who because of their seniority held large stakes in the firm but contributed little to the bottom line. Their shares could be redistributed to the large incoming classes.

Most Goldman Sachs partners have lived all their lives in highly competitive environments, arriving at their current status by repeatedly rising to the top. For some the announcement that a member of their class had managed to nose ahead of them was very difficult. "You've heard of the fight for an 'o5' [.05 percent]?" one former partner asks. "For some people it is devastating." A few became so consumed with the disappointment that, despite multimillion-dollar earnings and the stature of their position, they felt like failures. From the start, management was concerned about the emotional impact of the process of differentiation. But many former partners feel the firm struck the right balance, a difficult task. While making enough of a distinction to reward and encourage performance, there was some cross-subsidization that kept dissension to a minimum.

Although long anticipated, Rubin's departure shortly after the 1992 presidential election was a sad event for the firm. The newly elected Bill Clinton honored Rubin by selecting him for the post of national economic advisor. Immediately after accepting the job offer from the president-elect in Little Rock, Rubin made a detour on his way back to Washington. With only hours to spare Rubin had come to New York to say farewell to the firm and the people he had been so close to for the previous twenty-six years. A hastily convened—and therefore poorly attended—partners' meeting was held in the thirtieth-floor conference room. Rubin sat before his audience, eating breakfast as Friedman proffered a few words of introduction. Neither man was completely comfortable discussing in a public setting the intense emotions of the situation, and both were reduced to clichés to make their points. Friedman looked awkward as he tried to speak about the unique chemistry that existed between himself and Rubin and the sense of personal loss he felt.

Rubin confided to his partners that he had counseled Clinton to select Senator Lloyd Bentsen for the secretary of the treasury position, certain that the senator was the best candidate. Warren Christopher, the secretary of state designate, later had sounded him out about a job at the White House, and Rubin signaled his interest. It was the job he had always wanted. In his characteristic self-deprecating manner, he was modest about the impact he would have in government, suggesting simply that he would try his best.

In making his decision, Rubin had sought the counsel of his wife, Judy, and Friedman. His family, he admitted, was not enthusiastic, but he felt strongly that he had to go forward. In departing, Rubin dispensed with his prepared notes and spoke with carefully chosen words. He described the emotional closeness he felt to the firm and its people. Goldman Sachs had been the base of his life, and leaving was very difficult, he said. Looking down at his hands, he was visibly moved. Judy, he told his partners, could not believe he was leaving. He himself had only just come to realize how much the firm meant to him, how attached he had become.

Rubin knew he was leaving on an upswing. The management, he noted, was the strongest it had been in the firm's history. He admitted that he had not wanted to say this at the Christmas party only weeks earlier, afraid of offending some of the older retiring partners, but the firm's management was good enough to lead a country, not just an investment bank—particularly, he added with a note of humor, given the state of the country. The firm, he wisely predicted, would have great years going forward. Theirs was a cyclical business and one still obviously on the way up.

Rubin concluded by saying that if there was one man on the planet he would like to speak with in his new job it would be Steve Friedman—a ringing testament to their partnership. Out of sentiment and politeness, Rubin signaled that he would be back when he had more time to say his real good-byes and hoped to keep in touch. The latter would of course be impossible—once in office he would distance himself from the firm—but no one in that room could have doubted his sincerity. Rubin's partners gave him a standing ovation, and he stood next to Friedman. The two men, bound intellectually and emotionally by two decades of working closely together, awkwardly shook hands. Rubin's moving speech was a tough act to follow, and Friedman seemed almost at a loss for words. He was numb, he told his audience; with Rubin he had enjoyed an intense working partnership and, "wham," it was over.

Rubin's farewell memo to the employees of the firm was unusually personal: "Together with Judy and the rest of the Rubin family, I wish you all the best individually and collectively, as the amazing group of people that you are. You will always mean a great deal to us." This ability to speak directly and from the heart is one of the reasons for Rubin's almost universal popularity. Rubin went out at the top, his stellar reputation only enhanced by his success in public service.

Friedman would miss his colleague and friend, acknowledging that "no firm can face the departure of someone of Bob's stature without a great sense of loss." Yet other than his travel schedule, which would become increasingly demanding, Friedman said after Rubin's departure that nothing had changed; it was business as usual. The senior partner's job is one of both substance and style. The endless flag-waving would exhaust Friedman; the intense travel schedule to meet with clients and government officials would become a grinding chore that he now had to face alone. "You could literally fill up every day and night of the week and some Sundays with these commitments," he said. "Each of them taken independently is useful and informative and you meet very impressive people, sometimes fascinating ones. But you have to admit to yourself that in many ceremonial cases you're only adding value because you're physically there and you have an epaulet on your shoulder."

Reflecting on one particularly grueling European trip, in which Friedman visited clients, finance ministers, and heads of state in six European countries he said: "The whole time I kept looking at the pilot of the chartered plane we were in, and I thought to myself, you know he's a perfectly well-spoken guy, perfectly presentable. If I could just give this guy a nice blue serge suit, and teach him about eight lines, he could do the ceremonial parts as well as I could at these big receptions." The pressures on Friedman were great, and as 1992 and 1993 wore on, his schedule became more exhausting. But Friedman was fighting fit, a regular runner, and although tired, he felt up to the challenge. The relentless pace of change that Friedman set for himself and the firm never slackened. Strategic dynamism, as he calls it, is not "bruise-free stuff," and the intensity of the job never waned.

Some partners have suggested that Rubin's departure was immediately felt. Friedman, they say, was not entirely comfortable managing thousands of people and preferred dealing with the top people; he left mingling with the masses to his colleagues. But others who know Friedman well attest to his compassion for his employees.

Over time, Goldman Sachs had increasingly become a trading firm, and now there was no longer a trader at the top. Friedman would never be steeped in the technicalities of the firm's trading businesses—he had come to them too late. His background was in investment risk, valuing companies for the long term, not in short-term market risk.

Friedman chose not to name a number two. He worked closely with the management committee, meeting every Monday morning with its ten members and using this experienced group as a sounding board. Decisions of the management committee rarely surprised Friedman, and there was no question of who was in charge. When controversial issues left the committee deadlocked, Friedman, like the chief justice of the Supreme Court, cast the deciding vote.

The question of succession would be left wide open from the day Rubin went to Washington. Many would argue that the firm is best served with both a banker and a trader at the helm, but at the time of Rubin's departure Friedman did not feel ready to name a successor. In contrast to seven years earlier, when he and Rubin had been the only logical choices, there was now a relatively large pool of highly talented men who could succeed him. For seventy years, since the day Sidney Weinberg wrested control of Goldman Sachs from a disgraced Waddill Catchings, the honor of senior partner had been bestowed on one or two of the firm's most profitable partners. This was part of the firm's history. Still, as late as 1993, for Friedman the obvious choice to run the firm had not emerged.

The consequences of giving the nod too early, and later realizing that the wrong choice had been made, could be dire. Equally troubling, those bypassed might walk, depleting the firm of some of its top talent when in fact they still should have been in the running. Friedman was careful not to signal his impending departure. He wanted to follow the performance of his top lieutenants for as long as he could and to keep them involved. The palace intrigue resulting from the transition at the top had torn apart more than one firm.

Through different pairings—auditions of a sort—Friedman studied which top partners might produce the type of leadership he and Rubin or Weinberg and Whitehead had provided. Pairs of top managers were made nominal vice-chairmen for different areas of the firm. Friedman had for some time been pushing the combination of Jon Corzine, the co-head of fixed income, and Hank Paulson, the co-head of investment banking, giving them joint responsibility for some of the firm's activities in Asia. He wanted time to watch the mix, to assess the crucial synergies that might come from the relationship. In addition to the pairing of Corzine and Paulson, the firm's asset management business was overseen by Corzine and Roy Zuckerberg (co-head of equities); Winkelman took charge of Europe; and Corzine was responsible for the financial treasury functions of the firm. And although none of them seemed to know it, all were in the running.

"THE PEOPLE of Goldman Sachs are intense and proud," Friedman wrote in the firm's 1993 annual review, "and they aren't willing to settle for less than our being the very best in each of our significant operations. I share this viewpoint." By then, Goldman Sachs did not need to settle for much. It was the premier investment bank in the world. Its dominance across all major markets would be hard to exaggerate; no other firm came close. Moody's and Standard & Poor's both gave it top credit ratings in the industry. In the high-profile and fiercely competitive business of international mergers and acquisitions the firm was ranked first, with an astounding market share of 24.7 percent; in the domestic market it was also ranked number one with an equally impressive market share. *Euromoney* magazine conducted "the decathalon of investment banking," a ranking of the world's banks across all sectors of the investment banking business. Only Goldman Sachs placed among the top five banks in each area, including underwriting (where it ranked first), trading (fourth behind three commercial banks), and advising (first). On overall points the firm bested second-place Merrill Lynch by more than 30 percent. In a similar poll of American chief financial officers conducted by *Financial World*, the firm was overwhelmingly voted the best across the broad range of investment banking services. Goldman Sachs blew the competition away. By 1993 it had competitors in its various businesses but no real rivals overall.

By the early 1990s investment banking was an information processing business, not in the technical sense but in the sense of moving valuable financial information around the globe to the greatest advantage of the firm and its clients. Friedman would explain that, "It is vital that information flows smoothly within our firm: horizontally (across departmental, divisional, and geographic boundaries) as well as vertically (so that people on the front line feel comfortable in passing necessary but unpleasant information upward, or in making controversial suggestions)." Thus it stood to reason that those organizations with the least amount of friction in the flow of information would find the greatest success. Friction resulted from cultures in which employees were not used to a continuous dialogue and in which their efforts to communicate among themselves were neither encouraged nor rewarded. This facet of the firm's culture, its high degree of integration and the tangible rewards bestowed on those who cooperate, along with extreme dedication, allowed it to move away from the pack in the early part of the 1990s.

The work ethic at Goldman Sachs is exceedingly strong. Secretaries answer the phones from 7 a.m. on, and meetings often begin earlier or are scheduled for as late as 10 at night. Because of the firm's global coverage, conference calls can occur any time of the day or night. Breakfast, lunch, and sometimes even dinner are eaten at one's desk, unless there is a client involved. Increased seniority only heightens the time demands. Many partners at Goldman Sachs who had shown themselves to be stars were increasingly overburdened with responsibilities. The constant pressure of international travel, twenty-four-hour-a-day markets, and weekend meetings made Gus Levy's schedule look tame by comparison. Management committee meetings of up to twelve hours began on Friday nights, resumed Saturday morning, and ended in the afternoon; attendance was optional only at breakfast.

Fixed income, once the firm's weakest performing division, was the first department to make more than $1 billion, and in 1993 it earned more than the entire company had ever made until two years earlier. For years Corzine and Winkelman had worked slavishly to improve fixed income, cultivating clients, hiring talented traders and economists, and investing heavily in technology. By now they had effected a total turnaround, and in 1992, *International Financing Review* magazine named Goldman Sachs "International Bond Trading House of the Year," acknowledging the firm's preeminence as well as its innovation in trading fixed income products anywhere in the world.

In 1993 the world's bond markets rallied. The trading conditions were some of the most benign in recent memory, with the unbeatable combination of a strong trend in one direction and low volatility. Short-term interest rates (defined as twelve months or less) were low, and the firm earned money standing still. It made $600 million on interest alone—the differential between its borrowing costs and the yield on bonds it held in inventory. It was an extraordinary, record-breaking year.

There were a few canaries in the mine shaft, however—partners and traders who in the midst of plenty vehemently insisted all was not right. "Profits were going up so fast that no one worried about the fact that risk was going up faster," a former trader says. Although the firm's trading businesses were generating spectacular returns, one partner who was asked to examine the firm's trading risk argues that taking into account the amount of risk that was incurred, the firm's performance looked less impressive, and it was actually underperforming the market. A bull market, he explains, was mistaken for brilliance. It was not a message many wanted to hear, and in that one stunning year of 1993, when it all came together, few were listening.

By that time O'Brien had been with Goldman Sachs for eleven years, had been a partner for five of them, and was managing some of the firm's most profitable trading desks. His record as a trading manager was flawless; his departments had made money for Goldman Sachs every quarter of every year. Traders liked working for O'Brien, who wanted to be kept informed but rarely interfered, and many thrived under his loose management style. Both skill and luck are necessary to succeed in trading, and in 1993, O'Brien was so lucky that he made money even when he guessed wrong.

As the head of proprietary foreign exchange trading O'Brien often took large positions in currencies or bonds, focusing on a slightly longer time horizon than some of the other traders on his desk. He did it because he loved markets and hoped to set an example for the younger traders. In June 1993, O'Brien and his desk held a basket of currencies and European bonds, but within days of establishing the position O'Brien grew concerned as the market moved against him. O'Brien did not want to liquidate and began to contemplate a way to hedge against some of the risk. He consulted the firm's asset allocation models. These models showed that the position could be hedged in part by purchasing U.S. Treasury bonds. Following that advice O'Brien bought what some traders remember to be $1 billion worth of treasuries. This position would dwarf the regular trading undertaken by Goldman Sachs's government bond desk. The hedge worked perfectly. As the original trade dropped in value, O'Brien reached his pain threshold, losing as much as he felt the trade warranted and, showing discipline, liquidated his position. Treasuries then made what one trader called a "step function," soaring in price as yields fell from 7.25 percent to 6 percent in a matter of weeks. It was a nice start to a year in which O'Brien's traders made more than $500 million—close to 20 percent of the firm's profits. The majority of this was generated by the firm's proprietary traders.

The pressure to show spectacular profitability, to break all previous records, increased throughout 1993. The firm's expansion plans and the increased size of the partnership demanded it. While most employees thrived on the challenge, some were uncomfortable in this atmosphere, and a few departed for competitors. Equally important, some clients in the firm's trading businesses noticed a change. One fund manager whose closest banking relationship was with Goldman Sachs for almost a decade said that in 1993, internal positions became more important and client coverage slipped. The firm was now positioning many of the same instruments that this fund manager did, and in his opinion the firm was failing to show the kind of exceptional service that had won them his business in the first place. Other firms, less focused on trading for the house, still looked upon clients as their bread and butter. One long-serving bond trader believes that some clients became reluctant to show their cards to a player now in the same game. He thinks that in 1993, "Some customers felt alienated, threatened, and careful."

Although management believed there were few traders capable of managing large risk positions, making directional bets on broad-range markets, risk taking had spread quickly across the firm's trading floors. Many traders recognized that their careers would be enhanced with proprietary trading profits regardless of what their job description read. Now there were dozens of traders who for the first time were taking just such risks, and the results were groundbreaking. Experience and expertise were no longer preconditions for taking positions; brains and bravery would suffice.

The incentives created by the firm's compensation system in part encouraged this. As was the case at most other Wall Street firms, traders essentially were granted a free option by the firm. If in trading the firm's capital they were successful, they took home hundreds of thousands or even millions of dollars in bonuses at the end of the year. If unsuccessful, they still had their salaries. Each year the slate was wiped clean, and the scoring began again. In a worst-case scenario, after many consecutive years of losses employment might be terminated, but with Goldman Sachs on the top of a resume, jobs at other investment banks were instantly available. The firm bore all of the risk.

It was no surprise that as 1993 wore on everyone in the trading business wanted to be a proprietary trader. Compensation for a successful proprietary trader can be as high as or higher than that of the newer partners—without the personal risk of unlimited liability or the requirement that earnings be reinvested in the firm until resignation or retirement. Traders were paid out everything in the year in which they earned it. If a proprietary trader earned $60 million for the firm one year and lost $50 million the next, he would still be well compensated for the two years, with a bonus of perhaps $2 to $3 million the first year and maybe $100,000 in salary the next. However, a trader who made $5 million in each of two years would have only a fraction of the first trader's compensation to show for his efforts (perhaps $500,000 for the two years), while having earned the same amount of money for the firm. This system encourages traders to swing for the fences (although throughout its history the firm's culture had acted as a force of self-restraint). If they make it, millions of dollars and a promotion can be theirs. If they miss, it's not their problem. This is the nature of the industry, and during this period Goldman Sachs, like most other firms, suffered from it.

Some within the firm, particularly from the banking side, have deep misgivings about the system and would have felt much better about

swings in profitability had the proprietary traders been required to rein-
vest some of their considerable earnings with the firm, with the option of
withdrawing them only after a number of years. But several competitors
have experimented with such plans and then watched their best traders
stream out the door. The management committee had gone so far as to
consider the idea of a deferred compensation program in which some of
the highest-paid employees would leave a portion of their remuneration
with the firm for a period of years. The idea was rejected because it was
disadvantageous to the firm in tax terms, and because the firm's total cash
payout (unlike competitors with deferral systems) was viewed as a
recruiting asset when hiring from other banks. Also, the amounts the firm
could defer without the risk of losing people were deemed too small to be
relevant.

Groupthink is an insidious danger on trading floors everywhere; it
spreads like a virus, killing independent judgment and contrary position
taking. Trading floors are places where leaders—even gurus—are sought.
Get it right a few times, and others will follow you. Get it right with any
regularity, and you will be elevated to the status of a demigod. If you cannot spot a market trend (and it can be an extremely difficult thing to do)
the next best thing is spotting the guy who can. As livelihoods, status,
futures, and ego all hang in the balance, it is no surprise that traders are
serious about finding the right leader.

"It got to the point where I felt like I couldn't do a trade in the market
without a dozen people at the firm monitoring it and calling all their
accounts and saying 'Larry's buying,' " Becerra remembers. By 1993 his
success was contagious, and everyone was hoping to be infected.
Although Goldman Sachs had many able proprietary traders, most of
whom were having the best year of their careers, none was as closely
watched as the flamboyant Becerra. One of the biggest problems was the
"choo-choo traders." Once Becerra bought a derisory amount of silver, a
small hedge to a bond position he was holding, then returned to his desk
and watched the choo-choo traders leave their stations. One by one
traders filed over to the silver trading desk. Each loaded up on a small
amount of the metal before returning to his seat. Becerra felt under
increasing pressure to be right, not only for his own P&L but also for
other traders on the floor and for the salespeople recommending his
trades to clients. His influence had extended far beyond his reach.

David Morrison's success also contributed to the problem of groupthink. Morrison's market calls on the Italian lira, and the ERM had only
increased his credibility. By 1993 his views were followed widely both
inside and outside the firm. Early in his career at Goldman Sachs his preliminary forecasts provoked heated arguments in London and New York,

which occasionally led him to rethink and revise a report. Traders would sometimes follow his views, but they were just one of many inputs to be considered. Beginning in 1993 his recommendations were more and more often followed blindly and translated into positions on the firm's trading floors by some of its more inexperienced traders with only a minimum of discussion.

When groupthink is allowed to develop and the bets become more concentrated, gains and losses are greatly accentuated, like a crowd running from one side of a boat to the other. The effects can be both destabilizing and dangerous. "Lemming traders," as they were known, became the butt of jokes, and one group threatened to have ties made up with the acronym, DSOTFMT—"do some of that for me, too," a phrase often heard on the trading floor. Following an accepted view, as expressed either by the firm's economists or by its largest and most profitable traders, absolved individuals of responsibility. Traders may be slower to cut their losses and less willing to admit their mistakes when everyone around them is holding the same position. There is comfort in conforming, but on a trading floor where the risks being taken are rising sharply, this can be a costly thing. Conversely, it should be noted that in good times a meeting of the minds on the best trading opportunities can greatly expand the number of traders holding winning positions and amplify the firm's profitability.

Despite the huge success in the firm's trading, Friedman asked a senior trading partner in fixed income at the time to study the firm's trading risk. What the trader discovered was alarming. So focused was the firm on the absolute level of returns that it was not cognizant of some of its traders' underperformance. Traders, by and large, had no awareness of their return on capital; the only measure was dollars and cents. While absolute returns were nothing short of spectacular, when adjusted for the risk of loss the picture, for some, altered considerably. The traders' "sharp ratios," a measure of the quality of returns, were deteriorating. The declining ratios indicated that the firm was having to risk more of its capital to generate each dollar of profit. Profits were rising, but in some areas the risks were rising faster. Yet the partner studying the firm's risk suggests that his biggest frustration was not that a group of traders was trading in a way that might spell trouble, but that he felt he could not attract the attention of management to what he considered a very serious problem. Some former traders claim that management, blinded by high profits in absolute terms, ignored the deteriorating risk-adjusted return on some trading desks. Those within the firm strenuously disagree, explaining that the firm had accurate risk models that were studied carefully by all levels of management.

As RISK ROSE, traders made and lost in a matter of weeks what they had earned for the firm during the whole of 1992. This was not a development with which everyone at Goldman Sachs was comfortable. The management structure had done little to adapt to the increased size of the partnership. Lines of communication ran up through businesses and only spanned divisions at the management committee level. You live in your stovepipe, those at the firm are fond of saying, until you reach the top. There were no more than five or six people outside the management committee who understood how the entire firm operated. Many partners, particularly from the banking side of the business, were unaware of or failed to comprehend the market risk being taken by the trading departments in order to generate such incredible profits. Some had little understanding of the risk to which their capital was being exposed. When the full picture came to light during 1994, many were outraged.

Following Becerra's lead, the style of dress for some in London became decidedly more casual. "I walk in in my jeans and boots and do my thing and leave," Becerra said. "I don't live twenty-four hours a day for this firm, which is something else they want you to do." Becerra kept unusual hours, working hard when it was needed and taking time off when there was little activity in the markets. A few others who felt their profitability justified it started to follow suit, and some of the discipline, although not the department's performance, suffered. For Goldman Sachs this was a difficult problem. Culture has been defined at the firm as the way people behave when their boss is not looking over their shoulder, and at Goldman Sachs it was all-encompassing. Few had lived outside it, and their tenure had usually been brief. The culture of Goldman Sachs—the team ethic and long-term approach to business—had acted as a force for self-restraint, mitigating the need for rigid and formal controls. Long workweeks, business suits, and accountability to management were all part of the package. Loyalty to the firm and its partners meant that almost everyone had traded the firm's capital as if it were their own.

In 1993, Goldman Sachs made more than $2.6 billion in pretax profits. The firm's return on equity rose to more than 60 percent, to levels not seen since the early 1980s. To put this in context, that same year Microsoft made $953 million, Disney earned $671 million, and the firm's largest investment bank competitor, Merrill Lynch, saw profits of $1.3 billion. No securities firm had ever had a year like it. The press made much of this, and the competition stewed in frustration and envy. The *Guardian*, a left-wing British paper, asked its readers in a front-page headline, "What's the difference between Tanzania and Goldman Sachs?" The answer, in bold black letters, was: "One is an African country that makes $2.2 billion a year and shares it among 25 million people. The other is an investment bank that makes $2.6 billion and shares most of it between [*sic*] 161 people." A more adulatory American press, in the form of *Forbes* magazine, simply set down the challenge in a story about Goldman Sachs: "Top this, if you can."

The tremendous jump in profitability was a testament to the vision of the firm's leadership. While many things went right in this one spectacular year, the groundwork for the firm to capitalize on the current opportunities had been laid many years earlier. The principal investments area that Friedman had labored for so long to bring into being saw its revenues almost quadruple from 1992 to 1993 and accounted for 40 percent of the investment banking division's revenues. Friedman had recognized this potential long ago as he was investing a few hundred thousand dollars in companies nobody had ever heard of. Proprietary trading units all over the firm, whether in fixed income, equities, or J. Aron, saw their profits rise as much as fivefold in 1993. It was Rubin who had envisioned the possibilities of this particular business many years earlier, and now it had come to pass as well.

Bonus time 1993 was not business as usual. While the press feasted on the more than $4 million earned by each of the newest partners, one of the biggest stories inside the firm was the pay of a few traders in London. Compensation for proprietary traders had been the subject of many debates. Some in the firm's trading areas had argued that Goldman Sachs would never be able to maintain a first-class business in this area if it could not keep its staff, and the exodus of talented and experienced traders had to be stemmed. In the past proprietary traders had been paid as much as $1 million to $3 million, but some had still departed.

In 1993 it was determined that successful traders, while not being compensated by a strict formula, would be paid at higher levels. Individual traders had earned for the firm as much as $100 million in 1993; management felt its hand was being forced. The decision was made that some traders would be paid at the same level as junior partners—or even higher but without the risk to their personal capital.

For years the firm had taken pains to ensure that employees were paid based on the sum total of their contribution to the businesses of Goldman Sachs, not simply on the basis of profits. The problem is a complex one. Some businesses are highly competitive, and the possibilities for substantial profits are small. Yet many of these same businesses are integral parts of being a full-service, global investment bank, and top talent is needed to run them. Recognizing this predicament early on, Goldman Sachs gravitated toward a subjective system of compensation that relied on factors other than pure profitability. The firm hired industrial psychologists to help them improve the process. As a result of this consultation, discussions of performance were separated from talk about compensation. The psychologists had found that when the two issues are dealt with in the same meeting, an employee often hears only the dollar figure. A new process of "360-degree reviews" was put in place, whereby each professional employee, in an intricate and lengthy process, is evaluated by those on all sides—by his or her senior colleagues as well as by colleagues across disciplines and at lower levels. (By 1997 this complex and comprehensive system would mean that 150,000 reviews were completed.) During 1993, Friedman had bragged about the compensation system in a memo to the entire firm that discussed, as he puts it, "the necessity of thoughtful reviews and mentoring by managers in order to improve employee performance and career development and as a prerequisite for trust in the subjective process by which bonuses are determined. I explained why we preferred this approach to mechanistic formulas which do not encourage people to cooperate or focus on the firm's broader interests." Yet now proprietary traders who by and large contributed only profits to the firm were some of the highest-paid staff.

The change in compensation policy was the firm's worst-kept secret. As óne vice-president sitting on the London trading floor remembers, "The natural reaction was, 'Jesus Christ, what has he got that I ain't got, and what can I do to make that happen to me?' Everyone decided that they were going to become a proprietary trader."

AN UNUSUALLY LARGE group of partners departed at the end of 1993, prompting concern on the part of top management. Those who left were notable for their tenure and their youth. The average duration of partnership had been falling for some time, from eight years in 1986 to five years by 1994, in part because of the increasing class size, but half the partners who left Goldman Sachs in 1993 had been with the partnership for five years or less. This was a radical departure from days past when partners left the firm as old men. The effects of the partnership's abbreviated tenure could be felt throughout the firm. Trading desks benefit from having a few gray heads around, experienced hands who have traded through all the stages of an economic cycle. But the biggest advantage of seniority is probably on the relationship side, where client trust must be earned over many years.

As 1993 closed the firm had achieved the holy grail of investment banking. Profitability had soared across every division of the firm and not a single department had a losing year. While its competitors had seen their trading profits vacillate wildly, the firm had maintained its almost unblemished trading record for most of a decade. Over the years the profitability had come from trading centers throughout the firm and had not been concentrated in one or two traders' P&Ls. It was an astounding feat, yet as management looked forward to the new year it explicitly recognized the risks it faced. The firm's competitors, particularly U.S. investment banks and the largest U.S. and foreign commercial banks, had recovered from some of their difficulties in the 1980s and were stronger. But the firm remained vigilant in the face of the rejuvenated competition. Goldman Sachs has always been extremely concerned with its reputation. As the firm entered 1994 management recognized that that reputation was one of the most sensitive factors to manage in its business, always worthy of special attention.

In light of the firm's increased trading activity and principal investments, as well as its growing balance sheet, the management committee once again reviewed the idea of a public offering. The views among the various members differed, but before a decision could be reached Friedman shelved the idea. By early 1994 he had grown concerned about the firm's trading; the volatility of earnings, he felt, was too great to consider a public offering.

In the 1993 annual review, he praised the firm for its exceptional year. But he took time to remind all concerned that trees do not grow to the sky. Many within the firm now note that in some of the trading businesses by the end of 1993 confidence had turned into overconfidence, and a sense of infallibility had been allowed to develop. Goldman Sachs had achieved an unimagined level of profitability, but Friedman was aware of the perils that existed at the top. A lover of military history, he knew that after great victories in battle Roman generals would have a spectacular procession to mark the event. As they marched in the parade someone would follow a few steps behind whispering in their ear, "Remember you are mortal, remember you are mortal."

CHAPTER VI

1994

THE CURSE OF
SUCCESS

WHEN ASKED IN 1992 what could cause a firm to stumble, Bob Rubin replied, "Hubris, ego, arrogance, a sense of self-importance, if you allow them to develop. That's when you fall off the track." For years Rubin had led by example, issuing regular warnings on the dangers of overconfidence. But by 1994 he was gone.

In December 1993, the first month of the firm's 1994 fiscal year, Goldman Sachs looked unstoppable. In that single spectacular month the firm made record profits of $375 million, or more than one and a half times what it had made in an average month in 1993. In the next eleven months the firm would earn only $133 million, making its performance in 1994 the weakest in a decade.

Winkelman and Corzine had warned the partnership at its meeting in January that the exceptional level of profitability the firm was experiencing was just that, exceptional, and could not be expected to continue. Partners from the trading departments contend the information presented was understood on an intellectual level by all. But as the size of the partnership had increased, partners' familiarity with business outside of their narrow purview had decreased. Some banking partners feel the firm's risk models were not explained in sufficient detail until the spring of 1995, long after the information was needed. In good times few want to hear about darker days, and for those whose businesses were conducted at a great distance from the trading floors, it was an easy message to ignore.

When the management committee met in January, its focus was not on unsustainable revenue flows or increased cost controls but on culture, new business, and innovation. Still on a winning streak, the firm's top management wrestled with prospective opportunities such as China, investments in new technology, and an in-house hedge fund. On the agenda there was little discussion of contingency plans for the inevitable rainy day, although Friedman did ask his fellow management committee members to think about the impact a poor earnings performance would have on partner and employee morale. Instead, Friedman and his fellow management committee members were gearing up for a bright future.

To THE UNINITIATED, a trading floor looks like bedlam. In massive rooms measuring 10,000 square feet or more, traders and salespeople are seated only a few feet apart at row after row of long wooden desks. No concessions are made for seniority—the most experienced trader and the newest clerk have exactly the same amount of space. On the walls are mounted electronic tickertapes with up-to-the-second stock, bond, and currency prices from around the world flashing by in bright green lights. Televisions tuned to CNBC or CNN are scattered around the room. Every inch of every desktop is piled high with computers and other information retrieval screens and the many keyboards required to operate them. Notes are stuck to the edges of the screens, and financial reports, trade tickets, personal photos, newspapers, bottles of aspirin, half-finished cups of coffee, and half-eaten meals are stacked on every horizontal surface. Trading rooms have high ceilings to dissipate the noise and heat generated by hundreds of machines and human bodies. Under the false bottom floors is a thick tangle of wires. There is no privacy— every conversation, business or personal, is held within earshot of a dozen colleagues. The volume rises and falls with the ebb and flow of the market. Each trader has at his disposal two or three telephone receivers, which, at the push of a button, can be connected instantly to hundreds of traders and clients at other financial institutions, who are sitting at the same kind of cluttered desks half a mile or half a world away.

London's massive, open trading floor is punctuated by large square pillars. Some of these are adorned with digital clocks displaying the time in the world's major financial centers. Larry Becerra had wrapped the pillar closest to his desk in a seven-foot-long red flag with a life-size picture of a Native American. The flag could be seen from any spot on the floor. In 1993, Becerra had made more than $70 million for Goldman Sachs as one of the firm's most successful traders ever and had earned himself enough money to go ranch shopping. The conversation on trading floors had turned to second homes on snow-topped mountains, private airplanes, and helicopters, all sure signs of a market top.

In December 1993, Becerra liked Italian bonds so much that he had amassed an enormous position in them. When the Italian bond market rose sharply his positions alone made the firm $80 million in a single month—$80 million on a single trade, in a position so large it could not easily be exited. It was a huge leap in profitability for an individual trader, and Becerra gained another entry in the record books. A good month's profits for the entire firm were only twice that sum.

All bets were off. The numbers were so large that it seemed as if anything was possible if you were willing to take enough risk. As one former colleague commenting on Becerra's spectacular trading that month said, "The risk manual had been getting frayed at the edges; that just tore it up."

Nothing was too large now. The firm's proprietary traders felt confident that they could handle a position of almost any size. Large, concentrated bets were now the focus. As many partners have noted, the firm no longer focused on hitting singles and doubles; a home-run mentality permeated the trading floors. This new attitude did not go unnoticed. One area of the London trading floor became known as "testosterone alley" for the ribald conversation and daring trading practices.

The sense of overconfidence extended to the higher reaches of management. One trader of long standing had a disturbing conversation with a partner of considerable seniority in early 1994. "The end came for me when I went for a drink with this partner," he says. "He had recently met with the Fed [a member of the Federal Reserve Board] and was feeling good about the firm. 'We're too big to fail,' he told me. 'A $100 million loss, a $50 million loss, it means nothing. We're too big now, they won't let us fail.' " Hubris, the most deadly trading sin, had taken hold. "The only thing that kills franchises is prosperity," says Michael David Weill, the senior partner of the noted investment bank Lazard Freres, "because it goes to people's heads. They believe that if they are successful it is because they are particularly smart and then because they are particularly smart they can do anything." There was a growing feeling as 1994 began that trees did indeed grow to the sky.

Becerra had never taken the profits on his gargantuan Italian government bond position and instead rode it into February and the oncoming storm. Now he became doubly famous. No one had ever made $80 million in a month—and no one had made $80 million in a month and lost more than $100 million just thirty-one days later. If the first number had seemed incredible, the second was unthinkable.

In early 1994, the firm's expansion plans remained firmly in place. Since 1990, Goldman Sachs had opened offices in locations such as Beijing, Mexico City, Milan, Osaka, Seoul, Shanghai, Taipei, and Vancouver, and the professional staff had grown by 48 percent. With expansion the firm's expenses had risen substantially, increasing the demand for profits. In the first half of 1994 the firm's expenses were running at an annualized rate of $3.6 billion a year, or twice the rate they had in 1990. Costs that had risen with the opening of each new office were pushed up further by the expansion plans of competing banks. Large European banks looking for a toehold in New York offered lucrative packages to lure away highly trained staff. Experienced vice-presidents could not be replaced easily by cheaper, new M.B.A. hires but only by costly lateral hires, the bidding for whom increased salaries across the industry, putting immediate pressure on the firm to expand profits.

FOR MANY YEARS Bob Rubin had carried a battered legal briefcase, and when that gave out he switched to accordion folders, throwing them away when they became too tattered. Steve Friedman used an L.L. Bean canvas bag to tote the firm's most important documents. Now, despite the example from the top to play down the trappings of wealth, the overarching desire to do so had receded. The average Goldman Sachs employee could not be described as flashy or extravagant, given the general level of wealth, but after the unprecedented 1993 bonuses there were signs that things had begun to change. First the Lamborghinis appeared and then chartered airplanes. Penthouse flats in London, ranches in the Far West, and personal wine cellars were suddenly within reach, and two traders took their bonuses and turned them into helicopters. Partners, their wealth tied up with the firm, may have had to delay some consumption, but those who were now being paid like partners were free to spend as they pleased.

On February 4, 1994, the trading world changed for Goldman Sachs. In a largely preemptive move the Federal Reserve raised interest rates by one-half of 1 percent in an ultimately successful effort to contain the growing threat of inflation. This was the first of six interest rate increases over the course of ten months. Much of the speculative trading activity at Goldman Sachs and other financial institutions had benefited from a climate of falling interest rates. When the change came the firm's traders (as well as their peers in the industry) were slow to react. Bond markets all over the world went into a tailspin; the U.S. bond market dropped twelve points in the first quarter of the year. Bond markets, although much bigger and deeper than stock markets, do not make headlines, warrant congressional committee investigations, or provoke new legislation. But bond market declines can ultimately be much more damaging, driving up long-term interest rates (mortgages included) and increasing the costs of running a business. In other years a rise in interest rates might have caused a few investors and speculators, caught the wrong way around, to sell their bond positions, putting downward pressure on bond prices. But what happened in 1994 can only be described as an avalanche. Events conspired to make this the worst bear market in bonds since the 1930s. Both inside and outside Goldman Sachs the trading success of recent years had created ever larger pools of cash searching for short-term trading opportunities and the profits they could generate. The speculating community—investment banks, commercial banks, hedge funds, and others—had, through their successes, allowed their positions to increase dramatically, and by late 1993 they were all on one side of the market, their profits dependent on a continuing worldwide rally in bond prices. It became clear that speculative positions held by seemingly steady hands had grown larger than the markets could bear easily. The stampede of speculators all trying to sell bonds at the same time caused a downward spiral in prices. Liquidity in the marketplace dried up, making prices erratic and forcing bond values even lower.

In December 1993, one of the firm's most profitable traders had been bullish on the British pound, predicting its rise against the yen. The firm's appetite for risk had grown, and he established a large sterling-yen position that would benefit from the strengthening of the British currency against that of Japan. The pound rose gradually against the yen over the course of December and early January, but in February the British currency declined against the Japanese currency by 10 percent over fifteen trading days. By the time the position was fully liquidated, the loss totaled more than $80 million. The chorus of those concerned grew louder, and Winkelman and Corzine began to make more regular trips to London, spending long hours sitting on the trading desks. As risk taking had spread across the firm's trading desks, some of London's traders had now managed to lose most of their previous year's profits—and 1994 was still young.

Friedman spent opening day of the 1994 baseball season at Camden Yard in Baltimore, but he did not see the game. This would prove to be one of the worst trading days in the firm's history, and he spent the entire game holed up in a tiny office under the stands going over the problems with Corzine, who was in New York.

In 1994, Goldman Sachs was a highly diversified financial services company, and management could take comfort in the breadth and depth of its businesses. The firm, among other activities, traded coffee and lumber, underwrote bonds and stocks, arranged mergers, and invested its own capital in growing businesses. It was felt that an explosion could happen in any part of the firm—this was the risk of doing business—but that it would, to some degree, be counteracted by other areas left unaffected. In the stock market crash of 1987, for example, fixed income and

J. Aron were able to capitalize on a rising bond market and a falling dollar to compensate for some of the downturn in the equity businesses, and the firm ended the year profitably. Many partners believed that the firm's broad range of activities would shield it from a severe financial downturn. Partners have insisted that the firm's statistical models bore out this belief. However, some of this faith was misplaced. As the firm later explained, the profitability in 1993 was due "in large part to substantial and concentrated FICC [fixed income and currency and commodities] positions that benefited from declining interest rates and the decline in relative value of certain European currencies." When the Federal Reserve raised interest rates these large concentrated bets fell sharply in value. One partner says now that the firm drew too much comfort from thinking that 1994 could not happen because of its diversity, that investments as diverse as Euros, governments, U.S. equity capital markets, and coffee would not all go down in the same year. The J. Aron coffee department had never lost money, even when it was a separate company, until 1994. The firm had perhaps become, as one partner indicated, a bit "too smug" in its assurance that its bets were widely spread. As many have explained, this was a four standard deviation year. While equities, investment banking, some of the customer trading businesses within fixed income, and J. Aron did turn in solid performances, the losses from proprietary trading almost swamped their success.

"I think that it took a lot of time for traders to get their minds around the fact that 1992 and 1993 were a unique trading environment caused by a particular set of circumstances, a different world than 1994," Friedman said in 1996. "Nineteen ninety-four was a time for humility." While trading conditions had changed dramatically, with the bond market declining and volatility rising, Goldman Sachs was slow to react. Friedman feels that during this tumultuous period the firm no longer held the trading edge it once had. But adverse market conditions were not the only trials plaguing the firm.

The Maxwell affair had legs. However hard Goldman Sachs tried to put the uncomfortable facts of its association with the disgraced tycoon behind it, newspapers on both sides of the Atlantic refused to let the story die. Some financial debacles victimize a faceless horde of small investors who cannot be easily identified or put on the evening news. As a result, these episodes are deemed of little interest to the general public, and reporting on them is largely confined to the financial press. The Maxwell story was different. Seventeen thousand pensioners were facing lives of destitution as a result of his malfeasance, which had been aided by an array of wealthy American and European banks and accountants. The media had a big, juicy story and some very visible targets.

In 1993 the Securities and Exchange Commission looked into the firm's trading activities with Maxwell. Sheinberg was forced to testify, and all of his personal records—calendars, airline tickets, personal notes, and the like—as well as the firm's records relating to their trades were subpoenaed.

Although the SEC apparently did not charge the firm or Sheinberg with any wrongdoing, the pension funds brought lawsuits. The Maxwell pension trustees, staring at a £400 million hole left by Maxwell's thievery, decided that the best way forward in the spring of 1994 was to sue Goldman Sachs and Sheinberg in a U.S. court—before a sympathetic jury, if possible—on the charges of breach of contract and fiduciary responsibility, fraud, and conspiracy. The lawyers for the trustees argued that Goldman Sachs had conspired with Robert Maxwell to defraud pension participants, some of them elderly retired people, out of their life savings. They claimed that Goldman Sachs either knew of Maxwell's pilfering of shares or that it had reason to know, and that either way the firm aided him in his theft.

Goldman Sachs did not relish hearing these charges aired in open court. As one partner knowledgeable of the facts explained, while not admitting any wrongdoing in the Maxwell situation the firm did not do everything perfectly and it was anxious to put the episode behind it. The firm moved immediately to have the case dismissed, describing the charges as "invalid, misdirected, and represent[ing] an expensive and time-consuming distraction." Judge Beatrice Shainswit, sitting for the New York Supreme Court, did not see it that way. She said that defendants Goldman Sachs and Eric Sheinberg "virtually ignored all the allegations at the heart of plaintiffs' case." She denied the firm's motion to dismiss and ordered that the case go forward.

While Goldman Sachs exuded confidence publicly, inside the firm legal counsel Katz delivered a less optimistic message. Goldman Sachs was too rich and had been standing too close to the epicenter to walk away unscathed. And indeed a defense lawyer might be hard pressed to find a jury that would ignore the fact that the firm was $2.6 billion richer than a year ago while thousands of pensioners in Britain would be worrying about next winter's heating bills.

Goldman Sachs could not easily fight this case in court in either the United States or England. With a trial the story was destined to remain on the front pages and the publicity would have been terrible for business. Additionally, the risk-reward calculation for an investment bank in trying a case like this is very uneven. Jury polling in the past had shown that prospective jurors were not terribly sympathetic to investment bankers, and that complex cases of this sort were exceedingly difficult to try. If the firm were to be found guilty, a jury, eyeing the partners' $5 billion in capital, might decide that a high price should be paid for what the plaintiff lawyers had called "malicious, reckless and outrageous conduct." Moreover, if investment banks lose a case such as this, licenses can be revoked, businesses must be closed, reputations are destroyed, and firms can go under. The risk is simply too high.

Even before the case was filed in New York the firm had begun negotiations in London for a worldwide settlement between the banks involved and the pension funds. While staunchly maintaining its innocence, in 1995, Goldman Sachs agreed to pay $253 million to settle the cases on both sides of the Atlantic. Despite paying out a quarter of a billion dollars, the partnership had over-reserved in anticipation of such a financial charge. Management was anxious to put this episode behind them and a settlement would achieve just that.

Nonetheless, the resolution dismayed many partners who had believed the firm's optimistic statements in the press and were shocked when they received word of the size of the settlement. Some partners were angry with the management committee and with Sheinberg, and a few accused the management committee of lying to them about the scale of the problem. A battle also erupted between the general and limited partners (retirees who had left more than $1 billion in capital with the firm) as to who would bear financial responsibility. Katz had tried to prepare the limited partners for this event, but few of the more than one hundred limited partners had attended the meetings he held to discuss the Maxwell settlement. Moreover, the general partners, who receive monthly statements of the firm's accounts, could see the huge reserves the firm was making; the limited partners had no such opportunity.

Two well-respected limited partners, Fred Krimendahl and James Gorter, were asked to look into the matter on behalf of the limited partners. Their task was to examine the charges and suggest an allocation of responsibility for any financial settlement among the various partnership classes. Many limited partners, having been assured and reassured by management that the firm had done no wrong, expected Krimendahl and Gorter to reaffirm this view. The limited partners were stunned. After looking at the evidence of the case against the firm, partners who were there remember Krimendahl and Gorter concluding, in essence, "If we were the plaintiffs we would not settle."

The entire burden of the settlement fell on those who had been partners in 1989, 1990, and 1991, despite the fact that more than half of those required to pay were now retired. Limited partners who had never been given the details of the firm's actions with regard to Maxwell were told simply to take out their checkbooks.

The monetary costs of the Maxwell episode were tremendous. In addition to the massive settlement and four years of public relations and legal fees, at the time of the publisher's death the firm still had $62 million in outstanding loans and $29 million in unsecured foreign exchange transactions with Maxwell. When the British government revoked Salomon Brothers's mandate to underwrite the British Telecom offering in North America because of concerns over its possible role in the U.S. treasury bond scandal in 1991, it had given the nod to Goldman Sachs. The firm was required to assure the British authorities that nothing in its dealings with Maxwell or anyone else was improper. Two years later, when the British government floated the third tranche of British Telecom (in a deal known in the market as BT3), Goldman Sachs would be excluded from the list of underwriters. The press at the time reported that the firm's relationship with Maxwell lay behind the slight, although Goldman Sachs said only that they understood that it was because of some conflicts. Privatizations were lucrative, but more important, they brought the firms that led them prestige and priceless publicity. To be deliberately left out must have been a stinging rebuke.

The nonmonetary cost to Goldman Sachs of dealing with Maxwell was also enormous. The greatest damage was done in London, where for a time the names Robert Maxwell and Goldman Sachs became linked in the minds of the financial world. From the beginning, some partners within the firm had warned of Maxwell's shady reputation and practices. "We thought," said one partner, "that Maxwell was just another corner-cutting, tough-nosed businessman. We thought we could go down into the snake pit with him, armed with a stick and snake boots." Goldman Sachs did not need Maxwell; at any point the firm could have decided that dealing with him posed a risk to its own good name and walked away. Investment banks live and die by their ability to analyze the balance between risk and reward; in dealing with Maxwell, Goldman Sachs sorely miscalculated this crucial equation.

For more than a year the firm was bombarded by bad press. London publications from serious magazines like *The Economist* to tabloids, ran articles on the firm's relationship to Maxwell. Many second-guessed the firm's judgment in dealing with Maxwell and questioned its image of honesty and staking the moral high ground.

By April 1994 the Maxwell suit was not the firm's only problem. The second floor of the London office, which housed Goldman Sachs's fixed income and foreign exchange departments, had managed to lose $350 million since the start of the fiscal year. Concern at the size of the losses drove management for the first time in memory to tell its traders to curtail their risk. "Just don't lose any money" was the message most traders remember and trading risks, by and large, were scaled back considerably. By this point in the year, other trading operations, such as Bankers Trust, had told their traders to take some vacation and shut down many risk-taking accounts. Friedman took a different approach from the previous two years. "I got a little bit micro that year and started looking at some of the traders' books," he said, "and it was quite remarkable that some people had gone many, many months without making money. We reduced their limits."

At Goldman Sachs traders for the most part decided on their own when to close positions down. Management rarely intervened. Trading managers had sat on the desks for which they were responsible and were kept apprised of the thinking and actions of those who reported to them. Top management was kept informed through reports and informal channels of communication. It was a system that until now had worked well. The level of trust and comfort between staff and management was high, and until 1994 there seemed to be little need for a more formal approach.

In 1995, Goldman Sachs introduced an interdisciplinary, firm-wide risk management system, a risk committee that meets weekly, and a loss limit on every trading seat. At the push of a button, management can aggregate the firm's market and credit risks across the entire organization at any point during the day. Computers make all this possible; no longer is risk assessed with a series of phone calls and a quick tally on a scratch pad. Every week traders are required to defend their positions before a committee made up of representatives from throughout the firm. The committee acts as a qualitative filter, and only careful, well-reasoned, and researched bets get through. Each trader's chair has a risk limit—not a predetermined size for a position, but a set amount the firm would be comfortable losing before a trader is shut down. But none of this was in place in 1994.

O'Brien's genius and his weakness as a manger of traders was that he believed in hiring the best people and letting them get on with it, as long as he was kept informed. Traders who worked for O'Brien consulted with him and kept him informed, but by and large they were left to their own devices. Everyone loved the trading environment he created, and most thrived under these conditions. But for traders undeterred by the firm's culture, there were few formal management constraints.

Goldman Sachs continued to reduce its market risk, which was a little like chasing its own tail. Some in management remember that at times the risk was difficult to adjust because "as soon as you ratcheted it down in half, the volatility would double." Many within the firm have argued that it was the unprecedented volatility of the world's bond markets in 1994 that was the firm's undoing. Yet a study of bond market volatility by a former Goldman Sachs economist shows that while 1994 was a volatile year it was by no means unprecedented. European bonds had seen much rockier markets as recently as 1990, when the firm was earning record profits. The U.S. bond markets had been more volatile in 1980, 1984, and 1987, and in all three years the firm turned in a good performance. Certainly the firm's huge open risk positions caused problems. Some partners defend the 1994 performance by noting that the firm's models had accurately predicted the risk, and the trading losses of 1994 were simply a cost, albeit a high one, of doing business. Others, including many in positions of power in the firm today, view the events differently. Goldman Sachs, they argue, became too much like a hedge fund, taking large leveraged bets on the direction of markets with the risk of sustaining huge losses. Compounding the problem was an unwillingness to let go. One partner with considerable seniority explained that the firm had the arrogance to stay with their positions too long. Traders, he argues, reasoned that if they liked the position at a given point and it moved against them the opportunity only looked better. Some of the trades, partners have noted, were in illiquid instruments that "you just couldn't get out of." Another partner who was on the management committee at the time noted with some resignation, "Nineteen ninety-four we did to ourselves."

During 1993 and 1994, as the firm's positions increased and the volatility of profits rose, Bob Rubin's trading expertise was sorely missed. Some partners have speculated that if Rubin had stayed and Friedman had had his counsel, 1994 would have turned out very differently.

By the summer it was clear that Goldman Sachs's troubles were profound and the firm was undergoing, according to one partner, a remarkable stretch of making the wrong bet. Still, as Friedman acknowledges, "What had happened had been what the models had predicted would happen if the bets were wrong. The bad news was that the bets would continue to be consistently wrong." Later, looking back on this period, Corzine admitted, "We developed a pattern of success in macrotrading and allowed ourselves to overconcentrate our risk in those areas. That, along with outright poor market judgments, caused the bulk of the 1994 problems."

When the management committee met for a strategy session in August, the emphasis was no longer on new businesses or expansion. Friedman challenged his committee members to take a long, disciplined look at the firm's priorities and costs, to take a fresh approach and rethink their business strategies. He asked them to imagine that they had just sold Goldman Sachs and, as a requirement for getting paid, had to achieve some predefined rate of return. What would they do differently? Personally,

Friedman was convinced that the firm needed to cut expenses immediately, and he proposed a reduction in head count. He felt that the firm had invested too heavily in opportunities that would not come to fruition, and he urged retrenchment. He asked his fellow management committee members to keep an open mind and examine every option. On issues that could have a major effect on the firm, such as those involving legal and ethical concerns, Friedman felt that it was incumbent upon the senior partner to make a decision. But business issues like expansion and staffing would be put to a vote of the management committee. Earlier in the year, he had wanted to curtail the firm's plans for expansion but was outvoted by his fellow management committee members. Those members had been more optimistic about the organization's prospects, but by August, with Friedman pushing hard, a hiring freeze was agreed upon.

Friedman's first years as partner in the early 1970s—and later, in the 1980s, when the firm had some fixed income losses—had taught him that "this thing can go both ways." It was a lesson he would never forget, but as Friedman recalls, "At the beginning of the year there was too much of a euphoric sense of 'We can bet on our judgment about markets directions.' Some people said, 'Well, *everyone* got caught in the bad markets,' as they did, but you are entitled to exercise judgment and be smarter than other people and at least recognize when you no longer have an edge in the market. . . . I didn't find that people were real good at hearing that at the end of 1993." Many other firms were having a difficult year, but other than Salomon Brothers (which ended the year with a loss of $399 million, its London proprietary trading unit losing $400 million), Goldman Sachs was perhaps the most aggressive trading firm on Wall Street and as such would suffer one of the largest reversals in fortune.

Friedman was concerned but not alarmed. "No competitor with acceptable leverage suffered direly in the long term because of bad trading results in liquid markets," he says. His role as senior partner, he felt, was to safeguard Goldman Sachs from any threats to its existence. Bad assets (nonperforming loans and the like), liquidity problems, and lack of legal compliance are the three things that can bring down firms in a heartbeat. Friedman left the trading operation in the hands of his lieutenants, Corzine and Winkelman, although he watched it carefully. Corzine and Winkelman, both experienced and level-headed traders, had been through times of market turmoil before and never lost their nerve during this most recent crisis. While the management committee was less than thrilled by the trading losses accruing in their divisions, they knew the situation was being controlled by steady hands.

By autumn the firm had ceased most of its riskiest trading, but it was not clear how the hemorrhage would be stopped. Goldman Sachs was

losing money at the rate of $200 million a month. The firm's expense
structure, swollen in recent years, was crippling. There had been no firings, and the torrent of revenues usually produced by the firm's trading
businesses was now a mere trickle. Management needed to act quickly
and decisively to protect the integrity of the firm. For many partners
August, September, and October were very scary times, and it was hard
to see how and when the firm's fortunes would reverse. There was certainly a risk for partners remaining with the firm that their capital
accounts would be further diminished.

There was one big trade left. Mark Houghton-Berry had spent most of
his professional career at Goldman Sachs. A Brit with an Oxford degree
and a Stanford M.B.A., he was actively recruited to join J. Aron in the
fall of 1985. H-B, as he is known to everyone, has a plum-in-the-
mouth accent that betrays his upper-class background. An exceedingly
articulate man, his cynical sense of humor and first-rate analytical mind
made him a fixture on the London trading floor. Hanging over his desk
for many years was a sign copied off a Reuters screen that read in big letters, "It started in such a small way. Just doing it for kicks. It seemed
exciting and all my friends were doing it too. It got bigger though and
pretty soon I was doing it every day. I thought I could handle it but I was
wrong. Short sterling futures can really screw you up. Just say no."
Houghton-Berry's success in trading the treacherous short sterling interest rate contract (a futures contract that moves with the level of short-
term U.K. interest rates) was widely known, and many had envied and
imitated him. Yet the message taped to his computer would prove
strangely prophetic.

Houghton-Berry and Gavyn Davies, the firm's U.K. economist, were
friends. Hailing from opposite ends of the political spectrum, the two
shared a love of markets and golf. Davies had strong ties to the Labour
Party while Houghton-Berry came from an old staunchly Tory colonial
family. The two had often enjoyed a friendly argument over government
economic policy, but in the spring of 1994 they were in complete agreement. Over the course of 1993, interest rates in Britain had declined.
Eddie George, the governor of the Bank of England, following the lead of
the Federal Reserve, hinted that this trend might soon be reversed. Once
the market had accepted that rates would fall no further, it began to
anticipate the next round of rate rises (rates moved up in the market even
before the Bank of England formally raised them, as the market "discounted" the central bank's impending action). It was Davies's view,
shared by Houghton-Berry, that although rates in the U.K. would rise
over time, they would not reach the levels anticipated in the market nor
rise as quickly as current prices would suggest. Davies ultimately would

be proved right, but not before he and his partners suffered one final, staggering loss.

Houghton-Berry's short sterling position had been built up throughout the year, a cocktail of 50,000 options and futures designed to express his precise view on the magnitude and timing of the expected rate rises. It was a "house position" watched closely by four partners and one of the firm's most experienced traders. Like other trades in the past two years, it was so large that "you couldn't expect to trade out of it," Houghton-Berry remembers. Like other major bets the firm had taken in 1993 and 1994, Goldman Sachs had to be right or it risked losing tens of millions of dollars.

An unsuccessful bill tender (in which the central bank sells short-term bills) by the Bank of England in July sent shock waves through the market. Rates rose in the market one hundred basis points (1 percent), and on paper the position lost more than $50 million. "It was just complete mayhem. But it was a failed auction, not a change in official rates," Houghton-Berry recalls. There was no economic foundation for the market's move, and although extensive conversations were held with management, Houghton-Berry kept his nerve as well as the position. As the markets regained their senses with the realization that the Bank of England had not raised rates, the position recouped its losses, and by early September it was marginally profitable. On Wednesday, September 7, the bank held its monetary meeting to determine rates. The Bank of England's actions in the marketplace on Thursday suggested that there would be no rate rise, and the short sterling contract rallied on Friday. Over the weekend Davies published a column in the *Independent*, a national newspaper, saying that the Bank of England had decided to hold policy steady until November or later. Monday morning things looked even better; the position had recouped all of its losses and more and was up $10 million from a hole in Houghton-Berry's trading account of $70 million. But on that morning, September 12, both Steve Friedman and the Bank of England had surprises for Goldman Sachs.

For months Bob Katz was the only person at Goldman Sachs who knew Friedman's secret. He was Friedman's only internal consigliere, and the two met often to discuss Friedman's plans. On the morning of September 6, at a regularly scheduled management committee meeting, Friedman announced that he was resigning from the general partnership and would become a limited partner. Katz had kept this secret, and the response was shock. One investment banker turned to another and whispered, "Is this a joke?" Some inquired into Friedman's health, and he offered reassurances. But by his own admission he was physically worn out; the grueling hours, heavy travel schedule, and pressures of running an organization in the throes of change were all taking their toll. He had missed seeing his children grow up, he said, and wanted to see his grand-children grow up. A year earlier he had told his family of his plans to depart, but felt obliged to stay on for one more year. He still had many major projects in the works that he wanted to see to completion. And the succession question had not yet been resolved. In June 1994, Friedman had begun preparations for his departure. With the help of an unwitting partner (who was told they were preparing the "kidnap scenario," con-tingency plans should anything untoward ever happen to Friedman), pro-files of top management were assembled for the purpose of selecting a successor.

The relentless pace that had characterized Friedman's career at Gold-man Sachs from the beginning marked his departure. On September 6, he told his fellow management committee members that the identity of the new senior partner would be announced the following Monday, Septem-ber 12, at the regularly scheduled partners' meeting. He was in a hurry because the management committee knew the problems that plagued their competitors when they let the succession question linger. The process could be highly divisive and Friedman was certain that by accel-erating the decision this fate could be averted. A tight timetable also meant fewer leaks. There would be no intrigue, no hints in the news-papers or wild rumors flying around the office. But Friedman knew he was running a big risk. The Bank of England would meet on Friday, Sep-tember 9, and almost certainly report the following Monday. Friedman had watched Houghton-Berry's short sterling position, closely monitor-ing the daily swing in profit and loss, and he knew his would not be the only news the firm would receive on the 12th.

Friedman spoke to each member of the management committee during the week and encouraged them to speak among themselves. He asked the group to submit, in short written statements, suggestions about both the structure of the top management and the best occupants for the role. Many possibilities were considered, including another co–senior partner pairing, a triumvirate, or the eventual solution of a chairman and a vice-chairman. Gus Levy, in 1969, had been the last person to be designated a clear number one. Friedman and Weinberg had run the firm alone only after their co–senior partner had resigned. All agreed that one man should not be asked to shoulder the chairman's role alone as Friedman had done for the past two years.

As discussion began, it became clear that there was a strong consensus in the top partners' views of each other. However, when it came to self-analysis, the views were far more disparate, as members of the management committee were less objective about themselves. "Our management committee is like a college of cardinals. They're very talented people, and as in the college of cardinals, a substantial number of them have a reasonable, legitimate belief that they should be elevated," said Friedman.

During the week that Friedman was guiding the management committee toward one of the most important decisions of his tenure, he was not afforded the luxury of concentrating on the task full-time. He was not even in New York. Goldman Sachs had been courting the German government actively for years in an effort to be named one of the lead underwriters for the Deutsche Telekom privatization scheduled for 1996. Because of this relationship, Friedman was invited by Chancellor Helmut Kohl to attend the ceremonies at which Russian troops were to depart from Berlin. The Deutsche Telekom offering was the most important piece of business available to Goldman Sachs since the Ford Motor Company underwriting almost forty years earlier, and Friedman could not refuse this invitation. He took the red-eye flight to Germany, checked into his hotel, looked longingly at the crisply made bed, then headed straight to the ceremonies. It was important that Goldman Sachs "show the flag," and as the head of the firm, only he could perform the task.

Every member of the management committee agreed from the start that Jon Corzine was part of the solution. Years earlier, long before the succession issue was ever raised, Rubin had confided his belief that Corzine would one day lead the firm. Corzine had for a number of years been operating as chief financial officer of Goldman Sachs. Despite the problems now facing the trading businesses under his supervision, all agreed he would have the major role going forward. Friedman was heartened by this fact; personally, he saw Corzine and Hank Paulson, one of the co-heads of investment banking, as the best team, and he hoped his fellow management committee members would reach the same conclusion. In his view it was desirable to have a trader and a banker in the two top slots, providing the firm with leaders who had expertise across the firm's main businesses.

Back in New York, Friedman met with Corzine and Katz at his home on Saturday. He also had lunch that weekend with John Weinberg, and he spoke to John Whitehead by telephone. On Sunday the management committee met at a midtown hotel, and Friedman officially nominated Corzine for the position of senior partner, with Paulson as vice-chairman. Corzine and Paulson had a chance to say a few words and then stepped outside the room to watch a tennis match on television while their partners considered the future. The discussion focused on whether Corzine and Paulson should have equal titles or if Corzine should be made a clear

number one. The decision to go with Corzine and Paulson was unanimous, and Corzine was named the sole senior partner. After the two men
rejoined the group a toast was raised.

On Monday, September 12, several hours before Friedman was to
announce his departure to the partnership, the Bank of England raised
interest rates. Despite its actions of a few days earlier, the bank pushed up
short-term rates by half a percent to 5.75 percent, and the short sterling
futures contract plummeted. Friedman's first call that morning was from
Corzine. There was a problem in London; the firm had lost tens of millions of dollars in minutes. This was the beginning of the worst quarter
Goldman Sachs had experienced in decades. Friedman knew he could
become the target of heavy criticism if at one of the firm's bleakest
moments he became a limited partner, turning away from managing the
firm and shielding his own capital from further losses. He began to wonder whether he was making a mistake. Was this perhaps not the right
moment to leave? "I thought about it pretty carefully during the year,"
says Friedman. "Although we were having a crummy year and I pushed
us to tighten our belts on a number of occasions, after I announced my
retirement subsequent trading results in September, October, and November were particularly rotten. If the last quarter had happened earlier, I
would have changed my decision." But now it was too late. Corzine was
ready, and the clock could not be turned back.

Minutes after the Bank of England announcement Corzine telephoned
Houghton-Berry. He wanted to know where the markets were trading, how the position stood. Markets do not cope well with surprises,
and the news was all bad. "The market went into panic," Houghton-
Berry remembers. "People started talking about rates as high as 8 percent by Christmas." Prices moved down sharply, overshooting any
reasonable expectations, as markets prepared for a shock that would
never materialize.

Despite the pain, Goldman Sachs never completely lost heart. After
years of urging its traders to take risks and expressing confidence in their
talents, the firm was not going to order Houghton-Berry to get out completely. One former trading partner suggests that this is one of the firm's
strengths. They were smart to never close down a business, "never to
slash and burn," instead making their cuts judiciously. Proprietary trading had been an engine of profits in London and New York; they would
not shut down a business that had served them so well for eight years.
Just get the position way down, Houghton-Berry was told; reduce the
risk.

The magnitude of Goldman Sachs's exposure was common knowledge
in the market, so getting out was a little like playing a card game in which

everyone else knows your hand. The market was skittish and illiquid, but slowly Houghton-Berry managed to work the position off and in doing so moved the markets against himself and depressed prices further. In the end, the position lost $50 million. By Christmas, interest rates had risen to only 6.25 percent. Had Houghton-Berry carried the position until year-end, the futures and options would have made about $20 million.

As the end of 1994 approached some partners faced a decision they had not anticipated. The deadline for committing to the next two years' partnership agreement was the day after Thanksgiving, and many partners were reconsidering their decision to stay with the partnership. At a time like this the value of a partnership cuts both ways. It is clearly a disadvantageous structure when partners and their capital can depart easily in difficult times. Had the firm had another unsatisfactory year in 1995 it would have been better off as a public company, with the downside protection which that form could provide. But for management in 1994 there were advantages to running a private company. Public shareholders, in love with predictable recurring earnings, have shown little tolerance for substantial trading losses, and when they have occurred those shareholders have vented their disappointment on the company's share price. For the firm's management, explaining those losses to highly sophisticated investors, like the firm's general partners, its employees, and outside investors was far easier than standing in front of an overflowing auditorium of angry shareholders might have been.

"LET ME BEGIN by attempting to describe my feelings," Jon Corzine said to his partners at the September meeting. "I am excited, honored, and humbled." At this point in its history, Goldman Sachs was in need of a leader with the common touch, a man who could understand and appeal to what his partners were feeling. Some men, once in a position of power, develop a certain charisma; Corzine always had it. Until stepping down as co–chief executive in January 1999 he was an accessible leader who, like Rubin before him, was comfortable wandering the trading floors, chatting with staff in the elevators. His partners describe him as understanding and unpretentious, a leader whose door was always open. In his beard and signature sweater, he brought to the firm a more informal style—one that reflected the more casual atmosphere of a trading floor. It was an appealing image. Corzine says "thank you" to waiters and speaks graciously to hired drivers; he has the ability to relate to anyone within the firm, regardless of his or her rank or importance. In a company that can no longer be run simply by the will of its chairman, where consensus is more important than ever, these are essential characteristics.

Goldman Sachs needed a trader in the top job. The trading businesses at Goldman Sachs are newer and more volatile than the banking side of the firm and require more attention and experience from top management. Client businesses run more easily of their own accord and fit better with the firm's cultural instincts. Putting a trader in the top spot was in keeping with the times. When Gus Levy headed Goldman Sachs, his peers running competing firms were all bankers. By 1994 this had changed, and top posts at Morgan Stanley, First Boston, Salomon Brothers, and Lehman Brothers were filled with men who came from their firm's trading departments. Still, Corzine's appointment as senior partner was not without controversy. Some banking partners felt that rather than be elevated, Corzine should have been made to bear some of the responsibility for the firm's troubles, many of which originated in his division. One current partner feels that Corzine's appointment raised the level of concern among some of the firm's investment bankers. They no longer wanted to be part of an organization that engaged in the kind of risky trading Corzine had supervised. If he was going to the top, they were going out the door.

Corzine and Paulson inherited a firm in crisis. Unlike Friedman's own rise to power—which John Weinberg paved the way for three years before he vacated the top job—they would have no preparation, no transition period in which the firm or the outside world could adjust to the new arrangement. Partners, clients, and rating agencies were nervous. Many on the banking side did not know Corzine well and were suspicious. This was one of the ways in which Paulson, a lifelong investment banker, played an invaluable role. By providing those in his own department with reassurances of Corzine's abilities and leadership, he convinced many to remain loyal.

As Weinberg had done in the wake of the Penn Central fiasco and again after Levy's sudden death in 1976, Corzine and Paulson called on some of the firm's most important clients. Their message was one of reassurance and control. Lessons had been learned, they told them, and new risk controls would be put in place. Corzine put his credibility on the line when he took over. The rating agencies were nervous—large losses and volatile earnings are not their cup of tea. Rumors of a credit downgrade swirled in the market. Corzine went to the rating agencies and made a personal appeal. I have just taken over, he told them; your actions will be a judgment on me, and I have not even started. You owe me the time to try, he argued successfully.

Corzine was forty-seven years old when he was named head of the firm; Paulson was forty-eight at the time. An entire generation of partners now had to acknowledge that the road to the top job was blocked.

Corzine knew that resignations would almost certainly follow. "You have to acknowledge that this can be, is, a painful experience," he said. "You reach out. I don't know how else to do it. You sit down and try to appreciate how someone else might feel about the results." Corzine hoped the management committee members would stay on. "We've all learned over a long period of time how to work with each other. The chemistry is good." In early 1997 Corzine would elevate Paulson to the newly created position of president, and Roy Zuckerberg, a thirty-year veteran of the firm and head of its equity division, and Robert Hurst, the head of investment banking, to the posts of co–vice chairmen. By that time every other member of the management committee—including everyone who thought he was in contention for the leadership at that meeting in late 1994, with the exception of Katz—would be gone.

The first and most dramatic departure was Mark Winkelman's. Aside from Corzine and Paulson, Winkelman had been the most serious contender for a top spot. At the time of his departure he was the head of J. Aron and co-head of the fixed income area. Corzine praised Winkelman's talents publicly, calling him "one of the brightest, ablest people I've ever been around. Goldman Sachs is a hell of a lot better off with Mark helping build our future." It was a widely shared view. Some have suggested that Corzine had hoped to run the firm with Winkelman. Others refute this and point out that the firm, especially after the difficulties of 1994, could not be run by two traders.

The problem Goldman Sachs faced was not only one of financial losses but of a loss in confidence. Partnerships stand on confidence and trust. In the autumn of 1994, both of these were badly shaken. "The traffic around here was incredible," one current partner recalls, pointing to the hall in front of his office. Partners swarmed in and out of each other's offices, discussing their plans and fears and guessing who would resign next. Some spouses grew concerned as they watched their net worth slipping away. "September, October, November 1994 . . . there was ever more frenzied activity," one vice-president remembers, "partners looking over their shoulders at each other, wondering who was going to jump ship next. There was an air of barely controlled panic as you watched people watching each other trying to decide what to do as decision time approached."

In October of 1994 twenty-three partners had resigned since the last partnership agreement had been signed almost two years earlier. By Thanksgiving that number had doubled, as fully 30 percent of the partnership departed over a two-year period. In a matter of months the firm lost, among others, its senior partner, the co-head of fixed income and head of J. Aron, three members of the management committee, the head of research, the heads of government bond trading and corporate bond trading, and its chief international economist, as well as the partners in charge of the Tokyo, Hong Kong, and Los Angeles offices.

The partners who left the firm in 1994 were not doddering fools on the brink of senility, but men who only a few months earlier had thought themselves to be in the prime of their Goldman Sachs careers. These were men with substantive experience and institutional memories—what the firm likes to call its "culture carriers." They were the very people who otherwise would have been relied upon to train the next generation of partners. The experience and leadership of those who left would not easily be replaced.

Just when the partnership needed to stand firm and united, it was unraveling. The defections devastated morale across the firm, and the esprit de corps that had characterized the Goldman Sachs partnership was shattered. More would have left but for Corzine's and Paulson's persuasiveness. Many who knocked on their doors to announce their resignations were convinced to stay. But Corzine did not wait for others to knock; he went to small gatherings throughout the firm and spoke to anyone who would listen about his vision for the future. He romanced his audience, reminding his colleagues of what it meant to be a partner of Goldman Sachs and reassuring them that the fundamentals were still in place. What he conveyed was the depth of his own feelings about Goldman Sachs and his belief in the firm's future.

Other members of the management committee spoke to the disaffected as well. "One of the strengths throughout the firm is a preoccupation with focusing on those things that are not going well. This is not a place where people like to take victory laps," explains David Silfen, a member of the management committee and the co-head of equities at the time. "However, in 1994 when I talked to my partners I tried to concentrate on the glass being half full. I tried to make them aware of what was factual and what was not; as not everyone had access to all of the information. But there were still some individuals who continued to be uncomfortable. In those instances I would race to open the exit door for them, as it was clear they were not going to be good partners going forward."

Paulson concentrated on the banking partners, by all accounts the most shaken group at the firm. Bankers are by and large a conservative group, and for many of them the situation appeared simple. Banking was doing well, it continued to do well, and its profitability was being washed away by proprietary trading losses. They wanted Paulson to explain how it was going to stop. The greatest fear was among these bankers, who were the least knowledgeable about the firm's trading businesses. At a partnership meeting a few years earlier a top management consultant had come to talk about the firm's businesses. He had told the partners, strangely enough, that foreign exchange trading was not risky, which accounted for why the firm was making so much money in that area. Some investment bankers, removed from the trading businesses, seemed to have believed him, and to them the events of 1994 came as a rude surprise.

Paulson explained to the many partners who during the fall of 1994 seated themselves on the couch in his office that the situation was not out of control and that what happened would not happen again. The management committee had learned much in the past twelve months. Traders were not going to stick with losing positions for a long time, and the firm knew that it was not bigger than the market. In the future, he assured them, Goldman Sachs would take much more controlled risks, and formal mechanisms, like the risk committee, would prevent any new mishaps. Paulson told those who came to him that they could not have a better leader than Corzine.

As Corzine was busy cajoling partners to stay, he also extended invitations to fifty-eight new members to join. The class of 1994 was the largest to date, partially to replace the large number of partners who were leaving. One of those invited passed up the opportunity, preferring to take a job with an investment boutique, but the other fifty-seven fell into line. Upon seeing the details of the firm's finances for the first time, some of the new partners were unpleasantly surprised. One vice-president described the experience of not having been named a partner in 1994 as, "Rushing to the airport, racing through check-in, and tearing down the corridors, only to see the door of the airplane close and the aircraft taxi away from the gate. Standing at the window, cursing your own stupidity at having missed the flight, you watch the jet speed down the runway and explode on take-off." While this analysis may have been apt in the darkest days of 1994 and early 1995, three short years later the financial prospects of the partnership class of 1994 had become the envy of those working in the banking industry the world over.

Some of the staff became disaffected as they watched the management ranks change and their year-end compensation dwindle. Many at Goldman Sachs believed that there was a covenant, a pact between partners and their employees. Each year professionals were told that Goldman Sachs did not pay the highest compensation in the industry, but that the firm would stick by its employees in tough times. (While the firm staunchly denies that it pays less than the industry standard, the rating agency Standard & Poor's has noted that, "The partnership structure also helps to keep compensation low relative to other firms.") " 'We are saving it for a rainy day,' they said each year," one vice-president with substantial tenure in New York recalled. "Well, 1994 was a monsoon." Professionals now saw their compensation reduced by as much as 40 to 60 percent. No one would argue that these people were starving, but there was a sense of betrayal and distrust that arose from the pay cuts. The firmwide bonus granted to nonprofessional staff was cut from 30 percent to 8 percent—the lowest level since the early 1970s. The pact had been broken, and some employees' trust in the partners was destroyed. As trust faded, staff drifted out the door. The mammoth German bank Deutsche Bank alone would hire more than fifty Goldman Sachs employees. The moves were unprecedented. In the past, few with promising careers had left Goldman Sachs, and when they did it was usually for a top American competitor. Now seven-figure pay packages with multiyear guarantees from foreign banks proved hard to ignore, and in 1994 and 1995 the headhunters who work the Wall Street territories had the richest pickings within Goldman Sachs of their careers.

Many at the firm have argued strenuously that it is important to focus on the broader picture and look at Goldman Sachs's earnings over a two- or three-year period including 1994. During that period the firm earned on average $1.5 billion a year, making it one of the most successful firms on Wall Street. They maintain that to focus on a single twelve-month period is unfair and misrepresentative. But surely this misses the point. Nineteen ninety-four was a debacle not because the firm suffered large trading losses but because it lost so many experienced partners and their capital. The destabilizing effect of these departures and the ensuing turmoil that engulfed the firm was a much greater problem than the dollar losses themselves. Money can be made back easily, but losses of confidence, trust, and valued staff are infinitely more difficult to recoup.

Many partners who left in 1994 felt they had no choice. Goldman Sachs was no longer a firm they recognized; it had chosen to pursue a path of risk taking with which they did not agree. With the vast majority of their wealth tied up in the firm and the senior partner and many other high-ranking colleagues walking out the door, many wondered if they should preserve what they had and depart. Some of those who left during this period argue that the management committee became greedy in its pursuit of short-term profits; as a result the firm's risk was badly managed and partners suffered for it financially. With a loss of confidence in management, departures were inevitable.

Those who remained say that the defectors panicked at the first sign of trouble; after having enjoyed the largesse of 1992 and 1993 they left the firm as soon as its fortunes waned. Those who departed are viewed as weakhearted and unwilling to accept that Wall Street is a highly cyclical business with good years and bad. The departures, they suggest, were driven by personal greed. Some current partners are quite cynical about what was causing the departures: the fear that personal wealth was at risk. Some partners who remained at the firm were embarrassed by how certain elements of the partnership failed to stand up to tough times.

The partners' meeting on November 17, 1994, was billed as the most important in memory. Thirteen days remained until the partnership agreement needed to be signed, and Corzine spoke compellingly to his partners, telling them that the situation required "character, commitment, and action." The times, he said, called for consolidation and retrenchment. The firm would rebalance the mix, lowering its dependence on trading profits and refocusing on teamwork and clients. Quoting John Weinberg, Corzine said that they needed to "leave history to the historians and go forward."

Interest peaked when Paulson spoke. While Corzine explained philosophically how the firm would change and adapt, Paulson tackled the nuts and bolts. He presented his partners with three profit scenarios for the coming year, all of which he thought were ridiculously low. He spoke of his plans to take $1 billion off the firm's "run rate"—its ongoing costs—lowering expenses to $2.6 billion. In the first scenario the firm would make profits of $1.2 billion, in the second case $1 billion, and in the final case $900 million. Paulson showed his colleagues step by step, business by business, from where the firm's revenues would come and how the firm could easily generate $3.7 billion in revenues. Still there was skepticism, and the partners showered him with questions about the minutiae of his presentation. Paulson felt he had gone on too long, that the discussion was too detailed and tedious, but every time he looked up at his audience he saw that they were rapt, still furiously taking notes after two hours. He was speaking the words they hoped to hear, the details of how the firm would thrive going forward. One partner-designate from the class of 1994 (although not yet legally partners, the group had been invited to the meeting) grew concerned. If the firm earned $1 billion, $500 million immediately came off for outside investors. Of the remaining $500 million, each new partner would be entitled to roughly thirty basis points (this number is somewhat oversimplified, because some of each year's profits are on investments made in earlier years, and those profits do not accrue to the newest partners), or an annual income of $1.5 million or less. While on the face of it this looks like a more than healthy income, many on the staff already earned that much or more, and everyone in the room could have left the firm for a higher income elsewhere in the industry.

The partners who listened to Corzine and Paulson that afternoon and

then opted to stay with the partnership did so because of their unwaver-
ing belief in the firm's future and its leadership, not because of anything
top management was offering them now. Corzine concluded the meeting
by reminding his partners to "look at the horizon, not just at this moment
in time," and, with Paulson, invited them to "fight this battle with us."

The firm stated a small profit in 1994 in an unbroken string of profitable years that extended back to 1939, yet some partners have said that
their capital accounts rose in 1993 and fell back in 1994 and thus were
flat over the two-year period. Few partners could remember the last time
the firm's capital had declined. Goldman Sachs realized profits on investments the firm had made years earlier and brought back into the income
statement about $100 million in reserves made for contingencies.
Moody's Investors Services noted that profits from long-term investments, both realized and unrealized, "comprised a significant compo-
nent" of the year's earnings and "offset poor results in some other areas."
Corzine refuted articles that appeared in the press that the firm harvested
these gains to avoid having to report a loss. "We don't take merchant
banking gains to beef up earnings," he explained. "We sell our investments when it's the right time to sell them." While the firm recorded a
profit of $508 million, the interest and dividends owed to limited part-
ners and outside investors was $522 million. The London office, which
had made approximately $800 million in 1993, lost virtually all of it in
1994. The partnership capital declined by 10 percent, and the firm took
another equity infusion from the Hawaiian trust Kamehameha. It was the
first major decline in more than half a century.

Partnership sign-ups went right down to the wire. Top management
was in the office the Friday after Thanksgiving, the last possible day for
signing the next two-year agreement. One partner close to top management has described how a number of partners who had wanted to leave
in 1994—not because of the events of the year but because it was the
right time in their careers—signed the agreement as an act of solidarity.
The departures served as a weeding-out process for the partnership, and
only those who were the most committed to and focused upon the firm's
future remained. Some have described it as the day when the next generation of leaders looked each other in the eye and by their actions vowed to
rebuild the firm.

There is still much debate over the effect on the firm of Friedman's
departure. Some have argued that each of the partners who left did so for
personal reasons. Others are not so charitable. Friedman, they argue, led
by example, and when he left Goldman Sachs at its low point his departure hastened the flow. One of those who felt strongly that it was Friedman's responsibility to stick by the firm in 1994 was John Weinberg.

For months Weinberg had watched the firm's troubles accumulate, and by Thanksgiving he knew he had to do something. One late November day, the senior chairman made his way down to 85 Broad. He had been ill recently, and many of those who saw him say he looked in poor health, frail, and worn out. He was angry, and he had come to give the troops a sense of history—a history he personified for his listeners. His message was simple: Goldman Sachs would thrive if the interests of its clients remained paramount. There were good times and bad, but the shared values that made up the firm's culture were immutable.

Weinberg wandered the halls of Goldman Sachs holding informal meetings with partners and senior vice-presidents. (Later he took his message to London.) At one meeting in New York, shortly after 4 p.m., managers packed into a small fifth-floor conference room to listen to the revered scion of one of the great banking families of the twentieth century. The room was small, crowded, and almost no daylight shone through the windows. The long wooden conference table and comfortable leather chairs left little space for the packed listeners. Goldman Sachs is situated in a part of the city where the streets were designed for carriages or foot trade, and the buildings are set too close together; little natural light reaches the fifth floor. The audience leaned against the walls and windows, shifting their weight uneasily from side to side. Rumor had already reached them that something momentous was to be said, though the details were vague. Nervous jokes were traded to ease the palpable tension. Every man and woman in the room was concerned about the firm's future and their own. The unending string of astronomical pay raises had come to an abrupt and unpleasant halt, and to those who had never experienced anything but success this was a rude awakening.

Most who had come to listen to Weinberg remembered him from the early years of their careers; others knew him by reputation only. He was renowned for his plain speaking, like his father before him. The room was silent as he began. Weinberg rose slowly before his audience, the full weight of his years showing. He had a story to tell his young listeners.

Weinberg faced an audience of some of the richest and most powerful men and women on Wall Street, yet they listened in awe as he recounted events, many of which had occurred before they were born. Goldman Sachs had faced adversity before, dark days that seemed to linger but always faded. From these episodes the firm emerged stronger than ever. Partners were the keepers of a trust, and it was their job to protect and preserve it for the next generation. The crash of 1929 could have destroyed the firm, and for fifteen years afterward there had been little work and few fees. Goldman Sachs had skated close to the edge when its involvement with Penn Central in the early 1970s rained lawsuits down upon the firm. Bob Freeman's arrest and guilty plea a few years earlier had been a painful experience, but the firm went forward, only growing in stature. The current situation too, Weinberg told his listeners, would pass. The key to the future lay in understanding the past. He had come to remind them of who they were, to give them a sense of themselves.

Early in 1947, Sidney Weinberg found himself seated on the dais at a charity dinner next to one Thomas Watson, Sr., the founder of IBM. During the course of the evening, Watson convinced the investment banker of the merits of using a computer to run his complex business. Weinberg had little idea of what a computer was, but Watson assured him that it was the key to the modern age. Weinberg could not resist; anything this revolutionary was worth a try; by the end of the evening Watson had made a sale. Shortly thereafter an extremely large box, five or six feet across and four feet high, arrived at the firm's New York office. Emblazoned across the side were the letters IBM, meaningless to everyone who read them. The package was unexpected, and no one wanted to touch it. The firm's controller, George Perk, a bald-headed man with a fringe of short red hair, came into the office each morning and circled the strange box, shaking his head before walking away. One evening John Weinberg, who was working at his father's office as a summer intern, mentioned the box to his father over dinner. The next morning the elder Weinberg charged into the operations area and demanded that it be opened. Tools were located and the carton was stripped away to reveal a large gray metal box—an old-fashioned punch card system. The small crowd examined the machine. "What do you think it does?" Weinberg asked, but no one knew. Weinberg parroted Watson's words: "This is going to do great things. It will change everything." Still the crowd stared.

Sidney Weinberg, a man inclined to action, said, "Well, plug the damn thing in. Let's give it a try." The prehistoric computer was plugged in, and instantly the firm was plunged into total darkness. The telephones went dead, the elevator stopped, and the confused staff stood motionless. "Damn it," Weinberg shouted, "I'm going to get him." With his son John in tow, Sidney ran down the stairs to the ground floor, out into the summer sunshine, and down the street to the closest pay phone in a local bar. When Watson came to the phone Weinberg started cursing, "Damn it, you sold me this thing and all it did was blow out everything. The thing doesn't work; what does it do anyway? You get down here and get the this thing working again." Watson knew the value of a client, and the chairman of IBM came down to the Goldman Sachs offices himself. Although power was not restored immediately, the gesture was appreciated, and the firm continued to use IBM systems for the rest of the century.

Those at the gathering smiled. They had not known Sidney Weinberg, but they all knew what he stood for. He had dedicated himself above everything to the clients of Goldman Sachs. Throughout his long tenure, he had ignored many of the fancy new financial products being developed, choosing to leave that to other men or other firms. Even profitability had not concerned him overly much; he knew it would come in time. In his world, like that of Tom Watson, it was simple—the client always came first.

Many found John Weinberg's message inspiring, an acknowledgment that something needed to and would be done. They walked away proud to be associated with Goldman Sachs and its history. Others found Weinberg's words a sad reminder of what had once been and how the firm had changed.

Weinberg reminded the faithful that they needed to get back to basics, they needed to become Goldman Sachs again. He went on to say that by leaving in one of the firm's darkest hours, the man he had cultivated as his hand-picked successor had disappointed him. One current partner described Weinberg as being from the "buck stops here" school and says that the former senior partner found it unacceptable that a number of partners decided to depart the firm during one of its most difficult periods. Some of those who heard Weinberg speak remember that he was furious and he thought that it was Friedman's responsibility to make certain that the defections did not occur. They remember that in John Weinberg's world it was simple: 1994 was a cataclysmic event for Goldman Sachs and it was not acceptable to send a message to the organization that it was tolerable for partners to leave at this time.

For many at Goldman Sachs, Weinberg's statements were like a thunderbolt. These were drastic times, but Weinberg let those assembled know that, in his view, Goldman Sachs would not and should not be turned into a hedge fund. He reminded his audience that Goldman Sachs believed in teamwork and that the efforts of every person in the room mattered. "He talked about the management committee," one senior manager recollects, "and how they had lost touch with the common people. They needed to do what he was doing, which was getting out and letting people know that this was Goldman Sachs and it had a bad year, but not to worry." For 125 years the firm had served its clients above all, and it would not stop now. People and relationships—those were the things that mattered.

But times had changed, and many argue that Friedman and Rubin had successfully adapted to the new order. Clients always had come first, but as corporations issued their own commercial paper and operated finance companies one could be forgiven for being unable to distinguish between a client and a competitor. Change, Friedman believed, was needed to survive. "Every major company I have seen that has suffered by failing to adapt to the times has been too rigid in worshiping dysfunctional aspects of its prior culture," he says. Friedman had coaxed a world-class performance out of the firm to which he had dedicated his career, and he set a standard for performance and profitability that no other investment bank in the world could meet. He had built businesses that would take the firm into the twenty-first century as the premier investment bank.

"When eventually the first of December came around, there was almost a sigh of relief, if only because then for the first time the partners actually knew who they had left," one long-serving vice-president remembers. The annual partners' dinner dance held the first Saturday in December was a grim affair. Corzine dispensed with tradition and instead of naming each of the departing partners, simply thanked them as a group. Even the senior partners' message in the annual review no longer listed individually those who had left. The *Financial Times* explained that in 1994, Goldman Sachs had "lost partners, prestige, élan and morale." The firm had simply lost its way, one partner sadly stated.

The dead were promptly buried. When the mergers and acquisitions department held a conference call the Sunday after Thanksgiving to rally the troops, the mood was low. As one partner listed the names of those who had left, he was interrupted by an angry colleague: "Enough talk about those guys; those guys are dead," he said. Not gone—dead.

For many years a bronze plaque has hung on John Weinberg's wall. Inherited from his father, it lists the trials of Abraham Lincoln: the many business failures, political defeats, and personal disappointments he endured before he "achieved the highest success attainable in life and undying fame until the end of time." It conveys a message Weinberg hoped no one would forget. Nineteen ninety-four was a setback, but great successes would be born of failure.

CHAPTER VII

1995–1998

THE ROAD TO IPO

When Jon Corzine suggested to his partners in the January 1995 meeting that the firm would achieve profits of $10 billion over the next five years, some of his audience thought he had taken leave of his senses. Goldman Sachs had barely scraped by with half a billion dollars in 1994; in the fourth quarter the firm had actually lost $42 million, and market conditions had not improved dramatically. The profit projections Corzine set forth seemed like little more than a pipe dream. To most observers the firm's immediate prospects did not look bright. In the first quarter of 1995, Goldman Sachs earned a paltry $160 million, and unless things looked up, 1995 would not be much of an improvement over the preceding year. In fact, with the sudden increase after 1994 in the number of limited partners who would need to be paid a fixed rate on their capital out of the firm's pretax profits, the profit picture threatened to be even bleaker. Added to this, the abrupt transition had left management weakened. Corzine and Paulson were already trying to establish their authority with employees, rating agencies, and clients all over the world. Many partners who had been convinced to stay had done so as a personal bet on the new leadership; now top management had to deliver.

Corzine, the tall, dark-haired co-chairman, speaks softly in a deep, rich voice. A self-described "washed-up old trader," Corzine can be seen sprawled in a chair wearing his trademark sweater vest, a man entirely comfortable with himself. Self-deprecation, Goldman Sachs–style, is deeply embedded in his manner, but those who worked closely with him on the trading floor remember that when necessary he can be every bit the forceful trader, "whipping them around"—as traders like to describe the buying and selling of bonds—with the best of them.

Like most Goldman Sachs partners Corzine dwells on the role luck and fate have played in his phenomenally successful career. Michael David-Weill, the chairman of Lazard Freres, quotes his father when he says, "Don't trust self-made men because they think it's their fault." Not this one. While it would be naive not to recognize that talent and drive play an important role, to hear Corzine tell it, luck was the biggest factor in his ascendancy to the top job.

A Midwestern boy from a middle-class family, Corzine never dreamed of Wall Street; in fact, he did not even know what an investment bank was. "My parents were trying to make me a 4-H'er," he recalls. A basketball star and a Phi Beta Kappa graduate from the University of Illinois in 1969, he was about to begin a Ph.D. program in economics at UCLA when fate and the Vietnam War intervened. Corzine joined a reserve unit of the Marines that had been—but then stopped—sending all of its people to Vietnam. After the stint with the Marines he was unable to return to the Ph.D. program; now a father, he needed to work. Corzine took a job at Continental Illinois bank while he completed an M.B.A. at the University of Chicago. When he was looking for another job in 1974 the financial industry was deeply depressed, and Corzine found nothing on Wall Street. After a year trading bonds at Banc One in Ohio, the salesman from Goldman Sachs who covered Corzine introduced him to the firm, which offered him a job in 1975.

Corzine made his mark first in Goldman Sachs's fledgling fixed income department. He views his move to Goldman Sachs, characteristically, as fortuitous. At other Wall Street banks, with better-established fixed income divisions, the competition would have been greater. He was made a partner in five short years and given a seat on the management committee in 1985, even before he was asked to become the co-head of fixed income in 1988.

Corzine built the firm's formidable U.S. government bond trading operation through a combination of aggressive trading and focus on client needs. Perhaps most important, Corzine knew how to manage traders. He accepted losses as part of the trading process. Some of the firm's preeminence in the realm of proprietary trading is due to the fact that, like Rubin before him, he never lambasted traders for well-thought-out bets that went wrong. He showed enormous confidence in those who displayed ability and was openly receptive to new ideas and new businesses. Those who have worked closely with him describe his constant search for a new challenge or opportunity.

At the firm Corzine works out of a modest-sized office with just enough room for a couch, coffee table, three chairs, and a desk piled high with papers, books, reports, and trading and computer screens. Corzine watches the markets closely and is fully versed in the major moves of financial instruments around the globe. Trading vernacular peppers his conversation. On the wall behind his desk is a photo gallery of the firm's history—a dozen black-and-white prints of the firm's past leaders. Outside Goldman Sachs, Corzine is involved in programs aimed at improving urban schools and bringing cultural resources to blighted inner cities like Newark, New Jersey. He spends some weekends working with residents of Harlem and is described by those who know him well as crazy about sports. With his family, he closely follows the fortunes of the teams he supports.

Corzine's plain speaking, so reminiscent of John Weinberg, made him a well-liked and approachable leader. Partners have remarked on his ability to make people feel positive about themselves and their affiliation with the firm. As one partner explained, he can deliver bad news and make you feel good about it. Many who have known Corzine throughout his career at Goldman Sachs explain that by remaining close to his troops, even as his star rose, he was able to convey the depth of his feelings about the firm down to the grassroots level.

Like Corzine, Hank Paulson is a native of the Midwest. Unlike Corzine, who chairs a presidential commission for Bill Clinton and serves on the U.S. Treasury Department's borrowing committee, Paulson is a committed Republican who spent the early 1970s (after completing his Phi Beta Kappa B.A. from Dartmouth and an M.B.A. at Harvard) working in the Nixon White House before joining the Chicago office of Goldman Sachs in January 1974. Eight years later Paulson was selected as a partner and in 1990 was asked to co-head the firm's investment banking division and offered a seat on the management committee. No stranger to risk, for a number of years he successfully ran the firm's principal investments business. Paulson personifies many of the firm's values, living in the modest suburban house he bought when first starting out. In addition to Paulson's enormous responsibilities at the firm—he became sole CEO in January 1999—as head of the nonprofit Peregrine Society he is deeply involved in efforts to save birds of prey facing extinction. With his family, he has been a frequent traveler to the Amazon and is helping to establish the first national park in China, in order to aid preservation.

In those tense autumn days of 1994, Corzine and Paulson had focused almost exclusively on holding the partnership together. As partners dithered about whether to sign the new partnership agreement they were at first cajoled and later told that it was decision time—"Get into the boat or get out." Now that Corzine and Paulson knew the makeup of their team, their focus turned to discipline and morale. Corzine and Paulson traveled the world speaking to clients and staff in foreign offices. Paulson fielded questions at many of the firm's offices. At some gatherings he was lambasted, but he knew he needed to deliver the message on a personal level.

Corzine and Paulson had grand plans for the firm, a long-term strategy that would take Goldman Sachs into new businesses and new countries, but all that would have to wait. It did not take a calculator to see that if the firm's financial performance did not improve in 1995, none of these plans would be possible. Corzine and Paulson would need to rebuild morale, restore trust, and move the business forward, and they would need to do so quickly. Paulson, by nature an expansionist, leaned against the wind in early 1995, seeking ways for the firm to consolidate and strengthen itself. First Corzine and Paulson needed to stabilize the firm's earnings through a combination of new risk management systems and extensive cost cutting unlike anything the firm had ever endured. The firm could withstand one bad year, but two in a row would be an entirely different story. If the firm's financial situation did not improve there would be nothing to stop the flow of partners from streaming out the door with their capital.

In 1994 the firm's problems came from the execution of its strategy, not from a flaw in the strategy itself. Overseas expansion and proprietary risks both make sense for Goldman Sachs and would be part of the firm's future. In summing up the problems of 1994, Corzine would say that the firm had paced its growth too fast. It had also been slow to react to the changing market environment. Top management was determined to learn from the mistakes of 1994 and undertook a comprehensive review of all the firm's operations. Nothing was sacred. The study focused intently on the firm's cost structure, its risk-taking practices, and its governance procedures. All would be completely revamped.

At the beginning of 1994 many partners had felt that Goldman Sachs was lean and mean, but their opinions were revised when they looked again. In many areas the firm was running a Cadillac operation, with little regard for expenses. For years, some partners argue, management had focused on the top line—revenues—without serious enough regard for the bottom line—profits. That would change. Without favorable market conditions it was increasingly clear that the firm's fortunes would be revived in the short term only if the cost base could be drastically reduced. While it would have been nice just to dim the lights and close a few empty conference rooms, this would not scratch the surface. Investment banking is a service business, and between 70 percent and 80 percent of a firm's costs are in its people. Heads would have to roll.

Goldman Sachs had long enjoyed the reputation of being a benevolent employer, and the perception existed that the firm rarely fired its employees. The firm in fact had conducted cutbacks in J. Aron in 1983 and in its trading businesses in both 1987 and 1991. In the mid–1980s and particularly in the downturn that followed the stock market crash in 1987, the firm reduced staff by both attrition and firings by thirteen hundred, or 20 percent of the total. Each time the firm had let people go it was the result of an industry-wide downturn. Up until this point the partners had avoided firing large numbers of staff because of vicissitudes in their own business. Large-scale firings are not without risk: "For every one you lay off, you frighten four," says limited partner Roy Smith. "You're destroying loyalty in the interest of year-by-year profit management." Despite the fact that management was not new to this process, this round of firing was done with a certain amount of ineptitude—for one thing, it took a tortuously long time. While rumors circulated, tensions built and morale sank further. The manager of each area was asked to take a hard look at the bottom quartile, and later at the bottom decile, of those he or she supervised in terms of performance. Some managers, whose businesses had done well in 1994, began by saying they did not have anyone in the bottom quartile. When pushed, managers running businesses with twenty people would say, "Okay, I have one person in my bottom quartile."

The process took several months to complete, but to many who were there it seemed like it took forever. For Corzine personally, this was an extremely painful process and one that he felt was grossly unfair. In good years the partners reaped the majority of the firm's profits; in rough times some employees paid with their jobs. It was an inequality that had always existed in the securities industry, and Corzine was determined that under his management things would be done differently.

Partners met in glass-fronted offices while staff looked on fearing the worst. In some areas work ground to a halt as frightened employees sat around waiting for the other shoe to drop. No one could say for certain when the firm's fortunes would turn, so the size of the eventual cuts remained a mystery. The investment banking and equities divisions, while not enjoying record years in 1994, had turned in solid performances, and many within these divisions felt it was unfair that they should be forced to trim what were patently profitable businesses.

When the cuts came they were deep and untimely. By postponing the inevitable (Friedman had suggested staff reductions six months earlier), the firm had kept its high cost base throughout 1994, and now more draconian cutbacks were needed. In the end just over 10 percent of the firm was asked to leave. The depth of the staff reductions, while seemingly crucial at the time, would prove to be a mistake. The dismissals had been postponed for so long that almost as soon as Goldman Sachs finished firing, it began hiring.

In early 1995 it was essential that the new leaders demonstrate that they had taken control of the organization and that the losses would not be allowed to continue. At the time it appeared as though the profits generated in 1992 and 1993 accrued from market conditions that might not recur. These profits had allowed the firm to subsidize dramatic growth, yet there was no reason to believe that they would be sustained going forward. With perfect hindsight it is clear that the firm's core businesses were performing adequately, although its businesses in Europe and Asia would lose money in 1995. Despite the dramatic dip in profitability and the internal turmoil in 1994 the firm was still the preeminent investment bank and was ranked first in U.S. and foreign common stock offerings, initial public offerings, worldwide completed mergers and acquisitions, investment-grade debt, and U.S. equity research. The industry as a whole was not in distress, and the firm would have done well to stay the course. Ultimately, however, the cost reductions made the firm a stronger competitor, and as its fortunes improved it was a more tightly honed machine. Difficult decisions had to be made, and Corzine and Paulson showed the strength of their leadership from the first. If the conditions of 1994 had continued and the firm had not acted aggressively to control its costs, the results could have been disastrous.

During the early months of 1995, the proprietary trading businesses ground to a halt. The firm continued to risk its capital to service its clients and through its principal investments area, but large speculative positions in global capital markets were reduced to almost nothing until markets stabilized and the firm regained its footing. No one doubted that this was a temporary situation—management simply needed time to regroup, reassess, and establish new procedures.

NO FIRM HAS IMMERSED itself as deeply in the risky world of proprietary trading with the same consistent high level of profitability as Goldman Sachs. Despite one wretched year, proprietary trading went forward because it provides the firm with a sizable and diversified stream of revenue and can be complementary to its client businesses. When market conditions are inhospitable to underwriting and sales activities (for example, in a bear market for bonds and stocks), proprietary trading can be a source of substantial profits for the firm. Corzine had no intention of eliminating or even drastically scaling back the firm's risk taking over the long term, but things would be done differently. "The Goldman Sachs culture accepts that we'll be principal risk-takers," he says, "and frankly I think it has been reinforced post-1994. I think we went through a traumatic period and learned many lessons about how to manage, if not eliminate, risk going forward. There's probably a greater commitment to principal risk-taking within our business since that time."

Goldman Sachs is psychologically prepared, in a way that few others are, to operate proprietary trading businesses successfully. The firm has a long history of tolerating trading setbacks, of not abandoning traders or businesses that are deemed to be fundamentally sound even when they incur large losses. As a result of its history (the early preparation Levy provided and the years of experience top management has in the risk-taking business), its private status (allowing it to more easily weather uneven revenue streams), its position in the center of the world's capital flows, and the experiences of 1994, there was at this point no other banking institution as well positioned as Goldman Sachs to exploit trading and investment opportunities in the market as they arose.

The firm revived its proprietary trading businesses in 1995, and over the following three years many of the firm's businesses developed a proprietary element. As Goldman Sachs provided clients with more innovative products and investment opportunities, it invested its own capital alongside them. Throughout the firm small businesses developed where specialized trading and investment skills and the ability to risk a certain amount of partnership capital gave the firm an edge. Plans to buy a hedge fund were put on hold, but Goldman Sachs found a different route through which to enter the business. Acting as a "fund of funds," Goldman Sachs pools resources on behalf of its wealthy individual clientele and invests them in hedge funds and other investment vehicles. The firm carefully researches the large universe of hedge funds, giving the seal of approval and a chunk of capital to those it feels will deliver the best returns. In exchange for this service the firm earns itself a fee and a percentage of the profits. For clients it is an opportunity to diversify their portfolios by investing in a wide range of these risky vehicles in amounts ($5 million, for example) that would have been below the minimum investment required for many funds.

Through the total restructuring of the firm's risk-control systems, Goldman Sachs would benefit from having a trader in the top position. In 1995, Corzine established an interdisciplinary risk committee staffed by partners from all over the world. Every Wednesday at 7:30 a.m. New York time, the committee convenes by teleconference and examines all of the firm's major exposures, including the risks related to the market, individual operations, credit, new products and businesses, and the firm's reputation. Any trader wanting to put a substantial amount of the firm's capital at risk must defend his action before this group, explaining the rationale and proposed course of action. No one is exempt. For the first time there is a firm-wide standard for assessing risk on a comparable objective scale. The acceptable trade-off between risk and reward is no longer determined at the local level. The risk committee, which vastly strengthens both quantitative and qualitative risk controls, ensures that every area of the firm meets the same standards. Top management has stressed that had such controls been in place years earlier the firm would not have suffered the same level of trading losses in 1994.

Every trading seat is now given an unequivocal loss limit, an explicitly defined dollar figure below which losses must remain. The amount of capital at risk is no longer a subject of negotiation between an individual trader and his or her direct manager. Each trader is given the technology to analyze the size and scope of positions he or she can take under different market conditions while remaining within the limits established. Some of this was made possible by advances in the sophistication of the firm's risk models, but it was also the result of a degree of consensus across departments about the risk of loss the firm was willing to endure— a consensus that had not existed before 1994.

The firm's new methods marked a recognition that the informal controls used for so long—where individual trading managers set the standards for risk in their own areas with agreement from those above them—were no longer adequate for a global firm now experiencing higher levels of staff turnover. In the mid–1980s, when Goldman Sachs was two-thirds its present size, its positions were much smaller, its staff turnover was lower, and financial instruments were less complex, the less structured methods had worked well. With thirty-two offices and more than ten thousand employees, many of them relatively recent arrivals, informal controls and the firm's culture could no longer be as heavily depended upon to monitor behavior.

The development of new risk systems would pay off in many ways. Management control would be greatly enhanced, and individual traders would have a better sense of their parameters. The firm's new methods of monitoring risk are reputed by many in the market to be the best in the industry. So valued is the product that the firm is considering selling its in-house systems to clients; management has given its approval for trial arrangements.

The governance structure of Goldman Sachs, its ten- to fourteen-member management committee, had remained untouched since it was established by Sidney Weinberg twenty-five years earlier. Corzine and Paulson were of the strong opinion that a large global organization could not be run effectively by a group that was now eleven members strong. The management committee had been set up as a representative body, with the head of each major area of the firm holding a seat. Every Monday morning the partners on this committee were expected to act as advocates for their respective areas. Corzine and Paulson believed that the firm needed a smaller executive committee, with six members who would not represent specific constituencies but would take a firm-wide view.

Decisions in the new executive committee could be made and implemented more quickly, and there is complete agreement that it is a substantial improvement, although something has been lost. There are fewer partners at the firm who feel that they are sitting at "the big table." Input across departments cannot be as complete, and by necessity large areas of the firm are underrepresented at the highest reaches of management. While revolutionary for Goldman Sachs, these changes were not groundbreaking; they were, in fact, very much in keeping with trends on Wall Street. (In January 1999, the firm replaced the executive committee with a fifteen-member management committee.)

In assembling his executive committee Corzine turned to two members of the next generation of partners. Along with himself, Paulson, Zuckerberg, and Hurst, Corzine appointed John Thain and John Thornton (Thornton replaced David Silfen, who had served on the executive committee for a year), both men still in their thirties. Although they are both Americans, unlike their predecessors they have spent a large proportion of their careers overseas, which is now an important part of the training for any future leaders. Corzine feels that a leader passes on a culture not just by what he says and does, but also by whom he selects for the succeeding generation of leadership. Many expect that Thain and Thornton will one day run the firm. Their 1999 promotions support that.

Below the executive committee Corzine and Paulson established the operating and partnership committees. The large number of partnership defections in 1994 had made clear to management committee members just how few partners understood the breadth of the firm's business and its inner workings. Many partners had left because of their discomfort with the activity of the firm's trading businesses and questions about how it fit into the whole picture. A nineteen-member operating committee, with representation from every area of the firm, would be an attempt to address this problem. Those partners appointed to the operating committee, while still close to the day-to-day management of the firm's business, would now have input into the running of the entire organization. At the same time, a much larger group of partners has intimate knowledge of the firm's operations and its longer-term strategies. This committee is charged with responsibility for all operating matters, including reviewing proposals for new businesses and developing and implementing each year's budget. All of its first year was spent reviewing the revenues and costs of the firm's various departments. The partnership committee wrestles with thorny questions like the size and composition of the partnership and the compensation of its members.

By bringing a larger group of partners into the upper reaches of management, the culture of the firm, as transmitted by its leaders, could more easily be spread to a larger group of people. "You have to broaden the number of people who have a leadership mandate," Corzine said. "Against that you have to make sure that you don't dilute the value of the mandate. Now instead of debates in the management committee with twelve people, we have these committees, so that hopefully we'll reinforce the culture and mission among a broader group of people. The culture and mission are reinforced in the way debates are conducted and actions taken. Hopefully there are two-way flows of ideas and communication about what is working and what is not. In the old days, Gus Levy just called the three partners into his office and told them, 'This is the culture. Go out and do it.' Leadership today at Goldman Sachs is more complicated."

As 1995 wore on, five of the partners who had left at the end of 1994 asked to return to the partnership. With one exception—that of a partner who had "gone limited" but continued to work at the firm (and was a very substantial revenue generator)—all were turned away. The firm took a hard line with those it viewed as fleeing at the first sign of trouble; in the opinion of those who remained, they had shown themselves to be partners on whom the firm could not depend.

By the end of the year, the rigorous cost cutting had lopped $1 billion off the firm's $3.6 billion of overhead. Profits looked up in the second quarter, rising to $346 million, then reached $425 million by the third quarter. As a result of strong performances in equity trading and underwriting and a bumper year in the mergers business, the firm's profits for the year totaled $1.37 billion. While not a spectacular result this was a solid first step that would allow the firm's new leader to contemplate even more radical changes for the future.

With profitability back on track and morale revived, one overarching question remained. Was a private partnership, with its unlimited liability and inherently unstable capital, an outmoded form of ownership for a modern investment bank? Every other major firm in the industry had implicitly answered this question in the affirmative and over the previous two decades transformed themselves into public corporations. Now the partners of Goldman Sachs would need to reconsider it for themselves.

In a replay of events a decade earlier the Goldman Sachs partnership met in January 1996 once again to consider a public offering. The firm's governance had been entirely reorganized, but the capital and partnership structures remained untouched.

The events of 1994 had made for a good stress test, revealing to management weaknesses that would need to be resolved before Wall Street hit the next cyclical downturn. Many of the major issues affecting the firm's risk systems had been addressed, and now Corzine and Paulson were determined that drastic changes in the partnership and capital structure would be made. "Too many people with the ability to walk away with their capital caused a threat to the firm—a real one," says one partner. Top management had been surprised and distressed by the number of partners who had contemplated leaving or actually left in 1994. Paulson was certain that whatever ownership format the partners chose, the firm needed a more secure capital structure. In order to plan effectively for the future, management required better knowledge of the resources, human and financial, it would have available. As the most successful investment bank in the world Goldman Sachs had no trouble raising as much capital from the outside as it needed, either through debt offerings or private equity placements like the two (Sumitomo and Kamehameha) already in place. As the firm with the best debt rating and the highest long-term return on equity, locating sources of capital was not difficult, and the partners' own capital had compounded rapidly as of late. Yet the stability of this capital was a totally different matter.

The executive committee was in complete agreement about the problem but not the solution. Corzine and Paulson recommended a public offering, and the majority of the executive committee agreed with their leaders. Some who agreed to pose the idea of a public offering to the partnership at large now admit that while favoring the proposal at the time their support was not wholehearted, and the decision was a close one.

The approach to evaluating the public option would be more rigorous than a decade before. Corzine and Paulson were not going to allow half-baked proposals that could easily be shot down on matters of detail to be set before the partnership. They appointed a committee of partners with a wide range of experience and seniority to study the idea comprehensively in preparation for a proposal to the entire partnership. This group, led by a partner and specialist in the business of banking, would examine the firm's capital structure from every angle. The study was called "Pegasus IV," a follow-up to the 1986, 1991, and 1993 studies of the public option.

In early January, Corzine and Paulson first floated the idea to a combined meeting of the operating and partnership committees, where it had all the loft of a lead balloon. These two groups, the almost forty key partners below the executive committee, were the proposal's natural audience. As top performing partners with substantial seniority, they had the most to gain financially and should have been the group most receptive to the executive committee's recommendation. An external consultant, a compensation specialist, had been made available to the committees, and he was asked what would represent the average compensation of a managing director at a public investment bank. While the top five to ten managing directors at public investment banks did very well, the next one hundred fifty or so people below them were generally not compensated as well as those at Goldman Sachs. On hearing the figures, the members of the operating and partnership committees were genuinely surprised and unimpressed. This was not a level of earning to which anyone in the room aspired. Other partners, as had happened ten years earlier, felt that the partnership should be preserved for cultural reasons. One trading partner worried that he would no longer feel special as merely an employee of a public company, and that the firm itself would no longer be special.

Despite the support of both Corzine and Paulson, the almost universal consensus among the members of the operating and partnership committees was that a public offering was not the way forward. The group expressed to Corzine and Paulson its overwhelming desire to fix the capital structure through alternative means and its willingness to live with whatever that meant. Top management knew that without the support of these partners the idea could never go forward. First, it would be almost impossible to muster the necessary votes without the leaders of each department lending their support. Second, even if the votes could be found, it would be a disaster to proceed over the objections of the next generation of the firm's leadership.

Notwithstanding the disapproval of the two committees, the proposal for a public offering was presented to the entire partnership two weeks later. The plans to put forth the idea at a meeting of the full partnership had been solidified before the proposal was previewed by the operating and partnership committees. So the entire partnership would be given a chance to weigh in on the matter. There had been a great deal of "pre-selling" before the actual meeting, as management made its case to various partners on an informal basis. Before the meeting took place a series of articles had appeared in newspapers and business magazines, some of them as early as the summer before, speculating that a public offering was already in the works. Outside the firm a public offering began to look like a foregone conclusion, but the press had gotten ahead of itself.

Nineteen partners who attended the fateful meeting in 1986 were present in 1996. For this group the discussion was steeped in memories and inevitable comparisons. The partnership could no longer fit comfortably into the second-floor meeting room at 85 Broad Street, so the gathering was held at the Arrowwood conference center in a suburb just north of New York City. One partner said that in contrast to 1986, it felt like there were five hundred people in the room.

The format of the meeting was exactly the same. On Friday there was a presentation and everyone was given a chance to speak, and on Saturday the fate of the partnership was determined. Management sought the views of every partner, and on Friday small caucuses were held with designated leaders. Each leader was given a list of questions to tease out opinions from the group. Later the caucus leaders met to compare notes. But many things had changed in ten years. In 1986 the firm had considered a public offering from a position of strength; the fear of having insufficient capital to meet the expanding needs of the company had driven the partnership to examine the option. Now the firm was reviewing the issue from a position of weakness. The possibility of doing nothing, it was widely agreed, no longer existed. Despite its preeminence in the world of investment banking and its acceptable financial performance in 1995, the partnership was now considering a public offering because the weakness of a structure where partners and capital could easily depart had been revealed. Partners had always known that their liability was unlimited, but in 1994 they had been given a painful reminder of exactly what that meant. Fear of another year like 1994—not only the financial losses but the instability created by partners withdrawing their capital from the firm—drove them to consider a capital structure with more permanence and less personal exposure.

In 1986 the management committee had been nominally unanimous in its support for a public offering. This time the executive committee could not present a united front because John Thain, the youngest member of the committee and the firm's chief financial officer, was opposed to the proposal. At first few realized his opposition, but as the meeting wore on it became clear that the executive committee was divided, and that Thain had become a spokesman—many say inadvertently—for the younger generation. Like many of his cohorts he felt changes could be made that would allow the firm to continue in a private format. Although not an organizer of the opposition, Thain is a major opinion leader within the firm; because of his senior position his views carried a great deal of weight.

The Pegasus committee assigned to study the offering presented its report to the full partnership in what some remember as excruciating detail. They reviewed the myriad valuations and issues that would arise, down to dealing with the fate of each principal investment. Many of those who attended the meeting remember that over the course of the presentation it became obvious that the partners selected to study the public offering option did not themselves support it. The committee had included in its written presentation a "staying private" alternative, complete with the changes that would necessitate, and it became increasingly clear that the committee supported this proposal. Eric Dobkin, the long-standing partner in charge of global equity capital markets, and an experienced specialist in pricing large global equity offerings, rendered his professional opinion. Selling Goldman Sachs would be just such an offering, and Dobkin's opinion of the price the firm would achieve was extremely influential. Ten years earlier Morgan Stanley had offered shares to the public valued at almost three times book value; at the time, according to most assessments, Goldman Sachs would have sold for a higher price. Now, in light of market conditions and Goldman Sachs's recent performance, Dobkin believed that if the firm went to market it would sell for substantially less than two times its book value. Some on the executive committee vociferously disagreed with Dobkin's assessment, and a heated discussion ensued. Even those who may have thought that the arguments in favor of a public offering were compelling could see that if Dobkin's assessment was correct, the timing was inauspicious.

Again the issue arose of the newest partners getting their shot at the brass ring. At the time of the meeting ninety-two (or 53 percent) of the 172 partners had less than three years' tenure. This group could be expected to oppose the offering, as the newest partners had done in 1986, purely on the grounds of personal wealth creation. With little capital in the firm they would not receive a substantial portion of the equity in a public company. And whether the firm sold for one or two times its book value meant very little to those holding only slivers of the firm's capital.

Nonfinancial considerations loomed large in the 1996 meeting, as they had in 1986. Although much had changed at Goldman Sachs, forces similar to those of a decade earlier were at work. Many of the same issues involving legacy and recruiting the best talent were raised. One partner brought out a proposal to take the firm public that had been made twenty-eight years earlier, as if to emphasize that taking the firm public would not be a betrayal of the heritage of Sidney Weinberg and Gus Levy. Once again partners grappled with the unquantifiable value of the partnership. The issue of stewardship, of leaving to the next generation of partners a stronger business than the one inherited, was raised. It was an idea that traced its roots to Marcus Goldman and the firm he left for his heirs. No one attempted to argue that Goldman Sachs as a public company would remain the same; instead, the partners confronted the notion of how big a change public ownership would create.

Few argued with the contention that the possibility of becoming a partner at Goldman Sachs still served as the major source of motivation for its professional employees. What, many wondered, would take its place? There was a discussion of the merits of employee stock ownership options as an alternative method of bonding employees to their company. Yet everyone recognized that there is a certain cachet to a Goldman Sachs partnership that no amount of stock options can replace. Partners and their spouses receive huge psychic rewards from belonging. They feel an enormous pride in their association with and ownership of the firm, a feeling that would be impossible to duplicate in a public company. Every Goldman Sachs partner could, if he or she wanted, have walked out the firm's doors and into a managing directorship at one of its publicly owned competitors. Few had exercised this option. So it is natural that they would be wary of any measure that converted the firm into something similar to the institutions at which they had chosen not to seek employment.

Any proposal to go public would need to be supported by the partnership on economic, strategic, and cultural grounds. In 1986 the proposal had made sense on economic grounds and in terms of the firm's strategy for rapid expansion. It had failed on cultural grounds, as partners balked at the changes the firm would need to endure to become a public company. In 1994, Friedman had tabled the proposal on strategic grounds, as the firm's volatile earnings made it an unlikely candidate for a successful IPO. In 1996, the proposal did not make it past the first hurdle, that of economics.

Corzine and Paulson could easily see that the vast majority of the partners did not want to sell their firm. The opposition was overwhelming, cutting across both seniority and departmental lines. Paulson found the response moving. Going public was what the leadership thought it needed to do to hold onto the partners and stabilize the firm's capital. Now those very partners were asserting their wish to stay with the firm as it was.

Like Weinberg, Friedman, and Rubin before them, Corzine and Paulson never forced the issue; they would act on the will of the shareholders. At other firms partners had been pushed into signing agreements to sell their firms, but that would not happen here. Without forceful arguments by the firm's leaders there was no cheerleader for the proposal, no one to make the case. "These kinds of things, I don't think, are going to come from below," explained one partner who was at the meetings. "He [Corzine] was going to have to stand up there and say, 'This has to be this way, for these reasons,' if it had any chance."

Friday night the executive committee met in private to compare notes. The following morning a complex discussion on compensation in a public company was on the agenda. But it was already painfully obvious that such a session was entirely irrelevant, since the support among the partnership was so weak. The executive committee decided to table the motion.

When the partnership reconvened the following morning for additional discussion and what most presumed would be the deciding vote, Corzine announced that the subject was no longer under consideration. In an outburst of emotions, a spontaneous standing ovation erupted. The partnership was united. "At that moment he [Corzine] gained a lot of trust that he would never have had if he had tried to push it through," one partner remembers. But another partner made a prescient observation to a *Wall Street Journal* reporter: "He [Corzine] isn't going to jam it down the partners' throats; like anyone in that kind of position, he wants to keep his job. But he won't give up on the idea."

The partners rejected the option of going public in 1996 for many reasons. On a cynical level, the market had at one time valued the firm much more highly, and many believed that it would again. For some, the notion of a public company was rejected because they felt that the partnership allowed Goldman Sachs to stand apart from other investment banks. It was a question of balancing risks and rewards, and as one partner noted, "The premium that came from a public offering wasn't worth the threat to the culture."

Satisfied with the results, Corzine nonetheless believed that the partnership needed to revisit the issue of a public offering regularly. "This was one of those things I think you have to be a small 'd' democrat about," says Corzine. "The will of the shareholders ought to prevail, but there is one thing you need to do. You need to confirm that each generation of partners wants to go forward in this format, and this one very clearly did." Yet, as Friedman had told his partners a decade earlier, this was not an issue that would go away.

Some partners believe the 1996 meeting was completely bungled despite considerable preparation, and that the executive committee was forced to walk away with its tail between its legs. The leadership was too far out in front of the partners, seemingly unaware that not enough were following. "I thought it was a terrible piece of work," commented a partner who attended. "Corzine, it was clear to those in the audience, wanted to take the firm public, but despite his support he delegated most of the presentation to partners not on the executive committee. They all had a clear bias against it . . . so the whole thing was presented, I thought, rather halfheartedly by people who didn't believe in it. All sorts of sniping from the crowd was permitted to go on in a way that was uncontrolled." Some who were disappointed with the meeting speculate that Corzine might have been using it as a means to educate the partnership about the myriad issues it faced related to the capital structure, and that it was simply the opening stage of a much longer campaign to take the firm public. Lending credence to this view was the fact that after 1996 the firm made many changes to the partnership that were necessary for the firm to become a public company.

Others have suggested that had Corzine truly wanted to take the firm public he should have waited. He did not have the hold on the organization that John Weinberg had in 1986 or that he himself would shortly gain. "Jon was not presidential; there was no John Weinberg there to lead it," one partner remarked in 1997. "I think if it came up again he would be much more presidential, and that could have a big effect on the outcome." Others argue that Corzine got exactly what he wanted and in short order. While the partners did not follow the path Corzine had advocated, they gave him a blank check to make the changes necessary to shore up the firm's capital base. Many of the modifications of the capital structure effected immediately after the meeting would have been unthinkable only two years earlier, and they were urgently needed.

The first—and to the outside world the most dramatic—change was to do away with the title of partner. A new managing director title would be bestowed on all partners and hundreds of vice-presidents who were not partners. The managing directors who were not partners would be accorded all of the benefits of partnership—equal salaries and offices, attendance at partners' meetings, access to the partners' dining room (now the managing directors' dining room)—without an ownership stake in the firm. The creation of this new title accomplished a variety of things. For many years Goldman Sachs had had thousands of vice-presidents, but there had been almost no means for distinguishing among them in the eyes of those outside the firm. Almost anyone who had been with the firm for four years and seen his or her career thrive was granted the title of vice-president. Now those with the most seniority and responsibility, those who had met with exceptional success, possessed a title that more accurately reflected their role. This can be a valuable asset, particularly when calling on clients.

The managing director title would also make the firm more competitive in the recruiting wars that erupted in the late 1990s. As U.S. commercial banks and European banks sought a larger market share of the investment banking business, they lured top Goldman Sachs vice-presidents away with large guaranteed bonuses, stock options, and managing director titles. Conversely, when the firm made lateral hires from other banks, it had only the titles of vice-president (which would be a step down) or partner to offer managing directors. Now there was a comparable position available. The new title would also be a way of retaining those who would never be made partner but whose contribution was worthy of greater recognition. It encouraged people to stay at the firm without opening the partnership floodgates and diluting its economic value to the existing partners. As part of their compensation, employee managing directors would be offered "P-shares" (participation shares), whose values would be tied strictly to the overall profitability of the firm, not to the individual's or the department's performance. This helped to give all managing directors—employees and owners—the same firm-wide perspective.

The Goldman Sachs annual review, since its inception in 1970, has listed the partners in terms of their seniority by partnership class. Now the names of all managing directors, whether owners or not, are listed together, still by class. There is no public evidence to distinguish those with ownership stakes from those who, as managing directors rather than vice-presidents, are in the running for those stakes.

Goldman Sachs, long known for its flat management structure and few layers of organization, would suddenly take on many of the trappings of a public corporation. The title of managing director vastly increases the officer class, doubling the ranks of managers. The organization was larger, but much more important it now spanned the globe, delivering an increasing number of new products. (Much is made of the firm's rapid growth by those within it, but the actual rate of growth was much faster between 1976 and 1986, when the size of the staff quadrupled. It is not the firm's absolute size but its geographic dispersion and the complexity of new lines of business that have made many of these changes necessary.) Corzine felt strongly that he had to broaden the charter, democratizing the organization and making it more inclusive, thereby giving more people, as he calls it, the "mandate."

Goldman Sachs had never had a strict hierarchical structure. It is run by a concentric series of coinciding committees—diagrammed by one partner as overlapping amoebas—that look mystifying to any outsider. Any individual managing director might be on a number of committees. The dozen or so committees deal with everything from risk taking to charitable contributions. There is a diversity committee, established by Rubin in 1990, to address issues of equal opportunity, a subject of great concern to Corzine. (He has indicated that he will judge the success of his era in part on the firm's ability to hire and promote women and minorities. To this end, as one of its many efforts, the firm has established a warm and welcoming day care center on the premises for any parent who finds himself or herself in a child care bind.) There is a global compliance committee, chaired by one of the firm's lawyers, charged with establishing systems on a worldwide basis to ensure that the firm is in compliance with a dizzying array of regulations in dozens of countries.

As part of the structural reforms initiated in 1996, the unlimited liability partnership was abolished; in its place a private limited liability corporation was created. The only assets the managing director partners (known legally as participating limited partners) now had exposed were those invested with the firm. Private assets, such as homes and bank accounts, were shielded from liability should the firm's assets ever be in jeopardy. Since the time of Penn Central, Goldman Sachs partners had not faced any real threat to their personal assets, and most partners, Corzine estimates, had 90 percent of their net worth invested with the company, so the change, while perhaps psychologically comforting, made little material difference. The financial risk to the partners was primarily because the firm was private, not because it was a partnership, and in 1996 that had not changed.

Corzine did not make these changes without a note of regret. Much would be gained in facilitating effective management of the firm and disseminating its culture to a broader base, but something would be forfeited in terms of intimacy. He said:

> I'm a trader and I hate meetings, but I don't know how you convey a consistency of view without having larger groups of people see and learn how your value system actually works. It has to be transparent, otherwise people have to read extraordinarily complicated tea leaves. So you need lots of visible situations where people can observe the behavior of the leadership and how they react to different situations. From that they'll draw their own sense of who we are and what we're about. It all filters down. Also, now that we have around 275 m.d.s [managing directors] who come to partners' dinners, and quarterly and annual meetings, that again is where you set a tone. They are the line leaders. This is where we say what is important. And we don't even have to say "This is what we think is important because this is what the agenda is." It seeps throughout an organization, and in the fullness of time it becomes a pattern of values and behaviors that everyone accepts as being important.

The partners' dinner dance, once an intimate affair with a hundred or so partners and their wives at a midtown hotel, was transformed overnight. The 1997 dinner dance was held at the Museum of Natural History, and more than nine hundred people attended. Quarterly partners' meetings included all four hundred ten managing directors and were held at the Arrowwood conference center, since the firm's headquarters was unable to accommodate the crowd. "We deal with them in the spirit of partnership," Hank Paulson said at the time. Yet inside the firm the term partner has not died. Despite management's efforts, most employees are still conscious of who is on the way up and who has already made it.

Partners' capital, once a source of instability, was shored up in 1996, and the rules governing withdrawals were substantially altered. To share in the bounty of the firm henceforth has required a more enduring commitment. The payout period, which begins after retirement, was lengthened, and a complicated system of new capital accounts was introduced. In years when the firm did particularly well the partners would put some portion of their earnings into a longer-term capital account, with an eight-year commitment and a three-year payout period, which helped to increase stability.

Even as the partners cheered the defeat of the proposal to take the firm public, few believed that the issue of the Goldman Sachs partnership transforming itself into a public corporation was dead. The ownership of the firm's capital needed to be examined from time to time to make certain that the private format was still the will of the partnership and that it was consistent with the strategy of the firm going forward. Even after 1996, top management was not convinced that Goldman Sachs could remain a private company for the foreseeable future. "It may be that we'll have to end up being public so that we can broaden that leadership mandate out even further than where we are now," Corzine said in 1997. "We're stretching the rubber band about as far as we can within a private partnership format. I don't know how much more we can stretch it. Without growing the pie of economics, I think it's going to be hard to do that because you're not really going to have the currency to be able to motivate enough people."

As the firm's success in 1996 was compounded by its record performance in 1997 (when the firm's profits soared above $3 billion), the financial incentives to sell the firm became increasingly compelling. It was a remarkable turnaround, a credit to the firm's management and to those who had placed their faith in Corzine and Paulson. During the 1990s, Goldman Sachs pulled even further away from its competitors. Compared to its peer group of the eight major American investment banks in 1996, the firm had a much higher revenue base, more than twice the level of earnings, and a return on equity of 51 percent as against the industry average of 36 percent. Since 1994 the firm had been involved in many of the most important financings in the world, including the $13 billion privatization of Deutsche Telekom (the largest IPO ever), the $38 billion merger of Daimler-Benz with Chrysler Corporation (the largest industrial merger ever), the first privatization in China (China Telecom), and a $4 billion bond offering for South Korea (the largest sovereign debt deal in Asia). By early 1998 the financial press speculated that with a rising stock market and the increased value of the firm's franchise, the firm could almost certainly sell itself for 3.5 to 4 times book value, a far cry from twenty-four months earlier. But for Corzine and Paulson there was a larger issue beyond the firm's fluctuating value in the open market.

Corzine and Paulson's legacy began to take shape almost as soon as they took charge of the firm. Goldman Sachs would need to be a growth company, despite the fact that this runs counter to much of the firm's famed caution. The pace of change would need to be faster than anything Goldman Sachs had experienced before. Simply doing more of what the firm did well would not be enough for Corzine. "I am fundamentally an expansionist," he said. "I think our pace of expansion has been, and probably continues to be, too slow for my taste, because I think the pace of change in the world is faster than we're willing to accept. A great risk for Goldman Sachs is that because of our organizational structure and the kind of people we hire, our cultural instincts are to move slowly. We are naturally conservative." Corzine and Paulson forged ahead, and under their leadership new business in hitherto uncharted territory was explored. They attempted to steer the firm on an even faster track than their predecessors, while giving them credit for setting the course.

One of the lessons of 1994 was that too much of the firm's profitability had depended on a climate of falling interest rates, and too little of its income was generated by dependable fees. In contrast, a firm like Merrill Lynch has very limited exposure to proprietary trading, and through growth and major acquisitions has delved heavily into fee-earning businesses like fund management. The result for Merrill Lynch has been a consistent and rising level of income. Corzine and Paulson made strides to diversify the firm's revenue stream away from its traditional investment banking and trading businesses, into areas better insulated from the gyrations of the stock and bond markets.

Sidney Weinberg and later Gus Levy had avoided managing investors' money, first because of the bitter memories of the Goldman Sachs Trading Corporation and later because of the risk of competing with money managers who were themselves clients of the firm. Levy sold the firm's money management business in 1976 to the firm's old friend and business associate Kleinwort Benson. The stated reason for the sale was Goldman Sachs's desire not to compete with its clients, but some within the firm had feared that the Federal Reserve Board would eventually force it to sell and that they were simply getting out early when the price might be

better. This would turn out to be a mistake. The firm would never have
been forced to sell, and just a few years later investment banks would
make a headlong rush into the field of money management. At the time of
the sale the firm managed more than $500 million, a sizable operation
when one considers that Fidelity Investments, the money management
giant, was managing $3.1 billion at the end of 1975. In the 1980s the
firm realized its mistake and clawed its way back into the money management business, its early advantage lost. Whitehead acquired at no cost a
troubled money market fund, Institutional Liquid Assets, which in time
became a part of the much larger Goldman Sachs Asset Management
(GSAM). But even as late as 1994 some members of the management
committee had doubts about this business, which was underperforming
the firm's other divisions, and some felt the firm should sell it.

Under Corzine and Paulson, GSAM became the focus of top management attention and firm-wide resources. In 1995 the department had a
staff of two hundred fifty people; three years later there were a thousand
people working in it. For the first time since Goldman Sachs acquired
J. Aron in 1981, the firm made a series of acquisitions, buying a number
of small money management firms. Yet Goldman Sachs lags behind its
two major investment banking rivals, Morgan Stanley and Merrill Lynch,
in the amount of assets it has under management. Corzine had come to
the conclusion that the firm needed to act quickly to build up the dollar
amount under management and increase its expertise in the fund management area. At the start of the 1990s, GSAM had as its goal to have
$100 billion under management. In 1997 that goal was $200 billion by
the year 2000. The department also aspired to $200 million in bottom-
line profits. While increasing revenues in the short term, this business
would also provide a substantial asset if the firm went public. The multiples paid for a top fund management business exceed anything a simple
investment bank could expect to achieve. Those within the division hope
to create a business that would be valued by the outside world at $2 bil-
lion. The success of GSAM formed a cornerstone of Corzine's and Paulson's legacy.

The firm Corzine and Paulson envisaged would be entirely transformed
from the one they inherited. The opportunities, they believed, were endless. Taking a cue from its leaders, the 1997 annual review was titled "The
Art of the Possible." "We need to do something that challenges the
organization to be more than it is today," Corzine explained. "As the
regulatory environment changes, we can consider insurance and banking
functions. There is no reason we can't diversify horizontally over time
and extend our franchise into other financial functions, and I think we
will."

The $10 billion in profits Corzine envisaged the firm earning by 2000 was an amount that many thought fanciful in 1995, but now is easily within reach. In 1996 profits returned to the record levels of 1993, and firm-wide bonuses to nonprofessional staff rebounded to a healthy 25 percent. Goldman Sachs was the most profitable private company in the United States, eclipsing the United Parcel Service, Levi Strauss, and even Fidelity Investments. The foreign expansion, stalled in 1994, was renewed, and by the end of 1996 thirty-eight new partner managing directors had been named, along with 86 nonpartner managing directors, 47 of them from outside the United States. Things could have gone very differently. Stung by the events of 1994, management could have recoiled from aggressive trading and expanding what the firm likes to call its "global footprint." In doing so it would have missed some of the best years on Wall Street. However, after regrouping, Corzine and Paulson stayed the course set by their predecessors and pursued their goal of being the world's preeminent investment bank.

THE FIRM'S TRADING businesses reemerged strongly in 1997, but it was investment banking that really shone, accounting for 40 percent of the firm's revenues. In a market where the demand for IPOs was so great that the issues almost walked out the door, Goldman Sachs was king. In 1997, Goldman Sachs brought to market such companies as AMF Corporation and Lucent Technologies (the $3 billion spin-off from AT&T, the largest IPO to date), earning a 20 percent market share in this highly visible business. A second merger boom unlike anything seen since the late 1980s emerged in the late 1990s, and Goldman Sachs was one of its biggest beneficiaries. Despite the large number of new entrants into the investment banking business, the specialty of mergers and acquisitions continued to be dominated by the same small group of players; and the group was dominated by Goldman Sachs. In stark contrast to other parts of investment banking where margins have been squeezed, the mergers business has not been commoditized and fees have not been driven significantly lower. Not only did the firm hold onto its market share, but the number and size of deals done took a quantum leap. From the beginning of 1993 through the middle of 1998, the firm held the number one ranking in worldwide mergers and acquisitions and initial public offerings with a market share of almost 24 percent and 15 percent respectively. During this period Goldman Sachs's global market share in deals over $1 billion would be an incredible 37 percent. The firm's mergers and acquisitions department was now a billion-dollar business for the firm—a fourfold increase from 1993.

In the final quarter of 1997 the Asian equity markets, along with their currencies, suffered drastic devaluations. Declining values were accompanied by increased volatility—market conditions not unlike those seen in 1994. Yet the firm's new risk management systems were vindicated. Although some of the firm's competitors sustained huge losses—to such an extent that they felt the need to make public statements about their solvency—Goldman Sachs trading would remain in the black in this highly unsettled period.

In shoring up the firm after 1994, some have argued that Corzine was preparing it for a sale. They believed that slowly but surely the firm was being made to operate as much like a public company as it could, short of being one. Under the new governance structure, with its expanded managerial class and the increased emphasis on businesses with steady recurring earnings, Goldman Sachs had taken on some of the trappings of a public corporation, ensuring that if and when the transformation came, it would be easier than at any other time in the firm's history.

ON MAY 14, 1997, the spirit of Gus Levy hovered over Goldman Sachs's London office. Late in the afternoon his legacy, now half a century old, was to emerge in full force as Goldman Sachs competed for the biggest block trade in history. The Kuwaiti Investment Office (KIO), through its representative Shroeders, a U.K. merchant bank, was offering three banks a chance to buy a single block of British Petroleum (BP) shares worth $2 billion. For years the trade had been rumored in the market; newspaper articles had appeared, but until that afternoon, nothing concrete had been known.

Ironically, the shares being offered by the Kuwaiti government had been purchased in the wake of the 1987 stock market crash and held for the past ten years. Goldman Sachs and Salomon Brothers, both of whom would be bidding for the block, had acted as underwriters for the British government when it initially sold the state-owned oil company. As the offering foundered in the fall of 1987, the British government bought back the shares from the underwriters and later resold them to the KIO, which accumulated almost 22 percent of British Petroleum. At the time the KIO was hailed as a savior, but later the British government decided that such a substantial holding was unwise and might "operate against the public interest." As a result, by 1988 the KIO had dropped its ownership to 9.3 percent. Now that the value of the KIO holding had more than tripled, it was seeking voluntarily to reduce its stake again by selling 3 percent of BP onto the open market through a carefully orchestrated block trade.

For the KIO the issues were complex. While its traders hoped to sell the shares expeditiously at the best possible price, they would have to walk on eggshells to do so. As part of a sovereign body—the government of Kuwait—they had no desire to upset either the British financial authorities by putting downward pressure on the stock market (BP was the largest stock in the index) or the management of BP, as the KIO continued to hold over 6 percent of the company. They were also concerned that the shares were distributed widely, quickly, and into stable hands, not passed on to speculators who might immediately dump them for a quick profit. It was important that the market remain unruffled. Any panic selling by the investment bank holding the shares would reflect badly on the KIO, to say nothing of damaging the KIO's remaining holding. The Kuwaitis understood that only a bank with a vast global network of contacts and a great deal of experience in moving enormous blocks of stock could make this trade work. For Goldman Sachs the deal was a simple matter. The firm had invented block trading and brought it to Europe in the early 1990s. This would be a headline-grabbing trade that would show the firm's true mettle. It was a competition Goldman Sachs was determined to win.

For years banks from around the world had approached the KIO about selling its BP holding. In the summer of 1996 a team from Goldman Sachs had met with the KIO and offered an extraordinary proposal. Goldman Sachs would bid for the KIO's entire holding in BP, worth $5 billion at the time. One price, one trade, one shot. It was an astounding move designed to show the client that the market had unprecedented liquidity and appetite for a top name, and that the firm had the capacity to move a block many times larger than anything that had been attempted before. The Kuwaitis would naturally be cautious about the political ramifications of the trade, and Goldman Sachs reasoned that a transaction in which there would be no prior public knowledge, no pre-marketing, and no public announcement until the trade was over would appeal to them. Nonetheless, the KIO declined the highly unusual offer.

In the days and weeks leading up to the BP trade no one at Goldman Sachs had any idea that it was imminent, but it would not be fair to say the firm was unprepared. It had been widely rumored for some time that the KIO was looking to reduce its holding again. In February 1997 more than one client called Goldman Sachs to say that another American firm had been making inquiries in the market about a very large placement of an international oil stock. Goldman Sachs had heard nothing of the trade, but assumed that it was either a large block of BP or Shell for sale. The BP share price declined and a story repeating the rumor appeared in the papers the next morning. Goldman Sachs's traders assumed that the chances of the trade taking place had declined, since the element of surprise had been lost.

When the deal finally broke three months later, the KIO had reclaimed the element of surprise. Unbeknownst to Goldman Sachs, the Kuwaitis had determined that it was the right time to sell, and had enlisted Shroeders Bank to advise them and orchestrate the sale. Shroeders would find the buyer, take no market risk itself, and be paid a fee for its troubles. At 4:40 p.m. on May 14, a banker at Shroeders contacted three candidates: Goldman Sachs; a consortium composed of Salomon Brothers and Kleinwort Benson; and the Union Bank of Switzerland. These three were selected because of their prior proposals to the KIO, their experience in block trading, their oil analysts, and their expertise in the U.K. and U.S. equity markets. Each contender was asked to sign a confidentiality agreement in which it committed to refrain from dealing in BP shares for 48 hours and agreed not to alert its clients that the block was coming. While each competitor was informed that the group vying for the block was small, the specific names were not revealed. The banks were told that once the decision was made, the losers would not be given the winner's name, but the winner would be told which firms it had been competing against. Each contender was given just one hour to price the biggest block trade in history and submit its best bid: The final decision would be made shortly after 6 p.m.

When Wiet Pot, the managing director in charge of equity sales in London for Goldman Sachs, got the call, he knew he had to find Gary Williams immediately. Williams, the managing director who heads block trading in Europe, was at a routine meeting with regulators outside the office. For a year, since the firm had first bid for the KIO's entire holding, Williams and Pot had played the trade out in their minds. Assuming that one day the KIO would sell and they would have almost no time to prepare, the two strategized every conceivable move they could make if the call ever came. They had planned every minute detail of both their buying and selling strategy, including the question of how they would hedge such a mammoth position and the marketing approach they might employ. They had lined up client lists and contact numbers so that on the day of the deal, if it ever came, all they would need to decide was the price. And then they waited. Each afternoon for months at the close of business they would ask themselves if today was the day. As the weeks rolled by they began to wonder if the call would ever come.

Williams was interrupted at his meeting by his secretary on the telephone. She spoke hurriedly: "Wiet says the trade is on; get back here fast." Jumping up to leave, Williams grabbed the mobile phone of an equity salesman who was with him and dashed out the door, dialing Pot as he walked out of the building. Williams, an American who had not lived in Britain long, found himself lost in a maze of tiny London lanes. It was 5 p.m. and he could not get a cab. Frantically he walked toward where he thought the office was, talking on the phone and waving at each cab that passed.

By the time Williams climbed into the back of a cab ten minutes later, Pot had assembled a conference call with Zuckerberg, the firm's vice-chairman and head of equities; Thain, the firm's chief financial officer; and four other top managing directors in the equities division in New York. Williams was patched into the call, and the discussion focused on the one unresolved issue: price. BP had recently reported strong earnings, and the price of its shares stood at 744 pence. In order to interest clients in buying a chunk of the deal, Pot and his troops would need to offer them an incentive, a discount to the existing market. No investor would pay the market price knowing that a huge supply of shares was being released. But what would they pay? The partners reasoned that clients would be interested in the shares at 716 pence, maybe even a penny or two higher. They then priced in a spread of seventy-five basis points, which they felt was fair given the enormity of the risk they were taking on, and decided that they would bid 710.5 pence per share. The final price had been determined before Williams got out of the cab and walked into the firm's office. The pieces were in place. All that was left to do was tender the bid, wait for the call, and if it all went right put the long-planned strategy into action.

It is hard to exaggerate the risks inherent in a trade like this one. Once the KIO agreed to the price, whichever bank had submitted the highest bid would be holding 170 million shares of BP and be fully exposed to any movements in the price from that moment forward. Many trades like this one, although none as large, had gone badly wrong. Sometimes the shares proved difficult to resell; word got around the market quickly, and the price of the shares plummeted below the purchase price. Sometimes the market as a whole simply edged lower, taking the stock in question with it. Firms, including Goldman Sachs, had been forced to sit with large loss-making positions for months after buying a big block. Anything could happen. There were no guarantees, no safety valve—only a small buffer in price that could be wiped out in minutes.

Pricing was crucial. If the firm was the highest bidder but had bid too high to resell the shares easily, the losses could be considerable. The BP deal was worth fully 40 percent of the firm's equity capital, and while all of it was never at risk—as it seems impossible that the shares would ever be valueless—a substantial loss was always a possibility. The U.S. or U.K. stock markets or the oil price might suffer from some unexpected and unpleasant news. During the period in which the firm owned the shares some bad news about either BP or the KIO could push the price down. Although all of these risks were small, they needed to be considered.

"At the end of the day it's about risk tolerance—that's the true definition of block trading," explains Silfen, former co-head of the equities division. From a risk management standpoint the firm needed to envision a worst-case scenario, an estimate of the potential downside if it all went horribly wrong. One of the worst-case scenarios was that in the time between the moment the KIO accepted Goldman Sachs's bid and the investors confirmed their orders, a period that could last hours, days, or weeks, the stock market could crash, taking BP down with it. Knowing that investor demand for the shares was strong and that the selling period would likely be short, the firm considered a crash a very minor risk. If such a scenario played out, the BP shares would be only one of many problems with which the firm would need to deal.

A more realistic risk was that investor demand would turn out to be weaker than expected and the selling price would need to be lowered appreciably. Conceivably, the firm could lose $100 million, although this was considered highly unlikely. Potential losses of closer to $50 million were more realistic. Although it is very difficult to measure the trade-offs, some within the firm felt that it would be worth losing $25 million, if it came to that, in exchange for the elevated profile and sense of accomplishment such a trade would bring to Goldman Sachs. Breaking even was acceptable, although not desirable. The message from top management was "full steam ahead." There had been complete support when the firm bid for $5 billion worth of the shares the summer before, and nothing had changed. This time the message came back from top management: "Let's do it, don't miss this thing."

Against this backdrop, the top managing directors in the equity division considered the market. They knew that a number of large money managers in the United Kingdom were underweight in BP shares, and they felt it would not be difficult to sell $600 million to $800 million worth of the shares into the U.K. market. Another $1 billion could be moved easily into the United States. The general consensus was that there was a great deal of interest in the shares, and the firm would be able to sell most of them, if need be, in the 650–700 pence price range.

Finally, if it all went wrong the firm had a hedging strategy. In general Goldman Sachs does not hedge block trades (sell another instrument to reduce the market risk), but a strategy was needed to protect against a worst-case scenario. There was no good simple hedge available. "The danger is that the placement fails and the markets rally and you increase your risk exposure," says Pot. "We decided our best hedge was to put all our distribution power behind it." The block was too large to sell the shares of another oil company against it easily. The correlation between BP shares and the price of oil, over time, is poor. If the instrument used as a hedge does not have an extremely good correlation with the position, there is risk that the position and the hedge could both lose money. Then, instead of reducing the risk, it has been doubled. For this reason selling the shares of another oil company or futures contracts on the FTSE were ruled out. Only as a last resort would the firm buy put options on the FTSE, which would make money if the U.K. stock market collapsed (but lose nothing except the small premium paid if the market rose) before the BP shares had been sold.

Ten minutes after the bids were due Shroeders informed Goldman Sachs that it now owned the largest block of stock ever transacted, 170 million shares of BP, or roughly the amount of shares in the oil company that traded in a normal month. Salomon Brothers and Kleinwort Benson, many believe, had lost the bidding by one-half of one pence. The whole process from start to finish had been completed in ninety minutes, but it was only now that the real action would begin.

In a bold move the firm rejected all possible hedging strategies. Goldman Sachs would sell the shares, and it would sell them before the London stock exchange opened eighteen hours later. It was a monumental task, one that had never before been attempted, but those in control knew it was worth the risk.

At first the firm did nothing. The U.S. market would be open for another three hours, and the firm did not want to begin selling into New York only to have the buyers turn around and dump the shares onto the New York Stock Exchange. Instead, they conducted a series of internal conference calls among economists, strategists, and salespeople, dispersing information about BP to the sales force. The selling process was aided by the fact that BP is a huge, well-known company with a well-researched story. Stock analysts would be up to the minute on the company's status, and investors could be quickly apprised. Most investors who would be interested in the company were well versed in its fundamentals and knew the price at which they would have buying interest; they simply needed an update on any news. The sales effort was also aided by a strong bull market into which investor cash was still pouring at record levels. Goldman Sachs might have to sell investors on the stock but not on the strength of the market.

The temptation in a deal such as this is to move the stock as fast as possible, offloading it on a "first-come, first-served" basis, thereby reducing the investment bank's risk and locking in its profits. But this is not the best idea. For starters, investors begin to worry if sales are made too hastily and word gets around that shares are being dumped. "If a client responds by indicating demand for two million shares and you immediately confirm stock sold, that suggests desperation, which is not the impression you want to give," says Pot. Secondly, the firm felt it had an obligation to its European clients not to sell all of the shares into the United States. Long-term clients of the firm, particularly those in the United Kingdom, would not be pleased to wake up and find that the biggest block trade of the largest company in the country had been completed the night before and they had not been offered a single share. "Had we done that, we could never look our U.K. clients in the eye again," explained Williams. Although waiting until the following morning to sell all of the shares prolonged the firm's risk, it was deemed to be the right thing to do. Once the sales force was assembled and informed of the deal, they decided to test the waters. Up to five hundred people would be involved in the selling effort. The first calls went out to clients in New York at 8:10 p.m., a full two hours after the firm took possession of the shares. Instead of simply selling the shares, salespeople polled clients to determine their interest, taking orders and building a book. Clients were told that they would know their final allocations in a few hours.

It was clear by 9:30 p.m. that there would be no trouble selling the entire block, and that the firm could take its time in allocating stock. The big question, the strength of investor demand, was answered almost immediately. European clients, who had to be contacted at home, showed immediate interest in the stock. The firm soon realized that it was in the enviable position of being able to allocate the stock on what it deemed to be an equitable basis. A decision was made to hold back half the shares until the morning for the European markets. For the firm this would be a highly profitable deal, but the real success would come from the firm's eventual domination of the block trading market. It was with this trade, some believe, that the firm asserted its undisputed leadership role, finally vanquishing Salomon Brothers—a triumph whose roots run right back to Levy.

The following day the BP shares closed in London at 724.5 pence, down 20 pence from the day before but solidly above the 716-pence level at which Goldman Sachs had sold them to their clients. The shares later rallied to 737. A week later, when British Airways sold its 22 percent stake in USAir, it selected Goldman Sachs to handle the trade, which was valued at $500 million. Later in the year, when Michael Eisner wanted to dispose of four million shares of Walt Disney stock, he asked the firm to sell them for him. By the end of 1997, Goldman Sachs had come to dominate the block trading business. Its standing in this market seems only to confirm the point, hammered home many times by Friedman, that there is a substantial advantage to being an early innovator and leader in a new business, an advantage that could last a half century or more.

Once again, with the BP trade, Goldman Sachs forever changed the world of block trading. Despite earning a reputed $17 million in the trade, there was some downside. "The good news is that we did the trade successfully." observed Williams. "The bad news is that the trade helped to change the economics of the equities business for the worse. This trade demonstrated that in certain circumstances you can sell a huge amount of stock with very little preparation; the investment bank will make a lot less money, if any at all, and it has to take a lot more risk." The success of the BP trade meant that the standards were raised another notch. With each leap in the size and pricing of block trades, the economics of the business erode. Every time Goldman Sachs wins a piece of business, bidding the seller closer to the market for larger and larger size blocks, the firm is also aware that it is slowly destroying its own profit margins.

IN 1998, Goldman Sachs went from strength to strength, earning more than a billion dollars, a recordbreaking pace, in each of the first two quarters. Only twenty-four months after rejecting the notion of becoming a public company, the landscape—the firm's fortunes, the markets, and its competition—had changed entirely. In December 1997, Corzine had publicly stated that the majority of partners wanted the firm to remain private and that the issue of a public offering would not, he believed, be on the agenda in 1998. But the rampant bull market, which saw the Dow rise from 7400 to 9200 during the spring and continued to increase the valuations given to investment banks, as well as rapid consolidation in the securities industry, contributed to the firm's decision to reconsider its private status in a project aptly named Echo.

From 1995 to 1997, Goldman Sachs had watched Morgan Stanley merge with retail-based Dean Witter; Salomon Brothers combine forces with Smith Barney and Citibank (Glass-Steagall, which was phased out over the 1990s, was virtually eliminated, and the notion of the trading power of Salomon Brothers teamed up with the banking acumen of Smith Barney, both boosted by the capital of the largest bank in the United States, was a daunting prospect to the industry); Union Bank of Switzerland join with Swiss Bank Corporation; and Bankers Trust purchase niche-M&A expert Alex Brown. Many speculated that the size and breadth of these merged institutions would put Goldman Sachs at a competitive disadvantage, forcing it to look for a partner. It was indeed a sea change in the industry, and the firm's management, taking the actions of its competitors seriously, felt the need to reexamine its own strategy. But perhaps the biggest threat to the firm's continuing existence as a private independent investment bank came not from these mergers—after all, the same trend had existed in the mid-1980s and had not greatly affected the firm—but from Merrill Lynch's purchase of the massive Mercury Asset Management. Goldman Sachs may or may not have wanted to buy Mercury, but it probably did not have the option to do so. As a private company, with no stock, it would have been extremely difficult for the firm to spend the more than $5 billion Merrill Lynch paid for the British fund manager. Early in 1998 Goldman Sachs had considered purchasing a stake in Garantia, the premier Brazilian investment bank, but the deal fell through. As other opportunities like this arose in asset management or bargains cropped up in the battered Asian economies, the firm was hamstrung without public shares to use as an acquisition currency. Some of the financial opportunities, as in the case of Merrill Lynch taking over bankrupt Yamaichi Securities or Salomon Brothers's investment in Nikko Securities at a time when the value of Japanese assets was depressed, would be short lived, depending as they did on economic conditions that might soon change. The partners needed to act decisively and quickly if they were to capitalize on this window of opportunity.

"Structure follows strategy" was the watchword of the firm's newest committee, established in March as a subcommittee of the operating committee. Paulson led a group of eight department heads in a total review of the firm's strategy. The committee's motto meant that the firm would make no decisions on its structure, whether a public sale, an acquisition, or anything else, until it had determined its strategy. The rapid-fire schedule was set in March. Everything about the long-term direction of the firm would be examined in six short weeks. Management stressed emphatically that this was not a simple "should we go public or not?" discussion again, that the strategy exercise was one the firm needed to undertake even if it were to stay private. The strategy committee would report to the executive committee in mid-May, and its recommendations would be set before a meeting of the entire partnership on June 12. Never before had the genie been let out of the bottle so early to wander free, stirring up speculation.

The strategy committee was charged with surveying the terrain for the next five to ten years, imagining the world of 2008 and determining what kind of institution Goldman Sachs would be when it got there. The committee asked itself many questions: What are the major drivers of profitability, and what can the firm do to expand them? What does it mean to be global? Who are our clients? ("Good firms," Paulson told them, "worry about competition. Great firms worry about their clients.") How much emphasis should be placed on proprietary activities? Is the firm capital-constrained, and would it have more capital with public share-holders? Is it necessary to have an acquisition currency (that is, shares) in order to expand sufficiently? How great a disadvantage is the impermanence of the firm's capital? Does it need downside protection? What would be the impact of technology on the firm's business? Without the answers to these issues, the firm's management insisted, the question of a public offering could not be addressed. No one had forgotten 1994 and the painful cyclicality of the industry, but the biggest strategic question Goldman Sachs faced in the spring of 1998 was how fast to grow.

This time the decision to go public was born of good times, of a wealth of attractive business opportunities that mandated that the firm reexamine its priorities. The strategy committee would focus on determining the best way for the firm to remain on top, the direction it would take to ensure its preeminence. But some at the firm could not see past a public sale, and attention quickly focused on multiples the firm might earn in an initial public offering. Paulson, in a forceful speech given to all managing directors, refocused the discussion onto the points he felt were essential. He was determined to raise the level of debate, and taking a leaf out of John Weinberg's book, he adjured his audience to remember the question that all the firm's past leaders had asked themselves: What is in the best long-term interest of the firm? He reminded the managing directors of their responsibility to the next generation, something every leader had done in the past. People were acknowledged by Paulson as the firm's scarcest and most valuable asset, and the question remained: In which format can the firm attract and hold the best people in the industry? To date the answer had always been a partnership, but would it be different going forward? Those who heard Paulson found his words stirring and say that stewardship is something about which there is no cynicism at the firm.

In the weeks running up to the partnership meeting Paulson, who had supported the proposal to sell the firm in 1996, played a bit of the devil's advocate. The financial rewards for selling the firm would be so great that no one needed to be convinced of the economic merits of an IPO. Paulson felt a weighty responsibility to examine the issue from all strategic and cultural angles, focusing attention on any adverse consequences of becoming a public company. He and Corzine would not allow the firm to be swept up in the euphoria of a rampant bull market. Stewardship is about protecting the culture of the firm and leaving the next generation a stronger business. Could that be done in a public forum? they would ask their partners. Paulson would go into the strategy process openminded, unsure at the beginning where he would come down at the end. He was committed to the honesty and integrity of the process, determined that the outcome would not be rigged. The question he challenged the partners to ask themselves was, What would Goldman Sachs be like the day after it sold itself?

Partners were actively encouraged to express their thoughts to the executive committee through personal meetings, letters, or electronic mail. Corzine would try to speak to every partner personally, ensuring that this time the sentiments of the leadership would not stray from those of its partners. There was a risk in this approach. Partners lined up on both sides of the issue, convinced of the merits of their beliefs. This is the kind of debate that could tear some firms apart, a fate that would only be averted by stressing the importance of unity above any particular outcome.

As they had done before the 1996 meeting, the partnership and operating committees held a joint meeting in New York the last weekend in May to hear the strategy committee's report. This was a very different meeting than the one that had taken place two years earlier. And although most of the faces in the room were the same, the outcome would be entirely different.

At this two-day meeting the strategy committee laid before the most senior partners a plan for vigorous expansion. The report rejected the notion of Goldman Sachs joining the ranks of banking behemoths. The firm would not rush out and combine forces with Chase Manhattan Bank or J. P. Morgan, as had often been speculated. Goldman Sachs did not need to be a supermarket of financial services—the opportunities in its existing client and proprietary businesses were deemed more than ample for the firm to grow. Goldman Sachs would differentiate itself from its competitors, most of whom were making a headlong rush into retail businesses, by remaining a wholesaler of investment banking services. Top management believed that while retail businesses are a gold mine in good times, when more difficult conditions emerge the enormous overhead they carry is simply too great a liability.

Goldman Sachs would continue down the path it had been on, albeit at a much faster pace. The firm had ambitious plans for expansion. Over the next five years the firm planned to double the number of people working in its client-serving business, which, it believed, would more than double the amount of revenue it earns. With this dramatic growth the firm's leaders believed that Goldman Sachs would be able to increase its market share in most businesses, despite the fact that it is already number one or two in all of its major businesses and among the top five in all of its other businesses. Building the firm's asset management through organic growth or small purchases, which is what the firm had done to date, was rejected in favor of much more agressive acquisitions, particularly in Europe and Japan.

While there was widespread acceptance among the strategy committee that this was the way forward, there was less consensus on how it should be achieved. All the members of the strategy committee believed that the firm could execute their recommended plan for the future as either a private partnership or a public corporation. They had not been asked to make a recommendation on the structure that would best suit their strategy, and opinions differed widely.

Everyone on the operating and partnership committees listening to the strategy report knew there were enormous risks inherent in such an aggressive plan for growth. The list of companies that have expanded at the peak of an economic cycle, only to find themselves mired in financial turmoil a year or two later, is a long one. But the risk of not zealously embracing opportunity was deemed to be even greater. The joint meeting never formally endorsed the notion of a public offering—they were never asked to—but their support, estimated by some who were there as two to one in favor, paved the way for the firm's sale.

This time around the economic and strategic hurdles were not even bumps in the road. So bright were the firm's financial prospects in the spring of 1998 that the valuations bandied about during the early stages of this process were mouthwatering to those who would reap the windfall. Many of the important strategic arguments—the possibility of making a major acquisition, defraying partners' risk, and facilitating rapid expansion—strongly suggested a sale. The lone hurdle was the cultural issue. One current partner feels that the issue boiled down to, "How do you walk in here the next day and look a guy in the face who has worked here for eight to ten years and tell him you've just taken away his opportunity to be a partner of the firm?"

Tension built as the fateful meeting approached. Corzine told all employees early in June that they needed to hang on a little longer until there was resolution and that the management was glad to be facing this decision in a period of strength without the backdrop of financial anxieties. He also announced that Paulson would be named co-chairman and co-CEO of the firm, a position equal to Corzine's. It was a return to the past, to a management formula that had worked so well for the firm before.

Going into the June 12 meeting many felt the decision could go either way. Everyone knew that in 1996, Corzine, Paulson, Zuckerberg, and Hurst had supported a sale, and many believed that they would again, yet there were widespread reports of opposition by the youngest members, Thain and Thornton. As in the two previous partnership-wide meetings on this subject, no one doubted that management would not proceed with a sale if it lacked the overwhelming support of the firm's owners. And because of the division within the executive committee, the threshold for support among the partners would need to be high—a simple majority would not suffice. The proposal would also need vast support because, at the pinnacle of its industry, Goldman Sachs's strategy, its success, and its clients did not mandate a change. Doing nothing to reshape the firm—the alternative that had not been available two years earlier—was an option now.

There was one crucial difference from the two earlier meetings. In 1986 the newest class of partners had only been on the job for six days and had almost no equity. In 1996, the equity of new 1994 partners was also relatively small, since 1995 was not a particularly strong year. But when the 1996 partners were asked to consider a public sale in 1998 they had already booked one record year, and a second looked more than likely; therefore they would have much larger capital stakes to sell. Although it is always the most junior partners who are disadvantaged by a sale, in 1998, in part because of the inflated valuations the stock market had placed upon investment banks well into the summer months, for this group the economics would be compelling.

Goldman Sachs's one hundred ninety partners retreated on Friday, June 12, to the IBM Palisades Executive Conference Center north of New York City, where they cloistered themselves in a red brick and timber complex atop a hill. Security was high, with extra plainclothes security guards on duty, and the entrances to the compound were closed. The location of the meeting had been kept secret, and many members of the press congregated at the Arrowwood conference center, assuming the meeting would be there. Even with the stepped-up security one journalist climbed over the fence and another tried to infiltrate the meeting using a fake ID card. As rain poured down outside, the partners faced what Paulson called a decision of "grave importance . . . one of the most important things the firm will ever do."

As had been the case in 1986 and 1996, the format of the two-day meeting included a presentation by the committee studying the firm's options, a fifty-page folio of financial scenarios, and an open and spirited debate by the entire partnership. No one expected there to be a vote at this gathering; there was no formal proposal and nothing to vote on. The partnership would signal its interest to the executive committee, and later, if it was deemed to be the will of the group, a specific proposal would be drawn up on which the partners would then vote.

Paulson spoke at the first session on Friday morning, and his words set the tone for the next two days. People who heard him remember that, after he thanked his partners for electing him to share the top job and praised Corzine for turning the firm around over the previous three years, he launched into a discussion of solidarity. Those assembled may have entered this discourse with differing views but whatever the outcome of the following thirty-six hours, they would, he told them, emerge united.

For the partners there was a day of education and a day of contemplation. In his early remarks, Paulson tried to move the argument to the highest possible ground. While explicitly recognizing that there was a great deal of money involved in this decision, he asked his partners to banish it from their minds. "When you became a partner, you didn't have to buy in," Paulson told them. "You were able to earn your ownership interest in Goldman Sachs because prior generations of partners passed it on. And the understanding was that you would leave the firm in better shape. When the time came, you would gladly and graciously pass your ownership interest along to those who came after you. That we are now standing at a point of inflection which requires us to consider and perhaps even to decide to end this partnership in no way absolves us—every one of us—of this solemn trust."

Paulson's goal was to make all partners in the room reexamine their position and rethink any assumptions they might have held before the meeting. Partners remember that he made both cases, for going public and for staying private, in an exaggerated manner, causing everyone to consider the repercussions of their viewpoints. He threw down the gauntlet to those who wanted to remain private by asking them to consider the following possibilities: Employees cannot be locked in or motivated through ownership; capital is not permanent in a private format; there is no downside protection; the market for an IPO was incredibly strong; and remaining a partnership might represent an effort to cling to an outdated and no longer effective form of ownership. Then he crossed the fence, to those advocating a change, and asked them to reflect on the following: The partnership has allowed the firm to recruit and keep the best talent in the industry; the firm's culture rests on the foundation of its partnership, which has allowed Goldman Sachs to differentiate itself from other firms; public owners have a different agenda from partners and are not known to be "long-term greedy"; Goldman Sachs as a public company might no longer be a fun place to work. By stating the extremes Paulson moved everyone in his audience toward the center, where he wanted the debate to be focused.

Following Paulson's remarks the partners broke up for "Echo tutorials," small group sessions designed to give them a more solid grounding in the facts they would need to make this decision. There were sessions on the structure of an enhanced partnership, the structure of an IPO, valuations of an IPO, issues of capital structure, considerations of strategy. At the strategy workshop partners asked such questions as, "Is there any acquisition out there that we wanted to make that we couldn't because we were not public?" Everyone was encouraged to attend more than one session, and interest was so great that the meetings ran two hours longer than scheduled.

In the evening, the partners met for a barbecue and what was billed as an entirely social evening. The atmosphere was a little like that in a college dormitory, as many partners watched the NBA playoffs on television while others milled in and out of game rooms and congregated in small groups in hallways and on stairs to discuss the burning issue of the moment.

Saturday morning Corzine addressed the group on a subject close to his heart—fairness. But first he felt a responsibility to read a letter he had received from John Weinberg and John Whitehead the previous afternoon. The two Johns were opposed to the partners' selling the firm. They believed strongly that "If it ain't broke don't fix it." Both were committed to the notion that the partnership was one of the things that had made the firm great and that it would be a mistake to tamper with it. Corzine had spoken to Weinberg, who had assured his successor that he would wholeheartedly support whatever decision the partners made. Those who heard Corzine speak remember that he annotated these remarks by reminding those assembled that Weinberg, Rubin, and Friedman had each, along with their management committees, at some point recommended that the firm go public. Corzine, who had been a member of each of those management committees, had supported the proposal each time and, without strongly advocating it now, supported it again.

Greed, Corzine told the assembled in a heartfelt statement, would not be defined for him by the *Independent* or the *New York Post*. Many newspapers, those included, had made the case that selling the firm at a bull market price and reaping the rewards would be an act of pure selfishness on the part of the partners. Greed is a two-sided coin, Corzine argued, and a system in which 1.5 percent of the participants reap the vast majority of the rewards in good times and adjust the compensation and headcount of the other 98 percent of the firm in rough times also might be viewed as grossly unfair. Between 1987 and 1994, the firm had downsized six times in different divisions in response to disappointing earnings, and the employees—not the partners—had borne the full brunt of the adjustments. Perhaps, Corzine ventured, selling the firm in good times and spreading the largesse broadly, deeply, and generously would actually be less greedy.

By midmorning on Saturday the leadership was done talking, and it was time to hear from the partnership. What followed was an impassioned debate, but nothing like the emotional response that had poured out in 1986. As had been the case in 1986 and 1996 the floor was opened for discussion and more than one hundred partners stated their point of view. A discussion began in which the arguments, many of them eloquently framed, emerged in sharp relief. Each speaker emphasized his or her support for the outcome, whatever it might be, and after each speaker was finished there was a round of applause from the floor.

The debate focused on four main areas: equity, risk, strategy, and acquisitions. Those who spoke in favor of staying private emphasized the partnership as the firm's point of distinction, as what makes the firm special, and pointed to it as a formula that works. Teamwork—one of the most venerated aspects of the firm's culture—was a direct outgrowth of the partnership. The firm did not need to make this change, and it could potentially damage the very fabric of Goldman Sachs.

Some of those in favor of selling the firm argued that a partnership might not be the best way to hold onto top employees. Goldman Sachs, they suggested, can no longer be run by its one hundred ninety owners but requires up to a thousand leaders to maintain its high level of operation. The firm needs to hold onto these people and can do so more effectively if it can offer them stock. Those opposing the change pointed to the fact that Goldman Sachs was the employer of choice at most business schools and that the firm had little trouble attracting top talent from other firms. Those who came to Goldman Sachs did so in pursuit of a partnership, not stock options.

Goldman Sachs would never let a client have the capital structure the firm itself had, some partners argued. A major global business hoping to expand to more than twenty thousand employees cannot rest on a capital base that has no permanence. In a risky cyclical business it makes no sense to expose the resources of a handful of people to the whims of the world's capital markets.

Those for and against felt that they had the issue of strategy on their side. The firm would not be able to make a major acquisition without stock, and without this ability it might be relegated to being a niche player, unable to compete for all of the top business.

The discussion, which was expected to end before lunch, went on until 2 p.m., with people going out to get food and returning to eat at their desks.

As at the other two partnership meetings held to consider this question, the co-chairmen did not forcefully push the issue. "Jon is a very low-key guy who listens a lot and doesn't feel the need to dominate a meeting by speaking," said Robert Hormats, a managing director. "He would always take in a lot of different opinions before making a decision." The members of the executive committee, divided as they were, listened closely to their partners. For, ultimately, the decision about whether to remain a partnership is a political one—the partners must have the will to continue to be partners. Without that the firm would inevitably become a public corporation.

After the long open session each partner was asked to fill out an anonymous written questionnaire for submission to the executive committee asking which ownership format they preferred and why.

On Saturday at around 2:30 p.m. the meeting adjourned and the partners left the conference center, some driving back to the city, some to the airport. They did not know what would happen next; the fate of the firm had been left in the hands of six men of differing opinions. There had been the overwhelming sense that a majority of those present supported the idea of selling the firm, but Corzine and Paulson had made it clear that a supermajority would be needed. The executive committee cloistered itself for the next thirty hours to review, reflect, and decide. They emerged from this meeting united, and on Monday announced to the world their belief that Goldman Sachs should sell a portion of the firm to the investing public. A detailed proposal would be drawn up for the partnership to vote upon during the summer, and anticipating that there would be more than sufficient support from the partnership and hospitable markets, the firm would have an initial public offering in the fall of 1998.

Some were cynical about the firm's decision to go public. The same question asked two years earlier had yielded a resounding no. Partners talked endlessly about the value of partnership, but at the height of the greatest bull market in history they were willing to relinquish control of their firm. Others saw it differently, viewing the firm's continuing status as a private partnership as the result of inertia and nostalgia. A partnership, they believed, is an obsolete structure with which to operate a vastly expanding, global, risk-taking enterprise. The money, which they intended to spread to every employee of the firm, would only strengthen the organization. Those who supported the change point out that far from being greedy, Goldman Sachs's leaders pushed for this move in 1996, when the firm would have sold for not substantially more than its book value.

Very few partners were free from mixed emotions. Even those whose support for the IPO was the strongest felt enormous regret at the passing of the partnership and all the benefits it had engendered for the firm and its culture. "I am not without my own sadness about changing the partnership structure," Corzine said after the decision. "And I am not without my own concerns. However, in order to achieve the mission of this organization—to serve our clients and to sustain and strengthen the preeminence of this firm—I believe, on balance, that this is the right decision."

Some limited partners wondered about the wisdom of a public sale. Among those retired from the firm are partners who, when faced with the opportunity to sell as general partners, declined on the grounds that the partnership made the firm great. One limited partner went so far as to say, "A lot of us think there's a big danger here that you could kill a goose that, over the years, had laid an awful lot of golden eggs. . . . Why in God's name would you want to tamper with something that has worked so well?" On the other side, many limited partners had voted to sell the firm in 1986, or supported the idea in 1996, but from the standpoint of personal gain their timing had not been perfect. Publicly, Friedman characterized the move as a way to husband scarce partnership capital: "We're in the longest stock market boom and the biggest one in history," he said with some prescience. "What you do is you store up your seed corn in the event of a bad period. One hears the rumor there used to be a time when stock markets went down."

On the day following the firm's announcement, its co-CEOs were on the defensive. A barrage of press speculating on how rich they and their partners would become had, they felt, missed the point of the sale. "Contrary to what you might read, we are not doing this because of the money. This is not about money or cashing out," Corzine vehemently asserted. "We intend to be the preeminent, independent global investment bank. We are going to be damn tough, and we will have the capital to compete." Paulson stressed that the firm would not merge with a big bank or retail operation. The firm would use the capital provided by a public offering to do more of what it already did well, as a vehicle for growth.

Some of the post-mortems mourned the passing of the last great Wall Street partnership, decrying the end of an era. Yet the importance of this transition, while historically interesting, is minimal to the industry. Did it matter that the industry leader was a private partnership able to conduct its business without focusing on the short term and the smooth flow of recurring earnings that stock markets applaud? Probably not. Goldman

Sachs had slowly but surely been readying itself to become a public company. Now that the time for change had arrived, the transformation could be smoother and simpler than at any time in the firm's history.

WHEN THE PARTNERSHIP reconvened on August 10, the group assembled held the first and only vote in the firm's history on the question of a public offering. At this meeting, which was so shrouded in secrecy that the partners gleaned their information from a slide show (there was no written material to take away), the financial details of the offering were revealed. Issues covered included how the anticipated bounty would be spread among employees and limited partners and how the vesting would take place. The Goldman Sachs foundation, which would concentrate on funding projects in the field of education, was touched upon as well. But the purpose of this meeting was nothing more than edification; any lingering doubts those in the audience might still have held about the decision to go public were left unspoken.

After the presentation a vote was taken. One by one the partners filed into a room to sign an affidavit in front of a notary public. The two questions contained in the document—Are you in favor of proceeding with the plan as outlined? and If it proceeds would you wish to participate?—required separate signatures. The plan was almost uniformly endorsed.

Although the official figures were never released, many believe that payouts from a public offering to the one hundred eighty-eight general partners would have amounted to between $5 billion and $6 billion, enriching many individuals by between $50 million and $75 million, and some of the more senior partners by amounts in excess of $100 million. Senior and mid-level professionals would have been compensated based on performance, like a traditional discretionary bonus. Employees, it was expected, would be paid through a formula that entitled each to a windfall equal to 50 percent of their 1997 or 1998 compensation plus a bonus for each year of service. All shares distributed through the offering would have been restricted; they could not be sold for between three and five years.

On July 29 Corzine and Paulson met with the limited partners, a group of key people who felt they had a legitimate claim on the premium that would accrue from the sale. Were it not for their years of hard work the firm would not have the name, prestige, culture, or ethos it now enjoys. The one hundred ten limited partners, many of whom spent their entire working lives at the firm, had on average a longer tenure than most active partners (tenure has declined over time). The prospect of paying those who had been partners for less than two years a significant multiple of their stake while offering those who spent many decades as partners one and a half times the value of their investment in the firm was troublesome to some of the limited partners. John Whitehead, a vocal critic, emphasized the enormity of the limited partners' contribution and tried to impress upon management its moral obligation to those who had built the firm. The firm's leaders were caught between their debt to the past and their commitment to the future. The compromise hammered out—limited partners were to be paid a premium over book value of 25 to 55 percent, depending on whether they chose cash or stock—was acceptable to most limited partners, although few were overjoyed. In August, when the limited partners made their election, most opted for the more highly valued stock option.

Inside the firm some things began to change almost immediately. All of the employees now knew that they would be enriched by the sale, and some began to speculate on just what this would mean for their personal wealth. The newspapers were filled with speculation. As soon as the decision to go public was made, the firm began to use the prospect of stock as an enticement to recruit high-level talent into some of the fastest growing businesses.

The conditions that had prevailed in the financial markets during the spring, as the partners finally agreed to go public, had been almost too good to be true. But events unforeseen in June would by August overtake the firm. Even as the partners signaled their support for an offering to be held in early November, the financial world around them had already begun to change dramatically. The valuations for the entire firm presented to the partners in August (the proposal was to sell only a portion, 10 to 15 percent) ranged from what was thought to be a highly conservative $20 billion to a lofty $35 billion. These values were derived from the prices at which the firm's competitors, known as "the comparables," were trading on the stock market. In July, Merrill Lynch was trading at 4.1 times its book value and Morgan Stanley Dean Witter at 4.4 times its book value.

But in August, as the partners sat and listened to the plan that would make them and their co-workers even more fabulously wealthy, the value of their competitors and implicitly their own firm had in fact already passed the pinnacle. The Dow Jones Industrial Average had peaked at 9,367 in early July, and the Asian financial crisis and economic downturn that had begun almost a year earlier, and which many believed would be contained, had already shown signs of spreading to the United States and Europe. While the firm's own strategists were predicting that the Dow Jones Industrials would end the year between 9,000 and 10,000, doubt had begun to spread, and by the time the partners met in August the market had slipped to 8,500. Unforeseen was the fact that Russia was falling deeper into economic chaos. Enormous sums had been lent to Russia by banks, investment banks, and hedge funds, on the premise that it was of such geo-political importance to the West that it was "too big to fail." By the end of August the Dow had shed another 1,000 points and Russia had devalued the ruble and defaulted on its government debt. In excess of $100 billion was lent by Western financial organizations to Russia and more than 90 percent of this would ultimately be lost. As a result bank stocks were hit particularly hard, and as uncertainty in the market increased the torrent of IPOs completely dried up.

In the final week of August the firm filed its first registration statement with the SEC. While interest in what was billed as the largest IPO ever was intense, the document was most notable for its blank space. Even in what were thought to be the final stages of its private partnership, with the prospects for public ownership only weeks away, the firm could not abandon its long held policy of secrecy. The document contained very little new information and said nothing about the partners' compensation or ownership stakes, how profitable its individual businesses were, or even how many shares would be offered. Yet there were a few new insights to be gleaned. The proposal revealed that after the firm was no longer a partnership, the management still wanted its managing directors to think and act like partners. In an attempt to maintain some of the culture and incentive structure of the partnership a "partnership pool" was proposed as a mechanism by which managing directors' compensation would still be tied to the firm's overall performance. The document also showed how the firm's mix of profitability was shifting with its overseas expansion.

In the first half of 1998, 46 percent of pretax profits came from outside the United States. In 1995 the firm's overseas operations had earned nothing. The plan also contained a poison pill defense that would guard against a hostile takeover. Goldman Sachs, the firm that perhaps conducted more successful defenses than any other, would not be taken over themselves, at least not against their will. The offering document made it clear, with uncanny foresight, that "in the event of market downturn, our business could be adversely affected in many ways."

The firm's cost structure had been greatly swollen since the cutbacks in 1994 and in 1998 expenses were running at an annualized rate of almost $7 billion, up 61 percent from a year earlier. In a poor trading environment, which in truth had already begun by the time this document was made public, the firm admitted that its revenues could decline, and unless costs could be cut profit margins would be reduced as well.

The stock market gyrations that commenced in August, some of the wildest in memory, led to almost immediate speculation that the offering would need to be substantially revised or even shelved. As the price-to-book ratio of competitors Morgan Stanley Dean Witter, J. P. Morgan, and Merrill Lynch contracted sharply during this period and their share prices plummeted (dramatically underperforming the overall falling market), some wondered openly if the deal could be completed at all. As the Dow careened from 8,600 to 7,400 in a matter of days, the pressure to confront the mounting speculation increased. In an effort to counteract the climate of uncertainty, Corzine and Paulson told all the employees in a conference call the first week in September that the IPO was still on track, and that nothing had happened to derail it. Paulson told the employees to remember that the decision was driven by strategic objectives rather than economic considerations. "Nothing that is happening in the markets today or last week or tomorrow or next week should substantially change that objective or the positive outlook that we have for the firm over the next five to ten years." It was not a convincing argument. The market for IPOs had evaporated and no one knew this better than the firm that had brought the largest number of companies to market. The firm's bankers understood the value of the right market conditions for completing a successful IPO, and as the longest stretch of time without an IPO in over a decade passed, the existing conditions were anything but hospitable. Less than two weeks after Paulson and Corzine were reassuring their troops, some of their partners were leaking stories to the press that the deal was up in the air and that the decision to proceed could go either way.

By September 20 the firm, as valued by the price of other banking stocks, was worth 40 percent or $13 billion less than it had been two months earlier. Merrill Lynch had watched its stock price plummet 47 percent from its high, as Morgan Stanley Dean Witter had fallen by 44 percent. By early October the price-to-book ratio of the firm's two most formidable competitors was down to 1.59 and 1.88 respectively. Other competitors such as Lehman Brothers and Bankers Trust had seen their stock prices halve. The firm was perhaps now worth $17 billion (at a very optimistic 2.5 times book), far below the most conservative estimate three months earlier. There were some who argued that Goldman Sachs, because of its higher dependence on trading revenues and its smaller money management operations, would trade at a discount to some of its major competitors. Conversely, the firm has a better name and a larger market share in the most profitable areas of client driven investment banking.

By the end of September the worldwide economic situation had only deteriorated further, and world leaders and their finance ministers were already decrying this as the most unstable financial era in fifty years. The huge losses taken in Russia, in addition to those taken a year earlier in Asia, had caused investors to shun assets that were viewed as risky, sparking distressed selling in many markets and a flight to cash and government bonds. Stock markets all over the world had been hard hit, but it was in the bond market, in an eerie echo of 1994, that some of the most destabilizing influences were felt.

Rumors had circulated for weeks that some of the largest hedge funds were in dire financial trouble. Yet hedge funds publicly report little information and until some of the funds' CEOs wrote to their investors little factual information was known. On September 2, John Meriwether, a former vice-chairman of Salomon Brothers, sent a letter to his investors explaining the unusual market conditions his fund, Long Term Capital Management (LTCM), had faced, reporting losses of 52 percent of its capital in the year to date, and asking for further infusions of cash. LTCM was an interesting case. The fund, which Meriwether successfully ran for four years, had returned $2.75 billion of capital to its investors at the end of 1997, citing its inability to find adequate trading opportunities for such a large pool of cash. Events had moved so quickly that now, only nine months later, the fund was looking to these same investors for an increase in capital. LTCM's core business was to make highly leveraged bets with money borrowed from banks by seeking out aberrant price relationships between fixed income markets and then taking a position, often using futures, derivatives, swaps, and options, based on the likelihood that the relationships would return to "normal." This trading, which is not considered particularly risky and is known throughout the industry as "relative value" trading, was widely practiced by the commercial and investment banking industry and hedge fund community. For the most part it involves the purchase of debt of a lower credit quality, which may have fallen in price, and the simultaneous sale of government issued bonds. Like all leveraged trading, when it goes right the results can be spectacular, but in difficult times, losses are greatly amplified.

During the market conditions that existed from 1995 until the middle of 1998, this type of trading had been very successful and LTCM had returns of more than 40 percent in 1995 and 1996. Yet when the financial crisis developed in the summer of 1998 those bonds with lower credit ratings became worth even less, relative to U.S. treasury bonds, which, viewed as a safe haven, climbed steadily in value. The Federal Reserve had become increasingly concerned about the impact the LTCM portfolio could have on its highly exposed creditors and counterparties (by and large banks and investment banks), as well as those financial institutions that held similar positions of considerable magnitude on their own books. The Federal Reserve judged that a forced liquidation of LTCM, at fire sale prices in the already skittish marketplace might, according to Chairman Greenspan, "produce large losses or *worse*" to those exposed. Even more damaging, Greenspan indicated that "had the failure of LTCM triggered the seizing up of markets, substantial damage could have been inflicted on many market participants, including some not directly involved with the firm, and could have potentially *impaired the economies of many nations, including our own.*"

As the fund's losses mounted in September the Federal Reserve intervened, taking decisive action it believed was necessary to prevent further instability in the financial markets. It was a highly unusual move by the Fed in response to extraordinary market conditions. Thus on September 20, officials from the Federal Reserve and the Department of Treasury visited LTCM's offices to learn the details of their positions. As a result of this meeting, the determination was made by the Fed that to simply allow the fund to go into default would cause an unacceptable level of dislocation in the market. Indeed, given the size and scope of the portfolio and the fact that the market for many of these instruments had all but dried up, it is not clear whether a wholesale sell off of the fund's assets would even have been possible.

William McDonough, president of the Federal Reserve Bank of New York, convened a meeting in his office on the morning of September 22 with Goldman Sachs, Merrill Lynch, and J. P. Morgan, the three Wall Street institutions that he characterized as having "the greatest knowledge of the situation at LTCM and a strong interest in seeking a solution." These banks would form the core of a larger group that would rescue LTCM through an infusion of $3.6 billion in exchange for control and 90 percent ownership of the fund. (Goldman Sachs would put up $300 million, or just less than five percent of its partnership capital.) As negotiations proceeded at a breakneck pace for the next four days, Goldman Sachs would play a unique role. The firm, in addition to working with the banking group to hammer out acceptable conditions for taking over the hedge fund, was also negotiating with Warren Buffet and AIG in a separate potential bailout. In the end the terms offered by the alternate group were not deemed to be as attractive, and the bank consortium offer was accepted. It is an investment about which there are no guarantees, depending as it does on market conditions.

On September 28, with the LTCM rescue fresh in everyone's mind, the firm canceled its offering. Citing the unstable conditions of the financial markets, the firm's co-CEOs withdrew, rather than delayed, the prospective sale. The expansion plans, which in part precipitated the decision to go public, now looked to be in serious doubt as the firm's competitors announced their plans for immediate staff reductions and Goldman Sachs's profitability in the fourth quarter was a severe disappointment, with the lowest earnings since 1994. "I can't imagine we would advise a client, what with the volatility we have, the falling valuations, and uncertainty of earnings going forward, that this is a good time to go public," Paulson said. "You have to understand that these are difficult times." It was a way station on an incredible journey. The firm's management committee had been promoting the idea of a public sale, either privately among themselves or to the partnership, for twelve years—yet once again it was not to be. Even as Corzine and Paulson pulled the offering, they signaled their commitment to reviving the plan if the right conditions were to prevail again.

Thus the firm found itself at a crossroads: The partners had voted down a partnership, but a corporation had not come into being. Another class of partners was selected in the fall, the class that was never meant to be. As the landscape of the financial industry changed rapidly, the firm was by its own admission operating with a sub-optimal capital structure, without the flexibility it had hoped to gain by becoming a public company. There was widespread disappointment throughout the firm as employees and partners alike watched their visions of vastly inflated wealth evaporate, and Goldman Sachs entered a period of heightened uncertainty. In January 1999, Corzine resigned as co-CEO, retaining the title of co-chairman, while relinquishing day-to-day responsibilities. He would concentrate on the firm's plans for the IPO, although no one could say when the firm would have another opportunity to go public and if the conditions would ever be as ideal as they were in the spring of 1998. Yet it seemed that the legwork had been done, that the partnership had intellectually and emotionally crossed over a bridge to the idea of a public sale, and that although there would be a delay, there was no road back.

1999

THE INITIAL
PUBLIC OFFERING

F AST-FORWARD. It is October 1999, Goldman Sachs is no longer a
partnership, Hank Paulson is alone at the helm of the firm, and Jon
Corzine is running for the U.S. Senate from the state of New Jersey. For
almost three years I studied and wrote about the history of Goldman
Sachs but you can include my name on the list of those who remain
astonished.

The highly unusual transition of power from Corzine to Paulson came
at the end of 1998, a year of extraordinary events that would bring their
already strained relationship to the breaking point. On the face of it,
Hank Paulson's and Jon Corzine's partnership had seemed to be a replay
of the firm's recent history; a Republican and a Democrat, a banker and a
trader, but there were a number of strikes against it from the start. Many
of the difficulties originated from the hasty transition undergone by the
firm in 1994. Unlike the leadership changes in 1976 and 1990 this one
was not heralded. While there was broad consensus that Corzine should
be the CEO, Paulson was not the only candidate considered to work with
him; in the aftermath of his appointment, feelings were bruised and some
very senior partners departed. (Corzine's first preference was to work
with Mark Winkelman, with whom he had developed a strong partnership when they ran fixed income together.) Unlike their predecessors,
Corzine and Paulson had not worked together closely before they came
to power and were not on equal footing from the start. Looking back, it
seems that the process was too rushed and that not enough attention was
given to creating a durable consensus.

As the events of 1998 unfolded, strains in the relationship between

Corzine on the one hand and Paulson and the executive committee on the other began to be apparent to the more senior partners. This was not a simple clash of personalities but rather a serious disagreement of substance. Jon Corzine believed unstintingly that Goldman Sachs needed to sell itself to the public in 1998. He felt certain that as a private partnership Goldman Sachs would find it increasingly difficult to maintain its position at the top of its industry and that the breadth and scope of the firm's operations made it dangerous to continue to operate without the permanent capital enjoyed by a public company. He had believed this since 1986 and nothing that had happened in the intervening years had dimmed his belief. But without the overwhelming support from the six-man executive committee—only two of whose members supported his position—inertia alone would keep the partnership from acting.

Paulson's support was much more cautious, coming as it did only after the strategy committee had completed an in-depth study and he witnessed the growing support of his partners for the proposal. Corzine had been disappointed when the partners had rejected the notion of going public in 1996, Paulson had not. Corzine and Paulson could not agree upon the timing or approach to the initial public offering or many of the details the plan would include. Yet, Corzine knew if he did not push hard for the offering it would never happen; as the events of 1986 and 1996 had clearly shown, without forceful leadership Goldman Sachs would remain a private institution. The firm's top management had for many decades operated in a consensual manner, but for Corzine to see the public offering through he would have to back away from this practice. He would go out on a limb, prodding, persuading, using his enormous stores of charisma and loyalty to bring the partnership to the point of action. Over the course of 1998, Corzine was indefatigable in lobbying his partners on behalf of the IPO. While in the end his efforts were successful, and those within the firm now wax lyrical on the benefits to Goldman Sachs of being a public company, he put further distance between himself and the executive committee and Paulson.

In June 1998, on the eve of the decision to go public, Corzine and Paulson publicly expressed enormous enthusiasm and confidence in each other when they announced they would be resurrecting the Weinberg-Whitehead, Rubin-Friedman management style co-CEO. Paulson praised his co-senior partner in deferential language in front of all the managing directors, citing him as responsible for the firm rebounding from the depths of 1994. He held up the co-CEO partnership as setting the tone for how the entire partnership would work together, serving as an example and indicator of the unity of the whole firm. Paulson was hopeful that the co-CEO structure was a solution to some of the difficulties that had arisen within the leadership in recent years. He and the executive committee thought that this structure would lead to more consensual management and smooth out many of the rough spots. Despite the initial enthusiasm, Corzine and Paulson were to survive as equals for a mere seven months.

Trading conditions in the fall of 1998 were as treacherous and unexpected as any in recent memory. Triggered by Russia's default on its debt in August and the steep economic decline in the Far East, bond prices all over the world, and particularly the relationship between various bond prices, moved to levels considered by most risk models to be exceedingly unlikely (the four standard deviation move that traders are so fond of discussing). Trading in many instruments ground to a halt as liquidity evaporated, making markets dysfunctional and dangerous. Ironically, the firm had initiated its fixed income arbitrage unit only months earlier. This group sought to exploit trading opportunities that arose when bond prices became misaligned because of temporary and aberrant conditions in the marketplace. As a result, Goldman Sachs traders were holding many of the same "value trades" as Long Term Capital Management (LTCM, the highly leveraged hedge fund which found itself in serious financial trouble in the summer of 1998) and others, and when the market chaos descended there was no backing out. As a result of the trading losses in 1994, which had hastened the departure of a sizable contingent of partners, Corzine and Paulson had focused on the nuts and bolts of the firm's trading businesses and its risk management systems. They and their partners felt confident that the firm had in place systems which would prevent the kind of wrenching losses that the firm had experienced four years earlier. Management throughout the firm believed that the changes had been sufficient and that, while the firm would have its ups and downs, large concentrated losses resulting from lack of agility when exiting positions were a thing of the past. But, despite management's confidence, the firm's models, considered to be state of the art, had failed to account for "copycat" risk, the risk that other important players in the speculating community had made the same bets in substantial size. When it came time to reverse these positions there would be no liquidity, no one to take the other side of the trade—in short, no way out. The actual level of risk the firm held had been significantly underestimated because they had not accounted for the positions of other players in the market. Such systemic risk could not be accurately evaluated by models that relied on historical information to predict an event unlike anything that had happened in the past.

In each of the first three quarters of 1998, Goldman Sachs averaged a billion dollars in earnings. In the final quarter it barely scraped by with

$100 million. Losses in the firm's trading and proprietary investments exceeded $650 million. Many bankers within the firm were outraged. As in 1994, they stood by helpless as the firm's trading business took another severe blow. Some of those running the firm blame themselves, saying they had not fully prepared the bankers for the magnitude of the potential losses. Others say that most bankers simply do not understand trading well enough and the breach between the two halves of the firm is very difficult to bridge. It harkened back to the old Wall Street bugaboo, trading versus banking. It was a battleground that had torn other firms apart and one that management insisted did not exist at Goldman Sachs. (Corzine views this as one of the weaknesses of his and Paulson's leadership. Rubin and Friedman, a trader and a banker, had managed to successfully bring these two parts of the firm together. He and Paulson had not.) And although partners did not stream out the door as they had in 1994, as it was now much more difficult to withdraw capital and a once-in-a-lifetime IPO was in the cards, something equally important was at stake. For Goldman Sachs, which reduced its trading risk somewhat during the fall (many of its positions were not or could not be liquidated and when market conditions returned to normal the positions returned to profit), the greatest casualty of 1998's market chaos was the IPO. There was an unequivocal consensus that, in light of such extensive losses, the firm could not speak confidently to potential investors about its plans, profit projections, or its businesses, and the offering was canceled in September 1998. It was understood internally that as soon as the firm had one strong quarter's results the IPO would be revisited. Management was extremely anxious to complete the transition as quickly as possible.

In the midst of this difficult time another controversy was brewing inside Goldman Sachs over the role the firm should play in helping to rescue the ailing LTCM. Corzine felt strongly about this issue. In his view, the firm had benefited so greatly from the existing financial system that it was unconscionable not to come to the aid of that system when, as many believed, the system itself was in jeopardy as a result of LTCM's potential default. Corzine was certain that Goldman Sachs had a moral obligation to take a leadership role in any rescue plan. On a more mercantile note, he had always wanted to make a sizable investment in LTCM, and here was his opportunity. Corzine immersed himself in negotiations with the Federal Reserve and a group of major Wall Street firms, and conducted separate talks with Warren Buffet and the insurance giant AIG about a possible rescue. Recognizing that these were extraordinary times, the most unusual circumstances in the financial markets in the past fifty years, Corzine was certain that they required extraordinary actions. There was widespread belief that if LTCM failed a number of smaller Wall Street firms would also fail, generating increased chaos in the markets and damaging confidence among public investors. Many of Corzine's partners, including many in leadership positions, were not convinced. Some thought that Goldman Sachs should participate in a rescue but should not take a leadership role. Even the firm's risk committee did not agree on the need for the firm to participate in aid to LTCM. This was another issue where Corzine moved away from consensual management, frustrating and angering his colleagues. Again, those within the firm argued that he was out of step with the thinking of the executive committee, operating independently of the views of the majority of partners in management, and without what they considered adequate consultation. Certain of his views and driven by what he believed were the firm's obligations as a "corporate citizen," Corzine pursued negotiations and Goldman Sachs took a leadership role in the eventual LTCM rescue package.

The LTCM rescue was only one of the largest and most visible issues in 1998 on which Corzine and others in management could not agree. Corzine is an optimist, convinced of the unlimited opportunities that exist for financial services companies, and thus he was committed to the wholesale expansion of the firm. While CEO he uncovered many opportunities for the firm to make substantial investments in businesses in Russia, Brazil, and Mexico, for example. He saw many of these as unique opportunities that required leadership and decisive action. Some of those on the executive committee felt the firm needed to proceed with more caution, arguing that Corzine was off on his own and not engaging in sufficient consultation with the executive committee. (Ironically as a public company today, top management makes decisions more quickly and with a lower degree of consensus than when it was a partnership.) Paulson and Corzine could not agree on the direction or pace of the firm's expansion. Yet, the firm went ahead with deals with which Paulson did not agree, in Russia for example, further increasing the tension between its leaders.

Publicly, Goldman Sachs put on a very different face. Stories leaked by someone within the firm gave insight into the troubles brewing. But even after press reports surfaced in New York and London in the fall of 1998 that Corzine's and Paulson's relationship was on very shaky ground, speculating that Corzine would be pushed toward the exit, those within the firm continued to insist that the newspapers were reporting irresponsibly, pointing out how "un–Goldman Sachs–like" such an event would be. No one had been eased out of a leadership position at the firm since Sidney Weinberg and Walter Sachs bid farewell to Waddill Catchings in 1930. Corzine's and Paulson's deteriorating working relationship was like a family secret that those within the firm would not mention, hoping the problem would go away.

Elevating Paulson to a position of equal stature to that of Corzine had not increased the number of issues about which they agreed, nor did it smooth over their relationship. In the lull after the offering was pulled, the executive committee, ex Corzine, came to believe that something had to be done. Among those running the firm, the frustration level had reached a breaking point. It was clear that the issue of leadership, the direction the firm would take in terms of its expansion, the mix of its businesses, and even its managerial style needed to be determined before the offering was revisited. After a long series of meetings among the members of the executive committee it was determined that it was Corzine who would leave the firm, a solution to which he acquiesced.

On January 11, 1999, Paulson and Corzine recorded a voice mail message for all of the managing directors. Paulson spoke at length. Corzine would relinquish day-to-day responsibility for the firm and his title of co-CEO and co-senior partner. He would remain as co-chairman and concentrate on the public offering. As the force behind the IPO, he would stay on at the firm until it was completed at some indeterminate point in the future. Paulson insisted the changes were made at this point because there was what he termed a "window of opportunity," an interlude between the first and second IPO attempts. It was an inelegant solution, but one that allowed Corzine to complete and participate in the IPO. Paulson highlighted the new management committee structure; John Thornton and John Thain were promoted and officially named as co-COOs and, implicitly, heirs apparent.

Thus began the most awkward and uncomfortable period in the firm's management. Corzine was officially co-chairman, but he was no longer co-CEO. In his lame-duck position there was little he could do in the way of initiative, yet his presence at the firm could still be felt. Corzine's legacy to Goldman Sachs will undoubtedly be the IPO. Many argue that without him the IPO would not have happened during this period; moreover, had Corzine dropped the idea he would still be in a position of leadership today.

Corzine spoke only a few lines in the firm's announcement of his resignation, imparting little enthusiasm for the change. Yet his personal emotions shone through as he told those with whom he had spent his career how difficult this move was for him, stating that it was in the best interests of the firm. In speaking to the managing directors he said only that he was leaving in the interest of cohesion, nothing more specific—allowing those who owned and ran the firm to wonder and speculate. For such a cataclysmic change, he was brief almost to the point of being abrupt. And, although the word *coup* is banned from the Goldman Sachs vernacular, it seems clear that the decision was made for Corzine and this was not the moment he would have chosen to leave the firm.

The underlying message was a damning one. Teamwork at Goldman Sachs, valued above all else, had unraveled at the top. It is not surprising that those leading the firm are uneasy about discussing this episode. So much attention has been given to the spirit of teamwork that it is almost impossible to conduct an interview with any partner or employee without the term being used. Yet in this case the firm's ethos was not enough to hold together two men with such disparate leadership styles and enormous disagreements of substance.

The voice mail message detailing the management changes came as a shock to many partners, who were deeply saddened by it. As a leader, Corzine had engendered enormous personal loyalty and a large number of those at one remove from top management had not been aware of the full extent of the problems. The most senior partners, by and large, were not surprised. They had seen this coming or realized for the good of the firm a resolution like the departure of a co-CEO was in the offing. Some of those in positions of power expressed relief at Corzine's resignation, as the unity of top management was restored.

It was a clean break. Many partners, after they leave the firm, maintain offices and secretaries at Goldman Sachs, but if you call the firm today the switchboard cannot locate a Jon Corzine and the operator will ask you how you are spelling that name. Corzine has been described by those who know him well as the consummate trader. The most successful traders make their fortunes over time not by picking the biggest winners but by deftly cutting their losses, putting it all behind them and then moving on with an open mind. By early fall Corzine had announced his candidacy for the U.S. Senate. Today he can be found in slightly down-at-the-heels campaign offices in Newark focused on the issues of New Jersey's voters, with his life at Goldman Sachs clearly behind him. (Yet when challenged in the press on his lack of political experience, Corzine responded, "Political neophyte? I worked at Goldman Sachs!")

Over the decades, Goldman Sachs has shown resilience in bouncing back from even the most unsettling difficulties and, although in the space of six months it canceled an IPO, sustained large trading losses, and witnessed the departure of a CEO, the organization was remarkably unruffled. In the first quarter of 1999 the firm regained its enormous profitability and on May 3 Goldman Sachs sold itself to the investing public. In a prospectus very similar to the one issued a year earlier, Goldman Sachs sold 467 million shares, although initially only 69 million shares were sold outside the firm, at a price of $53 per share. During the first day of trading, enthusiasm for the shares was so great that the shares traded to a high of $77.25, but over the ensuing weeks they drifted down to $55, settling in the 60s by mid-October 1999. All of the firm's employees benefited financially from the IPO through a formula that gave them five-year restricted shares worth 150 percent of their previous year's take-home pay and that took into account the number of years worked at the firm. It was a windfall beyond what most had expected but, coming as it did after a year of tumult, enthusiasm was tempered by an element of relief. For many at Goldman Sachs the relief is palpable; the issue with which the firm's management had wrestled for thirteen years had finally been put to rest.

NOTES

The following abbreviations are used in the notes:

BW: *Business Week*

CUOHC: Columbia University Oral History Collection (memoirs)

F: Michael C. Jensen, *The Financiers: The World of the Great Wall Street Investment Banking Houses*

FT: *Financial Times*

FW: *Financial World*

G&G: Ken Auletta, *Greed and Glory on Wall Street: The Fall of the House of Lehman*

GSAR: Goldman Sachs Annual Review

IBA: Vincent P. Carrosso, *Investment Banking in America*

IDD: *Investment Dealers' Digest*

II: *Institutional Investor*

int.: Interview with author

IT&IC: Securities and Exchange Commission, *Investment Trusts and Investment Companies*

KA: Kleinwort archives

KB: Jehanne Wake, *Kleinwort Benson*

MAX: Tom Bower, *Maxwell: The Final Verdict*

ML: Charles M. Farkas and Philippe DeBacker, *Maximum Leadership: The World's Leading CEOs Share Their Five Strategies for Success*

MT: *Regina v. Kevin Maxwell et al.* transcripts.

NC: Judith Ramsey Erlich and Barry J. Rehfeld, *The New Crowd: The Changing of the Jewish Guard on Wall Street*

NYT: *New York Times*

obit.: Obituary

OC: Stephen Birmingham, *Our Crowd: The Great Jewish Families of New York*

SEC: Securities and Exchange Commission. Eric P. Sheinberg, witness before SEC in the matter of Maxwell Communications, November 3–4, 1993

Welch: *Welch Foods, C. E. Anthony Company and Yonker Brothers v. Goldman Sachs*

WES: Walter E. Sachs, Memoirs from Columbia University Oral History Collection

WSJ: *Wall Street Journal*

CHAPTER I

p. 3 storm out of the firm's headquarters: William Power and Michael Siconolfi, "How Goldman Sachs Chooses New Partners: With a Lot of Angst," *WSJ*, October 19, 1990, p. 1.

4 egg worth tens of millions of dollars: Michael Carroll, "Which Way Out," II, September 1995, p. 63.

4 an all-consuming job: GSAR, 1986, p. 66.

4 privacy than employees would be": int.

6 operating with considerably more capital: "Ranking America's Biggest Brokers," II, April 1987, p. 197.

6 lose Merrill Lynch $300 million): Michelle Celarier, "Four Legs Good, Two Legs Bad," *Euromoney*, January 1996, p. 27.

9 alternatives [to going public]": int.

9 or we can do a little of each": *G&G*, p. 235.

10 isn't that large," the partner responded: Beth McGoldrick, "Inside the Goldman Sachs Culture," II, January 1984, p. 65.

10 Goldman Sachs partners filled twelve places: Steve Swarz and Ann Monroe, "Goldman Sachs Strives to Adapt to Changes by Wall Street Rivals," *WSJ*, October 9, 1986, p. 1.

11 at book value, they should go out at book value": John Weinberg int., February 19, 1997.

11 Will this source of energy diminish?": *G&G*, p. 230.

11 $100 million if the deal went through: Robert A. Bennett, "Can Mighty Goldman Stay Private?" *NYT*, April 13, 1986, p. 33.

13 dinner that same night: In Michael Bloomberg with Matthew Winkler, *Bloomberg by Bloomberg* (New York: John Wiley & Sons, 1997), p. 4.

14 on our own culture": Geoffrey Boisi int., July 30, 1996.

14 do the right thing": Ibid.

15 underpromises and overdelivers to itself": John Corzine int., January 14, 1997.

15 complex and costly capital structure: Michael Carroll, "Which Way Out," p. 70.

15 majority of the firm's profits Ibid., p. 64.

15 not a studied decision": Jon Corzine int., January 14, 1997.

16 bond issues outside the United States: Robert A. Bennett, "Can Mighty Goldman Stay Private?" p. 33.

16 with the rededication": int.

17 training and development: Peter Mathias int., January 17, 1997.

17 seminal sin of the eighties on Wall Street": Martin Dickson, "Monday Interview: Premier Democrat on Wall Street," *FT*, August 10, 1992.

18 heartache in this business":
    Metz, Tim, "Goldman Sachs
    Avoids Bitter Take-over Fights
    but Leads in Mergers," Decem-
    ber 8, 1992, p. 18.

18 not even an outhouse":
    Weinberg int., February 19,
    1997.

18 stay in the business we had to
    do it": Weinberg int., February
    19, 1997.

18 garner an ever bigger market
    share: Beth Selby, "How Mor-
    gan Stanley Maps Its Moves,"
    II, June 1992, p. 53.

19 Morgan Stanley earned
    34 percent: "Managing Greed
    and Risk on Wall Street,"
    Economist, July 1986, p. 69.

19 Procter & Gamble among its
    best clients: GSAR, 1986.

19 washes a rental car": Steve
    Friedman int., December 12,
    1996.

20 cultural interest is to cooper-
    ate": int.

21 work with others, you have a
    problem": William Power and
    Michael Siconolf, "How Gold-
    man Sachs Chooses New Part-
    ners: With a Lot of Angst,"
    WSJ, October 19, 1990, p.
    A10.

21 thirty-three-year veteran part-
    ner of the firm: Beth Selby,
    "The Steve and Bob Show," *II,*
    December 1990, p. 70.

21 I never forgot that": Janet Han-
    son int., April 11, 1996.

21 below the industry average:
    Peter Mathias int., January 17,
    1997.

21 survive as just an employee":
    int.

22 two and a half times faster than
    anyplace else": int.

22 they have the use of a great
    amount of it": Gilbert Kaplan,
    "True Confessions," February
    1991, p. 53.

23 the entire firm cringed: Rob-
    ert A. Bennett, "Can Mighty
    Goldman Stay Private?" p. 33.

24 inside the firm and to the press:
    Steve Friedman speech, "Keys
    to Profitability in the 1990s,"
    June 1, 1993.

25 business in the early 1990s: int.

25 the mortgage business or devel-
    oping a capital markets
    group?" he asked in 1997:
    Friedman int., February 20,
    1997.

25 know how to compete against
    them": Beth Selby, "How Mor-
    gan Stanley Maps Its Moves,"
    p. 56.

25 things extraordinary well": int.

26 audacity, confidence, and
    maturity": Beth McGoldrick,
    "Inside the Goldman Sachs
    Culture," *II,* January 1984,
    p. 58.

26 save her career: Scott McMur-
    ray "Goldman Sachs Moves to
    Reassure Stanford
    Candidates."

26 we'll lose control": Henny
    Sender, "Too Big for Their
    Own Good," *II,* February
    1987, p. 63.

27 future is a public company":
    Alison Leigh Cowan, "An
    Exercise in Introspection Lets

Goldman Bare Its Soul," *NYT,*
January 25, 1990, p. D1.

27 convinced of that": William
Buckley int., September 24,
1996.

28 sold Wall Street": *II,* July 1992,
p. 146.

30 in the investment banking
industry": John Weinberg int.,
February 19, 1997.

30 opportunistic and innovative:
Matthew Winkler, "Goldman
Shakes Up Fixed Income Unit,
Displacing Some Key Partners,"
WSJ, July 15, 1988, p. 18.

30 eating our lunch": int.

CHAPTER II

32 Shopkeeper in Philadelphia:
WES, p. 3.

33 the National City Bank on Wall
Street: Ibid., p. 9.

33 "altitude of his hat": *OC,*
p. 111.

33 were known as "note shavers":
Robert Sheehan, "Let's Ask
Sidney Weinberg," *Fortune,*
October 1953, p. 173.

33 worth of commercial paper a
year: *OC,* p. 111.

33 housekeeping for her four
brothers: WES, p. 10.

33 all of it the senior partner's:
OC, p. 288.

33 forgave the final payment:
WES, p. 43.

34 deal for Goldman, Sachs: *OC,*
p. 289.

34 adopted its present name,
Goldman Sachs & Co: *IBA,*
p. 19.

34 1894 they had risen to
$67 million: WES, p. 45.

34 $200 million a day with
investors: E. M. Christner,
"Goldman Sachs Celebrates Its
First 100 Years," *IDD,* December 9, 1969.

34 almost tripled, to $1.6 million:
KB, p. 121.

34 sitting on $4.5 million of capital: KA.

35 every meeting strongly emphasized.": Paul Sachs to Herman
Andreae, October 28, 1912,
KA.

36 not be a single word of criticism": WES, p. 51.

36 this department alone were
$500,000: WES, p. 53.

36 their grandfather, Marcus Goldman, died: Ibid.,
p. 66.

37 now known came into being:
IBA, p. 79.

37 doubled, from 36.4 to 73.5: *F,*
p. 192.

37 and Knickerbocker: WES,
p. 29.

37 we knock off $750,000": *KB,*
p. 128.

38 business for the firm to pursue:
WES, p. 73.

38 twenty in 1898 to 173 by 1915:
IBA, p. 79.

38 clients and Lehman Brothers
had the money: *IBA,* p. 83.

38 much in the business world:
WES, p. 80.

39 retailer's net worth was a mere
$237,000: Ibid., p. 32.

39 common shares for themselves:
WES, p. 136.

40 traded down to only $25: WES, p. 33.

40 pay him about $9 million: WES, p. 27.

40 a five-and-dime shop: Paul Sachs, in CUOHC, p. 49.

40 much interested as you": Kleinwort partners to Paul Sachs, July 11, 1912, KA.

40 Continental Can Company, and Studebaker: *IBA*, p. 83.

41 little business to underwrite: WES, p. 88.

41 memorandum of understanding in 1936: *IBA*, p. 421.

41 bitterness existed between the two companies: Lucas Clay, in CUOHC, p. 1036.

41 open support for the enemy: *KB*, p. 142.

42 and your sterling account with us": Kleinwort partners to Goldman Sachs, July 12, 1916, *KB*, p. 143.

42 London business until after the war: *KB*, p. 142.

42 'a turning down office' ": Arthur Sachs to Herman Andreae, January 9, 1917, KA.

43 I have given all there is in me": Henry Goldman letter, October 29, 1917, KA.

43 his pro-German sentiments: *OC*, p. 395.

43 terms with any Sachses": Ibid.

43 and Sears Roebuck & Co: WES, p. 40.

43 and his wish was granted: Henry Goldman obit., *NYT*, April 5, 1937, p. 19.

43 enormous charm and person-

ality: Waddill Catchings obit., *NYT*, January 1, 1968, p. 15.

44 business—theory and practice": Ibid.

44 whatever the circumstances": Ibid.

45 to his position in the firm": WES, p. 44.

45 difficult to overrule: Catchings obit.

45 frenzy of stock buying: *IT&IC*, p. 3.

45 constant while issuance grew to $100 million: WES, p. 60.

45 trust sold out in a single day: Ibid., p. 33.

45 *The Great Crash of 1929:* Galbraith p. 89.

46 companies worth $500 million: *IT&IC*, p. 7.

46 Galbraith wrote: Galbraith p. 88.

46 is that you've no imagination": WES, p. 27.

47 caught with our pants down": Ibid., pp. 44.

47 a world of money": Ibid., p. 46.

48 amounted to about $13 million: Ibid., p. 48.

48 thirty years earlier: Walter Sachs deposition, December 16, 1948, United States District Court U.S.A.V. Henry S. Morgan, p. 131.

48 rise above $10 million: WES, p. 81.

48 stood by the wreckage: Ibid., p. 43.

49 he reluctantly submitted: Ibid., p. 48.

49 stop it in time": Ibid.

49 wasn't very bright": Sidney

Weinberg obit., *NYT,* July 24, 1969, p. 1.

50 most influential citizens": E. J. Kahn, "The Director's Director, *New Yorker,* September 15, 1956, p. 39.

50 liquor dealer of moderate means: Weinberg obit.

51 awful kid—tough and raw": E. J. Kahn, "The Director's Director," p. 65.

51 made good," he would say: Robert Sheehan, "Let's Ask Sidney Weinberg," *Fortune,* October 1953, p. 173.

51 "maybe one of these will help": E. J. Kahn, "The Director's Director II," *New Yorker,* September 22, 1956, p. 60.

52 alone went through fire": WES, p. 52.

52 clients, and Weinberg's talents: Ibid., p. 82.

52 he so much wanted to hear: Ibid., p. 171.

53 dozens of corporate boards: Ibid., p. 123.

53 way of thinking, unimportant": Ibid., p. 51.

53 one-third of the firm's profits: Weinberg obit.

54 very bleak banking years: WES, p. 189.

56 for his sins anyway": Robert Sheehan, "Let's Ask Sidney Weinberg," p. 208.

56 with all of them": E. J. Kahn, "The Director's Director II," p. 46.

56 tasted anything so delicious": E. J. Kahn, "The Director's Director," p. 48.

57 *shirts away"*: E. J. Kahn, "Director's Director II," p. 49.

58 percent of all underwritings: *IBA,* p. 465.

58 into the top seventeen: Ibid.

58 was only $7.5 million: Walter Sachs deposition, December 16, 1948, U.S.A.V. Henry S. Morgan, p. 131.

58 cleared for the first time in years": WES, p. 212.

58 even figure into this listing: In Ernst Bloch, *Inside Investment Banking* (Illinois: Dow Jones Irwin, 1986), p. 8.

60 because everybody came to him": Whitehead int., December 17, 1996.

61 Do you really want to do it?": Ibid.

62 open end, closed end, or no-end": Robert Sheehan, "Let's Ask Sidney Weinberg," p. 216.

62 as much as I have today": Weinberg obit.

62 means anything at all": E. J. Kahn, "The Director's Director II," p. 52.

62 had to like it": John Whitehead int., December 17, 1996.

63 therefore selected Gus": Ibid.

63 race track rather than in the classroom: *NC,* p. 30.

64 grow during this period": Cary Reich, "John Whitehead," *II,* June 1987, p. 28.

64 happen this afternoon," says Whitehead: Ibid.

65 Don't waste my time": Clay Chandler, "Treasury's High-Stakes Player," *Washington Post,* June 18, 1998, p. A01.

66 we do demand a full day":
Gilbert E. Kaplan, "Gus Levy
Answers 132 Questions About
His Firm, His Business—and
Himself," *II*, November 1973,
p. 35.

67 watched very carefully": Ibid.

67 rating was left in place: *F*,
p. 200.

67 rushed to redeem their securities: Welch, p. 1326.

68 investigation of the company: *F*,
p. 202.

68 at only $53 million at the time:
"Goldman Sachs Ordered to
Pay $3 Million Claim," *WSJ*,
October 10, 1974, p. 24.

CHAPTER III

71 $5,000 of it, in Goldman Sachs:
Cary Reich, "John
Whitehead," *II*, June 1987,
p. 27.

71 square-jawed appearance of
an ex-boxer": Anthony
Bianco, "John Weinberg," *BW*,
April 17, 1987, p. 224.

72 each time they will look different": John Weinberg int., February 19, 1997.

72 he used to say to me," says
John: Ibid.

73 a lot differently": Whitehead
int., December 17, 1996.

74 no question of a vote": Nigel
Adam, "The All-Round Magic
of Goldman Sachs,"
Euromoney, July 1981, p. 16.

74 things they weren't very good
at": Cary Reich, "John Whitehead," p. 28.

75 someday it will kill you":
Weinberg int., February 19,
1997.

75 it was their business": Whitehead int., December 17, 1996.

76 things went a little better":
Ibid.

76 Whitehead says proudly:
Ibid.

78 intellectual and commercial,"
says Paulson: Hank Paulson
int., December 15, 1997.

78 ready to switch his thinking":
Jacob Weisberg, "Traitor to
His Class," *Worth*, July/August
1997, p. 75.

79 stand by for twenty
questions' ": Beth Selby, "The
Steve and Bob Show," p. 73.

80 Geoffrey Boisi explains: Boisi
int., July 30, 1996.

80 you could suggest": Ibid.

81 break his leg": Friedman int.,
December 12, 1996.

82 world-class player": Boisi int.,
October 24, 1996.

82 set of socks": Friedman int.,
December 12, 1996.

83 a lot of clients": Ibid.

83 actual assignments": Boisi int.,
October 24, 1996.

83 dictates your schedule": John
Crudele, "Masterminding the
Mega-Deals," *NYT*, November
3, 1985, section 3, p. 6.

84 and lure clients: Tim Metz,
"Goldman Sachs Avoids Bitter
Takeover Fights but Leads in
Mergers," *WSJ*, December 3,
1982, p. 1.

84 loses out," says Friedman:
Ibid., p. 18.

84   with a predator": Boisi int., October 24, 1996.

84   fought for the other side": Margaret Park, "The Great Defender," *Sunday Times,* October 27, 1991.

85   advising on the side' ": Boisi int., July 30, 1996.

85   out of sight, out of mind: int.

86   specialist at Morgan Grenfell: Matthew Winkler, "U.S. Merger Specialists Invading Britain," *WSJ,* July 18, 1986, p. 24.

86   twitching twenty-four hours a day": Ibid.

86   making a lot of noise": Ibid.

86   we need emergency action": Margaret Park, "The Great Defender," *Sunday Times,* October 10, 1991.

87   £250 million price tag: Jack Willoughby, "Can Goldman Stay on Top?" *Forbes,* September 18, 1989, p. 160.

88   Weinberg admitted in the early 1980s: Nigel Adam, "The All-Round Magic of Goldman Sachs," *Euromoney,* July 1981, p. 23.

88   twelve and now there are fourteen": Whitehead int., December 17, 1996.

88   consultant to the firm: Mathias int., January 17, 1997.

90   annual review reads: GS Annual Report

91   twenty seconds": Jack Aron, Recollection: An Informal History of J. Aron & Company, Inc., April 10, 1981.

92   able to do that": int.

93   partner confesses: int.

94   J. Aron goldtrader: int.

94   infected the place": int.

94   too much money": int.

95   sold the company": int.

97   commodities division: int.

97   He was right": int.

98   risk-free arbitrage trading: John Gapper and Nicholas Denton, *All That Glitters* (London: Hamish Hamilton, 1996), p. 14.

98   if you lost money": int.

104   Aron broke that mold": int.

104   of people who made up the corporate bond department: Weinberg int., February 19, 1997.

105   according to Friedman: Friedman int., February 20, 1997.

106   You don't,' " Friedman says: Ibid.

106   company has already decided what to do": Beth McGoldrick, "Salomon's Power Culture," *II,* March 1986, p. 69.

108   accepting mediocre results": int.

108   instrument of change": Steve Kim int., April 4, 1996.

109   you were doing all the time": Clay Chandler, "Treasury's High-Stakes Player," p. A01.

110   you pay is no hindrance": In Martin Mayer, *Wall Street: Men and Money* (New York: Harper and Brothers, 1955), p. 199.

110   said about Levy in 1996: Kevin Muehring, "A Trader at the Treasury," *II,* January 1996, p. 43.

110 function effectively": Henny Sender, "Robert Rubin," *II,* June 1987, p. 473.

110 is the country?' ": Ibid.

112 influx of money into the business": Ibid.

112 man a genius: Connie Bruck, *The Predators Ball* (New York: Simon and Schuster, 1988), p. 318.

112 transactions did not look irregular": Lawrence Pedowitz int., February 19, 1997.

113 [*Wizard of Oz*]," Freeman recalls: Richard Stolley, "The End of an Ordeal," *Fortune,* October 4, 1993, p. 140.

113 handcuffs on him": Pedowitz int., February 19, 1997.

114 I couldn't remember": Richard Stolley, "The End of an Ordeal," p. 140.

114 old enough to be quite impressionable": Pedowitz int., February 19, 1997.

114 All of us will have scars from it": Kurt Eichenwald, "Transition at the Top for Goldman Sachs," *NYT,* August 15, 1990, p. D1.

114 $25 million of Goldman Sachs capital: "Wall Street's Shining Maiden," *Economist,* September 29, 1990, p. 110.

115 insider trading scandals: James B. Stewart, *Den of Thieves* (New York: Simon and Schuster, 1991), p. 586.

116 below lawyers," Pedowitz remembers: Pedowitz int., February 19, 1997.

116 on Freeman's actions: *DOT,* p. 654.

117 end the conversation.": James B. Stewart and Steve Swarz, "Why Robert Freeman, Previously Defiant, Agreed to Admit Guilt," *WSJ,* August 18, 1989, p. 1.

118 had saved the firm $548,000: Richard B. Stolley, "The End of an Ordeal," p. 146.

118 responsibility for what I did": Goldman Sachs memo, August 17, 1989.

118 only one right answer": Pedowitz int., February 19, 1997.

118 high negative expected value": Richard B. Stolley, "The End of an Ordeal," p. 146.

118 there was no sympathy": Ibid.

119 issues of law and fact": Goldman Sachs memo, August 17, 1989.

119 falsely accusing others: Letter from Freeman counsel to Wall Street Journal, October 18, 1991.

119 heartfelt sympathy": Management Committee memo to all Goldman Sachs staff, August 17, 1989.

CHAPTER IV

120 Whitehead and I did": Beth Selby, "The Steve and Bob Show," p. 73.

120 destiny, and not drooling": Weinberg int., April 29, 1998.

121 you better go ahead and eat it":

Kurt Eichenwald, "Transition at the Top for Goldman Sachs," *NYT,* August 15, 1990, p. D1.

121   was the heart of the place": Boisi int., October 24, 1996.

121   equals far more than two": Martin Dickson, "Premier Democrat on Wall Street," *FT,* August 10, 1992.

122   chief executive officer": Ibid., p. 71.

122   ask a lot of questions": Beth Selby, "The Steve and Bob Show," p. 71.

122   something he already knows": Ibid.

122   took action faster than he had: Ibid.

123   even want the job?": *ML,* p. 180.

123   process of reinvigoration": Ibid., p. 181.

124   the kingdom was happy and prosperous": Ibid.

126   payoff," says Friedman: Steve Friedman, "Keys to Profitability in the 1990s." Speech before the Securities Industry Association, June 1, 1993.

126   start competing with our clients": Stephen Taub, "The View from the Top," *FW,* January 20, 1987.

127   the mighty Fidelity Investments: Randall Smith, "Closing Water Street," *WSJ,* May 3, 1991, p. 1.

127   sought better terms: Floyd Norris, "Goldman Phasing Out

Big 'Junk Bond' Fund," *NYT,* May 3, 1991, p. 1.

127   spokesman for the firm: Ibid.

128   best for your client": Beth McGoldrick, "Wall Street Puts Its Own Money on the Line," *II,* June 1984, p. 74.

129   someone I want you to talk to' ": Friedman int., April 28, 1998.

129   he said at the time: Beth McGoldrick, "Wall Street Puts Its Own Money on the Line," p. 75.

129   let's go for it' ": Friedman int., April 28, 1998.

132   a year of record profits: Beth Selby, "Scraping by on $750,000 a Year," *II,* June 1991, p. 63.

132   remainder in the firm: Michael Carroll, "Which Way Out?" p. 65.

132   took home $5.3 million: Stephen Taub and David Carpy with Alison M. Smith, "Wall Street's New Austerity," *FW* July 21, 1992.

132   its nearest competitor: Beth Selby, "Scraping by on $750,000 a Year," *II,* June 1991.

133   an earthquake," Rubin remembers: Clay Chandler, "Treasury's High-Stakes Player," *WP.*

133   decisions," Rubin said: Kevin Moehring, "The Trader at the Treasury," *II,* January 1996, p. 43.

134   will also be no profits": Henny Sender, "Robert Rubin," p. 473.

136 promoted ahead of his class: ML, p. 195.

136 interest of the firm": Philip Maher and Ron Cooper, "Image and Reality at Goldman Sachs," IDD, October 4, 1993, p. 20.

137 "If you do that, you'll kill me": SEC, p. 553.

138 publicly quoted company": MAX, p. 21.

138 spirit of the law": MT, p. 412.

139 Maxwell was offering: SEC, p. 36.

139 macho game in town": Peter Lee, "The Most Macho Game in Town," Euromoney, May 1991.

140 craziest thing I ever saw: SEC, p. 131.

141 We soon hated them": MAX, p. 26.

142 ignore what they knew": int.

142 bank, was the brightest": "An Honour System without Honour," Economist, December 14, 1991, p. 103.

142 presidents, you know": SEC, p. 61.

143 estimated at £1.2 billion: MAX, p. 81.

143 wants to do a trade": SEC, p. 267.

143 dead meat, all right": Ibid., p. 587.

144 London could question him: Ibid., p. 24.

144 he was in trouble: Ibid., p. 81.

144 the outstanding shares of MCC: Tom Bower, Maxwell:

The Outsider (New York: Viking, 1988), p. 417.

144 72 percent of the transactions: "MCC Moved in a Mysterious Way," Economist, December 21, 1991, p. 99.

144 half of this year [1991]": "An Honour System without Honour," p. 103.

144 Sheinberg had told him so: MT, October 18, 1995, p. 41.

145 bears out of the market.": Ibid.

145 under such conditions: Ibid., p. 43.

145 incredible £400 million: MAX, p. 116.

145 but that's life: SEC, p. 42.

145 nobody liked him": Ibid., p. 91.

146 most of the shares: Ibid., p. 92.

146 10 percent lower: Ibid., p. 96.

146 managed the risk himself: Ibid., p. 97.

146 out of the air," he said later: Ibid., p. 124.

146 was intrinsically worth: Ibid., p. 140.

147 He just said, 'Done': Ibid., p. 127.

147 the closed period began]": SEC, p. 157.

147 $120 million and $160 million: Ibid., p. 177.

147 Cut it back: Ibid., p. 177.

148 public must own some": Ibid., p. 200.

148 any more shares," says Sheinberg: Ibid.

148 I could have dreamed": Ibid., p. 591.

148 getting the shorts": Ibid., p. 201.

148   we had the shares": Ibid.,
      p. 250.

149   and do something else": Ibid.,
      p. 593.

149   on the wrong side of it."): Ibid.,
      p. 155.

150   extent, it still is": Ibid.,
      pp. 60–61.

150   shares between buyers and
      sellers": Ibid., p. 310.

151   pension fund trustee MAX, p.
      142.

151   as "self-financing": *MAX*,
      p. 141.

151   by the Maxwell-owned BIT:
      Correspondence from Gold-
      man Sachs to Kevin Maxwell,
      May 29, 1991.

151   have been different: SEC,
      p. 339.

151   the sale to BIT": MAX, p.
      142.

152   so goddamn important?' ":
      SEC, p. 414.

152   they're attacking," Maxwell
      cried: Ibid., p. 414.

152   it's a foundation": Ibid., p. 428.

152   connected with these": Ibid.,
      p. 429.

153   I was holding air": Ibid.,
      p. 445.

153   anybody if you do this":
      Ibid.

153   clean with you": Ibid., p.
      447.

154   ones with us": Ibid., p. 451.

154   200 percent of the loan: Ibid.,
      p. 490.

154   Robert solemnly answered:
      Ibid., p. 491.

154   they thought it was": MT,
      October 26, 1995, p. 39.

155   to give him that money": SEC,
      p. 516.

156   people who were broke": Ibid.,
      p. 560.

157   was time to talk about pay-
      ment": MT, September 22,
      1995, p. 14.

157   on the £25 million loan":
      Ibid.

158   him again in my life": SEC,
      p. 554.

158   selling the shares": MT, Octo-
      ber 26, 1995, p. 43.

158   whatever you want with the
      shares: SEC, p. 568.

160   Kevin explained: MT, Septem-
      ber 22, 1995, p. 32.

160   heard him loud and clear:
      Ibid.

CHAPTER V

161   any other bank in the world:
      "Goldman Tops Cross-Border
      Euro Bid League at Pounds
      4.4," *Evening Standard,* Febru-
      ary 12, 1991.

166   not a problem' ": Larry Becerra
      int., November 18, 1996.

166   came some notoriety":
      Ibid.

167   at the time remembers: int.,
      February 12, 1998.

168   their own personal interests":
      ML, p. 184.

170   is the greatest disease": Debbie
      Galant, "Fast Cars and Loose
      Exchange Rates," *II*, May
      1992, p. 57.

170   "a betrayal of our future":
      Philip Stephens and Emma
      Tucker, "Major Stresses, Solid

Opposition to Devalua-
tion," September 11, 1992,
p. 1.

171   reserves in two or three days:
Philip Stephens, Peter Marsh,
and Stephen Fidler, "Sterling Is
Suspended within ERM," *FT,*
September 17, 1992, p. 1.

173   as fast as we can": int.

173   as much as 75 percent:
Robert E. Norton, "Upheavals
Ahead on Wall Street," *Fortune,* September 14, 1987,
p. 72.

175   had almost fifty fewer partners:
Michael Carroll, "Which Way
Out?" p. 64.

176   it is devastating": int.

178   great deal to us": Robert Rubin, memo to Goldman Sachs
staff, December 10, 1992.

178   a great sense of loss": Steve
Friedman, memo to Goldman
Sachs staff, December 10,
1992.

178   epaulet on your shoulder": *ML,*
p. 184.

178   as I could at these big receptions": Ibid., p. 185.

180   credit ratings in the industry:
Anita Raghavan, "Goldman
Quietly Raises More Capital
but Has to Pay Almost 9.5%,"
WSJ, March 28, 1995.

184   buying,' " Becerra remembers:
Becerra int., November 18,
1996.

186   they want you to do": Ibid.

187   between [*sic*] 161 people":
"People," *II,* January 1994.

187   if you can": Robert Lenzner
and Riva Atlas, "Top This if

You Can," *Forbes,* December
6, 1993, p. 42.

188   firm's broader interests": Steve
Friedman, memo to Goldman
Sachs staff, April 15, 1993.

188   happen to me?': int.

CHAPTER VI

190   fall off the track": Richard
House, "Why Goldman Ran-
kles Its European Rivals," *II,*
December 1992, p. 107.

190   average month in 1993: Anita
Raghavan, "Limited Loyalty,"
WSJ, December 16, 1994.

192   that just tore it up": int.

192   won't let us fail' ": int.

192   they can do anything": Padraic
Fallon, "The Last of the David
Weills," *Euromoney,* April
1993, p. 42.

194   bear market in bonds since the
1930s: "The Moonies Come to
Market," *Economist,* June 20,
1998, p. 89.

195   certain European currencies":
Goldman Sachs SEC filing,
August 24, 1998, p. 66.

195   was a time for humility": Friedman int., April 28, 1998.

196   heart of the plaintiffs' case":
MCP Pension Trustees Ltd. and
MGN Pension Trustees against
Goldman Sachs & Co. and Eric
Sheinberg. Judge Shainswit
orders, January 24, 1995.

198   because of some conflicts: John
Jay, "Goldman Chastened,"
Sunday Telegraph, June 20,
1993.

198   stick and snake boots":

Richard House, "Why Gold-man Rankles Its European Rivals," *II,* December 1992, p. 103.

199   We reduced their limit": Friedman int., February 20, 1997.

200   couldn't get out of": int.

200   we did to ourselves": int.

200   bulk of the 1994 problems": Michael Carroll, "Which Way Out," p. 74

201   end of 1993": Friedman int., February 20, 1997.

201   reversals in fortune: Leah Nathans Spiro, "Turmoil at Salomon," *BW,* May 1, 1995, p. 150.

201   liquid markets," he says: Friedman int., February 20, 1997.

203   Houghton-Berry remembers: Houghton-Berry int. October 4, 1995.

203   Houghton-Berry recalls: Ibid.

203   until November or later: "Tee-Hee and Sympathy," *Daily Telegraph,* September 26, 1994, p. 27.

205   they should be elevated," says Friedman: Ibid.

206   changed my decision": Friedman int., December 12, 1996.

206   8 percent by Christmas": Houghton-Berry int., October 4, 1995.

207   honored, and humbled": int.

209   The chemistry is good": Michael Carroll, "Inside the College of Cardinals," p. 11.

209   Mark helping build our future": Ibid.

209   decision time approached": int.

210   to be good partners going forward": Silfen int., May 8, 1997.

211   explode on takeoff": int.

211   relative to other firms": Standard & Poor's, October 1, 1996, p. 3.

213   was at risk: int.

214   results in some other areas": Anita Raghavan, "Merchant Banks Become Profit Boosters," *WSJ,* February 23, 1995.

214   time to sell them": Ibid.

217   did not occur: int.

217   but not to worry": int.

218   prior culture," he says: Anita Raghavan, "Limited Loyalty: Goldman Faces Pinch as Partners Leave, Clubby Culture Wanes; It Loses Some Top Talent and the Firm Has Had a So-So Year in Trading the New Boss Cuts Costs," *WSJ,* December 16, 1994.

218   vice-president remembers: int.

218   élan and morale.": FT, "Alas, poor Warburg" February 14, 1995.

218   until the end of time." A. A. Strelson

CHAPTER VII

219   had not improved dramatically: Anita Raghavan, "Goldman Sachs Pre-Tax Profits Fell 46% in First Period," *WSJ,* May 9, 1995.

220 think it's their fault": Padraic
Fallon, "The Last of the David
Weills," *Euromoney*, April
1993, p. 45.

220 4-H'er," he recalls: Corzine int.,
January 14, 1997.

223 year-by-year profit management": Phillip Maher and Ann
Schwimmer, "The End of the
Gravy Train," *IDD*, May 6,
1996, p. 15.

224 business since that time":
Corzine int., January 14, 1997.

228 is more complicated: Ibid.

229 real one," says one partner: int.

233 if it had any chance": int.

234 one partner remembers: int.

234 won't give up on the idea":
"Goldman Sachs Drops Idea of
a Public Sale," *WSJ*, January
21, 1996.

234 threat to the culture": int.

234 very clearly did": Corzine int.,
January 14, 1997.

234 that was uncontrolled": int.

235 on the outcome": int.

236 promote women and minorities: Wall Street Journal, *Guide
to Who's Who and What's
What on Wall Street* (New
York: Ballantine Books, 1998),
p. 240.

237 made little material difference:
Clay Chandler, "Goldman's
Golden Chance," *WP*, June 7,
1998, p. H01.

237 as being important: Corzine
int., January 14, 1997.

238 spirit of partnership": Paulson
int., December 15, 1997.

238 motivate enough people":
Corzine int., January 14, 1997.

238 industry average of 36 percent:
Moody's Investors Service, July
1997.

239 debt deal in Asia): Clay Chandler, "Goldman's Golden
Chance," p. H01.

239 We are naturally conservative":
Corzine int., January 14, 1997.

240 managed more than $500 mil-
lion: Gilbert Kaplan, Gus
Levy, *II*, November 1973,
p. 34.

240 and I think we will": Corzine
int., January 14, 1997.

241 even Fidelity Investments: Steve
Kichen, Tina Russo McCarthy,
and Peter Newcomb, "The
Private 500," *Forbes*, December 2, 1996, p. 151.

241 in this highly visible business:
GSAR, 1997, p. 32.

241 a fourfold increase from 1993:
Leah Nathans Spiro, "Inside
the Money Machine," *BW*,
December 1997.

244 get back here fast": Peter Lee,
"Goldman Shifts Oil Without a
Spill," *Euromoney*, June 1997,
p. 14.

246 co-head of the equities division:
Gregg Wirth, "Macho Men,"
IDD, June 16, 1997.

247 power behind it": Peter Lee,
"Goldman Shifts Oil Without a
Spill," *Euromoney*, June 1997,
p. 14.

248 want to give," says Pot:
Ibid.

248 in the eye again," explained
Williams: Gary Williams int.,
March 27, 1998.

249 a lot more risk": Ibid.

249   on the agenda in 1998: "Inside
      the Money Machine," *BW,*
      December 1997.

250   worry about their clients,":
      Paulson speech.

253   partner of the firm?": int.

254   the firm will ever do": Anita
      Raghavan, "Goldman, Wall
      Street's Holdout, to go Public,"
      WSJ, June 15, 1998, p. 24.

255   this solemn trust": Paulson
      speech.

258   opinions before making a deci-
      sion": Bloomberg News profile,
      June 13, 1998.

259   is the right decision": Corzine
      int., June 25, 1998.

259   has worked so well?": Clay
      Chandler, "Goldman's Golden
      Chance."

259   markets went down": Bloom-
      berg News, June 15, 1998.

259   the capital to compete": Joseph
      Kahn, "Goldman Goes for a
      Bit of Gusto," *NYT,* June 16,
      1998, p. 4.

262   affected in many ways": Gold-
      man Sachs Form S-1.

263   next five to ten years": *WSJ,*
      September 9, 1998.

265   fire sale prices: Greenspan testi-
      mony before House Banking
      Committee, October 1, 1998.

265   *including our own*": Ibid.

265   seeking a solution": McDon-
      nough testimony before House
      Banking Committee,
      October 1, 1998.

266   these are difficult times": *NYT,*
      September 29, 1998.

BIBLIOGRAPHY

Books

Aron, Jack R. *J. Aron & Co. 1898–1981: An Informal History.* April 10, 1981, unpublished.

Auletta, Ken. *Greed and Glory on Wall Street: The Fall of the House of Lehman.* New York: Random House, 1986.

Bernstein, Peter L. *Against the Gods: The Remarkable Story of Risk.* New York: John Wiley & Sons, Inc., 1996.

Birmingham, Stephen. *Our Crowd: The Great Jewish Families of New York.* New York: Dell Publishing, 1967.

———. *The Rest of Us: The Rise of America's Eastern European Jews.* New York: Little Brown & Company, 1984.

Bloch, Ernst. *Inside Investment Banking.* Illinois: Dow Jones Irwin, 1986.

Bloomberg, Michael, with Matthew Winkler. *Bloomberg by Bloomberg.* New York: John Wiley & Sons, 1997.

Blume, Marshall, Jeremy J. Siegel, and Dan Rottenberg. *Revolution on Wall Street: The Rise and Decline of the New York Stock Exchange.* New York: W.W. Norton & Company, 1993.

Boesky, Ivan. *Merger Mania Arbitrage: Wall Street's Best Kept Money-Making Secret.* New York: Holt, Rinehart and Winston, 1985.

Bower, Tom. *Maxwell: The Final Verdict.* London: HarperCollins, 1995.

———. *Maxwell: The Outsider.* New York: Viking, 1988.

Brooks, John. *Once in Golonda: A True Drama of Wall Street 1920–1938.* New York: Harper & Row, 1969.

Bruck, Connie. *The Predators Ball.* New York: Simon and Schuster, 1988.

Cantor, Eddie. *Caught Short.* New York: Simon and Schuster, 1929.

Carpenter, Donna Sammons, and John Feloni. *The Fall of the House of Hutton.* New York: Henry Holt and Company, 1989.

Carrosso, Vincent P. *Investment Banking in America.* Cambridge: Harvard University Press, 1970.

Chamberlain, Lawrence, and William Wren Hay. *Investment and Speculation.* New York: Henry Holt and Company, 1931.

Chernow, Ron. *The House of Morgan.* New York: Simon & Schuster, 1990.

Eccles, Robert G., and Dwight B. Crane. *Doing Deals: Investment Banks at Work*. Boston: Harvard Business School Press, 1988.

Erlich, Judith Ramsey, and Barry J. Rehfeld. *The New Crowd: The Changing of the Jewish Guard on Wall Street*. Boston: Little Brown & Company, 1989.

Farkas, Charles M., and Philippe De Backer. *Maximum Leadership: The World's Leading CEOs Share Their Five Strategies for Success*. New York: Henry Holt and Company, 1996.

Ferris, Paul. *The Master Bankers*. New York: William Morrow and Company, 1984.

Fisher, Kenneth L. *100 Minds That Made the Market* Woodside, CA: Business Classics, 1993.

Flynn, John T. *Investment Trusts Gone Wrong!* New York: Forbes, Abner, 1931.

Galbraith, John Kenneth. *The Great Crash of 1929*. New York: Penguin Books, 1987.

———. *A Short History of Financial Euphoria*. New York: Penguin Books, 1990.

Gapper, John, and Nicholas Denton. *All That Glitters: The Fall of Barings*. London: Hamish Hamilton, 1996.

Greenslade, Roy. *Maxwell*. New Jersey: Carol Publishing, 1992.

Grove, Andrew S. *Only the Paranoid Survive*. New York: Doubleday, 1996.

Hayes, Samuel L. III, and Philip M. Hubbard. *Investment Banking*. Boston: Harvard Business School Press, 1990.

Henriques, Diana B. *Fidelity's World*. New York: Scribner, 1995.

Institutional Investor. The Way It Was: An Oral History of Finance 1967–1987. New York: William Morrow, 1988.

Jensen, Michael. *The Financiers: The World of the Great Wall Street Investment Banking Houses*. New York: Weybright and Talley, 1976.

Mayer, Martin. *Wall Street: Men and Money*. New York: Harper and Brothers, 1955.

———. *Nightmare on Wall Street: Salomon Brothers and the Corruption of the Marketplace*. New York: Simon and Schuster, 1993.

McKay, Charles, and Joseph de la Vega. *Extraordinary Popular Delusions and the Madness of Crowds and Confusion de Confusiones*. New York: John Wiley & Sons, 1996. Originally published 1841.

Securities and Exchange Commission, *Investment Trusts and Investment Companies 1939–1942*.

Smith, Roy C. *Comeback: The Restoration of American Banking Power in the New World Economy*. Boston: Harvard Business School Press, 1993.

Smith, Roy C., and Inco Walter. *Global Banking*. New York: Oxford University Press, 1997.

Sobel, Robert. *N.Y.S.E.: A History of the New York Stock Exchange 1935–1975*. New York: Weybright and Talley, 1975.

Stewart, James B. *Den of Thieves*. New York: Simon and Schuster, 1991.

Trachtenberg, Jeffrey A. *The Rain on Macy's Parade*. New York: Times Business, 1996.

Twentieth-Century Fund Report. *Abuse on Wall Street: Conflicts of Interest in the Securities Markets*. Westport, CT: Quorum Books, 1980.

Wake, Jehanne. *Kleinwort Benson*. Oxford: Oxford University Press, 1997.

Wall Street Journal. *Guide to Who's Who and What's What on Wall Street*. New York: Ballantine Books, 1998.

Wells, Chris. *The Last Days of the Club*. New York: E.P. Dutton & Co., 1975.

Documents

Friedman, Stephen. "Keys to Profitability in the 1990s." Speech before the Securities Industry Association, June 1, 1993.

Goldman Sachs Annual Reviews, 1970–1997.

Goldman Sachs Form S-1, filed with the SEC August 24, 1998.

Kay, Scholer, Fierman, Hays, and Handler, Robert Freeman's attorneys, and Peter Kann, the chairman and publisher of the *Wall Street Journal*. Correspondence, October 18, 1991. Courtesy of Goldman Sachs.

MCP Pension Trustees Ltd. and MGN Pension Trustees, (as trustee of the Mirror Group Pension Group) v. Goldman, Sachs & Co. and Eric Paul Sheinberg, filed April 29, 1994. Index numbers 112177/94 and 112178/94.

MCP Pension Trustees Ltd. and MGN Pension Trustees, (as trustee of the Mirror Group Pension Group) v. Goldman, Sachs & Co. and Eric Paul Sheinberg, filed June 27, 1994. Memorandum of law in support of defendants' motion to dismiss pursuant to CPLP rules 3211 and 3015. Index number 112178/94.

MCP Pension Trustees Ltd. and MGN Pension Trustees, (as trustee of the Mirror Group Pension Group) v. Goldman, Sachs & Co. and Eric Paul Sheinberg, filed January 24 1995. Judges orders on motion to dismiss complaint. Index number 112178/94–002

Moody's Investors Service, report on Goldman Sachs Group, 1996–1998.

Regina v. Kevin Maxwell, Ian Maxwell, Robert Henry Bunn, Larry Steven Trachtenberg, Albert Joseph Fuller and Michael Stoney. United Kingdom the Crown Court. July 27, 1995; September 4, 22, 1995; October 6, 17, 24, 26, 1995; and November 2–3, 6–8, 21–22, 1995.

Sachs, Samuel, Paul Sachs, Arthur Sachs, and partners of Kleinwort. Personal correspondence, 1898–1920. Courtesy of Dresdner Kleinwort archives.

Sachs, Walter E. (1956 and 1964), Paul Sachs, Paul Cabot, and Lucas Clay. Memoirs in the Columbia University Oral History Collection.

Sachs, Walter E. Testimony before the United States Senate hearings on stock exchange practices, May 20, 1932, p. 566–83.

Sheinberg, Eric P. Witness before the United States Securities and Exchange Commission in the matter of Maxwell Communications, November 3–4, 1993.

Standard and Poor's Credit Analysis on Goldman Sachs & Co., 1993–1998.

United States of America v. Henry S. Morgan. U.S. District Court. Deposition of Walter E. Sachs, December 15–17, 21–22, 1948.

Welch Foods, C. E. Anthony Company and Yonker Brothers v. Goldman Sachs. U.S. District Court. Gustave L. Levy trial transcript, September 23, 1974. Judgment December 30, 1974.

Selected Articles

Adam, Nigel. "The All-Round Magic of Goldman Sachs," *Euromoney,* July 1981.

———. "Goldman Travels Badly," *Euromoney,* June 1987.

Agins, Teri. "Ralph Lauren Sells 28% Stake in Polo Concern; Goldman Fund Becomes First Outside Investor, Putting Up $135 Million," *Wall Street Journal,* August 24, 1994.

"Alas, poor Warburg," *Financial Times,* February 14, 1995.

"Another Diver in the Buy-Out Pool," *Economist,* April 15, 1989.

"Asset Allocation: A Newcomer on the Catwalk," *Economist,* March 2, 1991.

"Balancing Ability With Humility: A Conversation with Sidney J. Weinberg of Goldman, Sachs & Co.," *Nation's Business,* December 1965.

Baxter, Andrew. "Quiet American Makes a Big Noise in M&A," *Financial Times,* January 16, 1991.

Bender, Michael, et al. "A Magic Year for Fees," *Investment Dealers' Digest,* February 17, 1997.

Bennett, Robert. "Can Mighty Goldman Stay Private?" *New York Times,* April 13, 1986.

Bevan, Judi. "From Goldman to Governor?" *Sunday Telegraph,* May 25, 1997.

Bianco, Anthony. "John Weinberg," *Business Week,* April 17, 1987.

Bird, Laura, and Wendy Bounds. "Ralph Lauren Hopes Investors Like His Style," *Wall Street Journal,* April 9, 1997.

Bleakley, Fred R. "Goldman's Rise in Real Estate," *New York Times,* June 17, 1985.

Blitz, James, and Paul Abrahams. "Sterling Still Faces Hurdles," *Financial Times,* September 14, 1992.

Blitz, James, and Peter Marsh. "Dollar Hits New Low against D-Mark," *Financial Times,* September 2, 1992.

Boulton, Leyla. "Russia Enlists Goldman Sachs to Attract Cash," *Financial Times,* February 18, 1992.

Bray, Nicholas. "International: Maxwell Said to Prop Up Shares; Britain Is Studying Goldman Link," *Wall Street Journal,* December 13, 1991.

———. "Probe Discloses Scheme to Boost Maxwell Stock," *Wall Street Journal,* January 23, 1992.

Buckingham, Lisa. "Bankers under the Maxwell Shadow," *Guardian,* July 18, 1992.

Byrnes, Nanette. "Wall Street's Finest," *Financial World,* March 16, 1993.

Carey, David. "Wall Street's Finest," *Financial World,* July 26, 1988.

———. "Wall Street's Finest," *Financial World,* January 24, 1989.

Carey, David, and Stephen Taub. "The Wall Street 100," *Financial World,* July 21, 1992.

———. "The Wall Street 100," *Financial World,* July 6, 1993.

———. "The Wall Street 100," *Financial World,* July 5, 1994.

———. "The Wall Street 100," *Financial World,* July 4, 1995.

———. "The Wall Street 100," *Financial World,* October 21, 1996.

Carroll, Michael. "Inside Goldman's College of Cardinals," *Institutional Investor,* October 1994.

———. "Which Way Out?" *Institutional Investor,* September 1995.

———. "Rockefeller Center: The Ultimate Insider's Game," *Institutional Investor,* February 1996.

———. "Johns on the Spot: The Thain-Thornton Team at Goldman," *Institutional Investor,* October 1996.

———. "Dave's World," *Institutional Investor,* December 1996.

Cassidy, John. "Maxwell Meltdown. Faced with Heavy Losses and Collapsing Share Prices, Robert Maxwell Looted Pounds 770m from the Treasuries and Pension Funds of Mirror Group Newspapers and Maxwell Communications Corporation," *Sunday Times,* December 8, 1991.

———. "Four Legs Good, Two Legs Bad," *Euromoney,* January 1996.

Celarier, Michelle. "With Friends Like These," *Euromoney,* July 1997.

Chandler, Clay. "Goldman's Golden Chance," *Washington Post,* June 7, 1998.

———. "Treasury's High-Stakes Player," *Washington Post,* June 18, 1998.

"The Changing Face of Goldman Sachs," *Business Week,* November 22, 1976.

Christner, E.M., "Goldman Sachs Celebrates Its First 100 Years," *Investment Dealers' Digest,* December 9, 1969.

Cohen, Norma. "Goldman Urged to Return Maxwell Funds," *Financial Times,* July 12, 1993.

———. "Bank Accused over Maxwell £55m Switch," *Financial Times,* May 3, 1994.

Cohen, Norma, and Bronwen Maddox. "Goldman Broke Rules Over Maxwell 'Loans.' " *Financial Times,* June 17, 1993.

Cohen, Roger. "Maxwell Inquiry Focus: Goldman," *New York Times,* December 14, 1991.

Connelly, Julie. "Goldman, Sachs for the Defense," *Institutional Investor,* November 1977.

Corrigan, Tracy. "Traders Turn a Swift Foreign Exchange Profit," *Financial Times,* September 18, 1992.

Corrigan, Tracy, and William Lewis. "Goldman Sachs Plans to Use Flotation as Spur for Growth," *Financial Times,* June 16, 1998.

———. "Goldman filing reveals scale of capital trading," *Financial Times,* August 25, 1998.

Cowan, Alison Leigh. "An Exercise in Introspection Lets Goldman Bare Its Soul," *New York Times,* January 25, 1990.

Crudele, John. "Masterminding the Mega-Deals," *New York Times,* November 3, 1985.

Dickson, Martin. "Premier Democrat on Wall St.—Robert Rubin," *Financial Times,* August 10, 1992.

Eichenwald, Kurt. "Transition at the Top for Goldman, Sachs," *New York Times,* August 15, 1990.

———. "Business People; A Leading Deal Maker Quits Goldman, Sachs," *New York Times,* November 27, 1991.

———. "Insurers Buy an Interest in Goldman," *New York Times,* December 3, 1991.

"The '80s Revisited," *Institutional Investor,* January 1992.

Evans, Garry. "The Weinberg Interview," *Euromoney,* June 1990.

Evans, Rob. "Maxwell Pledges Share 'Already Held by Another Bank.' " *Financial Times,* July 13, 1995.

"Everybody's Broker: Sidney Weinberg," *Time,* December 18, 1958.

Fairlamb, David. "Can Anyone Get Globalization Right?" *Institutional Investor,* August 1995.

Faith, Nicholas. "Takeover Threat to LVMH Recedes," *Sunday Independent,* September 8, 1991.

Fallon, Padraic. "The Last of the David-Weills," *Euromoney,* April 1993.

"Family Retains Control of Ford," *New York Times,* January 18, 1956.

Fidler, Stephen, et al. "Sterling Was Being Sold like Water Running out of a Tap," *Financial Times,* September 19–20, 1992.

Field, Peter. "The Attack on the M&A Barons," *Euromoney,* May 1985.

Forman, Craig. "A Hot New Export to Europe Takes Hold: The Hostile Takeover," *Wall Street Journal,* April 19, 1988.

"For Richer or Poorer? Goldman Sachs Had Decided to Remain the Odd-Bank-Out on Wall Street," *Economist,* January 27, 1996.

French, Martin. "The Street Gets Mean; How Wall Street's Big Six Line Up," *Euromoney,* November 1991.

Friedman, Alan. "Trying to Escape the Maxwell Maze," *Financial Times,* December 27, 1991.

Friedman, Jon. "How Playing the Tortoise Paid Off for Goldman Sachs," *Business Week,* May 7, 1990.

"From Beyond the Grave," *Economist,* June 19, 1993.

Galant, Debbie. "Fast Cars and Loose Exchange Rates," *Institutional Investor,* May 1992.

———. "Communicating 'Commumacopia.' " *Institutional Investor,* May 1993.

Gapper, John, and Andrew Jack. "Commanding Views," *Financial Times,* January 11, 1997.

"German Rate Cut May Stave Off UK Increase," *Financial Times,* September 13, 1992.

Glynn, Lenny. "Robert Mnuchin, Partner, Goldman, Sachs & Co," *Institutional Investor,* June 1987.

"Goldman Has Life After Maxwell," *Independent,* September 16, 1992.

"Goldman Is Being Aggressive in Bidding for Firms' Bonds," *Wall Street Journal,* January 9, 1985.

"Goldman Sachs Picks Rubin and Friedman for Fixed Income Unit," *Wall Street Journal,* August 5, 1985.

"Goldman Sachs Profit Sank 59% in First Half as Interest Rates Rose," *Wall Street Journal,* August 11, 1994.

"Goldman Sachs Slims Down Its Management Structure," *Institutional Investor,* December 1995.

"Goldman Sachs Tells Employees IPO Will Go Ahead," *Bloomberg News,* September 8, 1998.

"Goldman Sachs IPO Value Declines as Financial Shares Tumble," *Bloomberg News,* September 20, 1998.

"Goldman Sachs Ordered to Pay $3 Million Claim," *Wall Street Journal,* October 10, 1974, p. 24.

"Goldman Sachs to Buy J. Aron, a Global Trader," *Wall Street Journal,* October 30, 1981.

"Goldman Tops Cross-Border Euro Bid League at Pounds 4.4bn," *Evening Standard,* February 12, 1991.

"Goldman's Public Debate," *Economist,* August 19, 1995.

Goodman, Wes. "Goldman to Sell a $275 Million Chunk," *Investment Dealers' Digest,* November 11, 1991.

Gourlay, Richard. "Goldman Sachs Sold Maxwell Collateral," *Financial Times,* November 7, 1991.

———. "Spotlight on Goldman Sachs Ties with MCC," *Financial Times,* November 7, 1991.

Graham, George. "LVMH Puts On Steady Performance," *Financial Times,* March 26, 1991.

Greenslade, Roy. "Fatherland," *Sunday Times,* January 21, 1996.

Gribben, Roland. "Kuwait BP Share Sale Nets £700m," *Daily Telegraph,* May 16, 1997.

Hamilton, Kirstie. "Big Hitters Push for Goldman Float," *Sunday Times,* April 26, 1998.

———. "Troubled Goldman Float May Be Put Off," *Sunday Times,* September 20, 1998.

Hansell, Saul. "Arbitrage Like It Oughta Be," *Institutional Investor,* April 1988.

———. "Merrill Lynch Visits the Fat Farm," *Institutional Investor,* November 1990.

———. "Playing for the House," *Institutional Investor,* April 1991.

Heffernan, Paul. "Ford Stock Set at $64.50; First Deals Drive Up Price," *New York Times,* January 18, 1956.

"Henry Goldman, 79, Banker, Dies Here," *New York Times,* April 5, 1937.

Hertzberg, Daniel, and William Power. "Delay of Trial in Insider Case Sought by U.S," *Wall Street Journal,* May 12, 1987.

Hertzberg, Daniel, and James B. Stewart. "Goldman Sachs Ex-Aide Target in Levine Probe," *Wall Street Journal,* July 9, 1986.

———. "Judge Refuses to Delay Trial of 3 Arbitragers," *Wall Street Journal,* May 13, 1987.

"Holiday Is No Respite for Pound and Dollar," *Financial Times,* September 1, 1992.

"An Honour System without Honour," *Economist,* December 14, 1991.

Horowitz, Jed. "Record Revenues in Store for Goldman's Bankers," *Investment Dealers' Digest,* December 2, 1996.

House, Richard. "Why Goldman Rankles Its European Rivals," *Institutional Investor,* December 1992.

"How the House of Cards Came Tumbling Down," *Financial Times,* December 6, 1991.

Hughes, Raymond, and Bronwen Maddox. "More Light Thrown on Goldman Sachs Dealings with Maxwell," *Financial Times,* April 2, 1992.

"International: Hanson Sells Stake of 2.8% in ICI to Goldman Sachs," *Wall Street Journal,* May 11, 1992.

Jack, Andrew. "Maxwell Support for MGN Shares Discovered," *Financial Times,* March 19, 1992.

———. "French Banks Lose Out in M&A: League Tables Show Goldman Sachs and Others Making Inroads," *Financial Times,* January 15, 1997.

Jackson, Tony. "Goldman Reveal Maxwell Stakes. Holdings Used as Collateral for Loans to UK Publisher-Broker Regrets Late Disclosure," *Financial Times,* August 15, 1991.

———. "Bank for Millionaire Monks: A Look at the Changes in Management and Profitability at Goldman Sachs," *Financial Times,* September 17, 1994.

Jay, John. "Goldman Chastened," *Sunday Telegraph,* June 6, 1993.

Kahn Jr., E. J. "Profiles: Directors' Director," *New Yorker,* January 1956.

Kahn, Joseph. "The Public Ambition of a Private Firm," *New York Times,* June 10, 1998.

———. "Goldman, Sachs Expected to Become a Public Company," *New York Times,* June 15, 1998.

———. "Goldman, Sachs Tries to Soothe Limited Partners," *New York Times,* July 30, 1998.

———. "Goldman, Sachs Partners Vote to Take Firm Public," *New York Times,* August 11, 1998.

———. "Goldman Keeps It Private Even in Going Public," *New York Times,* August 25, 1998.

———. "Goldman Staff to Discuss Stock Move," *New York Times,* September 8, 1998.

———. "Goldman Plan to Sell Stock is Canceled," *New York Times,* September 29, 1998.

Kahn, Joseph, and Timothy O'Brien, "How Goldman Sachs Escaped the Russian Economic Bloodbath," *The New York Times on the Web,* October 18, 1998.

Kahn, Virginia Munger. "Goldman's Guideposts: One Firm's Path to Success," *Investor's Business Daily,* April 16, 1993.

Kaplan, Gilbert E. "Gus Levy Answers 132 Questions about His Firm, His Business and Himself," *Institutional Investor,* November 1973.

———. "True Confessions," *Institutional Investor,* February 1991.

Karp, Richard, and Joe Kolman. "The Home-Run Hitters," *Institutional Investor,* March 1988.

Kichen, Steve, et al. "The Private 500," *Forbes,* December 2, 1996.

Kristoff, Nicholas. "Japanese Maverick Expands," *New York Times,* August 7, 1986.

Lambert, Richard. "Wall St. Meets Madison Ave," *Financial Times,* April 19, 1983.

Langton, James. "When the Stealing Had to Stop. Robert Maxwell Hoped to Beat the Old Adage about Fooling All of the People All of the *Time.* But Even as He Flew to His Yacht-and Death-He Knew He Had Been Rumbled," *Sunday Telegraph,* December 8, 1991.

Lazere, Cathy. "The New Generation of M&A Bankers," *Institutional Investor,* May 1989.

Lee. Peter. "International Equities: The Most Macho Game in Town," *Euromoney*, May 1991.

———. "The Start of a Global Bulge Bracket," *Euromoney*, April 1993.

Lee, Peter. "The Mighty Monoculture," *Euromoney*, October 1993.

———. "Which Is the Real Goldman Sachs?" *Euromoney*, October 1993.

———. "Goldman Shifts Oil without a Spill," *Euromoney*, June 1997.

Lenzner, Robert, and Riva Atlas. "Top This, If You Can," *Forbes*, December 6, 1993.

"Lessons from Maxwell. They Are Not as Obvious as They First Appear to Be," *Economist*, December 14, 1991.

Lewis, William. "Global Review Launched by Goldman," *Financial Times*, March 25, 1998.

Lewis, William, and Tracy Corrigan. "Goldman Sachs Partners to Discuss $20bn Flotation," *Financial Times*, April 18, 1998.

Liebowitz, Michael. "Goldman Raises $200 Mil in Private Debt Market," *Investment Dealers' Digest*, September 21, 1992.

Light, Larry, and Leah Nathans Spiro. "The Street's Big Holdout May Have to Go Public," *Business Week*, November 25, 1991.

"Lira Devalued 7% in EMS," *Financial Times*, September 14, 1992.

Maddox, Bronwen. "Verbal Basis of Goldman Deals Shocks City," *Financial Times*, January 28, 1992.

Maddox, Bronwen, and Peter Martin. "DTI Was Looking into MCC Share Deal in October," *Financial Times*, December 4, 1991.

Maher, Philip. "Goldman Partner Exodus Continues to Thin Ranks," *Investment Dealers' Digest*, November 8, 1993.

Maher, Philip, and Ron Cooper. "Image and Reality at Goldman Sachs," *Investment Dealers' Digest*, October 4, 1993.

———. "The New Bulge Bracket (II)," *Investment Dealers' Digest*, December 2, 1996.

Maher, Philip, and Anne Schwimmer. "Goldman Sachs Revamps Its Governance Structure," *Investment Dealers' Digest*, November 27, 1995.

———. "The End of the Gravy Train," *Investment Dealers' Digest*, May 6, 1996.

Makin, Claire. "The Americanization of British M&A," *Institutional Investor*, October 1988.

"Managing Greed and Risk on Wall Street," *Economist*, July 5, 1986.

Marckus, Melvyn. "Maxwell: The Credibility Factor," *Observer*, December 8, 1991.

"Marcus Goldman Dead," *New York Times*, July 21, 1904.

Marsh, Peter, et al. "Pound Falls to New Low in ERM," *Financial Times*, September 16, 1992.

Martinson, Jane. "GSAM Set to Target Europe," *Financial Times,* February 23, 1998.

Mason, John. "Kevin Maxwell Describes Awe of Father," *Financial Times,* October 17, 1995.

———. "Goldman Sachs 'May Have Wrecked' Deal," *Financial Times,* October 19, 1995.

Mattlin, Everett. "Winning without Home Runs," *Institutional Investor,* May 1988.

"Maxwell Meltdown," *Economist,* December 7, 1991.

"Maxwell: The Net Closes," *Sunday Times,* December 15, 1991.

McCarthy, Donald. "Here Comes Wall Street," *Institutional Investor,* March 1991.

McCarthy, Joseph L. "The Natural," *Chief Executive,* October 1995.

McCarthy, Robert. "Maxwell Case Probes Clear U.S. Banker," *Washington Post,* May 20, 1992.

"MCC Moved in a Mysterious Way," *Economist,* December 2, 1991– January 3, 1992.

Mcgee, Suzanne. "Superblock Trades Are the Rage in Wall Street's Seller's Market," *Wall Street Journal,* August 11, 1997.

McGeehan, Patrick. "Goldman, in Gutsy Bidding, Edges Out Salomon in Godzilla-Size Block Trades," *Wall Street Journal,* May 28, 1997.

———. "Goldman Gives Early Details for Stock IPO," *Wall Street Journal,* August 25, 1998.

———. "Goldman Shelves Indefinitely Its IPO," *Wall Street Journal,* September 29, 1998.

McGeehan, Patrick, and Anita Raghavan. "Goldman Plans to Use IPO Funds to Bolster Most-Profitable Lines," *Wall Street Journal,* June 16, 1998.

McGoldrick, Beth. "Inside the Goldman Sachs Culture," *Institutional Investor,* January 1984.

———. "Salomon's Power Culture," *Institutional Investor,* March 1986.

———. "Wall Street Puts Its Own Money on the Line," *Institutional Investor,* June 1984.

McLean, Bethany, and Andrew Serwer, "Goldman Sachs: After the Fall," *Fortune,* November 9, 1998, p. 128.

McMurray, Scott. "Goldman, Sachs Moves to Reassure Stanford Candidates," *Wall Street Journal,* February 14, 1985, p. 14.

———. "Institutions Rank Merrill Lynch & Co. Top Brokerage," *Wall Street Journal,* March 13, 1984.

Metz, Tim. "Goldman Sachs Avoids Bitter Takeover Fights but Leads in Mergers," *Wall Street Journal,* December 8, 1982.

Miller, Michael W. "Freeman's Case Looms Large, May Be U.S.'s Toughest Fight," *Wall Street Journal,* February 17, 1987.

"Moet Deal Gets Up Paribas' Nose," *Daily Telegraph,* March 26, 1991.

Monroe, Ann. "Salomon Brothers Was Lead Manager of 25% of Public Securities Issues in '84," *Wall Street Journal,* January 2, 1985.

————. "Salomon Leads '85 List of Underwriters of Securities Offerings by U.S. Issuers," *Wall Street Journal,* January 2, 1986.

————. "Salomon Stays First among Underwriters of U.S. Issuers, but Rivals Are Gaining," *Wall Street Journal,* January 4, 1988.

————. "Merrill Wants It All," *Investment Dealers' Digest,* May 27, 1996.

"The Moonies Come to Market," *Economist,* June 20, 1998.

Muehring, Kevin. "A Trader at Treasury," *Institutional Investor,* January 1996.

————. "Second- (and Third-) Guessing the Fed," *Institutional Investor,* November 1996.

Nash, Nathaniel C. "Goldman's Japan Tie Is Cleared," *New York Times,* November 20, 1986.

"The Next Generation of Financial Leaders," *Institutional Investor,* January 1990.

"The 1993 M&A Sweepstakes," *Institutional Investor,* March 1994.

"The 1992 M&A Sweepstakes," *Institutional Investor,* March 1993.

Nisse, Jason. "Goldman Sachs May Have 4% of Maxwell," *Independent,* July 22, 1991.

————. "Goldman Sachs Moves to Allay Fears over MCC," *Independent,* November 9, 1991.

Norman, Peter et al. "UK Will Borrow D-Marks to Aid £," *Financial Times,* September 4, 1992.

Norris, Floyd. "Market Place; Goldman Phasing Out Big 'Junk Bond' Fund," *New York Times,* May 3, 1991.

————. "3 at Goldman Leaving; Were in 'Vulture Fund.' " *New York Times,* July 25, 1991.

Norton, Robert E. "Upheavals Ahead on Wall Street," *Fortune,* September 14, 1987.

O'Harrow Jr., Robert. "Goldman Sachs Plan to Go Public Is Endorsed," *Washington Post,* June 2, 1998.

Owen, David. "A Turbulent Day in Whitehall," *Financial Times,* September 17, 1992.

Park, Margaret. "The Great Defender," *Sunday Times,* October 27, 1991.

Parker-Jarvis, George. "Maxwell's Shady 'Support' for MCC—During the Last Months of His Life Robert Maxwell Resorted to Desperate Means to Shore Up His Near Bankrupt Empire," *Observer,* December 15, 1991.

"Partners in Pain," *Economist,* December 3, 1994.

"Partners Leaving Goldman," *New York Times,* November 2, 1994.

Peers, Alexandra. "Who's News: Corrigan, Ex-Head of New York Fed, Joins Goldman," *Wall Street Journal,* October 20, 1993.

———. "Goldman Sachs Leads Wall Street Pack with a '93 Pretax Profit of $2.7 Billion," *Wall Street Journal,* March 8, 1994.

Peltz, Michael. "Psyching Out the Bond Market," *Institutional Investor,* December 1995.

"People," *Institutional Investor,* January 1994.

Peston, Robert et al. "SFO Probe into Maxwell Share Deals with Goldman," *Financial Times,* December 13, 1991.

Petre, Peter. "Merger Fees That Bend the Mind," *Fortune,* January 20, 1986.

Picker, Ida. "Ebb Tide on Wall Street," *Institutional Investor,* December 1987.

———. "Wall Street: Take the Money and Run," *Institutional Investor,* July 1988.

Porter, Mark S. "A Scorching Year for M&A," *Investment Dealers' Digest,* January 20, 1997.

Power, William. "Two Plead Guilty to Criminal Charges of Passing Information to Dennis Levine," *Wall Street Journal,* September 5, 1986.

———. "Who Will Be Rich? How Goldman Sachs Chooses New Partners: With a Lot of Angst," *Wall Street Journal,* October 19, 1990.

———. "Moving In: Salomon's Big Loss Could Well Become Goldman Sachs's Gain; With Many of Its Competitors Weakened, Partnership Is Stronger Than Ever." *Wall Street Journal,* September 19, 1991.

———. "Hawaiian Investor Puts $250 Million in Goldman Sachs," *Wall Street Journal,* April 28, 1992.

———. "For New Chairman, Hair Apparent Still Applies," *Wall Street Journal,* September 15, 1994.

Power, William, and Michael Siconolfi. "Goldman Chiefs Made over $15 Million Each," *Wall Street Journal,* July 22, 1992.

Preston, Robert. "Goldman Claims Maxwell Duped Firm on MCC Deals," *Financial Times,* December 21, 1991.

Quint, Michael. "Two Maxwell Pension Groups Sue Goldman over Funds," *New York Times,* May 2, 1994.

Raghavan, Anita. "Commodities: Goldman Sachs Is Raking In Big Bucks in Risky World of Commodities Trading," *Wall Street Journal,* November 9, 1992.

———. "Goldman Scrambles to Find $250 Million in Equity Capital from Private Investors," *Wall Street Journal,* September 15, 1994.

———. "Goldman Dealt Blow by Loss of Winkelman," *Wall Street Journal,* November 10, 1994.

———. "Goldman Is Said to Prepare to Lay Off up to 900 People, 10% of Its Work Force," *Wall Street Journal,* December 15, 1994.

———. "Limited Loyalty: Goldman Faces Pinch as Partners Leave, Clubby Culture Wanes; It Loses Some Top Talent and the Firm Has Had a So-So Year in Trading the New Boss Cuts Costs," *Wall Street Journal,* December 16, 1994.

———. "Partners' Capital at Goldman Sachs Fell in Fiscal '94," *Wall Street Journal,* February 13, 1995.

———. "Merchant Banks Become Profit Boosters," *Wall Street Journal,* February 23, 1995.

———. "Goldman Quietly Raises More Capital but Has to Pay Almost 9.5%," *Wall Street Journal,* March 28, 1995.

———. "Goldman's Partners Contend with Maxwell Legacy," *Wall Street Journal,* April 12, 1995.

———. "Goldman Sachs Pretax Profits Fell 46% in 1st Period," *Wall Street Journal,* May 9, 1995.

———. "Goldman Sachs Banking Arm to Buy Bowling-Center Operator," *Wall Street Journal,* January 8, 1996.

———. "Goldman's Pretax Profits Climbed 60% to $905 Million in Near Record Quarter," *Wall Street Journal,* March 19, 1997.

———. "Merger Route: A New Way Goldman Could Go Public," *Wall Street Journal,* August 5, 1997.

———. "Goldman, Wall Street's Holdout, to Go Public," *Wall Street Journal,* June 15, 1998.

———. "Goldman Sachs IPO Plan on Track, Co-Chairman Says," *Wall Street Journal,* September 9, 1998.

———. "Goldman IPO Wins Backing of Partners," *Wall Street Journal,* August 11, 1998.

Raghavan, Anita, and Michael R. Sesit. "Battle Brews as Goldman Mulls an Offering," *Wall Street Journal,* November 17–18, 1995.

———. "Goldman Sachs Drops Idea of Public Sale," *Wall Street Journal,* January 21, 1996.

Raghavan, Anita, and Michael Siconolfi. "Friedman Steps Down as Goldman Chairman," *Wall Street Journal,* September 14, 1994.

Reich, Cary. "John Whitehead, Former Co-Chairman, Goldman, Sachs & Co," *Institutional Investor,* June 1987.

———. "Wall Street's Management Muddle," *Institutional Investor,* May 1988.

"Resignation at Goldman," *New York Times,* November 11, 1994.

"The Rise and Rise of a Global Firm," *Euromoney,* October 1993.

Rosenberg, Hilary. "Salomon's Idea Machine," *Institutional Investor,* November 1988.

Ross, Irwin. "How Goldman Sachs Grew and Grew," *Fortune,* July 9, 1984.

Rutberg, Sidney. "Goldman, Sachs Buys Into Ralph," *Women's Wear Daily,* August 24, 1994.

Salomon Brothers. Annual Report, 1985.

"Samuel Sachs, 83, Banker Is Dead," *New York Times,* March 3, 1935.

Sandler, Linda. "Heard on the Street: Is Goldman Sachs's Water Street Fund Sinking Fast?" *Wall Street Journal,* January 16, 1991.

Selby, Beth. "Wall Street: The Steve and Bob Show," *Institutional Investor,* December 1990.

———. "Scraping By on $750,000 a Year," *Institutional Investor,* June 1991.

———. "How Morgan Stanley Maps Its Moves," *Institutional Investor,* June 1992.

Sender, Henny. "Investment Banking: Too Big for Their Own Good?" *Institutional Investor,* February 1987.

———. "The Client Comes Second," *Institutional Investor,* March 1987.

———. "Robert Rubin, Partner, Goldman, Sachs & Co," *Institutional Investor,* June 1987.

"722 Underwrite Stock Sale," *New York Times,* January 18, 1956.

Sheehan, Robert. "Let's Ask Sidney Weinberg," *Fortune,* October 1953.

Siconolfi, Michael. "Goldman May End Explosive Growth of Partnerships," *Wall Street Journal,* September 18, 1990.

———. "Merrill Lynch, Goldman Plan More Layoffs," *Wall Street Journal,* January 23, 1991.

———. "Goldman Sachs Said to Cut Staff as Earnings Soar," *Wall Street Journal,* March 7, 1991.

———. "Who's News: Boisi, 44, Retires from No. 3 Post at Goldman," *Wall Street Journal,* November 27, 1991.

———. "Goldman Sachs Is Earnings King on Wall Street, with Record '91 Pretax Profit of $1.15 Billion," *Wall Street Journal,* September 22, 1992.

———. "With Rubin Going, Friedman to Solo at Goldman," *Wall Street Journal,* December 11, 1992.

"Sidney Brings Them In," *Business Week,* January 27, 1951.

Sloane, Leonard. "Gustave Levy, Investment Banker Who Led Goldman, Sachs, Is Dead," *New York Times,* November 4, 1976.

Smith, Alison et al. "Bank Wars on Fall in Pound," *Financial Times,* September 30, 1992.

Smith, Randall. "Goldman Bought Bonds of Tonka Knowing Mattel Had Mulled Bid," *Wall Street Journal,* March 8, 1991.

———. "Goldman Plans to Shut Down 'Vulture' Fund," *Wall Street Journal,* May 3, 1991.

———. "Heads of Water Street Plan to Quit Goldman," *Wall Street Journal,* July 25, 1991.

——. "Goldman Traded Heavily in Maxwell Shares," *Wall Street Journal*, December 20, 1991.

——. "Goldman Sachs Gets Commitments for New Fund," *Wall Street Journal*, April 6, 1992.

Sommar, Jessica. "Two Bond Trading Chiefs to Retire from Goldman," *Investment Dealers' Digest*, November 1, 1993.

Spiro, Leah Nathans. "Money Machine," *Business Week*, June 10, 1991.

——. "Goldman's Deep Bench May Keep the Streak Alive," *Business Week*, September 26, 1994.

——. "Inside the Money Machine," *Business Week*, December 12, 1997.

——. "Turmoil at Salomon," *Business Week*, May 1, 1995.

Steinhauer, Jennifer. "Ralph Lauren Hopes to Raise $600 Million by Going Public," *New York Times*, April 9, 1997.

Stephens, Phillip. "Lamont Fends off Criticism with Strong Rejection of Devaluation," *Financial Times*, September 9, 1992.

——. "Major Stands Firm on Europe and Economy," *Financial Times*, September 10, 1992.

——. "Major Faces the Most Serious Test of His Career," *Financial Times*, September 17, 1992.

Stephens, Phillip, and Emma Tucker. "Major Stresses Solid Opposition to Devaluation," *Financial Times*, September 11, 1992.

Stephens, Phillip et al. "Sterling Is Suspended within ERM," *Financial Times*, September 17, 1992.

Sterngold, James. "Sumitomo of Japan Plans to Buy a Stake in Goldman, Sachs," *New York Times*, August 7, 1986.

——. "The Tense, Secret Talks behind Goldman Move," *New York Times*, August 8, 1986.

——. "Too Far, Too Fast," *New York Times*, January 10, 1988.

Stevens, Charles. "Sterling Surges, Causing Action by Central Bank," *Wall Street Journal*, May 10, 1988.

Stewart, James B. "Trading Charges against 3 Dismissed, but U.S. Is Free to Seek New Indictment," *Wall Street Journal*, May 20, 1987.

Stewart, James B., and Janet Guyon. "Damage Control: How GE and Kidder Managed to Ward Off an Impending Disaster," *Wall Street Journal*, June 8, 1987.

Stewart, James B., and Daniel Hertzberg. "Investment Bankers Feed a Merger Boom and Pick Up Fat Fees," *Wall Street Journal*, April 4, 1986.

——. "Street Bombshell: Insider-Trading Scandal Implicates High Aides at Goldman, Kidder," *Wall Street Journal*, February 13, 1987.

——. "The Wall Street Career of Martin Siegel Was a Dream Gone Wrong," *Wall Street Journal*, February 17, 1987.

———. "Goldman Official Traded Heavily in Takeover Stocks, Record Shows," *Wall Street Journal,* March 6, 1987.

———. "Three of Wall Street's Top Arbitragers Indicted on Insider-Trading Charges," *Wall Street Journal,* April 10, 1987.

———. "Judge Refuses to Delay Trial of 3 Arbitragers," *Wall Street Journal,* May 13, 1987.

———. "Prosecutor Asks Judge to Dismiss Charges against Three Arbitragers in Insider Case," *Wall Street Journal,* May 14, 1987.

———. "Wall Street Inquiry Focuses on 11 Stocks," *Wall Street Journal,* May 22, 1987.

———. "Suspicious Trading: New Evidence Links Arbitrager at Goldman to Insider Stock Deals," *Wall Street Journal,* February 12, 1988.

Stewart, James B., and Steve Swartz. "Abrupt Confession: Why Robert Freeman, Previously Defiant, Agreed to Admit Guilt," *Wall Street Journal,* August 18, 1989.

Stewart, James B., and John D. Williams. "Levine Analysis Shows Goldman Sachs, Lazard in Many Deals Cited by the SEC," *Wall Street Journal,* May 20, 1986.

Stolley, Richard B. "The Ordeal of Bob Freeman," *Fortune,* May 25, 1987.

———. "The End of an Ordeal," *Fortune,* October 4, 1993.

"Success Story under Threat," *Independent,* December 11, 1991.

"Sumitomo Bank Extends Goldman Sachs Investment," *Wall Street Journal,* December 12, 1991.

"Sumitomo Takes a Bite of Wall Street's Ripest Plum," *Economist,* August 9, 1986.

Supple, Barry E. "A Business Elite: German Jewish Financiers in Nineteenth Century New York," *Business History Review,* Summer 1957.

Swartz, Steve. "Consensus Said Emerging at Goldman on Need to Raise Additional Capital," *Wall Street Journal,* December 10, 1986.

———. "Goldman Sachs Boisi Will Direct 3 Combined Units," *Wall Street Journal,* August 28, 1987.

———. "Goldman Sachs Names Two Aides as Vice Chairmen," *Wall Street Journal,* November 23, 1987.

———. "Goldman Sachs Gets $225 Million as an Investment from 7 Insurers," *Wall Street Journal,* March 30, 1989.

———. "Goldman Is Likely to Fire Over 200 after Major Study," *Wall Street Journal,* May 18, 1989.

Swartz, Steve, and Ann Monroe. "Goldman Sachs Strives to Adapt to Changes by Wall Street Rivals," *Wall Street Journal,* October 9, 1986.

Taub, Stephen. "The View from the Top," *Financial World,* January 20, 1987.

Taub, Stephen, and David Carey. "Wall Street's New Austerity," *Financial World,* July 21, 1992.

"Tee-Hee and Sympathy," *Daily Telegraph*, September 9, 1994.

Teitelman, Robert. "The Man behind the Morgan Mask," *Institutional Investor*, October 1991.

———. "Morgan," *Institutional Investor*, March 1996.

"Three Ex-Goldman Partners Working on New Hedge Fund," *Investment Dealers' Digest*, October 2, 1995.

Train, Mark. "Lauren Fashions a £244m Windfall," *Guardian*, May 23, 1997.

Truell, Peter. "Goldman, Sachs Names 2 Vice Chairmen," *New York Times*, February 20, 1997.

———. "Setting the Value of Wall St. History," *New York Times*, June 6, 1998.

———. "The Wall Street Soothsayer Who Never Blinked," *New York Times*, July 27, 1997.

———. "Rubin Likely to Miss Big Windfall," *New York Times*, August 11, 1998.

Truell, Peter, and Joseph Kahn. "Goldman Sachs Nears Decisive Talks on Going Public," *New York Times*, June 7, 1998.

"Two Resigning at Goldman," *New York Times*, November 2, 1993.

Van Duyn, Aline. "Poll of Polls, The Decathlon of Investment Banking," *Euromoney*, October 1993.

Vartan, Vartanig G. "Two Levy Partners Expected to Lead at Goldman Sachs," *New York Times*, November 5, 1976.

"Vuitton Dumps Excess Baggage," *Daily Mail*, March 23, 1991.

"Waddill Catchings, Economist and Investment Banker, Dead," *New York Times*, January 1, 1968.

Waggoner, Walter H. "Walter E. Sachs, 96, of Financial House," *New York Times*, August 23, 1980.

Wallace, Anise C. "Wall Street: Investing Goldman's New Money," *New York Times*, June 3, 1990.

"Wall Street's Shining Maiden," *Economist*, September 29, 1990.

Walsh, Sharon. "Designer Could Fashion a Record Payday with Initial Public Offering," *Washington Post*, June 6, 1997.

Waters, Richard. "Goldman Sachs Heads towards a Half-Way House," *Financial Times*, June 12, 1991.

Wayne, Leslie, "Goldman Names 37 Partners," *New York Times*, October 16, 1986.

———. "Fabled Firm Turns to a Trader Again," *New York Times*, September 14, 1994.

Wayne, Leslie, and Saul Hansell. "Point Man for Economic Agenda," *New York Times*, January 18, 1992.

Weberman, Ben. "Goldman's Gilt," *Forbes*, February 24, 1986.

Webster, Justin. "Sheinberg, the Man Wedded to His Firm," *Independent*, December 11, 1991.

"Weinberg's Private View," *Financial Times*, August 1990.

Weisberg, Jacob. "Traitor to His Class?" *Worth*, July/August 1997.

——. "The Calculator," *New York Times Magazine*, July 19, 1998.

White, James A. "Top Goldman Stock Picker Is Going Solo," *Wall Street Journal*, July 2, 1991.

Whitman, Alden. "Sidney J. Weinberg Dies at 77; 'Mr. Wall Street' of Finance," *New York Times*, July 24, 1969.

"Who's News: Conway Turns Down Offer of Partnership at Goldman Sachs," *Wall Street Journal*, December 2, 1994.

Willoughby, Jack. "Can Goldman Stay on Top?" *Forbes*, September 18, 1989.

——. "Goldman's Equities Co-Head Will 'Go Limited' Nov. 30," *Investment Dealers' Digest*, September 16, 1996.

Winkler, Matthew. "Goldman Shakes Up Fixed-Income Unit, Displacing Some of Its Key Partners," *Wall Street Journal*, July 15, 1988.

Winkler, Matthew, and William Power. "Client Cash Rains Down on Two Firms," *Wall Street Journal*, July 27, 1989.

Wirth, Gregg. "Macho Men," *Investment Dealers' Digest*, June 16, 1997.

Zuckerman, Laurence. "The Good Life after Goldman," *New York Times*, October 16, 1994.

Zweig, Phillip L. "Goldman Sachs' Spectacular Road Trip," *Business Week*, November 1, 1993.

——. "Where Does Goldman Sachs Go from Here?" *Business Week*, March 20, 1995.

ACKNOWLEDGMENTS

I must say at the outset that I felt, like most of those whom I have interviewed, grateful for having had the opportunity to work at Goldman Sachs, side by side with many of the brightest, and certainly the most ambitious, people I will ever meet. Some of these people became my friends—one of them became my husband—and I held great store by those friendships. Goldman Sachs displayed a level of trust and confidence in its employees that was extremely liberating, and this remains one of its greatest strengths. This encourages employees to do their very best and may be one of the most essential and unwritten facts about the firm's culture.

The first person to give me professional encouragement on this endeavor was my agent, Geri Thoma. She saw the potential for this project and gave me endless support along the way. Geri helped me to find Ann Pappert, who has acted as a tireless researcher for the past two years. Without Ann's ability to locate almost any piece of information, I would still be wandering the stacks at the New York Public Library.

At Knopf, my editor, Jonathan Segal, has patiently endured every mistake made by a first-time author, all the while providing the guidance, encouragement, and confidence that any author needs. Jon took a chance on my inexperience, which undoubtedly made his task much more difficult, and I am very grateful.

Early in the project I prevailed upon Ron Chernow to give me some words of wisdom and he seemed only too happy to assist a new writer. Ron's guidance, and his willingness to listen to my troubles over long lunches and to read a portion of the manuscript, were more generous that I had a right to expect.

There are a number of people I would like to thank for giving me their time and answering my questions. Each of them gave me an insightful, often complex, view of the firm. I am particularly indebted to Munroe Cobey, Larry Epstein, and Mark Houghton-Berry. Thanks also go to David Allenson, Larry Becerra, Henry Bedford, Gavin Boyle, Richard Breslow, Jason Cox, Ida Giragossian, Janet Tiebout Hanson, Jeff Hanson, Noreen Harrington, Christian Hore, Steve Kim, Robin MacDonald, Dan MacEvoy, John Maltby, Peter Mathias, Ed Novotny, Xavier Rolet, Susheil Wadwani, and Jehanne Wake.

Larry Pedowitz gave me enormous help in recreating the events surrounding Bob Freeman's difficulties and the implications it held for the firm. There are dozens and dozens of others who spoke to me on the condition of anonymity to whom I would simply like to say thank you.

I was fortunate to be able to interview three of the firm's former senior partners, John Weinberg, John Whitehead, and Steve Friedman. Each gave generously of their time, recalling their years at the helm in great detail. It is no wonder that under their leadership, and that of their successors, the firm found such success.

Jon Corzine and Hank Paulson have ushered in a more open period in Goldman Sachs's history. This and the hours they devoted to my questions has greatly helped in preparing this book. Both men were refreshingly candid about the firm's triumphs and difficulties. I must thank Goldman Sachs for its cooperation regarding this project, about which they were undoubtedly not thrilled, but to which they graciously resigned. Their attitude moved quickly from trepidation to cautious yet earnest assistance and for this I am exceedingly thankful. In the end I conducted more than eighty interviews with current and retired partners. Their views on Goldman Sachs differed widely but they were uniformly proud of their association with the firm, and I am grateful to all of them.

In addition, at Goldman Sachs, I am especially indebted to Robin Neustein and John Rogers. Robin, who is the firm's chief of staff, has been a font of information. Her recollections and perspective tinged with anecdotes and humor have been invaluable. Even through her busiest days, as the firm took on the challenge of an IPO, she gave unstintingly of her time. I am in awe of anyone who can juggle as many balls as she seems to have aloft. John, the head of corporate communications, was always willing to answer a direct question, elaborate on difficult points, and relay real insight—not hype. I hate to think where I would have been without his support for this undertaking.

Without the support of my friends and family, who indulged my need to talk endlessly about this project and endured my extended state of distraction, I would still be on the first draft. For this I would like to thank in particular Eric Endlich, Harold and Shirley Endlich, Keith Endlich, Leatrice Endlich, Lili Endlich, Roselle Endlich, Liz Epstein, Simon Gillis, the late Lazar Gurwith, Pam and Leslie Harris, John and Janet Heffernan, Ilene Herscher, Bob Holtzman, Kathy Keitch, Kris Krok, Mark and Sherry Kronenfeld, Pamela Nichols, Sue and Ant Normand, and Steve and Evelina Swartzman.

My most heartfelt thanks goes to two people without whom this book would never have been completed. The first is my lifelong friend, Michelle Miller-Adams. When Michelle discovered, at the completion of her dissertation, that I was attempting to write this book without a sufficiently detailed outline, she swung into action. Since that fateful day she has read every word I have written, and edited, questioned, and improved almost every paragraph. It is no exaggeration to say that she coaxed out of me a better book than the one that I was writing.

To my husband, Mark, "Thank you" seems barely enough. For the past ten years he has shown unflagging faith and confidence in me, for which I am profoundly grateful. He inspired me to write this book, and he read and reread every word, giving invaluable insights on every page. For the past three years he has shown superhuman patience as I immersed myself in this project. Writing this book is just one of the many things I could not have dreamed of doing without him.

INDEX

accounting division, 22, 76, 119
Adam, Rick, 122
African Americans, 4, 236
Alex Brown, 249
American International Group (AIG),
    126, 265, 270
Ameritech, 126
AMF Corporation, 131, 241
annual reviews, 89–90, 99, 189, 236
antitrust case of 1947–53, 57–8
arbitrage, *see* risk arbitrage
Argentina, 123
Aron, J., *see* J. Aron
Aron, Jack, 90, 91, 94
Aron, Jacob, 91
art collection, 24
AT & T, 46, 241
Austria, 100
Aztec Oil, 82

Bankers Trust, 124, 199, 249, 263
banking crisis of 1907, 40, 50
bank mergers, of mid-1990s, 249–50,
    252
Bank of England, 42, 101–2, 171–2,
    202–4, 206–7
Baring Brothers, 98

Bear Stearns, 28
Beatrice Corporation, 117–18
Becerra, Larry, 165–6, 172, 184, 186,
    191–2
Bedford, Henry, 166–7
Beijing office, 192
Belmont, August, 36
Bentsen, Lloyd, 177
Berlitz language schools, 141
Berry, Thomas W., 3
Birmingham, Stephen, 43
BIT, 151
Black, Fisher, 146
Blair, Tony, 102
Blankfein, Lloyd, 104
block trading, 66–7, 79, 139; British
    Petroleum deal, 242–9; in Europe,
    139–41, 162, 242–9; Maxwell,
    139–43; LVMH deal, 140–1
Blue Ridge Corporation, 46
Boesky, Ivan, 31, 109; *Merger Mania,*
    112; 1986 insider trading scandal,
    31, 112, 116
Boisi, Geoffrey, 14, 20, 80–5
bond trading, *see* fixed income trading
bonuses, 133, 137, 168, 169, 183, 187,
    188, 211–12, 235, 241, 260; *see also*
    compensation system

Boston office, 37
Bower, Marvin, 73–4
Bower, Tom, 151
Branson, Richard, 162, 163
Brazil, 100, 250, 271
bridge loans, 31, 72, 125
British Airways, 87, 248; British
    Caledonia merger, 87
British Petroleum (BP), 18, 19; 1997
    deal, 242–9
British Telecom, 198
Brody, Ken, 155–7
Brosens, Frank, 118
BTR, 85–6
Buckley, Bill, 27
Buffet, Warren, 265, 270

Cabot, Paul, 60
Canada, 93
Cantor, Eddie, 48
capital, 5–7, 9, 14–15, 29, 121, 132,
    134–5; of 1869–1976, 33, 34, 44, 46,
    48, 51, 52, 69; GSTC turmoil, 45–8;
    IPO considerations, 5–15, 31, 137,
    175, 189, 228–66; limited partner,
    14, 28–31, 134–5, 174–5, 197, 206,
    219, 259, 260–1; of 1976–90, 16,
    18–19, 90, 93, 114, 119; of 1990–91,
    126, 129, 132; of 1992–93, 164,
    174–5; of 1994, 212, 214, 231; of
    1995–98, 219, 224, 225, 228,
    229–34, 251, 254, 257, 259; payout
    periods, 238, 260; Sumitomo deal,
    28–31, 174, 175, 229
Catchings, Waddill, 43–9, 52, 179, 271;
    The Road to Plenty, 44
Champion Paper and Fiber, 56
Chase Manhattan Bank, 157, 252
Chemical Bank, 95
Chicago, 38, 39, 93, 94, 98

Chicago office, 37
China, 191, 192, 221, 239; equity
    market, 241–2
China Telecom, 239
Christopher, Warren, 177
Chrysler Corporation/Daimler-Benz
    merger, 238–9
Citibank, 44, 95, 124, 249
clients, 17, 37, 44, 120, 131–2, 163,
    257; cold-calling, 18; corporate list,
    19, 54–6, 58–9; of 1869–1976,
    37–41, 44–8, 54–5, 58, 60–2, 68, 73,
    126; focus on, 17, 18, 21, 62, 79,
    88–9, 126, 217; of 1976–90, 75–6,
    88–9, 101, 126; of 1990–91, 121,
    125–32, 137; of 1992–93, 162, 164,
    168, 173, 182–3, 188; of 1994, 208,
    217; of 1995–98, 219, 224, 225, 235,
    238, 241, 244, 248, 250, 252, 263;
    "red book," 73; *see also specific
    clients*
Clinton, Bill, 77, 176, 177, 221
CNBC, 134, 191
CNN, 191
Columbia Business School, 21, 101
Columbia Trust Company, 37
commercial banks: and erosion of
    Glass-Steagall Act, 124, 249; mid-
    1990s mergers, 249–50, 252; *see also
    specific banks*
Commercial Investment Trust
    Company, 43
commercial paper, 32–43, 53, 61, 67, 79,
    105, 126; Penn Central fiasco, 67–9
commission system, 106, 108
commodities trading, 4, 90–104; J.
    Aron, 90–104, 132–4; of 1976–90,
    90–104; of 1990–91, 132–4; of 1994,
    194, 195
common stock, early valuing practices,
    39, 40

compensation system, 10, 106, 108,
132, 136, 168–9, 175, 183–4, 187–8,
211–12, 235–6, 256; IPO, 260–1;
payout periods, 238, 260–1; for
proprietary traders, 183–4, 187–8;
see also bonuses; salaries
Continental Can Company, 40
Corzine, Jon, 15, 79, 108, 135, 167,
179–81, 190, 194, 200, 201, 266;
background of, 220; IPO
considerations, 229–34, 238, 242,
249–66, 268–70, 272; LTCM
considerations, 270–71; leadership
with Paulson, 205–6, 208–14, 221–8,
238–41, 253–4, 267–72; management
style, 207–14, 219–21, 223, 226–8,
234–40, 268–69; resignation of,
272–73; Senate campaign, 267, 273;
senior partnership, 205–6
Coster, Donald, 55
Credit Suisse, 30, 125
culture, 12, 14, 16, 19–28, 55, 62, 81,
88–9, 96, 98, 114, 134–6, 163, 169,
183, 185, 186, 215, 217, 232, 255,
257; of 1990, 120–6, 134–5; of 1992–
1993, 163, 167–8, 173–6, 180, 184–6; of
1994, 190–1, 207, 208, 210; of 1995–
1998, 223, 224, 226, 228, 237, 251, 273
Curran, Paul J., 115
currency trading, 4, 44, 90–104, 113; J.
Aron, 90–104, 113, 132–4; of
1990–91, 132–4; of 1992–93, 162–8,
170–4, 182–7, 195; of 1994, 194,
195, 202–7, 210–11

Daily Telegraph, 161
Daimler-Benz/Chrysler Corporation
merger, 238–9
David-Weill, Michael, 220
Davies, Gavyn, 102–3, 166, 202–3

Day, Corbin, 81
day care center, 236
Dean Witter, 28; Morgan Stanley
merger, 249, 261, 263
DeLucia, David, 107
Department of Trade and Industry (DTI),
Maxwell investigation, 138, 141
Depression, 48, 49, 64, 72; Goldman
Sachs operations, 52–7
Deutsche Bank, 188, 212
Deutsche Telekom privatization, 205, 238
Dillon Read, 58
Disney, Walt, 186, 248
Dobkin, Eric, 232
Doonan, Thomas, 113
Dow Jones Industrial Average, 37, 67,
90, 143, 249; 1998 declines, 261–3
Drexel Burnham Lambert, 24, 30, 39,
45; bankruptcy, 125; fixed income
business, 30, 105, 107; 1986 insider
trading scandal, 111–15
Drexel Trading, 95
Dreyfuss, Ludwig, 34
Dulles, John Foster, 46
DuPont, 126

Eastman Kodak, 46
Economist, The, 142, 144, 198
economy, 44; of 1930s, 52; 1998 global
crisis, 261–5, 269
ego, 7, 17–18, 20–1, 184
Einstein, Albert, 43
Eisenhower, Dwight, 57
Eisner, Michael, 248
Electric Storage Battery (ESB), 80–2
Engelhard Minerals Corporation, 91–2
equal opportunity, 6, 236–7
equities, *see* stock trading
European Exchange Rate Mechanism
(ERM), 169–73, 184

Eurobonds, 30, 182, 195, 199–200

Euromoney, 139, 180

Europe, *see specific countries and cities*

executive committee, of 1995–98, 226–34, 250, 252, 254, 258, 268, 271, 272

Federal Reserve Bank of New York, 70, 265

Federal Reserve Board, 29–30, 192, 202, 239; 1994 interest rate increases, 193–5; LTCM investigation, 264–5, 270; Penn Central fiasco, 67–8

Fidelity Investments, 127, 139, 240, 241

Financial Times, 218

Financial World, 132, 180

Finland, 123

First Boston, 28, 58, 71, 105, 208; bridge loans, 125; merger boom, 81, 84, 125

Fisher, Richard, 132

fixed commissions, 108

fixed income trading, 4, 6, 30, 46, 54, 92, 97, 104–9, 164, 168, 220; international, 16, 191–2; of 1976–90, 97–100, 104–9, 194, 200, 201, 220; of 1990–91, 125, 133–4, 163; of 1992–93, 162, 165, 169, 172, 173, 181–2, 185, 195; of 1994, 191–4, 195, 199–200, 209, 210; of 1995–98, 264–5, 269

Forbes, 187

Ford, Edsel, 58, 59

Ford, Henry, Sr., 58, 59

Ford, Henry II, 58–9

Ford Motor Company, 54, 55, 56, 58–60, 89; as Goldman Sachs client, 58–60, 73, 129–30, 205

foreign exchange trading, 4, 44, 113; J. Aron, 90–104, 132–4; in London, 100–104, 133, 162–8, 170–4, 186, 194, 202–7; of 1990–91, 132–4, 147; of 1992–93, 162–8, 170–4, 182–7, 195; of 1994, 194, 195, 202–7, 210–11; *see also* international operations; *specific cities*

Fortune, 55

France, 41, 75, 140; stock trading, 140–1

Freeman, Robert, 110–19, 144; "bunny" charge, 116–18, 19; 1986 insider trading scandal, 112–19, 135, 216

Friedman, Richard, 130–1

Friedman, Stephen, 4–7, 11, 13–19, 24, 64, 76–9, 89, 156, 165, 169, 185, 191, 223, 233, 248, 256; background of, 79; co-leadership with Rubin, 76–9, 105–9, 120–5, 132, 173, 175–9, 217, 270; fixed income trading, 105–9; INCO-ESB fight, 80–2; as limited partner, 203, 206; M & A operations, 79–85; management style, 79, 105–6, 121–4, 128–9, 136, 174, 178–9, 188, 189, 193, 217–18, 268; 1994 losses, 194–5, 199–206; principal investment business, 126–31, 187; retirement of, 203–6, 214, 217

FTSE-100 index, 143, 247

fund management, 45, 239–40

Galbraith, John Kenneth, *The Great Crash of 1929,* 45, 46

Garantia, 250

Gell-Mann, Murray, 106

General Electric, 19, 28, 46, 54, 56, 115, 126

General Foods, 19, 44, 75

General Motors, 59

George, Eddie, 202

German Jews, 32, 33, 38, 41–3, 95

Germany, 32, 38, 101, 123, 205;
Deutsche Telekom privatization, 205,
238; mark, 170, 171; Nazi, 43;
World War I, 41, 42

gilt market, 166–7

Glass-Steagall Act, erosion of, 124, 249

Goldman, Bertha, 32, 34

Goldman, Henry, 34, 35–43, 50, 51, 52,
54, 64

Goldman, Julius, 38

Goldman, Marcus, 32–5, 53, 71, 126,
232

Goldman & Co., Marcus, 32–3

Goldman and Sachs, M., 33–4

Goldman Sachs & Co., 34, 45; of
1869–1976, 32–69, 73, 126, 129,
174; of 1976–90, 3–31, 70–119, 126,
132, 174, 194–5, 229–33, 240; of
1990–91, 120–60; of 1992–93, 131,
161–89, 195, 224; of 1994, 190–218,
222, 224, 231, 239; of 1995–98, 209,
211, 219–66; *see also* accounting
division; block trading; capital;
clients; commercial paper;
commodities trading; compensation
system; culture; currency trading;
fixed income trading; foreign
exchange trading; growth;
international operations; investment
banking; IPO; J. Aron; legal division;
limited partners; London office;
mergers and acquisitions; New York
office; office buildings; partnership;
principal investments; profitability;
proprietary trading; recruitment; risk
arbitrage; risk management systems;
secrecy; *specific employees, partners,
divisions, and offices;* staff; stock
trading; underwriting

Goldman Sachs Asset Management
(GSAM), 240

Goldman Sachs Currency Analyst,
170

Goldman Sachs foundation, 260

"Goldman Sachs in Perspective"
(training session), 89

Goldman Sachs Trading Corporation
(GSTC), 45–9, 55, 64, 72, 239;
liquidation of, 47–8

gold trading, 90–9; J. Aron, 93–104

Goodrich, 19

Gorter, James, 197

government bonds, 98, 99, 105, 106,
173, 182, 198, 220, 264

grain trading, 133

Great Britain, 18, 19, 36, 41, 85–8,
101–2, 108, 138, 161, 202, 242, 248;
ERM explosion, 170–3; Maxwell
affair, 137–60, 195–7; 1992
government, 166–7, 170–1; 1993–94
interest rates, 202–4, 206–7; sterling,
170–3, 194, 202–4, 206–7; *see also*
London; London office

greed, 7, 18, 173, 256; of 1992–93,
173, 212

Greenspan, Alan, 265

growth, 16, 26–7; of 1869–1976,
32–48, 64; IPO considerations, 5–15,
31, 137, 175, 189, 228–66; of
1976–90, 18–19, 26, 75–6, 88–90,
96, 126; of 1990–91, 121, 123; of
1992–93, 161, 173–6, 180–9; of
1994, 190, 192–3, 201–2, 222; of
1995–98, 219, 222–4, 239–41, 249,
251–3, 262, 265

GS Capital Partners I, 130

GS Capital Partners II, 130

Guaranty Trust, 44

Guardian, 186–7

Gulf War, 134

Gutfreund, John, 22, 63, 107, 125

Hanson, Janet Tiebout, 21

Hanson Trust, 85, 86

Harvard Business Review, 56

Harvard Business School, 70, 92, 101

Harvard University, 44

Hasbro, Inc., 127

hedge funds, 149, 168–9, 172, 191, 194, 200, 225, 261; 1998 crash, 264–5

hedging strategies, 246–7

Hertzberg, Daniel, 116

high-yield debt, 83

Hindenburg, Paul von, 43

Hitler, Adolf, 43

Hong Kong, 16, 210, 241–2

Hormats, Robert, 258

hostile takeovers, 19, 80–5, 110, 127, 262; INCO-ESB fight, 80–2; *see also* mergers and acquisitions

Houghton-Berry, Mark, 202–4, 206–7

Hurst, Robert, 156, 209, 227, 253

Hutton, E. F., 115, 125

IBM, 216

Imperial Group, 86

INCO-ESB fight, 80–2

Independent, 152, 203, 256

India, 123

Indonesia, 131

inflation, 90, 92, 133, 193

insider trading, 109–19; Goldman Sachs role, 31, 111–19; 1986 scandal, 31, 111–19

Institutional Investor, 28, 102

Institutional Liquid Assets, 240

insurance companies, 47, 126, 174

interest rates, 92, 162; European, 162, 171, 202–7; of 1970s, 90; of 1993, 181; of 1994, 193–5, 202–7, 239

Internal Revenue Service, 59

International Financing Review, 181

International Money Market, 100

international operations, 6, 15–16, 30, 36, 75, 85–8, 108; of 1869–1976, 36; fixed income trading, 16, 191–2; Maxwell affair, 137–60, 161, 195–8; of 1976–90, 75–6, 85–8, 100; of 1990–91, 123–4, 36, 137–60; of 1992–93, 161–89; of 1994, 191–2, 202–7, 210, 214, 222; of 1995–98, 224, 227, 232, 238–9, 241, 241–9, 253, 262; recruitment, 87–8; *see also specific cities and offices*

investment banking, 4–5, 13–14, 221; antitrust case of 1947–53, 57–8; of 1869–1976, 36–48, 54, 58–63; Ford deal, 58–60; of 1976–90, 80–8, 90, 92, 126; of 1990–91, 123–31; of 1992–93, 180, 187; of 1994, 194, 195, 208, 210–11; of 1995–98, 223, 224, 231, 241, 252, 263; *see also specific divisions*

Investment Banking Services (IBS), 13–14, 60–1, 81

investment trusts, 62; of 1920s, 45–9

IPO, 5–15, 31, 137, 175, 189, 228–66; 1986 meeting, 5–15, 31, 229–33, 254, 257, 259, 268; 1996 meeting, 228–34, 252, 254, 257, 258, 259, 268; 1998 decision for, and later cancellation, 258–66, 268–70; 1998 meeting, 249–260, 261; 1999 decision for, 273–74

Irving Trust Company, 37

Israel, 131

Italy, 171, 192; bonds, 191–2; lira crisis, 170, 172–3, 184

J. Aron, 4, 77, 78, 90–104, 113, 165, 195, 202, 222, 240; clients, 96, 101; Goldman Sachs's acquisition of, 90–104; management style, 96–7, 101; of 1990–91, 132–4; of 1992–93, 165; of 1994, 195, 209, 210; recruitment, 95–6, 101

Japan, 9, 136, 165, 192, 250, 253;
  equity markets, 25, 241–2, 250;
  Goldman Sachs office in Tokyo, 15,
  25, 30, 76, 100, 104, 136, 210; 1998
  financial crisis, 261, 264; Sumitomo-
  Goldman Sachs deal, 28–31; yen,
  165, 194
Johnson Mathey, 91
junk bonds, 30, 31, 109
Justice Department, antitrust case of
  1947–53, 57–8

Kamehameha Schools/Bishop Estate,
  14, 174, 214, 229
Kansler, Mrs. Ernest, 59
Katz, Robert, 155–60, 196, 197, 203,
  209
Kidder Peabody, 28, 112, 115, 125
Kim, Steve, 108
Kleinwort, Alexander, 36, 37
Kleinwort, Herman, 36
Kleinwort Benson, 239, 244, 247
Kleinwort Sons & Co., 36, 39, 40, 41,
  42
Knickerbocker Trust Company, 37
Kohl, Helmut, 205
Kohlberg, Kravis, Roberts and Co.
  (KKR), 116–17
Komatsu, Koh, 29
Korean War, 57, 71
Kraft Company, 44, 56
Kravis, Henry, 117
Krimendahl, Fred, 197
Kuhn Loeb & Co., 37, 58
Kuwaiti Investment Office (KIO), 242–7

Lasker, Bernard "Bunny", 117
Lauren (Ralph) Company, 130, 131
Lawson, Nigel, 101

layoffs, 99, 202, 222–3; of 1980s, 99,
  108; of 1995–98, 222–4
Lazard Freres, 111, 123, 192, 220
Leeson, Nick, 98
legal division, 6, 22, 38, 56, 67, 113,
  119; Freeman defense, 113–19;
  GSTC lawsuit, 48; Maxwell affair,
  155–60, 161, 195–8; Penn Central
  lawsuit, 67–9, 208, 215, 237
Lehman, Philip, 38, 41
Lehman Brothers, 7, 39, 58, 120,
  208, 263; early relationship with
  Goldman Sachs, 39–41; Shearson
  American Express merger, 11, 28,
  125
leverage, of 1920s, 46–7
leveraged buyouts, 9, 11, 28, 83,
  116–17; Beatrice, 116–18; Goldman
  Sachs's lack of involvement in, 72
Levine, Dennis, 111
Levi Strauss, 241
Levy, Gus, 5, 17, 18, 54, 62–9, 73, 90,
  104, 109, 181, 204, 208, 225, 228,
  232, 242, 248; background of, 63–4;
  block trading of, 66–7; management
  style, 64–6, 122, 126, 139, 239; Penn
  Central fiasco, 67–8, 208; risk
  arbitrage, 65, 109–10
Levy, Peter, 64
Lewis, Michael, *Liar's Poker*, 135
limited partners, 14, 134–5, 174–5,
  197, 203, 206, 219, 259; IPO
  compensation, 260–1
Lloyd's Bank, 87
London, 30, 36, 42, 85, 161–2; gilt
  market, 166–7; gold market, 93;
  1986 deregulation of financial
  markets, 86–7, 108; stock market,
  141–3, 149, 162, 242–9
London office, 16, 18, 25, 36, 42, 76,
  84–8, 138–9; BP deals, 18, 19,

242–9; building, 161; foreign
exchange trading, 100–104, 133,
162–8, 170–4, 186, 194, 202–7;
gilt market, 166–7; Maxwell affair,
137–60, 161, 195–8; of 1976–90,
85–8, 100–104, 108; of 1990–91,
133, 138–60; of 1992–93, 161–8,
170–4, 186–9; of 1994, 191–2, 194,
198–9, 202–7, 214, 215; of 1995–98,
242–9; proprietary trading, 103–4,
164–8, 170–4, 186–9, 191–2, 194,
198–9, 202–7; recruitment, 87–8;
trading floor, 191–2
Long Term Capital Management
(LTCM), 1998 crash and rescue of,
264–5, 269, 270–71
Los Angeles office, 210
Lucent Technologies, 241

McDonough, William, 265
McKesson and Robbins, 55–6
McKinsey and Co., 29, 73–4
Macmillan Publishing Company, 147
Macy's, R. H., 19
Major, John, 166, 170
management, *see* partnership; *specific
managers*
Mathias, Peter, 17, 88–9
Maughan, Deryck, 132
Maxwell, Kevin, 138, 141, 145–7,
150–60
Maxwell, Robert, 137–60, 195; death
of, 137, 141, 159–60; as Goldman
Sachs client, 139–60, 161, 195–8;
business practices, 138, 141–3,
147–60, 196, 198
Maxwell Communications Corporation
(MCC), 139, 142–60
May Department Stores, 40, 43
MCA, 163

Medina, Harold, 58
Menuhin, Yehudi, 43
merchant banking, 28
Mercury Asset Management, 250
mergers and acquisitions, 5, 9, 18, 21,
54, 62, 77, 79–85, 109, 110, 117,
131, 162–3; in Britain, 85–8;
INCO-ESB fight, 80–2; J. Aron,
90–104; of 1976–90, 79–85, 90–104,
110; of 1990–91, 121, 131, 133; of
1992–93, 180; of 1994, 194, 218; of
1995–98, 224, 228, 241; policy on
hostile takeovers, 84–5
Meriwether, John, 264
Merrill Lynch, 6, 19, 28, 58, 105, 132,
135, 180, 186, 239, 240, 250, 261,
263, 265
Merton, Robert, 146
Mexico, 93, 123, 192, 271
Mexico City office, 192
Microsoft, 186
Milan office, 192
Milken, Michael, 39
Mirror Group News (MGN), 154, 158
MIT, 101
Mocatta Metals, 91
Moët Hennessy Louis Vuitton (LVMH),
140–1
money management, 239–40, 263
Monsanto, 19
Moody's Investors Services, 180, 214
Morgan, J. P., 37, 40, 41–2, 44, 71, 80,
95, 124, 252, 263, 265
Morgan Grenfell, 86
Morgan Stanley, 18, 19, 25, 29, 54,
58, 59, 71, 75, 131, 132, 208, 240;
Dean Witter merger, 249, 261, 263;
INCO-ESB fight, 80–2; merger boom,
80–1, 84; 1986 IPO, 28, 232
Morrison, David, 102–3, 134, 170–1,
184–5, 188

Mortara, Michael, 107
mortgage-backed securities, 109, 193
Moscow office, 174
municipal finance, 54, 105
Musica, Philip, 55–6

National City Bank, 44
National Dairy Products, 44, 54, 56
New Deal, 56–7
New Yorker, The, 49
New York office buildings, 23–4, 34,
    53, 63, 71, 88, 122, 215
New York Post, 256
New York Stock Exchange, 34, 38, 66,
    108, 110, 247
New York Times, 23, 26, 60, 62, 155
Nikko Securities, 250
Nye, Dick, 117

O'Brien, Mike, 103–4, 133, 162,
    163–4, 181–2, 199; foreign exchange
    trading, 163–6, 182
Odlum, Floyd, 48, 62, 72, 125
office buildings, 23–5; London, 161;
    New York, 23–4, 34, 53, 63, 71, 88,
    122, 215
oil, 90, 99, 131; trading, 133, 242–9
operating committee, of 1995–98,
    227–30, 252
options trading, 145–7, 151
Osaka office, 192
Overseas Airline Guide (OAG), 141,
    147
Owens-Corning Fiberglas, 54

Paribas, 140
Paris office, 140
partnership, 3–4; annual dinner dance,
    218, 237–8; annual reviews, 89–90,
99, 189, 236; compensation system,
    10, 132, 136, 168–9, 175, 183–4,
    187–8, 211–12, 235–6, 256; Corzine/
    Paulson co-leadership, 205–6,
    208–14, 221–8, 238–41, 253–4,
    267–72; culture, 20–8; resignations
    of 1994, 209–18, 227, 228, 229;
    early animosities, 41–3; of
    1869–1976, 32–69, 73, 126, 129,
    174; family feeling, 10, 23, 32–69,
    71, 91, 121; Freeman arrest, 112–19,
    135, 216; Friedman/Rubin co-
    leadership, 76–9, 105–9, 120–5, 132,
    173, 175–9, 217, 270; GSTC scandal,
    45–9, 55, 64, 239; invitation process,
    3–5, 135–7, 211, 214; IPO
    considerations, 5–15, 31, 137, 175,
    189, 228–66; J. Aron and, 90–104,
    132–4; limited partners, 14, 134–5,
    174–5, 197, 203, 206, 219, 259,
    260–1; of 1976–90, 3–31, 70–119,
    126, 132, 174, 194–5, 229–33, 240;
    of 1990–91, 120–60; of 1992–93,
    131, 161–89, 195, 224; of 1994,
    190–218, 222, 224, 231, 239; of
    1995–98, 209, 211, 219–66; Penn
    Central, 67–9, 208, 215, 237;
    seniority, 11, 13, 175, 188, 229–30,
    232, 235, 236; strategy for future,
    241, 250–3; structure, 22–3, 74, 121,
    134, 175, 180, 186; structure
    reforms, 226–8, 235–42, 250, 259;
    title changes, 235–7; turnover, 21,
    120–5, 169, 175–80, 188–9,
    203–18, 226; Weinberg/Whitehead
    co-leadership, 70–6, 88, 89, 122,
    179; *see also* culture; *specific partners
    and divisions*
partnership committee, of 1995–98,
    227–30, 252
Paulson, Hank, 77–8, 85, 179, 205–6;
    background of, 221; IPO

considerations, 229–34, 250–66;
leadership with Corzine, 205–6, 208–
214, 221–8, 238–41, 253–4, 267–72;
management style, 221–2, 251, 268–69
Pedowitz, Lawrence, 112–14, 116, 118
Pegasus IV (study), 229–34
Penn Central Railroad, 6; fiasco of early
1970s, 67–9, 208, 215, 237
Pergamon Press, 147
Philadelphia office, 37
Philip Brothers Corporation, 13, 28, 91,
93
Port, Fred, 80–1
Pot, Wiet, 244–8
press, 102, 103; on Goldman Sachs, 25,
26, 49, 60, 114, 127, 134–5, 160,
170, 181, 186–7, 195–8, 204, 214,
230, 234, 239, 254, 256, 259–63,
271; on Maxwell affair, 152, 153,
155, 160, 195–8; on 1986 insider
trading scandal, 111, 114, 116; *see
also specific publications*
principal investments, 6, 128, 221;
Ralph Lauren, 130, 131; of 1990–91,
126–31; of 1992–93, 187, 189;
Water Street Corporate Recovery
Fund, 126–7
Private Client Services (PCS), 27, 168
private limited liability corporation, 237
Procter & Gamble, 19, 54
profitability, 20, 34, 121, 132; of
1869–1976, 34; of 1976–90, 7, 76,
82, 90, 93, 100, 104, 106, 109, 132,
195; of 1990–91, 125, 127, 130,
132–5, 141; of 1992–93, 131, 161,
164, 166, 168–9, 172–4, 180–9, 190,
195, 224; of 1994, 190–4, 200, 210,
212–14, 224, 231, 239; of 1995–98,
213, 219, 228, 238, 240–1, 249, 260,
262, 265
promissory notes, nineteenth-century,
32–4

promotions, 13
proprietary trading, 6, 63, 103–4, 109,
131, 161–89, 220; gilt market,
166–7; in London, 103–4, 162–8,
170–4, 186–9, 191–2, 194, 198–9,
202–7; of 1990–91, 131, 133, 163; of
1992–93, 161–89; of 1994, 191–2,
194, 195, 202–7, 210–11, 239; of
1995–98, 224–5, 250
P-shares, 236
public offering, *see* IPO
Pura, Tom, 107

QUE, 160

racial discrimination, 6, 236
railroads, 33, 37, 54; bond trading, 33,
35, 37–8, 54; Penn Central fiasco,
67–8, 208, 215, 237
RCA, 19
Reagan, Ronald, 7, 70, 76
real estate, 23–5, 31, 47, 124
recruitment, 12, 19, 20, 65–6, 75, 87,
89, 96–7, 105–8, 165, 169, 184, 232,
255; for foreign offices, 87–8, 165;
interviews, 20, 26, 97; J. Aron, 95–6,
101; lateral hires, 165, 169, 193,
235; 1994 freeze on, 201, 223; of
1995–98, 223–4, 232, 261; from
Salomon Brothers, 106–9
risk arbitrage, 9, 31, 54, 65, 77, 78,
109–19, 131; of 1976–90, 109–19;
1986 insider trading scandal,
111–19; of 1990–91, 121, 131, 133
risk management systems, 199; of
1995–98, 199, 222, 225–8, 229,
242
Roosevelt, Franklin D., 56–7
Rosenwald, Julius, 38–9, 40
Rothschild, N. M., 36

Rubin, Robert E., 4–7, 11, 13, 14, 16, 23, 24, 54, 65, 76–8, 114, 156, 187, 190, 205, 220, 233, 256; background of, 77; in Clinton administration, 77, 124, 176, 177; co-leadership with Friedman, 76–9, 105–9, 120–5, 132, 173, 175–9, 217, 270; fixed income trading, 105–9; J. Aron and, 97, 100, 101, 102, 104, 133–4; management style, 78, 110, 121–4, 133–4, 174, 193, 200, 236, 268; retirement of, 176–9, 200; risk arbitrage, 109–19, 133

Russia, 57, 93, 100, 174, 205, 271; 1998 economic crisis, 261–2, 264, 269

Sachs, Arthur, 36, 40, 42, 43, 45, 52
Sachs, Emelia, 38
Sachs, Harry, 33, 34, 42
Sachs, Howard, 52, 58, 85, 139
Sachs, Louisa Goldman, 33, 43
Sachs, Paul, 35, 36, 40, 43, 50–1
Sachs, Peter, 85, 139
Sachs, Sam, 33–43, 50, 51, 52, 55, 75, 85
Sachs, Walter E., 33–5, 44–9, 52–3, 55, 58, 271
St. Louis office, 37
Salomon Brothers, 4, 6, 13, 22, 24, 30, 132, 164, 198, 208, 250, 264; BP bid, 242, 244, 247, 248; commodities business, 93; fixed income business, 30, 105, 106–9, 198; London proprietary trading, 201; SEC investigation, 125; Smith Barney merger, 249; sold to Philip Brothers, 28, 93
SAS Airlines, 87
Scholes, Myron, 146
Sears, Richard, 38, 40
Sears Roebuck & Co., 19, 28, 39–40, 43, 129

secrecy, 10, 89, 111, 131, 134–5, 203, 254, 260, 262; Ford deal, 59–60; Sumitomo deal, 28–30
Securities and Exchange Commission (SEC), 68, 111, 125, 145, 149, 151, 262; Maxwell investigation, 145, 149, 151, 196–7; 1986 insider trading investigation, 111, 116–19
Securities Industry Association, 73
Seligman's, 33
Seoul office, 192
Shainswit, Beatrice, 196
Shanghai office, 192
Shearson American Express, 7, 111; Lehman Brothers merger, 11, 28, 125
Sheinberg, Eric, 104, 132, 137; background of, 139; Maxwell affair, 137–60, 196, 197; LVMH deal, 140–1
Shenandoah Corporation, 46
Shroeders Bank, 242, 244, 247
Siegel, Martin, 112–19
Silfen, David, 210, 227, 246
silver trading, 93, 95, 184
Smith, John, 171
Smith, Roy, 223
Smith Barney, 135; Salomon Brothers merger, 249
Soros, George, 172
Sotheby's, 12
South Africa, 93, 94, 100
South Korea, 239
specialization, process of, 61
Speyer, Jimmy, 37, 38
Speyer & Co., 37, 38
Standard & Poor's, 180, 211
Standard Chartered Bank, 87
Stanford University, 101
Stewart, James, 116; *Den of Thieves*, 115, 119
stock markets, *see* Dow Jones Industrial

Average; New York Stock Exchange; specific cities; Wall Street
stock repurchasing, 83
stock trading, 4, 5, 92; block trading, 66–7, 139–43, 242–9; BP trade, 242–9; of 1869–1976, 38, 39–40, 44–8, 54, 63, 64–7; GSTC scandal, 45–9, 55, 64, 239; Maxwell affair, 139–60, 195–8; LVMH deal, 140–1; of 1976–90, 117; of 1990–91, 139–60; of 1992–93, 162, 168, 173, 180; of 1994, 194, 195; of 1995–98, 223, 224, 228, 239, 241, 242–9, 262
strategy committee, 250–3
Studebaker, 40
Sullivan and Cromwell, 155
Sumitomo Bank, 9, 14, 15; Goldman Sachs deal, 28–31, 174, 175, 229
Sunday Times (London), 102
Swiss Bank Corporation, 249
Switzerland, 15, 16, 100, 249

Taipei office, 192
technology, 191, 251; *see also* computers
Thailand, 123
Thain, John, 85, 227, 231, 245, 253, 272
Third World loans, 124
Thorn EMI, 87, 162, 163
Thornton, John, 85–6, 162, 163, 227, 253, 272
Tilling, Thomas, 86
title changes, of 1996, 235–7
Tokyo office, 15, 25, 30, 76, 100, 104, 136, 210
Tonka Toys, 127
treasury bonds, U.S., 99, 106, 182, 198, 264
Truman, Harry, 57
Trust Company of America, 50
Tully, Daniel, 132

Underwood Typewriters Corporation, 40
underwriting, 92, 129; of 1869–1976, 36–48, 54, 57–8, 129; of 1976–90, 104–9; of 1990–91, 130, 141; of 1992–93, 173, 190; of 1994, 194, 205; of 1995–98, 228
Unilever, 19
Union Bank of Switzerland, 244, 249
United Aircraft, 81
United Cigar Manufacturers, 39, 40
United Parcel Service, 241
USAir, 248
USG Corp., 127
utilities, 37, 46; bond trading, 35, 37, 54

Vancouver office, 192
Virgin Atlantic Airlines, 162
Virgin Music Group, 87, 162, 163
Vuitton family, 140

Walker, Peter, 148, 152, 153
Wall Street, 53; antitrust case of 1947–53, 57–8; effect of computer on, 98; 1907 banking crisis, 40, 50; 1929 crash, 46–9, 69, 110, 215; of 1970s, 67–9, 90; 1980s mergers, 28, 112; 1986 insider trading scandal, 111–19; 1987 crash, 18, 138, 194–5, 242; 1998 bull market, 249, 251, 254, 259; 1998 market decline, 261–5; "star system," 21; World War I, 41–2
Wall Street Journal, 111, 116, 234
Wall Street Week, 134
Water Street Corporate Recovery Fund, 126–7, 135
Watson, Thomas, Sr., 216, 217
Weill, Michael David, 192

Weinberg, Helen, 51

Weinberg, Jimmy, 13–14, 51

Weinberg, John L., 3–4, 14, 17, 20, 28, 53, 56, 68, 80, 89, 102–5, 120, 204, 205, 208, 213–18, 221, 233, 251; background of, 71–2; co-leadership with Whitehead, 70–6, 88, 89, 122, 179; Freeman arrest, 114, 118, 119; IPO considerations, 3, 7, 10–13, 235, 256; management style, 75, 84, 88, 89, 125, 126, 268; 1994 speech to partners, 214–18; retirement of, 120–1; Sumitomo deal, 28–30

Weinberg, Sidney, 3, 5, 7, 13–14, 17, 37, 47, 48, 49–62, 63, 68, 71–3, 84, 90, 129, 179, 216–17, 226, 232, 271; background of, 50–1; death of, 62; Ford account, 58–60; McKesson scandal, 55–6; management style, 50–62, 228, 239; 1930s-40s operations, 52–8

Welch's Foods, 68

Wells Fargo, 162

Wharton Business School, 98, 99, 101

Whitehead, John, 7, 9, 17, 21, 36, 53, 57, 60–3, 81, 85, 120, 205, 240; background of, 70–1; co-leadership with Weinberg, 70–6, 88, 89, 122, 179; IPO considerations, 256, 261; IBS and, 60–1; J. Aron acquisition, 90–104; management style, 75, 84, 88, 89, 92, 128, 129, 173, 268; in Reagan administration, 70, 76; retirement of, 76

Williams, Gary, 244–5, 248, 249

Winkelman, Mark, 23, 97–104, 108–9, 113, 133–4, 163, 164, 179–81, 190, 194, 201, 267; retirement of, 209

women, 3, 4, 26, 236

Wood, Garland E., 3

Woods, Larry, 153

Woolworth Company, F. W., 40

World War I, 37, 41–2, 51

World War II, 29, 43, 48, 54, 57, 64, 66, 70, 71

Yamaichi Securities, 250

Zuckerberg, Roy, 155, 179, 209, 227, 245, 253

Zurich office, 15, 16, 100

PHOTOGRAPHIC CREDITS

The photographs in this book are used by permission and courtesy of the following:

Goldman Sachs: p. 1, p. 2 (bottom), p. 3 (top right and bottom), p. 4, p. 6 (top), p. 8

UPI/Corbis-Bettmann: p. 2 (top)

Corbis-Bettmann-Reuter: p. 7 (bottom)

New York Times Pictures: p. 3 (top left)

Vic DeLucia/*New York Times*: p. 5 (top)

John Sotomayor/*New York Times* Pictures: p. 5 (bottom)

WWD/David Turner: p. 6 (bottom)

Artur Walther: p. 7 (top)

Jerry Bauer: p. 7 (middle)